CISTERCIAN STUDIES SERIES: NUMBER THIRTY-SEVEN

STUDIES IN MONASTIC THEOLOGY

by

ODO BROOKE OSB

HOLY CROSS ABBEY NOVITIATE

Cistercian Publications
Kalamazoo, Michigan
1980

CISTERCIAN STUDIES SERIES: NUMBER THIRTY-SEVEN

STUDIES IN MONASTIC THEOLOGY

BY ODO BROOKE OSB

HOLY CROSS ABBEY
NOVITIATE

Available in Britain, Europe,
and the Commonwealth from
A. R. Mowbray & Co. Ltd.
St Thomas House
Becket Street
Oxford OX1 1SJ

Library of Congress Cataloging in Publication Data

Brooke, Odo, 1901-1971.
    Studies in monastic theology.

    (Cistercian studies series ; no. 37)
    Bibliography: p.
    CONTENTS: Studies on William of St. Thierry:
William of St. Thierry. The trinitarian aspect of
the ascent of the soul to God in the theology of
William of St. Thierry. The speculative development of the trinitarian theology of William of
St. Thierry in the Aenigma fidei. [etc.]
    1. Guillaume de Saint-Thierry, 1085 (ca.)-
1148?--Collected works. 2. Monastic and religious
life--Collected works. 3. Theology--Collected
works. I. Title. II. Series.
BX4705.G7464B76 1980   230'.2'0924   79-23103
ISBN 0-87907-837-5

With gratitude and respect

this volume is

dedicated

to the memory of

DOM ODO BROOKE, OSB

Monk of Farnborough

1909 - 1971

Like William of Saint Thierry, of whom he
wrote so well, Father Odo was a Black Monk
who greatly enriched the White Monks and
all who seek sure guidance in the ways of
the Spirit.

TABLE OF CONTENTS

I. STUDIES ON WILLIAM OF ST THIERRY

STUDIES BY ODO BROOKE

'Monastic Theology and Saint Aelred.' *Pax* 49 (1959) 87-93.

'The Trinitarian Aspect of the Ascent of the Soul to God in the Theology of William of St. Thierry.' *Recherches de Théologie ancienne et médiévale* RTAM 26 (1959) 87-127.

'The Speculative Development of the Trinitarian Theology of William of St. Thierry in the 'Aenigma fidei'.' RTAM 27 (1960) 193-211; 28 (1961) 26-58.

'William of St. Thierry's Doctrine of the Ascent to God by Faith.' (RTAM) 30 (1963) 181-204.

'Ascent to God by Faith (II).' RTAM 33 (1966) 282-318.

'Towards an Integral Theology.' *Pax* 54 (1964) 63-68.

'Natural Religion in the Supernatural Existential.' *The Downside Review* 83 (1965) 201-218.

'Faith and Mystical Experience in William of St. Thierry.' *The Downside Review* 82 (1964) 275-290.

'Towards a Theology of Connatural Knowledge.' *Citeaux* 18 (1967) 275-290.

'The Exigence for Theology.' *The Downside Review* 86 (1968) 377-384.

'The Human Person and Community Structures.' *Monastic Studies* 5 (1968) 7-18.

'William of St. Thierry.' *The Month* 214 (1968) 377-384.

'God is a New Language.' *Monastic Studies* (1969) 95-102.

'The Self and the Other.' *The Downside Review* 87 (1969) 351-357.

'The Church: Sacrament of Mankind in Christ.' *American Benedictine Review* 21 (1970) 79-87.

'The Monk and the World.' *The Downside Review* 88 (1970) 150-159.

'The Theology of William of St. Thierry: A Methodological Problem.' *Cistercian Studies* 6 (1971) 261-268.

BOOK REVIEWS

R. O. Johann. *The Meaning of Love* in *Pax* 49 (1959) 131.

V. White. *Holy Teaching. The Idea of Theology According to St.
Thomas Aquinas* in *Pax* 50 (1960) 34.

O. Casel. *The Mystery of Christian Worship and Other Writings* in
Pax 52 (1962) 134-135.

Mysterium Salutis, Dogmatique de l'Histoire du Salut in *The Downside Review* 88 (1970) 307-308.

J. Leclercq et al. *The Spirituality of the Middle Ages* in *Ample-
forth Journal* 75 (1970) 269-270.

PRESENTATION

Dom Odo Brooke's unexpected passing, quiet, peaceful, alone, at the early age of fifty-one, could not help but bring to mind the similar passing of two others who in different but complementary ways contributed most significantly to the renaissance of Cistercian studies in the English-speaking world: Father Louis (Thomas) Merton of Gethsemani, of whose death on December 10, 1968 the whole world was apprised, and Father Basil Morrison of Mount Saint Bernard's Abbey, who peacefully responded to the Lord's final call while kneeling in prayer in his cell making his thanksgiving after Mass on Sunday, January 16, 1969.

Father Louis, with his thirsting genius and deep spiritual insight, drank deeply of the Cistercian Fathers during his novitiate years, and later with a prophetic voice aroused the same thirst in others and inspired the undertaking of Cistercian Publications. Father Basil, as Master of Students in the General House of the Order, during what proved to be its most significant years, oriented the whole Order toward the revival of a monastic approach to studies. Together, then, these two prepared a receptive audience that wanted and needed the kind of scholarly offerings that Father Odo Brooke generously shared and that are again made available in this volume. Hopefully their publication here will bring them to a much larger audience and give them the permanence they deserve.

As we read through the rich pages of this volume, we cannot help but think how well prepared Father Odo Brooke must have been that Tuesday afternoon when, sitting at his desk which was in many respects his altar, he quietly responded to his Lord. Indeed, his whole scholarly life seems to have been a constant preparation for entering into the vision of the Trinity. We are fortunate that his life, which in its essentials was not different from that of many other monks, was gifted with a special grace of communication and that fraternal love which undertakes the laborious task of seeking to share the fruits of contemplative study. We are the richer for it.

Perhaps no medieval author can speak so directly to our age as can the open-minded and open-hearted Abbot of Saint Thierry. William's humble sharings, coming directly out of his own life experience like clear refreshing waters from a living spring, were meant to flow immediately into the life-currents of other open hearts. He wrote sometimes for novices, to help them learn how to pray, and these writings, clear and limpid, can immediately refresh even the beginner. But at other times his own profound depths, both as a scholar and a mystic, are shared with the reader in vibrant currents of thought that are too much for

pedantic prose and must leap about in analogies, reach out in all
directions for similes and burst forth in cascades of poetry.
Here, if the reader is not to be overwhelmed by the powerful flow
of thought, he stands in need of a sturdy guide who with sure
foot can tread his way through the flowing tide. And it is here
that Father Odo, after a long, prayerful and studious preparation,
generously offers his services.

Not every student of William of Saint Thierry will agree
with all of Father Odo's interpretations of the great medieval
mystic. Perhaps, to some extent, Father has too readily accepted
the assertions of Dom Déchanet in regard to William's sources,
especially among the Greeks. But the beginner can confidently
take him for guide, for Father surely touches on some of the deepest currents of William's experience and seems to have entered into them. The reader senses that the young Benedictine of the
twentieth century did indeed have something of the same lived experience as his fellow monks of the twelfth century.

Central to Father Odo's concern with William is the Abbot's
teaching concerning the development of faith to its fullest flow-
ering in the inner experience of the Trinity. He felt the theory
of the trinitarian mystical experience is William's most original
contribution to trinitarian theology and the orientation of faith
towards that trinitarian experience is his most original contribution to the patristic and monastic *credo ut experiar* (I believe
that I might experience).

In general, the short articles from *Pax* and *Downside Review*
are the more exciting and challenging, for in these Father Odo
sets forth in broad, bold strokes the basic insights which he la-
boriously and clearly grounds in the weightier scientific articles.

In the brief article from the *Month*, 'William of St. Thierry',
we find not only a brief biography of William but Father Odo's
basic insight into the nature of William's trinitarian theology
and mysticism, their relation and their essential movement. The
following articles, substantially the doctoral thesis Father Odo
so ably defended at San Anselmo, the Benedictine Pontifical College in Rome, fill out in a thoroughly scholarly way the content
of the first. It is in the latter that the spiritual unction of
William's and Father Odo's writings is more fully experienced.

Again, we find William's penetrating analysis of the dynamic
movement of faith toward vision summarily and popularly presented
in an article from *Downside Review*, and then fully and profoundly
elaborated in the two succeeding articles originally published in
Recherches de Théologie Ancienne et Médiévale.

In William's writing Father Odo found two distinct presentations of this development of faith. The one could be summed up

in the **expressions** *forma fidei, ratio fides* and its goal, *credo ut intelligam;* the reception of the formulas of faith from authority and the exploration of them by reason to attain understanding, the *cognitio fidei.* The emphasis here was on the acceptance of faith as the starting point, the role of authority, and the understanding of the intellect. It was essentially William's answer to Abelard.

Its weakness seems to lie in the refusal of *ratio fidei,* beginning only from what faith gives, to admit the value of developing a metaphysics in its own right, the contribution of a scholastic theology which would still subordinate reason to faith.

The other course is summed up in *ex fide in fidem, intellectus fidei - affectu cordis* and its goal *credo ut experiar.* The movement here is from the faith received to an inner penetration of it, not so much by reason as by a connatural intention based on love and caused by the illuminating **grace** of the Holy Spirit, giving birth to the *cognitio amoris.* This is the course which is central to William's thinking and Father Odo's concern.

Father Odo subscribed to that school of theologians who maintain that at the basis of even the initial act of **faith** there is a certain connaturality between the believer and the Divine revealed, and he saw in this the remote basis for a development toward mystical experience. Faith and the image of God in man are essentially dynamic, in movement toward union and likeness and ultimately vision. And the two are intimately linked. The image of God in man is a dynamic imprint, supernatural from the start, impelling the soul toward union with the Trinity through a transition from image to likeness. This is brought about by the Holy Spirit and is essentially a participation in the Holy Spirit, who is the unity of the Father and the Son. It comes about through experiential mystical knowledge proportioned to the restoration of the likeness; likeness causing connatural knowledge, which in its turn causes greater likeness, etc., until complete fulfillment in the beatific vision. Father Odo perceives the primacy of mystical experience in William's life and how his theology is an attempt to share and describe the reality which he has experienced, 'evolving a theology of the Trinity that is essentially mystical and a mystical theology that is essentially trinitarian.'

The articles in the second section, 'Studies in Monasticism and Theology,' are not divorced from those of the first; rather, they flow directly from them. Father Odo's deeply enriching personal experience of the theology of William of St. Thierry made him realize how much an experiential theology had to offer to our times, which in large measure have known only the more arid theology of the scholastics. He broadens his base for this insight by his considerations of monastic theology in general and of St. Aelred of Rievaulx in particular. But he does not simply propose a return to their 'kneeling theology.'

For me, one of the most exciting articles is his 'Towards an Integral Theology.' Here Father contrasts scholastic theology, which, basing itself on the perennial philosophy, seeks the metaphysical grounding of the facts of Revelation and the experiential theology of the Fathers and the medieval monks of the Cistercian school, which concentrates on salvation history and man's personal assimilation of this in responding to it. And then he goes on to point out that not only do we need to refind this approach to theology when the theologian goes beyond thinking and talking to living and experiencing, but that the theologian now has wonderful tools in existentialist and personalist philosophy and depth psychology, in the works of Heidegger, Marcel and Jung, to help man to see the Christian message as the fulfillment of his inner aspirations.

Unique in this collection is the final article, 'The Monk and the World.' It is indeed a piece apart, a witness that Father Odo was alive to the currents of monastic renewal and debate that were swirling around him as he pursued his quiet, scholarly ways. In this article he modestly offers 'a few tentative reflections' on the role of the monk in the world today. Seeing it as a witness to the world that is to evolve out of this present world, he presents a pluralistic solution to the debate between 'active' and 'contemplative' monks as to how best to achieve this witness, and asks the significant question, 'whether a monasticism centered in a deep experience of prayer is necessarily incompatible with a greater openness and freedom in our institutional structures and in our contacts with the surrounding world.'

I never had the privilege of meeting Father Odo Brooke personally, though we **corresponded** frequently. But in these articles I do think I have met him in a very deep way. I have met more than his thought, certainly, something of his inner spirit and heart. What he wrote of the Cistercian Fathers I think can aptly be applied to himself:

> For these theologians were concerned predominantly not with the history of Salvation in its purely objective, external, collective aspect but with the assimilation of that history through the connatural experience of the individual believer. Moreover, this was a personal assimilation in the experience of the theologian himself. It was not simply an analytical reflection on the meaning of this experience according to the testimony of others. These theologians did not only know about connatural knowledge. They knew connaturally. Their reflections about

this kind of knowledge were grounded in their own
personal experience.

Father Odo's shared experience of William and of that kind
of mystical experience of which William wrote has truly enriched
my life. Dom David has told us that Father Odo had a genius for
true friendship. Undoubtedly that is why he understood and
brought out in his article, 'Toward a Theology of Connatural Knowledge.' the key significance for our times of Aelred's teaching
on friendship. A shy man, Father Odo has best expressed the true
Christian quality of his friendship by his generous sharing of
himself and the fruit of his quiet scholarly labors through these
written words.
    We can be grateful to Cistercian Publications for making them
permanently available to us, and for publishing them as a lasting
tribute to Dom Odo Brooke - a tribute so richly deserved.

                                        M. Basil Pennington OCSO

St. Joseph's Abbey
Spencer, Massachusetts

PREFACE

DOM ODO BROOKE

VICTOR BROOKE was born in London in 1919. His father's side of the family were staunch Ulster Protestants; Victor was a cousin of Lord Brookeborough, the former premier of Northern Ireland, and, after the death of his parents, a ward of Viscount Alanbrooke. Of the years before his entry into monastic life little is known; Fr. Odo said little about this period of his life and it was characteristic of him to be more interested in other people, their problems and their joys. However, it seems that he went to a prep school in Sunningdale and thence to Eton. Victor being a bookish person was not the type to plunge into compulsory games with much enthusiasm, but he enjoyed his experiences as a "wet bob," or membership of the rowing club, even if, as on one occasion, his efforts at coxing were disastrous. A well-known figure at Eton at that time was Dr. Henry Ley, who was in charge of chapel music. Victor, like many others, found obligatory attendance in chapel distasteful and throughout his life always campaigned for more liberty in every sphere. He found the ethos of public school worship unattractive and this, no doubt, influenced him to a certain extent in the important step which he was to take later. From Eton he went in 1938 to New College, Oxford, where in due course he took a degree in modern languages. He was improving his knowledge of German by living with a family in Vienna when Hitler's troops entered the Austrian capital; and when war was at last declared between Britain and Germany he became—to the great disapproval of his family—a conscientious objector. Continuing to live in Oxford, he spent his time in market gardening and so developed a liking for this form of work at which he spent an hour or so every day after joining the community. In 1943 a further decision to be received into the Roman Catholic Church led to the breaking off of connections between himself and his relations.

Three years after his reception into the Church, Victor Brooke became, like many converts, interested in monasticism and, at the suggestion of the author Robert Sencourt, his close friend, he paid a visit to Prinknash. At first sight not the most likely candidate for a community in which manual work had a large place, he nevertheless sought admission and was clothed as a novice in 1947. As a novice he sometimes drove those who had to instruct him in practical matters to desperation and stories of his ineptitude in the kitchen and in church ceremonial were frequently related. On one occasion he served up the cocoa in soup tureens with ladles and on another, when told to turn out the oven gas, was found a little later trying in vain to blow it out. His

gifts lay elsewhere; and when, after making his profession, he began his studies for the priesthood, his destination was obviously
Sant' Anselmo, Rome. Here he eventually took a doctorate in theology, his thesis being 'The Trinitarian Aspect of the Ascent of
the Soul to God in the Theology of William of St. Thierry.' In
1959 an extract from this was published in Louvain and a further
extract appeared in 1966 in *Recherches de Théologie ancienne et
médiévale*. It would appear that the writings of the Benedictine
abbot turned Cistercian held a special interest for him, for he
wrote an article entitled 'William of St. Thierry' for the *Month*
in 1962 and 'Faith and Mystical Experience in William of St.
Thierry' for the *Downside Review* in 1964. In the following year
appeared 'Natural Religion in the Supernatural Existential' *(Downside Review* 1965) and 'The Self and the Other' *(Downside Review*
1969). He reviewed a number of books for PAX and for the *Ample-
forth Journal*, but his articles for PAX were surprisingly few.
'Monastic Theology and St. Aelred' (1959) and 'Towards an Integral Theology' (1964). He was ordained priest at Farnborough in
1954 and two years later completed his studies in Rome. On his
return, although originally assigned to Farnborough, his services
were in demand at Prinknash and accordingly he spent the next ten
years there teaching theology. When he finally came back to Farnborough in 1967 he settled down to more intensive study. The
following articles were written during this period: 'Towards a
Theology of Connatural Knowledge' *(Citeaux: Commentarii Cister-
cienses*, 1967), 'God is a new language' *(Monastic Studies*, 1969),
'The Church: Sacrament of Mankind in Christ' *(American Benedictine Review*, 1970), and 'The Monk and the World' *(Downside Review*,
1970). A deep thinker, his written output was, as can be seen,
not large; he never published a book. But he was often called
upon to give talks and sermons, was an excellent conversational-
ist and wrote witty letters.

His sermons were never without interest, based as they obviously were on careful reflection, and he was invariably chosen to
preach on special occasions; his last sermon was given at the
Christmas midnight Mass.

Although **Fr.** Odo held surprisingly liberal views on a number
of questions (he used to describe himself, with a smile, as a
conservative anarchist) he was unrelentingly conservative where
liturgy was concerned. In choir his love of the traditional
Latin liturgy was more often expressed by an interior than an exterior participation, and outside choir, although something of a
pianist, he would regularly spend an hour or so every Sunday lis-
tening to records of his favourite composers. The new vernacular
mass was at the beginning a great trial to him, and his efforts
to carry it out in obedience to authority in both monastery and
parish were often the source of no little amusement and

exasperation to the onlookers. Yet his devotion to the regular celebration of Mass was such that he never omitted daily celebration, except on the day he died when he was sent back to bed. It was also his invariable custom to remain behind in church for prayer after Vespers and Compline each day.

Some weeks before Christmas he developed asthma very badly and his condition deteriorated. He died quite suddenly of bronchial pneumonia on January 12th. In the community he will be remembered for his sympathy and understanding, for his cheerful presence and example.

DAVID PLACID HIGHAM
from PAX: A BENEDICTINE
REVIEW 326 (1971) 42-44

CHAPTER 1

WILLIAM OF ST THIERRY*

THE MYSTERY OF THE BLESSED TRINITY is at the very center not only of Christian doctrine but also of Christian spirituality.[1] This statement cannot be contested, yet it asks a challenging question. Do we think of God above all as the Trinitarian revelation, and is our life and especially our life of prayer formed after the pattern of that dogma? Surely the tendency is to think rather of 'God' and of his providence, than of the Father as the origin of the whole Trinitarian plan of salvation, expressed so forcefully at the beginning of the Epistle to the Ephesians: 'Blessed be that God, that Father of our Lord Jesus Christ . . . who has chosen us out, in Christ, before the foundation of the world, to be saints . . . marking us out before hand (so his will decreed) to be his adopted children through Jesus Christ . . . In him you learned to believe, and had the seal set on your faith by the promised gift of the Holy Spirit.'[2] Then from 'God,' our mind moves spontaneously to the Incarnation and Redemption. But are we always aware that through Christ, and as is so often forgotten, in the Holy Spirit, we are drawn into a Trinitarian relationship?

If asked why we are not more alive to the place of the Trinity in our lives and in our prayer, the reason may be that we think of the Trinity too exclusively in terms of the Processions within themselves and of the speculative theological problems arising from the mystery of three persons in one identical nature. However important this is for theology, if the Trinity is viewed almost entirely from this angle, it will inevitably appear remote from the lives of the faithful. The perspective is changed once it is realized that Revelation presents the Trinity first of all as the intervention of the persons for our salvation, according to the relationship 'From the Father, through the Son, in the Spirit to the Father,' with the life of the Trinity in itself as the ultimate foundation of this plan. Through this pattern, the Church lives her faith in the official prayer of the liturgy.[3] In Scripture and in the Liturgy, the Trinity is presented not only with an emphasis on the intervention in the history of salvation, but also on the persons in their distinct relationship rather than on their unity of nature.[4] A further question arises. How is the dogma of the Trinity lived in the spirituality of the individual Christian, and especially how is it lived by the mystics? The doctrine of William of St. Thierry is an important contribution towards an answer. His approach, though not to be identified simply with that of Scripture and the liturgy, is a further testimony to the relevance of the Trinity for Christian life. The

intervention of the persons in the history of salvation is now
concentrated on their intervention in the history of the individual soul. The spiritual life at its deepest level is seen as an
experience of the Trinitarian life of the Holy Spirit. Mysticism
is here shown to us not primarily as an advance in states of
prayer to be analyzed and charted. It is shown as the ultimate
meaning of man, and that meaning is to be found in the Trinity.

Nothing is known of William's early life, except that he was
born at Liége of noble parentage, in the second half of the elev-
enth century. It is very probable that he made his studies in
the famous school of Laon, under its master Anselm, and in the
company of Peter Abelard. We do not know, either, how long he
spent in the academic world; only that he was there long enough
to acquire a vast fund of intellectual learning which enabled him
later on to argue with confidence against the errors of Peter
Abelard and William of Conche. He first took the monastic habit
in the Benedictine Abbey of Saint Nicaise at Rheims; and in 1119-
20 he became abbot of Saint Thierry just outside Rheims. Here he
was intensely occupied for more than fifteen years with a temporal
administration which involved all the complex relations inherent
in a feudal régime with the nobility, the bourgeoisie and the
villeins. He had at the same time the direction of his monks, and
was playing a prominent part in the monastic revival which was
animating all the abbeys of his part of France. During this period he was wrestling with two personal problems, wretched health
and a burning desire for the eremitical life. He found himself
constantly drawn, as his own interior life developed through
prayer and study, to the Cistercian ideal as he encountered it in
Bernard himself. And yet, during these years as abbot, he wrote
his two great treatises on the love of God, *De contemplando Deo,*
and *De natura et dignitate amoris;* his treatise on man, *De natura
corporis et animae;* on the Blessed Sacrament, *De Sacramento Altaris,* and a commentary on the Epistle to the Romans.

Finally in 1135 he retired from St Thierry and joined the
Cistercian community at Signy in the Ardennes. There he remained
until his death in 1148. It was there that he wrote his treatises
on the faith against Abelard, *Speculum fidei* and *Aenigma fidei,*
his great commentary on the Canticle of Canticles and his Life
of St Bernard.

We know of only one absence from Signy during those thirteen
years: a visit to the Carthusian Monastery of Mont-Dieu. It pro-
duced the famous treatise on the eremitical life the *Epistola ad
fratres de Monte Dei,* which has come to be known as the Golden
Epistle.

Within the various trends of monastic theology,[5] the Cistercian theological movement, represented principally by St Bernard
and William of St Thierry, is of particular interest for the

question of the relationship of dogma to the spiritual life. In
contrast to those theologians among the black monks, as for instance Rupert of Deutz,[6] who tended to view the mysteries of
Christianity more in the broad outlines of the history of salvation, the Cistercians dwelt principally on the reflection of this
history as experienced within the individual soul. Their theology
is dominated by the theme of the journey of the soul to God.
This trend is admirably illustrated in the trinitarian theology
of William of St Thierry, always related in some way, either directly or indirectly, to this ascent of the soul, and moving ultimately towards a mystical experience of the Trinity. Despite a
more technical treatment of the subject in the *Aenigma fidei* and
in the polemical works against Abelard and Conche, he views the
Trinity more as a principle of life than as a problem to be scrutinized. His deepest convictions can be found in the words of
his friend Bernard: 'To subject this mystery to profane scrutiny
is rashness, to believe in it, true piety; to know it is life,
and eternal life.'[7]

Though William uses the Augustinian 'created trinity' of memory, intellect and will as a metaphorical illustration of the Trinity and the order of the Processions,[8] he is not really interested in the discovery of created analogies of the Trinity. His aim
was not to give a metaphysical explanation of how the Son proceeds
from the Father and the Holy Spirit from the Father and Son. Nor
was it even to give that kind of insight described by St Augustine
in his *De Trinitate*, when the mind is led, pedagogically, to a
contemplative perception of the uncreated Trinity through the medium of created images.[9] For William, the image of God in man is
the basis of the ascent of the soul to God. It is an imprint of
the Trinity[10] which gives to the soul its initial capacity to
achieve its final state of perfect likeness, *similitudo*. The *similitudo* is therefore the perfection of the *imago*.[11] As a mystical
theologian, William was more interested in this likeness than in
the image. For the likeness, as we shall see, implies his whole
doctrine on the experience of the Trinity. But even where he
gives a more complete analysis of the image as such, the whole
trend of his thought is to portray the image as a dynamic force
impelling the soul towards its perfection in the likeness.[12] The
analysis of trinities in the soul is seen as less important than
the movement of the soul towards the Trinity. The aim is not so
much to illustrate the Trinity by metaphor as to reach out towards
union with the Trinity.

In the *Aenigma fidei* William speaks of the ascent to God by
three theological stages, the way of faith, of the reasoning of
faith *(ratio fidei)*, and finally of 'experience.'[13] A great point
of interest in this important text is its close parallel with a
text in the *Golden Epistle* describing the spiritual ascent through

the three states, *animalis, rationalis, spiritualis*,[14] rooted ultimately in a psychological trichotomy, *anima, animus, spiritus*.[15]
There is no indication that William intended this trichotomy as a
metaphorical illustration of the three Persons of the Trinity.
Nor should the trichotomy be interpreted as a psychological division of the soul into three parts. It is a question more of
three aspects of the life of the soul in the spiritual ascent.
This relationship of theology to spirituality and to psychology
offers an interesting example of theological method. For it is a
theology developing in successive stages, each of which is proportioned in turn to the life of the senses, of the reason and of
the spirit. Thus grounded in the spiritual life of the soul, William's theology shares in the movement of what Louis Bouyer has
rightly called 'Une dynamique de l'âme.'[16] This movement is directed towards that state of likeness *(similitudo)*, the experience
of the Trinity which foreshadows the final vision of God in eternity.

    The first theological stage, that of faith, is related to the
status animalis, when man is under the dominion of the senses and
needs the guidance of an external authority to rule his life.[17]
This stage is closely connected with the Incarnation and the
whole temporal economy as a pedagogic preparation leading man by
degrees through what is perceptible to the senses towards the
eternal, immutable life of the Trinity.[18] The Incarnation is seen
as a *sacramentum*, not as we use the term for the sacraments strictly so called, but in the patristic sense of the word, implying the
whole range of signs whereby what is eternal, spiritual and invisible should be manifested through the medium of what is temporal,
material and visible: 'This is to be seen most clearly in the
person of the Mediator, who, though he is God eternal, became man
in time; in order that through him who is eternal and subject to
time, we may pass from the temporal to the eternal.'[19]

    The second stage, that of the reasoning power of faith,
brings us to the more technical and speculative development of
William's thought in the polemical works, particularly the *Aenigma
fidei*. His writings against Abelard and Conche are directed
against what appeared to him as a rationalism destructive of the
mystery of the Trinity.[20] The *Aenigma fidei* is a further development, to give an example of a more positive, constructive trinitarian theology as a counteraction to Abelard. Here William comes
forward as the Irenaeus of the twelfth century, the champion of
Orthodoxy and tradition, opposing the sources of the Faith in
Scripture and the authority of the Fathers to the dangerous rationalistic speculations of some of his contemporaries.[21] But as
Père Déchanet has shown, his return not only to St Augustine, but
also to the 'Light from the East' of the Greek Fathers, held in
suspicion by the conservative theologians of that time, reveals

considerable originality in the choice of these sources.[22]   In
opposition to Abelard, William's *ratio fidei* places reason wholly
under the dominion of faith, and from this angle he approaches the
metaphysical problems of the Trinity.   The central and more speculative section of the *Aenigma fidei* shows both the weakness and
the strength of this reaction.   In the attempt to push further
the analysis of such problems as that of the meaning of person
in the Trinity, it can hardly be said that on the metaphysical
plane he equals the best achievements of the contemporary scholastic movement.   His contribution lies rather in the fine dialectic
with which he leads us at every turn towards the ultimate mystery
of the Trinity.   After approaching the Trinity from almost every
viewpoint, the emphasis of the Latin Fathers on the unity of nature alternating with that of the Greek Fathers on the distinction
of Persons, *ratio fidei* confronts us at each conclusion with the
impenetrable mystery.   We are told that the human mind never
understands the Trinity so well as when it is understood to be incomprehensible.[23]   The initial mystery of the God who is both
three and one is never lessened, yet William's speculations always
explain more exactly just where the mystery lies in every aspect
of the problem.

From speculative problems William passes to the final stage,
mystical experience.   Thinking about the Trinity gives way to
experiencing the Trinity.   For *ratio fidei,* even though so ener-
gized by faith that it becomes a unique power *(ratio sui generis)*[24]
is still human reason, whereas in the final phase we pass beyond
reason to the sphere of the Spirit.   Here man's knowledge of the
Trinity is not his own; it is that which the Trinity has of itself: 'Those to whom the Father and the Son reveal each other
know exactly as the Father and the Son know each other.'[25]   This
knowledge is from the Holy Spirit; more, it is a share in the
very life of the Spirit.   It comes wholly from within the Spirit;
and it is a stage of transition from faith to sight.   It is an
anticipation, however remote, of the final vision of God.   *Ratio
fidei* led to the incomparable mystery.   This new knowledge, or
rather the *amor-intellectus* 'love-which-is-understanding,' gives
a kind of insight.   The mind is no longer perplexed by the antithesis of three and one.[26]   This does not mean that there is no
longer a mystery, that the antithesis is now reconciled by reason,
so as to see how three and one are compatible.   It means that the
mind has passed out of the realm of conceptual knowledge, where
the question whether reason can in any way explain the mystery no
longer arises.

What is meant by the statement that this kind of knowledge
is from within the Trinity and that it is the very life of the
Holy Spirit?   The explanation lies in the nature of knowledge,
and the strict equation between knowledge and likeness to the

thing known. From an analysis of sense knowledge, William describes how the eye cannot see unless it is somehow transformed into what is seen, nor can the ear hear unless it is in some way
transformed into what is heard.[27] So on an incomparably higher
plane we cannot know God in the way in which he knows himself, unless we have been transformed into his likeness. This relationship between knowledge and likeness acts in reciprocal causality.
Not only do we become like God in so far as we know him, but, reversing the text of St John, it is equally true that we know him
only in so far as we become like him: 'To be like God there
[namely, in the final vision] will be to see God, to know him.
We shall see him, know him in the same proportion as we are like
him. We shall be like him to the precise extent that we see him,
know him. For to see God, to know him, is to be like him; and to
be like him is to see him, to know him.'[28] We become like him
when the image of the Trinity in the soul has been perfected and
brought back to a perfect likeness, the *similitudo*, the most perfect union between the soul and God compatible with the distinction between Creature and Creator.[29] It is achieved when the
soul is raised to a created participation in the life of the Holy
Spirit, who is the uncreated mutual union of the Father and the
Son.
        The *raison d'être* of this experience is the life of the Holy
Spirit, as can be seen from the sequence of the argument. The
foundation of the experience is likeness, and the foundation of
the likeness is the Holy Spirit as the mutual union of the Father
and the Son. William goes so far as to say that the experience
is the Holy Spirit, though he guards carefully against any panthe-
istic interpretation:

> We may say that the life of the Spirit is this union,
> not merely because the Holy Spirit effects it or that he
> brings man's spirit to it, but because he, the Holy Spirit,
> God, Love, is this union (*ipsa ipse est Spiritus sanctus*).
> For he is the love, the union, the sweetness and the good-
> ness of the Father and Son; he is their kiss, their em-
> brace and whatever is common to them both in that trans-
> cendent union which is truth, in that truth which is union.
> Through him, then, all that belongs to the Son by sub-
> stantial union in his relationship to the Father, or to
> the Father in his relationship to the Son--all this is
> given in due proportion to man in his relationship to God;
> and man, in the possession of this blessed experience,
> when Father and Son kiss and embrace, finds himself in
> some way in their midst. Through the Holy Spirit, the
> man of God becomes in some ineffable, incredible way--not
> God exactly; but what God is by nature, man becomes by grace.[30]

Nor does he hesitate to say that the Holy Spirit is himself the love by which we love God--*ipse enim est amor noster*.[31] Love and knowledge are so closely united in this experience that he describes it as a knowledge-in-love *(cognito amoris)*; by which he means, not a formal identification of the faculties of intellect and will, but their interpenetration and union, in this knowledge of God which is *sui generis*. And the root of it is the trinitarian life.

William's mysticism is essentially trinitarian in the sense that its whole meaning is to be found in this theme. Through the Holy Spirit we share in that mutual knowledge by which Father and Son know each other: 'Those to whom Father and Son reveal each other know exactly as Father and Son know each other; that is, they have written in them the mutual knowledge that Father and Son have of each other; they have their unity, their will and their love; and all this is the Holy Spirit.'[32] This is an experimental knowledge which foreshadows the final vision:

> The sweet awareness (*sensus*) and experience of this
> infinite good, this indeed is life, the truly blessed
> life--even though in this wretched life it cannot be
> complete. But in the future life, life and its happi-
> ness will be brimming over, all the time, for ever.[33]

Does this imply a direct intuition that the Holy Spirit is the mutual love and union of the Father and the Son? Such a possibility cannot be excluded, but it is not the most likely explanation. A more probable interpretation can be given on the lines of Henri Bremond's illuminating analysis of the experience of the Venerable Mary of the Incarnation.[34] He argues convincingly that mystical experience as such is on a different plane from conceptual, scientific, theological knowledge. According to his interpretation, Mary of the Incarnation, in reflecting on her experience would have attempted to express it in terms of the current theological concepts. These concepts would evoke psychologically the memory of the intuition. As a result, she would pass imperceptibly from its description to its expression in theological concepts. So in the case of William of St Thierry, first of all there would be the initial experience of union with the persons of the Trinity. This would be followed by its theological expression in terms of the Augustinian Theory of the Holy Spirit. There is the clearest indication that William is talking of insight on the mystical plane, yet the explanation of this insight is given in terms of a theological theory. These two planes are so closely interwoven that in his writings they are inseparable.

Despite allusions to an experimental knowledge of the Trinity in the writings of the Fathers, there was no fully developed

theology of this experience. The great contribution of William
of St Thierry is to have evolved a theology of the Trinity which
is essentially mystical, and a mystical theology which is essentially trinitarian. He is therefore the initiator of the tradition of **trinitarian** mysticism, which is to be found especially in
the writings of Ruysbroeck, Eckhart, Tauler and Suso.[35]
     The structure of this theology is persuasive in its unified
sequence of thought. But how far does its ultimate value depend
on the initial premiss of the theory of the Holy Spirit as the
mutual love and union of the Father and the Son, a theological
opinion dating princapally from St Augustine?[36] Could it for instance be applied to the trinitarian economy, *Ex Patre, per Filium,
in Spiritu,* to be found throughout the New Testament and the liturgy, or to the theological explanations of the Greek Fathers
based on this economy? The force of William's trinitarian spirituality lies precisely in the Holy Spirit as the bond of union,
in whom we are united to the Father and the Son. The *similitudo,*
the 'likeness,' with its divine mode of knowledge received in
proportion to this likeness, follow strictly from this basis.
But in the Scriptural or 'Greek' trinitarian economy no less than
in the Augustinian theory, the Holy Spirit is the bond of union,
whereby we are linked with the other persons. The only difference
lies in why this is so. According to the theology of the Greek
Fathers, the Holy Spirit is the last person in the sequence of the
descending movement from the Father through the Son in the Holy
Spirit, and is therefore the first person with whom we make contact and in whom we are **drawn** in the sequence of the ascending
movement through the Son to the Father. As this initial point of
contact with the other persons, the Holy Spirit is the link, the
bond of union, in whom we participate in the Trinitarian relations.
William's mystical theology, despite its basis in the Augustinian
theory of the Holy Spirit, can throw light also on the whole Scriptural and 'Greek' Trinitarian tradition.
     In conclusion, William teaches us that to discover our true
selves is to discover the life of the Trinity. Created with the
imprint of the trinitarian image, the soul is impelled towards the
recovery of the perfect likeness to its archetype. In so far as
the soul achieves this likeness, it is given an insight which
passes beyond all that can be known by the senses or by human
reason. In a finely developed sequence of thought, he shows how
this experience of the Trinity is grounded in the Holy Spirit as
the bond of union, giving us a share in the mutual communion and
knowledge of the Father and the Son. This is to realize the pro-
mise of Christ to send the Holy Spirit to his apostles. 'In that
day you shall know that I am in my Father: and you in me, and I
in you.'[37]

NOTES

*Published in *The Month* 214 (1962) 342-52; and in *Spirituality Through the Ages*, ed. James Walsh (New York: Kenedy, 1964).

[1]Cf., M-M Philipon, 'La Trinité clé de roûte des mystères Chrétiens,' *Revue Thomiste* 58 (1958) 5-19.

[2]Eph. I, 3-14.

[3]See C. Vagaggini, *Theological Dimensions of the Liturgy*, translated by L. J. Doyle (Collegeville, 1959) 106-39, and C. Davis, *Liturgy and Doctrine* (London, 1960) 20-35.

[4]Cf the testimony of the more general teaching of the Greek Fathers, and also of the Latin Fathers before Nicaea: de Régnon, *Etudes de théologie positive sur la Sainte Trinité* (Paris, 1892) Vol. 4, 532.

[5]Cf., J. Leclercq, *L'amour des lettres et le desir de Dieu* (Paris, 1957); 'S. Bernard et la théologie monastique du XIIe siècle,' *S. Bernard Théologien, ASOC 9* (1953) 7-23, and 'The Monastic Tradition of Culture and Studies,' *American Benedictine Review* 11 (1960) 99-131.

[6]For example, the Prologue to his *De trinitate* (PL 167, 199) aims to show how the Trinity acts through the 'Book' of Creation and Redemption and divides history into three main phases, attributed respectively to the Father, the Son, and the Holy Ghost.

[7]*De consideratione*, PL 182, 799C. The tendency of William and St Bernard to minimize the value of human reason and philosophy should be seen in the light of the rationalism of Abelard and his disciples.

[8]Nat am, PL 184, 382C-D; Nat corp PL 180, 721B-C.

[9]PL 42, 1035; 1088. But note that William's approach is also to be found in Augustine: Ibid., 1051 and 1055.

[10]Nat corp, 721 CD.

[11]Ep frat PL 184, 348C; 341D.

[12]Nat am PL 184, 382A-383A; Nat corp 721B-721A; Spec fid PL 180, 365B-368C.

[13]Aenig, 414B-415D.

[14]Ep frat, 315C-316B.

[15]Ibid., 340C; 348CD-349A.

[16]L. Bouyer, *La Spiritualité de Citeaux* (Paris, 1954) 121.

[17]Ep frat, 316C-317D.

[18]Aenig, 402A-D; 403C-404A.

[19]Spec fid, 382-282A.

[20]A persuasive defence of the orthodoxy of Abelard on tri-nitarian theology has been given by J. Cottiaux, 'La conception de la théologie chez Abélard,' RHE 28 (1932) 247-95, 533-51, 787-828. But even if this is admitted, the expressions of Abelard were am-biguous, and there was the further danger from his disciples.

[21]Aenig, 432C: 'Non de fontibus nostris, sed de fontibus Salvatoris, ex Scripturis Sanctis, et certissimis auctoritatibus sanctorum Patrum.'

[22]See especially Déchanet, *Le Miror,* 200-9; and his *Aux Sources de la spiritualité de Guillaume de Saint-Thierry* (Bruges, 1940).

[23]Aenig, 426C.

[24]Ibid., 417B.

[25]Spec fid, 393A; of Aenig, 415A.

[26]Med, PL 180, 214CD.

[27]Med, 213 AB; Spec fid, 390D-391A; of James Walsh, SJ 'Guillaume de Saint-Thierry et les Sens Spirituels,' RAM 137 (1959).

[28]Spec fid, 393C; Aenig, 399AB.

[29]Spec fid, 393B.

[30]Ep frat, 349AB.

[31]Spec, 393AB.

[32]Contemp PL 184, 376B.

[33]Ibid., 394BC.

[34]H. Bremond, *Histoire littéraire du sentiment religieux en France* (Paris, 1926) vol. VI, 30-48. See Mary Denis Mahoney *OSU* 'The Venerable Mary of the Incarnation,' *The Month* (May 1961) 261-76.

[35]See L. Reypens, art. 'Dieu (Connaissance mystique)' in *Dictionnaire de Spiritualité* III (Paris, 1957) 883-929.

[36]See *De trinitate,* PL 42, 1079; 1087.

[37]Jn 14, 20.

CHAPTER 2

THE TRINITARIAN ASPECT
OF THE ASCENT OF THE SOUL TO GOD
IN THE THEOLOGY OF WILLIAM OF ST THIERRY*

PREFACE

WITHIN THE LAST THIRTY YEARS increasing attention has been
given to the study of William of St Thierry, and the importance of
his theology is at last winning due recognition. Among other
works, those of Jean-Marie Déchanet have been particularly outstanding. He has undertaken an extensive research into the
sources, giving special attention to the influence of the Greek
Fathers.[1] There have been his translations of some of William's
chief works, a critical latin edition and translation of the *Speculum fidei,* and a detailed analysis of many of the principle
themes underlying his theology.

These works reveal the importance of his doctrine of the Trinity and various aspects of this subject have already been brought
to light.[2] Yet there had been no study of his trinitarian doctrine as such. The need to fill this gap was evident from the in-
tricacy of his thought. He presents this dogma in many various
ways, sometimes even showing what appears to be almost a contradiction in method. The vital question was the interrelationship
of this complex pattern. Above all, was there any one dominant
trinitarian theme? If so, how did this relate to the other elements in his trinitarian thought? This was the chief purpose of
a thesis on this subject. It was an attempt to present William's
doctrine of the Trinity as a whole, and in doing so to show its
value in the light of the historical background, both of the contemporary theology of the twelfth century and of the preceding
history of the dogma of the Trinity. In addition there was the
need for a more complete analysis of the speculative development
in the *Aenigma fidei,* and particularly to examine more closely the
question of the interplay of the 'Greek and the 'Latin' approach
to the Trinity. New problems on the construction of the *Aenigma
fidei* have risen in the light of the discoveries of Père Déchanet
from original manuscripts and his own unpublished theories on that
subject, which he so generously allowed to be introduced into this
thesis.

When the decision was taken to publish parts of this work in
separate articles, the difficulty at once arose as to how the
structure of this whole doctrine could be preserved. It has nevertheless been found to be possible to give its most important aspects in two articles. In the first article the aim is to centre
the attention on what has been found to be the dominant trinitarian

theme and the root of his spirituality. This article is constructed from chapter I, the main points of chapter II, and chapter VIII.
This new adaptation has at least the advantage of bringing together the main chapters on the Trinity in relation to the spiritual
life. The second article will be on the speculative development
in the *Aenigma fidei*. The plan for these two articles will help
to accentuate the contrast between those aspects of his trinitarian theology which are related most closely to his doctrine of
the spiritual life and the more technical speculative evolution
in the *Aenigma fidei*, showing a less immediate connection with
that doctrine. It must be admitted that this will mean a sacri-
fice of the organic structure of William's whole trinitarian theology, which the original plan of the thesis intended to convey.
The intention then was to arrange the chapters so as to present
his doctrine of the Trinity in relation to the ascent from the
initial image of the Trinity through the three theological stages
related to the underlying spiritual states, *animalis*, *rationalis*
and *spiritualis* leading to the final 'resemblance' and participation in the trinitarian life through mystical experience.

My thanks among others are due especially to the following:
to Dom Odo Lottin OSB who has undertaken to publish these articles;
to Dom Jean-Marie Déchanet OSB for suggesting the subject of this
thesis, his most generous offer of his own unpublished discoveries
and his constant help and advice; to Dom Cyprian Vagaggini OSB for
his invaluable guidance as Moderator of the thesis, and to Dom
Jean Leclercq OSB for his help in the final revision.

INTRODUCTION

The distinction between the two middle ages, monastic and
scholastic, is already well known to theologians through the writings of Jean Leclercq.[1] Within each of these two broad divisions
of theology there are however various trends. Monastic theology
in general is in line with the tradition of the *sapientia* of the
Fathers as contrasted with the rising *scientia* of the scholastics.[2]

Yet within the framework of this general patristic tradition,
there is a development of particular interest, which is one of the
most distinctive marks of the specifically "monastic" development.
As against the tendency of the black monks to stress the objective
aspect of revelation,[3] the mystery of salvation as manifested
throughout the broad lines of sacred history, the white monks,
and in particular St Bernard and William of St Thierry, stressed
the reflection of this history within the individual soul.[4] In
this way the white monks imparted a special accentuation to the
patristic *sapientia* by an interiorization, or one might prefer to
say by a special emphasis on the more "interior aspects" of the
theology of the Fathers.[5] Both St Bernard and William of

St Thierry were primarily mystic theologians with their interest
centered on the history of the soul in its journey towards union
with God.

The importance of this development in the writings of William
of St Thierry lies in its specifically trinitarian character.
Therefore despite the number of important works[6] on William's
spirituality and theology, it is hoped that a study of William's
doctrine from this particular angle will be of some value. One
of the principle aims of this article will be to attempt to show
what is the main theme at the heart of William's trinitarian theology and its relationship to this journey of the soul and to pro-
vide the foundation for a further article on the mere technical
development of **trinitarian** theology, the *Aenigma fidei*.[7]

THE IMAGE OF THE TRINITY

THE *De Trinitate* of St Augustine has given such a classic exposition of the Trinity as illustrated through created images,
that we tend almost inevitably to think of the image of the Trinity in those terms.

To understand William's treatment of the subject, we must
change our perspective. Although, as we shall see, William uses
the Augustinian illustrations, the main interest of his thought
lies elsewhere. We shall see here how the Augustinian images
undergo a profound transformation, through William's greater emphasis on the dynamic conception of the 'image' as an imprint impelling the soul towards the final 'resemblance' of participation
in the trinitarian life.

The theme of image-resemblance.

'Une des clefs--sinon la clef--de sa spiritualité.'[8] This is
the judgment of Père Déchanet on the distinction between image
and resemblance. He describes this distinction in these terms.
The image is an aptitude, a capacity, an imprint of the divine
life. Resemblance is the divine life itself, the realization of
the supernatural powers which constitute the image.[9] This distinction appears clearly in the works of William.[10] But it is
more than a mere distinction. It represents the two poles of the
journey of the soul, forming one of the basic themes of his spirituality, and intimately related to his doctrine of the Trinity.

The image as an illustration of the Trinity.

William accepts the general principles of St Augustine that

everything in creation reflects the Trinity,[11] though he develops
this theme much less extensively.[12] For instance among the psychological images of St Augustine he selects only that of memory,
intellect and will. The following text from the *De natura et dig-*
nitate amoris gives an example of this psychological image of the
Trinity, illustrating both the Trinity in unity and also the order
of the processions.

> *Memoria de se genuit rationem: et memoria et ratio*
> *de se protulerunt voluntatem. Memoria quippe habet*
> *et continet quo tendendum sit; ratio quod tendendum*
> *sit; voluntas tendit: et haec tria unum quiddam*
> *sunt, sed tres efficaciae; sicut in illa summa Tri-*
> *nitate una est substantia, tres personae: in qua*
> *Trinitate sicut Pater est genitor, Filius genitus,*
> *et ab utroque Spiritus sanctus; sic ex memoria ra-*
> *tio gignitur, ex memoria et ratione voluntas pro-*
> *cedit.*[13]

The image as a means of Union with the Trinity.

The image of the Trinity in man is an illustration of the
Trinity. But it is more than an illustration. It is a means of
union with the Trinity. The following pages will show how this
is evident from the context in which William places the psychological illustration of memory, intellect and will. The same approach can be observed in his treatment of the virtues of faith,
hope and charity, when this illustration[14] of Trinity in unity is
placed in a context where these virtues are seen as a means of
salvation and of union with the Trinity.[15] In fact wherever he
treats of the image of the Trinity it is clear that he was less
interested in the analysis of the Trinity within the soul, than in
the movement of the soul towards the Trinity.

An imprint of the Trinity.

Immediately after the analogy according to the Augustinian
pattern, in the text from *De natura corporis et animae,* the theme
of the imprint is introduced.

> *Formatus es, non ipse formator. Recede ab his quae*
> *infra te sunt, minus formata, minusque formosa quam*
> *tu es; accede ad formam formatricem, ut possis esse*
> *formosior, eidemque semper adjungere, quia tanto ab*
> *illa specie amplius accipies, quanto te illi majori*

*charitatis pondere impresseris. Ab illa enim obtinebis
imaginis hujus indemutabilem statum, a quo sumpsisti
principium.*16

The words *forma formatrix, impresseris* convey the notion of
a form imprinted by the Trinity.17

Is this imprint natural or supernatural?18   In the *Epistola
ad fratres de Monte Dei,* the image which belongs to man necessarily according to his nature is distinguished from the further degrees of likeness which depend on the will and the Holy Spirit.19
This text refers directly to the image of God rather than to the
Trinity, but the existence of this natural foundation of the image
of God together with the association of the image of the Trinity
with the faculties of memory, **intellect** and will, suggest that
there is at least a natural basis for the image of the Trinity.
Père Malevez supports this opinion when he writes of 'la double
ressemblance naturelle,' the image of God and the image of Trinity.20
But William does not conceive this natural image of the Trinity
independently of the supernatural order, as is evident from the
text in the *De natura et dignitate amoris,* where the faculties of
memory, intellect and will are placed directly under the dominion
of the Persons of the Trinity: 'Memoriam sibi vindicat Pater;
rationem **Filius**; voluntatem ab utroque procedentem ab utroque procedens Spiritus Sanctus.'21   This 'prise de possession,' in the
words of Père Déchanet,22 draws the soul into a direct relation
with the Persons of the Trinity, and supernaturalizes the image
of the Trinity in man by implanting from the first moment of creation a tendency towards a supernatural end.

The dynamic tendency of the image to return to resemblance.

We can now see how such a conception emphasizes the dynamic
character of the image.   It is essentially an imprint impelling
the soul **towards** its archetype;23 and its whole *raison d'être* is
to realize this union: 'in ejus quasi quadam arce vim memorialem
collocavit, *ut* creatoris semper potentiam et bonitatem memoraret;'
'ut ergo Deo inhaereret. . .memoriam sibi vindicat Pater. . .'24
The foundation for this inclination is the **principle** that 'like
seeks like.'25   The purpose of the creation of man in the image of
the Trinity was that he should seek union with his creator 'simili
naturaliter ad simile recurrente.'26

But the impression must not be given of an impulse towards
an archetype conceived in a purely philosophical and **Plotinian**
sense.   William's image is essentially historical.   Shortly after
the text from the *De natura corporis et animae* he refers to the
creation and the fall into the *regio dissimilitudinis.*27   This is
an allusion to the whole history of the 'image-resemblance' given

in a text from the *Meditativae orationes* in its complete cycle, the creation of the image and resemblance, the original paradise, the expulsion from paradise into the *regio dissimilitudinis,* and finally the restoration of the initial harmony of the faculties in submission to the creator.[28]

The image of the Trinity is thus placed in a context which refers to the whole history of the soul in its successive phases of creation, fall and redemption. The appeal is made to realize the innate tendencies of the affinity to the Trinity, which exists even despite the fall through the imprint of the Trinity on the very faculties of man's soul, and to return to the original resemblance. The Augustinian analogies of the Trinity are placed within this framework showing that William is not interested primarily in giving an illustration of the Trinity, but in portraying the image as a dynamic force impelling the soul towards union with the Trinity. Père Malevez has rightly drawn attention to the significance of the phrase *cui intendendo* in the text "non jam tam delectatur in sua formositate quam in forma formatrice, *cui intendendo* semper efficitur formosior."[29] This phrase implies that the present image *sua formositas* is only the point of departure for a far more perfect degree of resemblance.[30] This final resemblance is developed fully in the texts which treat specifically of the *unitas spiritus,* and is already suggested in the passages which follow these texts on the image. The Holy Ghost acts on the soul so as to form a union *unum etiam quodammodo ipsa divinitate.*[31] The concluding passages of *De natura corporis et animae* following shortly after the texts on the image stress this historical context further with a description of the stages of the ascent of the soul, ἀναβαθμόσ, with the alternative of the descent, καταβαθμόσ.[32]

The realization of resemblance through the faculties of the image.

We have seen how the Augustinian analogy is given the nature of an imprint from the Persons of the Trinity and placed in the context of the return to resemblance. We have now to see how this return is effected through the faculties constituting the analogy,[33] in such a way that memory, intellect and love are treated as stages in a hierarchical order of ascent to God.[34] The image is seen here no longer as a mere capacity for resemblance but in the very process of actualization.

The text in question[35] does not treat explicitly of an image of the Trinity, but the relationship is implicit through the reference to the faculties of memory, intellect and will, which have elsewhere been explicitly related to the Trinity.[36] The hierarchical order is indicated by the words: 'Dei enim non reminisci, pecoris est; reminisci, non ad intelligendum, plus aliquid pecore, sed minus homine est; reminisci ad intelligendum hominis est; intelligere usque ad amandum, vel amando fruendum, jam hominis perfectae rationis.'[37]

There is a clear allusion here to the three stages, animal, rational and spiritual, which will shortly be explained. Memory alone suggests the animal state, less than a man and approaching the state of a brute beast. *Reminisci ad intelligendum* is the specifically human and rational state. *Intelligere usque ad amandum* is the state of *hominis perfectae rationis*. This last state suggests the whole doctrine of *amor intellectus* associated with the final stage of mystical knowledge given through the Holy Spirit. This impression is confirmed by the terms used to explain this transition of intellect into love *amor ipsi affici, ipso frui, esse sicut ipse est*.[38] The term *affectus* is associated by William with the mystical state,[39] and *esse sicut ipse est* refers to the *unitas Spiritus* which will be described when we treat of the Holy Spirit and resemblance.[40]

The significance of this doctrine for trinitarian theology in the twelfth century, a psychological, a metaphysical and an historical approach to the doctrine of the image.

An interesting comparison can be made between the different lines of development following on the conception of the soul as a created image of the Trinity. From the starting point of St Augustine, who forms a basis for the further evolution of trinitarian theology in the Middle Ages, two contrasting tendencies can be observed. St Anselm[41] and William of St Thierry both received the influence of St Augustine's psychological images of the Trinity. Each of them develops this idea in a different direction.

The value of the psychological analogy, the development of the Augustinian image by St Anselm in a metaphysical direction.

There is disagreement among historians of the dogma of the Trinity as to whether St Augustine intended his psychological image of memory, intellect and love as a metaphor or as an analogy of proper proportion. There are good reasons for following Perino's opinion in support of de Regnon as against Schmaus that the psychological image in St Augustine's doctrine is a metaphor.[42] The very nature of St Augustine's theology of the Trinity is not a systematized metaphysical analysis, but a series of psychological illustrations designed to induce contemplation of the Trinity.[43] rather than to give a metaphysical explanation of the manner of the Processions.

St Anselm develops this psychological image and forms the bridge between St Augustine and St Thomas.[44] The illustrative

psychological image of St Augustine is given the value of an analogy of proper proportion, giving a metaphysical insight into the
life of the Trinity itself.[45] In this process the purely psychological analysis is reduced to a minimum, and the whole attention
of St Anselm is focussed on the metaphysical value of the image.[46]
William on the other hand gives not the slightest indication
of extending the value of the illustration beyond that given to
it by St Augustine. Whatever is said on that question about St
Augustine is *a fortiori* true of William. The whole tenor of his
theology is to stress the transcendance and the mystery of the
Trinity and to show the incapacity of human words and concepts to
express this mystery.[47]
We have seen how the emphasis on his doctrine of the image
has been not on its illustrative value but on its capacity to act
as a means towards union with the Trinity.[48] It is noticeable
also that the images of faith, hope and charity, faith, intellect
and love are treated in a similar manner to that of memory, intellect and will.[49] The analogies of faith, hope and charity, faith,
intellect and love are obviously not intended as an analogy of
proper proportion, and there is no reason to suppose that he intended to give a different value to the image of memory, intellect
and will. There can therefore be no doubt that in so far as William uses the psychological analogies of St Augustine to illustrate the Trinity, he intends these analogies as a metaphor and
not as a metaphysical explanation through an analogy of proper
proportion.

*The development of the Augustinian image by William in an
historical direction.*

William retains from St Augustine the illustrative value of
the image as a metaphor of the Trinity. But this conception is
subordinate to his more fundamental theme of the image as a dynamic imprint, supernatural from the very start, impelling the soul
towards union with the Trinity through the transition from image
to resemblance.[50] This is the theme of the history of the soul
in its spiritual development. In this sense of the term 'history'
we can say that the image of the Trinity is treated psychologically
by St Augustine, metaphysically by St Anselm, and historically by
William.
Despite occasional suggestions in St Anselm of William's
approach,[51] the general trend of his theology is so different that
the contrast is immediately evident.[52] In the case of St Augustine,
the difference is less obvious. St Augustine's whole scheme of
psychological illustrations is in fact directed towards the contemplation of the Trinity,[53] and his theological method of *sapientia*
relates all his theological speculations to the ultimate salvation

of the soul.[54] Both William and St Augustine are therefore united
in so far as they direct their theology of the image ultimately to
the contemplation of the Trinity.[55] The difference lies in the
method of achieving this contemplation. St Augustine's method is
to prepare the mind pedagogically by the means of a progressive
series of created images leading gradually to a perception of the
Trinity in the mirror of these images. Finally the most perfect
mirror is achieved when memory, intellect and love are directed
not towards themselves but towards God. The contemplative aim of
St Augustine's trinitarian theology is therefore linked insepara-
bly with his psychological analogies.[56] This is very different
from William who directs the soul towards union with the Trinity
not primarily through a psychological reflection on created analogies, but through the transition of the image in its very nature, through the evolution from image to resemblance. The plane
is ontological and historical rather than psychological.[57]

William, as we shall see, bases his contemplation of the Trinity, not on the psychological **perception** of created analogies as
a mirror for the uncreated Trinity, but on the ontological **achievement** of resemblance. Contemplation of the Trinity is attained
when the soul becomes in its very nature united in *unitas spiritus*
with the Trinity. This also explains how the 'created image' is
for St Augustine the center of attention, whereas for William it
is the point of departure for the final resemblance.[58]

Comparison with St Bernard.

The exact nature of St Bernard's doctrine of the image is
difficult to determine. Standaert writes: 'S. Bernard n'a pas eu
une doctrine mais des doctrines de l'image.'[59] Nevertheless there
is a substratum in common between these various doctrines. This
substratum is the conception of the image as the history of the
soul in its creation, fall and return to the creator through that
element which makes the soul to be *capax Dei*.[60] Whatever differences there may be in the treatment of the image by St Bernard and
William,[61] there is at least this basic point of resemblance in
this conception of the image in terms of the history of the soul.[62]

Moreover both St Bernard and William place the images of the
Trinity within this context. There is the text of St Bernard
where the image of faith, hope and charity is seen as a means of
raising up the original psychological trinity of memory, reason
and will from the depths to which it had fallen and restoring it
to beatitude.[63] This treatment of the psychological analogy in
the context of the history of the soul shows that William's doctrine has basically a greater affinity to that of St Bernard than
to that of St Augustine.

*Conclusion on the historical significance of William's doctrine
of the image and its value for trinitarian theology.*

The Augustinian psychological image was developed by St Anselm into a metaphysical insight into the Trinity according to an analogy of proper proportion. William from the same Augustinian basis transfers St Augustine's doctrine to the plane of St Bernard's conception of the image in terms of the history of the soul. He applies this doctrine to the Trinity, and through a synthesis of Augustinian elements together with elements from the Greek Fathers and the Platonic tradition portraying the image as imprint, forms a doctrine centering on the image as a means of union with the Trinity. This doctrine is evolved from a synthesis of traditional elements, but in relation to the twelfth century is of considerable originality, in that it directs trinitarian theology towards a very different plane of thought from the theology either of St Augustine or St Anselm.

This line of development was soon to be checked by the rising scholasticism leading to the full development of the metaphysical treatment of the psychological analogy in St Thomas. The existence of a different approach, treating of the image in close relationship with the spiritual life and primarily as a means of union with the Trinity is both of importance historically and also of value for our present theology of the Trinity, which has not yet given full value to this theme.

THE THREE THEOLOGICAL STAGES

The trichotomy.

A general study of the works of William soon reveals the presence throughout of a trichotomy, theological, spiritual and psychological, and it is impossible to treat any of his trinitarian doctrine without showing its relationship to this fundamental structure. It would however be misleading to give the impression that the relationship of his trinitarian doctrine to this trichotomy, is that of an illustration based on an analogy between the trichotomy and the trinity of persons after the pattern of the Augustinian analogies of Trinity in unity.[64]

The question to be considered is of a very different kind and arises from the construction of his theology according to three stages and the relationship of these stages to their spiritual foundations and ultimately to the trichotomy of the soul. This theme will be found in intimate relationship with that of the return to 'resemblance,' towards which the image of the Trinity was directed.

Terminology.

This theme appears throughout William's works in varying
terminology. The final formulation of the three states *animalis
--rationalis--spiritualis,* and the trichotomy of the soul *anima--
animus--spiritus,* is only perfected in the *Epistola ad fratres de
Monte Dei,* though it is already foreshadowed in his earlier
works.[65]
Despite the varying terminology, each formula tends to show
certain fixed characteristics. The expressions *fides, sensus,
imaginatio, corpus, animalis, anima,* frequently recur in relation
to the first term, conveying a predominant impression of the life
of the body, the senses, and in the case of faith, of knowledge
received externally. The middle term is primarily characterized
by *ratio, intellectus, ratio per fidem, scientia, rationalis,
animus,* suggesting the domain of the rational life. The last
term is described chiefly by *spiritus, amor, sapientia, rationes
sui generis, intelligentia desursum, internus mentis obtulus,* implying a spiritual activity **transcendant** of the life of reason and
the senses.[66]

The theological stages.

The most important of these texts for our purpose is that of
the three theological stages in the *Aenigma fidei.* The text in
question is placed in the midst of his principal work on the Trinity and follows immediately after the discussion on the problem
of number and Person in the Trinity. The opening words suggest
at once the main theme:

*Tribus enim intelligentiae gradibus proficerent
fidei ascendendum est ad Deum et ad cognitionem ejus.
Primus gradus est diligenter investigatum habere, quid
sibi de Domino Deo suo sit credendum; secundus, quomodo
de eo quod recte creditur, recte nihilominus ei cogitandum sit et loquendum; tertius ipsa jam rerum experientia est in sentiendo de Domino in bonitate, sicut
sentiunt qui simplicitate cordis quaerunt illum.*[67]

This text from the *Aenigma fidei* on the three theological
stages is closely parallel to the text from the *Meditativae orationes* on the three spiritual states, 'animal,' 'rational,' and
'spiritual.'[68] The initial theological stage in the *Aenigma fidei*
described as faith grounded in authority[69] corresponds to the
first of the spiritual states based on submission to authority by
the man who is under the dominion of the senses and is unable to
govern his own life.[70] The theological stage of *ratio fidei*[71] is

paralleled by the understanding of the faith in the rational stage
of the spiritual life.[72] The final theological stage with its
sensus divinitatis and *sapor sapientiae*[73] communicated by a special mode of knowledge given by the Holy Ghost[74] and suggesting
already an anticipation of the beatific vision[75] is parallel to
the *affectus*[76] of the *sapientes*[77] in the last of the spiritual
states, when the soul is led by the Holy Ghost towards the final
'resemblance'[78] and ultimately to the vision of God.

The psychological roots.

The spiritual states are rooted ultimately in the psychological trichotomy of the soul, *anima, animus, spiritus.*[79] This division suggests rather varying aspects and modes of existence of
the soul rather than an ontological trichotomy in the philosophical order.[80] Despite the element of psychological equilibrium,[81]
William's psychology depicts primarily the evolution of the soul,
reflecting the development of the spiritual states and has been
well described by Père Bouyer as 'une dynamique de l'âme.'[82]

The sources.

Among the contemporaries of William, there is evidence of
the use of a trichotomy also by St Bernard, but the influence of
William on St Bernard on this point is more probable than that of
St Bernard on William.[83] The division of *sensus, ratio* and *intellectus*[84] is to be found in Anselm of Laon.[85] William was a student of Anselm and may have been influenced by him in the use of
this terminology.[86]

On the question of the ultimate sources, there is the possibility of the influence of Erigena for *sensus, ratio* and *intellectus,*[87] despite certain notable differences.[88] More important
there is the theological division of *fides, scientia* and *sapientia*
in Origen,[89] his hierarchy of the senses of Scripture as related
to the structure of the soul, *corpus, anima, spiritus*[90] and his
trichotomy of ψυχή-νοῦσ-πνεῦμα,[91] with its similarity to William's
anima-animus-spiritus.[92]

The most important aspect of these sources for our present
study lies in the dynamic character of the various psychological
elements in Erigena and Origen.[93] This has its ultimate roots in
Plotinus.[94] It has been said that for Plotinus: 'L'âme est un
élan, un mouvement, plus encore qu'une chose.'[95] If pressed to
summarize the quintessence of William's psychology, it would be
hard to find anything more apt than those words.

The mainspring of William's trinitarian theology.

It is now clear that the theological stages of the *Aenigma fidei* are not merely an arbitrary theme casually introduced in the course of the discussion of trinitarian problems. They arise as it were inevitably from the underlying structure of the spiritual states and ultimately from the psychological trichotomy of the soul.

As a result of this relationship, William's theology shares in the character of his spirituality and psychology. This explains the dynamic impetus of the theological stages. The theological stages, as we have seen, took the form of a movement towards the final **stage** of experimental knowledge through the Holy Ghost, with all the characteristics of the final spiritual state of perfect resemblance. This movement towards 'resemblance' is indeed the dominant inspiration of William's spirituality and also of his trinitarian theology. Whether we approach his thought from the angle of the 'image', or from the angle of the theological stages with their spiritual and psychological roots, we always find that these themes converge in the central one of the impetus towards resemblance through experimental knowledge given by the Holy Ghost.

Importance for the contemporary background.

The foundation of theology on a spiritual and psychological trichotomy has a further **significance,** which becomes of special importance in the light of the contemporary background. It implies that his **psychology** and spirituality determine to a considerable extent his theological method, demanding a consideration in turn of those aspects of his theology, which are proportioned to their corresponding psychological roots. If an element exists in man which is under the dominion of the senses and is wholly dependant on external authority, it is impossible for theology to pursue a course which does not take this element into consideration there must be some pedagogic process adapted to the nature of man in this state, giving special prominence to the life of the senses and to the basis of faith, before it is possible to approach **the mystery** of the Trinity from the angle of reason.[96] Finally after the rational consideration of the Trinity,[97] those elements in theology must be introduced which are proportioned to the highest state of man under the dominion of the Holy Spirit. This inclusion of elements both below and above reason, treated in their own right as essential stages in the evolution of the knowledge of the Trinity, contrasts strongly with the tendency of the rising scholasticism, represented by St Anselm[98] and Peter Abelard, to approach the Trinity almost entirely from the angle of metaphysics and logic.

RESTORATION OF RESEMBLANCE

The whole question of *ratio fidei*, and the speculative treatment of trinitarian problems, which dominates his main trinitarian
work, the *Aenigma fidei*, cannot be included here. It is hoped
that this will in itself be the subject of a future article. It
will then be shown how *ratio fidei* reaches its furthest point when,
having approached the Trinity from every angle, it finds that the
Trinity is best understood when it is understood to be beyond understanding.[99] This is the conclusion of the second stage in theology. But there is the further stage of a divine mode of knowledge, which preserves the mystery while giving in some sense a
positive insight into the trinitarian life. This insight is not
a rational penetration of the mystery, but an experimental, mystical knowledge, proportioned to the restoration of resemblance
and given through the Holy Ghost, so that we can in some way experience the Trinity without understanding the mystery rationally.
This aspect of William's theology is his most personal contribution to the theology of the Trinity, and is not directly or primarily polemical in character, but it is an important element in
William's counteraction to his scholastic contemporaries. It is
complementary to his bare assertion of the mystery of the stage of
ratio fidei.[100] In this way he attempts to direct trinitarian
theology away from the efforts at what was in his judgement a rational penetration of the mystery and to orientate it towards an
experience of the Trinity communicated through a divine mode of
knowledge, attained in proportion to our likeness to the Trinity.[101]

The Holy Ghost as the mutual union of the Father and the Son.

The foundation for this doctrine lies in the Augustinian theory of the Holy Ghost as the mutual bond between the Father and
the Son, a trinitarian theme of great importance in William's theology.
But whereas with St Augustine the Holy Ghost is conceived primarily as mutual love according to his psychological illustration
of the Trinity in terms of the Son as intellect and the Holy Ghost
as love,[102] William's conception is primarily that of the Holy
Ghost as the unity between the Father and the Son: 'quidquid
commune est ambobus.'[103] Admittedly a tendency sometimes to describe the Holy Ghost solely in terms of the 'will' and of 'love'[104]
shows that he found these terms particularly expressive of this
union. But he never conceived the Holy Ghost exclusively or even
primarily as love. The dominant theme is that of mutual union

which explicitly includes also knowledge.[105] It is the note of
the 'mutual' which characterizes the Holy Ghost. It is not knowledge as such, but mutual knowledge,[106] nor charity as such but
the reciprocity of charity which is proper to the Holy Ghost.[107]

Resemblance.

The Holy Ghost is therefore conceived primarily as the mutual
union between the Father and the Son, which is the foundation for
the doctrine of the restoration of resemblance, a participation
in the life of the Holy Ghost by sharing in the mutual union of
the Father and the Son. This is described in terms of daring realism, portraying a unity of spirit, whereby the soul becomes as
it were the life of the Holy Spirit himself. At the same time he
guards carefully against the danger of pantheism. A text from the
Epistola ad fratres de Monte Dei gives a clear expression of this
doctrine.

> *Dicitur autem haec unitas Spiritus, non tantum quia*
> *efficit eam, vel afficit ei spiritum hominis Spiritus*
> *Sanctus, sed quia ipsa ipse est Spiritus Sanctus Deus*
> *charitas: cum per eum qui est amor Patris et Filii,*
> *et unitas, et suavitas et bonum et osculum et amplexus*
> *et quidquid commune potest esse amborum in summa illa*
> *unitate veritatis et veritate unitatis; hoc idem homini*
> *suo modo fit ad Deum, quod cum substantiali unitate*
> *Filio est ad Patrem, vel Patri ad Filium; cum in am-*
> *plexu et osculo Patris et Filii mediam quodammodo se*
> *invenit beata conscientia; cum modo ineffabili in-*
> *excogitabilique fieri meretur homo Dei non Deus, sed*
> *tamen quod Deus est ex natura, homo ex gratia.*[108]

This passage conveys the idea of a participation in the intratrinitarian life with forceful realism. In this state of 'unitas Spiritus' the soul really shares in the very life of the
Holy Ghost, 'hoc idem homini suo modo fit ad Deum.' Man in a mysterious but real way becomes this mutual unity. This union is
not merely the effect of an **extrinsic** action of the Holy Ghost:
'Non tantum quia efficit eam vel afficit ei Spiritum hominis Spiritus Sanctus,' nor is it merely a psychological union of mind and
will. It is a real union of being on the ontological plane,[109]
and in a certain sense *is* the Holy Ghost: 'ipsa ipse est Spiritus
Sanctus.'

The reservation in this text that this is not a **substantial**
union with God 'non Deus,' but a union through grace, 'quod Deus
est ex natura, homo ex gratia,' is expressed more strongly in a
similar text from the *Speculum fidei* where a series of antitheses

accentuates this distinction.[110]

But this distinction does not obliterate the reality of a real participation in the life of the Holy Ghost,[111] and the reconciliation of these two apparently incompatible ideas is expressed in the term *similitudo* as opposed to *unitas*. Although there is *unitas spiritus* between man and the Trinity, man does not become the actual *unitas* between the Father and the Son, which is the Holy Ghost himself in substantial uncreated union. He becomes the *similitudo* of this unity,[112] a term which conveys the sense of a real participation in the mutual unity of the Father and the Son, without actually being that unity substantially. This is the meaning of the doctrine of the restored 'resemblance,' the term of the image of the Trinity in man.

Amor ipse intellectus est.

This state of restored resemblance is inseparable from the theme of the experimental knowledge of the Trinity characteristic of the third stage in theology, as is evident from William's strict equation between knowledge and likeness in the last of the theological stages. We not only become like God in so far as we know him, but we also know him in so far as we become like him.[113] This experimental knowledge acts in reciprocal causality with the restored resemblance, likeness causing knowledge, and knowledge causing a further degree of likeness until the final union of knowledge and likeness is achieved in the beatific vision.[114] It is therefore only through being in a manner what the Trinity is, that we can arrive at the highest knowledge of the Trinity.

It is a knowledge of love as contrasted with that of faith.[115] It has a certain analogy with knowledge of the senses and of the rational intellect, the basis for this analogy being a conformity between the knower and the thing known.[116] But it is a higher mode of knowledge,[117] and is like a sense of the soul in relation to the things of God.[118] It is of its nature incommunicable and can only be known through experience,[119] and is a divine mode of knowledge.[120]

Knowledge in the strict or only metaphorical sense?

There has been considerable discussion as to whether *amorintellectus* is knowledge in the strict sense of the term, or as to whether it is merely an affection of the soul acting as a substitute for knowledge or as a preparation for knowledge through the restoration of likeness by charity.[121] On this point the judgement of Père Déchanet is more convincing than that of Gilson. William refers clearly to this knowledge as *cognito* and *intellectus*,[122] and the equation between knowledge and love is expressed

in the famous phrase: *amor quippe Dei intellectus est.*"123
There is no reason why these terms should not be accepted with
their literal force, unless the term knowledge is limited to purely conceptual, rational and discursive knowledge,124 or unless
amor ipse intellectus est is interpreted as a formal identification of the faculties of reason and love,125 which is contrary to
the texts of William.126 Furthermore this knowledge is presented
as an anticipation of the beatific vision. It is a *medium quid*127
between the knowledge of God in this life and the full beatific
vision. The eschatological character of this experimental knowledge, as a real anticipation of the final vision leaves little
doubt that it is knowledge in a strict and not merely metaphorical
sense, though a knowledge which is *sui generis* and transcendant
both of sense and of reason.

Amor-intellectus *and the mystery.*

The eschatological aspect of *amor-intellectus* raises the
question as to whether this knowledge in any way unveils the mystery of the Trinity. In contrast with the rational knowledge of
scientia the experimental knowledge which comes through love reveals God in some way directly as he is in himself: 'ipsum vero
quod est idipsum.'128 It is not merely knowing about God, but
knowing God. It is described as a beginning of a knowledge which
is not that of faith.129 Moreover it implies that the soul really
becomes in a manner what God is, 'unum Spiritum cum Deo esse,'130
just as the restored resemblance gives a real participation in
the intratrinitarian life.
    There is certainly a marked contrast between the confidence
with which William describes the powers of *amor-intellectus* and
his extreme reserve shown in the speculative parts of the *Aenigma
fidei* on the powers of reason in the face of the mystery.131
Can it be possible that this description implies some kind of
knowledge of the mystery itself? Despite this contrast, the mystery still remains even with the divine mode of knowledge given
in *amor-intellectus,* which, although a direct knowledge of God as
he is in himself, remains obscure, *per speculum et in aenigmate*132
and is *quaedam docta ignorantia.*133 The conclusive text is from
the *Meditativae orationes,* which definitely asserts that the mystery still remains. The divine mode of knowledge given through
the Holy Ghost is not an unveiling of the mystery, but induces
a recognition of the incomprehensibility of God which comes precisely from the mystery of Trinity in unity and unity in Trinity.
'Etiam ad hoc ei valeant unitas Trinitatis et Trinitas unitatis,
ut pio et sobrio intellectu comprehendat non comprehendo majes-
tatem divinae incomprehensibilitatis.'134 Yet despite the incomprehensibility of the mystery, the soul under the influence of

this knowledge is no longer disturbed by the mystery. The antithesis of Trinity and unity is in some way overcome, in so far as
the focus of the mind on the Trinity does not prevent a simultan-
eous perception of the unity, nor does the unity prevent a simul-
taneous perception of the three Persons.[135]

Amor-intellectus *and the Holy Ghost.*

The essential element in *amor-intellectus* is the Holy Ghost.
All the characteristics of this mode of knowledge, its divine
character, its eschatological implications, its power to transform the soul into a likeness to God, producing *unitas spiritus,*
are explained ultimately by this relationship with the Holy
Ghost.[136] With the same realism that we observed in the restored
resemblance, this knowledge through love in a certain sense really
is the Holy Ghost, 'ipse enim est amor noster,'[137] and is therefore the very mutual knowledge which the Father and the Son possess
of each other.

Quibus ergo revelat Pater et Filius, hii cognoscunt,
sicut Pater et Filius se cognoscunt; quia habent in
semetipsis notitiam mutuam eorum; quia habent in se-
metipsis unitatem amborum, et voluntatem vel amorem;
quod totum Spiritus Sanctus est.[138]

A personal experience or a theological construction?

How far is *amor-intellectus* and the whole doctrine of 'resemblance' the expression of a personal experience? A definite answer to this question is ultimately beyond the scope of theology.
We can only tentatively put forward the solution that seems most
probable. It is difficult to believe that the author who wrote
with such understanding of this mode of knowledge had not been
given some personal knowledge of this kind,[139] yet at the same
time we are struck by the manner in which he presents it. He does
not appear to be describing primarily a personal experience. The
general tone of the texts is far from subjective. It is not a
personal, subjective description of a vision of the trinitarian
life, but a highly objective exposition of a theological theme,
presented, as we have seen, according to a unified and logical sequence of thought, with the exact theological distinctions needed
to express this profound and mysterious doctrine.[140]
   The most probable answer to this difficult question lies in
the supposition of some intuition of union with the trinitarian
life. Afterwards he would have attempted to give some explanation
in terms of philosophy and theology, through the Augustinian theology of the Holy Ghost with all the consequent deductions in

relation to the restored resemblance and *amor-intellectus*. The final result is not a mere description of an experience, nor a purely academic exposition of a theological thesis, but a theology of an experience, based on it and attempting to explain and justify it according to theological doctrine.

The terminus ad quem *of William's theology.*

We have seen how the three theological stages arise from their basic structure of the animal, rational and spiritual states, representing the evolution of the soul in its return to union with the Trinity. This structure imparts an essentially dynamic character to William's theology expressing a continual movement towards a progressively higher mode of knowledge culminating in the divine mode of knowledge communicated through the Holy Ghost. This scheme presupposes the creation of the soul in the image of the Trinity, and the subsequent fall into the *regio dissimilitudinis* from which the soul has to return to union with the Trinity by means of these three spiritual states. The theme of the image of the Trinity is impregnated with the same dynamic character as that of the three theological stages. Fundamentally it represents the initial imprint given by the Trinity at the moment of creation impelling the soul **towards** union with the Trinity through perfect 'resemblance.'

We can now see how the basic theme of William's theology and its underlying spiritual and psychological structure is that of a dynamic impulse towards the goal of 'resemblance' which is identical with the last of the theological stages and consists in a participation in the life of the Trinity, giving an experience of the Trinity through the Holy Ghost. It is therefore beyond doubt that the whole of William's trinitarian doctrine is ordered towards the participation in the intratrinitarian life which is the subject of this chapter.

The personal role of the Holy Ghost ad extra in the work of sanctification.

In the *Aenigma fidei* William implicitly accepts the doctrine of appropriation. The question remains as to whether his treatment of our relationship to the Persons *ad extra* and in particular to the Holy Ghost is entirely explained by this doctrine. We are struck by the contrast between the texts on appropriation with their emphasis on the unity of the Persons in their action *ad extra*,[141] and the texts which describe the Holy Ghost in realistic terms as the source of every gift throughout creation,[142] and especially the texts quoted here in relation to the role of the Holy Ghost with regard to the restoration of resemblance and to the gift of experimental knowledge[143].

The problem of our special relationship in the work of sanctification to each Person of the Trinity as distinct from the other Persons is not explicitly considered by William. But the question remains as to whether his doctrine definitely excludes this possibility and as to whether it is fully intelligible in any other way. In answer to this question it should be noticed that the texts treating of appropriation are concerned with another problem from that of the texts on the restoration of resemblance. The texts treating of appropriation are concerned with the attributes of the divine essence in opposition to Abelard's supposed attempt to make the attributes of power, wisdom and love constitutive of the Persons, whereas the texts treating of resemblance are concerned with our participation in the life of the Holy Ghost, conceived as the mutual unity of the Father and the Son. The difficulty in the texts on 'resemblance' is partly that he is treating primarily of the union of the soul with the Trinity, and not technically of the trinitarian problems of the inseparability of the Persons as in the texts treating of appropriation in the *Aenigma fidei* and in the polemical works. There is no explanation of what is meant by such expressions as: 'Dicitur autem haec unitas spiritus, non tantum quia efficit eam vel afficit ei spiritum hominis Spiritus Sanctus,'[144] or: 'hic autem facit illud in eo in quo fit, et faciendo per gratiam in ipso est'[145] referring to action of the Holy Ghost in effecting our resemblance.[146] However it can be presumed that he did not intend to contradict his assertion of the traditional doctrine of the unity of the operation of the Trinity *ad extra*, known later as the unity of efficient causality. But the essential point of these texts does not lie in the conception of an action *ad extra*, but in the participation in the life of the Holy Ghost in what William conceived as proper to the Holy Ghost, the mutual unity of the Father and the Son: 'non tantum quia efficit eam. . .sed quia ipsa ipse *est* Spiritus sanctus. . .in amplexu et osculo Patris et Filii mediam quodammodo se invenit beata conscientia.'[147] The question here is that of *participation in a relationship* and not of an *action ad extra*. The arguments for appropriation do not apply in this case, and there is no evidence that William intended to exclude any other explanation than that of appropriation. Furthermore the meaning of a participation in what is *proper* to the Holy Ghost cannot be explained in terms of the doctrine of appropriation, which presupposes that the attribute or action appropriated is common to the whole Trinity.

A further reason for the existence of this special relationship lies in William's conception of the Holy Ghost as the initial link, the bond of union relating us to the Father and the Son, parallel to the argument used for supposing the existence of a

special relationship to the Holy Ghost in the work of sanctification in the Greek Fathers, as for instance St Cyril of Alexandria.[148] This argument is applied to the traditional scheme 'ex
Patre, per Filium, in Spiritu, ad Patrem,' and its strength lies
in the conception of the Holy Ghost as the 'bond of union' between ourselves and the Trinity, leading us through the Son to
the Father. Analogously, is it unreasonable to apply this argument to William's conception of the Holy Ghost as the mutual bond
between the Father and the Son, and therefore the initial link,
the 'bond of union' between ourselves and the Father and the Son?

Moreover this relationship of our sanctification to the Holy
Ghost is not a casual theme in William's theology, suggesting a
merely rhetorical significance, but it is at the very core of his
whole doctrine of the return of the soul to God through the res-
titution of resemblance, which is conceived in strict dependance
on what is proper to the Holy Ghost.

In conclusion it can be said that William gives no explicit
teaching on this subject, but the existence of a special relationship to the Holy Ghost in our sanctification is implicit in his
doctrine.[149] The question of a special relationship to the Father
and the Son is less apparent. Through the Holy Ghost as the mutual bond the soul is related in a personalistic manner to the
Father and the Son 'in amplexu et osculo Patris et Filii,'[150] but
the relationship precisely to what is proper to the Father and
what is proper to the Son is less clearly in evidence than with
the Holy Ghost.

Emphasis on the Persons rather than the nature.

Throughout these texts treating of our participation in the
life of the Trinity through resemblance, it is the Persons of the
Trinity and especially the Holy Ghost who are in the foreground,[151]
which contrasts strongly with the entitative sections of the *Aenigma fidei* treating of the mystery of the Trinity through the analysis of the divine nature. This illustrates one of the characteristics of William's trinitarian theology. In general, when he
treats of the Trinity entitatively *quoad se* or polemically, the
emphasis is on the divine nature. When he treats of the Trinity
quoad nos, the emphasis is on the Persons.

The historical origins of amor-intellectus.

William chooses the text from St John 'similes ei erimus quoniam videbimus eum sicuti est'[152] as the basis for his equation
between knowledge and likeness. He reverses the text showing that
it is equally true to say that we shall know God because we shall
be like him as to say that we shall be like him because we shall

know him.[153]

The immediate origin of the formula *amor ipse intellectus est* is St Gregory the Great.[154] But there are frequent references to this mode of knowledge among the Fathers;[155] which have their ultimate source in Plotinus.[156] This traditional doctrine becomes an important element in twelfth century monastic theology not only with William but also with St Bernard,[157] although with St Bernard this doctrine takes a rather different form and is not given the complete theoretical development that is found in William's theology.[158] The themes of knowledge through likeness, a mystical experience based on the restoration of resemblance, becomes one of the dominant features of twelfth century cistercian spirituality. The special contribution of William in this respect lies in his close application of this theme to the dogma of the Trinity.

The foundation of a tradition of Trinitarian mysticism.

In general William is a representative of what Dom Cuthbert Butler has called 'Western mysticism.'[159] In particular it is of interest to note that the Dionysian tradition, which is so much in evidence in his treatment of *ratio fidei* in the sections of the *Aenigma fidei* on the divine names [160] has not exercised any deep influence on the more specifically mystical aspects of his theology. Despite allusions to the *theologia negativa*,[161] the actual descriptions of the experience of *amor-intellectus* express a mysticism of light rather than darkness, of illumination rather than the way of unknowing,[162] and illustrate the contrast observed by Dom Cuthbert Butler, when he distinguishes in this respect the mystical theology of St Augustine, St Gregory and St Bernard from that of Dionysius. In line with this general tradition, William nevertheless offers his own contribution, which is of considerable importance both for the theology of mysticism and for the theology of the Trinity. This is due to the profound relationship which he establishes between *amor-intellectus* and the dogma of the Trinity. We have already observed the doctrinal expression of the experience of *amor-intellectus* which integrates this experience into a closely reasoned theological structure. This introduces a strictly theological element which distinguishes William's treatment of this kind of knowledge from the eminently 'practical,' 'descriptive' character which Dom Cuthbert Butler sees as one of the dominating features of 'Western' mysticism. The dogmatic element in this experience consists above all in the intimate relationship between *amor-intellectus* and the Trinity.

This doctrine is based on the text of St Matthew: 'nemo novit Filium nisi Pater; neque Patrem quis novit nisi Filius, et cui voluerit Filius revelare.'[163] A knowledge of this kind is suggested in the text from St John referring to the coming of the Holy

Ghost: 'in illo die vos cognoscetis quia ego sum in Patre meo, et
vos in me, et ego in vobis,'[164] indicating a special knowledge
given through the Holy Ghost.

It is one of the most important contributions of William's
theology to have developed this doctrine into a fully formed theology. Before William there are references to an experimental
knowledge of the Trinity,[165] but there is no real theology of this
subject. Reypens in his article in the Dictionary of Spirituality
'Connaissance mystique de Dieu' shows how in this respect William
is the founder of a whole tradition of a trinitarian mysticism.[166]
The special importance of his theology on this point lies in the
relation of *amor-intellectus* to the Trinity. It is not merely an
experience of the Trinity without an intrinsic connection between
this knowledge and its basis of trinitarian doctrine. On the contrary this knowledge is so closely connected with the Trinity that
it has its whole raison d'être in William's conception of the Holy
Ghost as the mutual unity of the Father and the Son. It is therefore a mysticism which is *essentially* trinitarian in so far as
theologically it is unintelligible in this structure except in relation to the Trinity. Moreover this experience of the Trinity
is not only an accidental element in his theology. It is the culmination of his central theme of the transition of the soul from
image to resemblance. The whole of his theology is ordered towards
this point. It is in this sense we can say that his theology is
an original contribution to the history of the dogma of the Trinity.

Comparison with St Augustine.

It is clear by now that this is the heart of William's trinitarian spiritual and psychological doctrine. The interest of his
doctrine of image-resemblance is above all that it centers on this
experimental participation in the intratrinitarian life. The difference in accentuation from St Augustine's treatment of the image
in relation to the Trinity is still more in evidence than in the
comparisons made in the first chapter. Although, as was shown,
St Augustine's doctrine of the image is directed ultimately towards the contemplation of the Trinity, the whole direction of St
Augustine's thought centers round the Trinity in creation, whereas the whole trend of William's thought is towards the participation through image-resemblance in the *uncreated* Trinity. The
distinction could almost be summarized by saying that St Augustine
is interested in showing the Trinity in the image of man, whereas
William is interested in showing the term of the image of man in
the Trinity.

Comparison with St Bernard

This doctrine of William's can be compared with that of St
Bernard's in two ways, illustrating both the similarity and the
differences in these two representatives of twelfth century Cistercian monastic theology. Like St Bernard, William's theology
is based on the theme of the journey of the soul as the image of
God. Both of them give that special emphasis on experience, on
the 'interiorization' of theology. But there are important differences, which help us to see the specific contribution of William.
St Bernard is interested primarily in the analysis of love,[167]
despite his allusions to *amor-intellectus*. William is concerned
above all with the union of the two faculties, giving an experience *sui generis* which is really knowledge in the strict sense
although it is not knowledge of a rational kind. Moreover in this
knowledge through love there is a much more explicit relationship
to the Trinity than in the mystical theology of St Bernard. The
union of the soul with the Word is at the center of the doctrine
of St Bernard, union with the Holy Spirit at the center of the
doctrine of William.[168] It is precisely this foundation in William's conception of the Holy Spirit as mutual union of the Father
and the Son which gives to his mystical theology its special character of the experience of the trinitarian life. Therefore we can
summarize these differences in the general way. St Bernard's mystical theology is primarily that of the soul as image in the journey to union with the Word through love. William's mystical theology is primarily that of the soul as image in the journey to
union with the Trinity through the Holy Ghost, giving the experience of *amor-intellectus*, which is not only love but also knowledge in the strict sense.

In this way William's doctrine meets the scholastic *fides
quaerens intellectum* more closely on the plane of *knowledge*. We
can detect the implied antithesis between what he conceived as
Abelard's attempt to penetrate the mystery of the Trinity through
the knowledge of reason and his own doctrine of the experience of
the Trinity through the *knowledge of amor-intellectus* in the Holy
Ghost.

Image-resemblance and the Greek conception of deification.

The *orientale lumen* is reflected throughout William's works
in various ways. One of the most interesting aspects of this influence is the apparent antithesis of transcendance and immanence.
Throughout the passages of the *Aenigma fidei* treating of *ratio
fidei* there is the constant Dionysian theme of the transcendance
of God over human reason.[169] The Trinity was only understood when
it was understood to be beyond our understanding. In these more

mystical passages of William's works, relating to the final stage
in the ascent of the soul, it is rather the immanence of the Trinity to the soul which is accentuated. We participate in the trinitarian life through the Holy Ghost by means of the restoration
of the 'image' to the completed 'resemblance.' This conception
of the return to the divine life in terms of conformity with the
original impulse of our nature historically as the image of God
is in line with the general mentality of Oriental thought. Grace
in Oriental thought is conceived less as a free action of God
superimposed on man from without and offering him an entirely new
life, than as a return to the deepest historical roots of his nature.[170]

An original synthesis.

This is undoubtedly William's finest theological achievement.
It rests on a blend of traditional elements, which are not merely
juxtaposed, but form an organic and unified **synthesis**, resulting
in an original conception of the relation of the Trinity to the
spiritual life. The basis is the Augustinian doctrine of the Holy
Ghost in the intratrinitarian life, though even here William gives
to this doctrine his own special emphasis. This is developed
through a highly realistic conception of the role of the Holy
Ghost *ad extra*, reminiscent of the emphasis of the Persons in
Scripture and the Greek Fathers. The element of *amor-intellectus*
comes ultimately from Plotinus. Finally there is the affinity
with the Greek conception of deification immanent to the soul in
close conformity with the nature of man in the historical sense
as image of God. Each of these elements is shown in **intrinsic**
and necessary mutual relationship, and fused so as to form a doctrine of the experience of the Trinity, which is peculiar to William.

The theoretical value of this doctrine.

This synthesis constructed from the doctrine of the Holy
Ghost as the mutual union of the Father and the **Son** is persuasive
in its unity and its logic. The question is how far its objective
value depends on the initial premise of the doctrine of the Holy
Ghost, which is only a theological opinion dating principally from
St Augustine.[171] If this opinion is not accepted, has William's
doctrine nothing to contribute?

We have already referred to the role of the Holy Ghost in the
traditional economy, *ex Patre, per Filium, in Spiritu,* as the bond
of union between ourselves and the Trinity. It seems that it is
possible to transpose William's doctrine to this traditional
scheme and to show that it can offer an important contribution to

the traditional teaching on the action of the Persons *ad extra*.
Fundamentally William's doctrine rests on the idea of the
Holy Ghost as the bond of union between ourselves and the Trinity.
It is through the Holy Ghost, the substantial bond of union between the Father and the Son that we achieve 'resemblance' which
is participated union. This participated union gives rise to an
experimental knowledge which comes precisely through our degree of
likeness to the Trinity. If we apply his doctrine to the traditional scheme, we find that the basic doctrine with all its consequences of the Holy Ghost as the 'bond of union' between ourselves and the Trinity is still valid. The only difference lies
in the reason *why* the Holy Ghost is the 'bond of union.' In William's doctrine the reason lies in the Augustinian conception of
the Holy Ghost as the mutual union between the Father and the Son,
whereas in the traditional economy the reason lies in the place
of the Holy Ghost in the scheme: *ex Patre, per Filium in Spiritu*.
This application of William's doctrine on the experience of
the Trinity to the traditional trinitarian scheme of the economy
of the Persons *ad extra* enables us to see that mystical experience
is trinitarian in its deepest foundations and arises from an assimilation to the Holy Ghost drawing us into union with the Trinity
and so communicating to us an experimental knowledge arising from
that unity. It suggests also that mystical experience, in view
of its basic trinitarian roots, tends of its very nature towards
some experience of the trinitarian life.

Conclusion.

The basic theme of William's trinitarian theology is undoubtedly that of the Holy Ghost as the mutual unity of the Father and
the Son, effecting the restored resemblance to the soul and communicating an experimental knowledge of the Trinity. The reason
for this conclusion lies in the existence of the basic theme of
the return to resemblance which is the main impulse of William's
thought on the psychological, spiritual, and on the theological
plane. Therefore the trinitarian theme which gives the whole
raison d'être to this resemblance is on a different plane from
those other aspects of William's trinitarian theology, which we
hope to consider in a later article. It is essential to his most
basic doctrine in the sense that if this key point is removed, the
doctrine of the restored resemblances loses its whole *raison d'être*.
Furthermore, as the experimental knowledge of the Trinity is
inseparable from the doctrine of the Holy Ghost and the restored
resemblance, we can say with equal truth that this experience of
the Trinity is at the very heart of his doctrine and is the end
to which whole doctrine, theological, spiritual and psychological
is directed. It is precisely here that we discover the originality

of William's contribution to the history of the dogma of the Trinity. Against the historical background of the approach through psychology with St Augustine, through metaphysics with St Anselm and through logic with Peter Abelard, William's approach is predominantly through mystical experience. In this respect he was the founder of a tradition which was to develop with the school of Eckhart, Suso, Tauler and Ruysbroeck. This is an important moment in the history of theology both for the study of mysticism and for the study of the theology of the Trinity. For William developed a theory of mystical experience which was *essentially* trinitarian, and an approach to the Trinity which was *essentially* mystical.

Finally we touch here on questions of great importance not only historically but also for the whole theoretical treatment both of mystical and of trinitarian theology. William's theology recalls to us the need to understand the true relationship of the dogma of the Trinity to the whole psychological and spiritual development of man, and also suggests possibilities of further reflection on the question of the dogmatic roots of the mystical life.

NOTES

*Published: *Pontificum Athenaeum Anselmianum* (Louvain, 1959), and RTAM 26 (1959) 87-127.

PREFACE

[1]J.-M. Déchanet, *Guillaume de Saint-Thierry, l'homme et son oeuvre* (Paris, 1942) gives a table of sources (200-209) and J.-M. Déchanet, *Aux sources de la spiritualité de Guillaume de Saint-Thierry* (Bruges, 1940). For his theories on the influence of Plotinus, see J.-M. Déchanet, 'Guillaume de Saint-Thierry et Plotin,' *Revue de moyen âge latin* 2 (1946) 241-260.

[2]See especially Déchanet, *Guillaume de Saint-Thierry,* 89-109 (an introductory analysis of the trinitarian doctrine of the Aenig; Déchanet, *OEuvres choisies de Guillaume de Saint-Thierry* (Paris, 1943) 30, 249-251, and *Aux sources de la spiritualité,* 14-15, (the doctrine of the image of the Trinity in the soul); Déchanet, 'Amor ipse intellectus est,' *Revue du moyen âge latin* 1 (1945) 349-374 and *Meditations et prières* (Brussels, 1945) introduction, the doctrine of *amor-intellectus*; and L. Malevez, 'La doctrine de l'image et de la connaissance mystique,' *R sc rel* 22 (1932) 178-205, 257-279, (The relationship of the doctrine of the image-resemblance to the experimental knowledge of the Trinity). Finally there is L. Bouyer, *La spiritualité de Citeaux,* 118-154 developing the relationship, originally discovered by Père Déchanet, between the three theological stages and the three spiritual states, *animalis, rationalis, spiritualis.*

INTRODUCTION

[1]J. Leclercq, *L'amour des lettres;* and 'S. Bernard et la théologie monastique du XIIe siècle,' *S. Bernard théologien,* 7-23.

[2]Cf C. Vagaggini, *II senso teologico della liturgia,* especially 493-495 for an excellent analysis of *sapientia* and *scientia.* In the light of the later scholastic distinction *ex fine operis* and *ex fine operantis,* the patristic theological *sapientia* is shown as a *genus mixtum,* in which the scientific element, still in a state of imperfection in this theology, was *ex fine operis* ordered towards the perfection of man as a whole including all that could in the broad sense be described as an experimental and mystical knowledge of God. The author contrasts this theological ideal with that of the *genus purum* of theological science pursued

ex fine operis solely according to the strict demands of that science. Moreover this ideal of *scientia* for the mediaeval scholastics was conceived predominantly according to the pattern of Aristotelian philosophical, deductive science. The whole question of mediaeval monastic and scholastic theology can only be fully understood in the light of this transition from the patristic to the scholastic ideal. For further references to the patristic and scholastic theological method cf. M. R. Gagnebet, 'La nature de la théologie speculative,' *Revue thomiste* 44 (1938) 1-39 and 213-255. R. Perino, *La dottrina trinitaria di Sant' Anselmo* (Rome, 1952) 37-40 and J. Maritain, *Les degrés du savoir* (Paris, 1932) 577-613.

[3]Cf J. Leclercq, *L'amour* 208. This contrasting tendency of the black monks is well illustrated in the works of Rupert of Deutz. See *De victoria* (PL 169, 1217-1502) which treats above all of the objective divine economy throughout history. The prologue to Rupert's *De trinitate* (PL 167, 197-200) shows the manifestation of the Trinity throughout the work of creation and redemption, dividing history into three main phases, attributed respectively to the Father, the Son and the Holy Ghost (199 AB). See also in the work itself (247 AB): 'Sanctae Trinitatis gloriam per opera ipsius quasi per speculum contemplari.'

[4]Although the white monks constantly refer to the objective historical mysteries of the redemptive work of Christ, their interest is primarily to see how these mysteries are experienced in the individual soul. See J. Leclercq, *L'amour* 210, and P. Bonard, 'La Bible expression d'une expérience religieuse chez S. Bernard,' *S. Bernard théologien,* 24-25.

[5]This element is present in patristic theology, as is evident from the very nature of *sapientia,* as for instance in the works of Origen; See *L'amour* 211, referring to H. de Lubac, *Histoire et esprit* (Paris, 1950) [ET: *History and the Spirit* to appear as CS 55] But there is a difference of emphasis between this development in monastic theology as compared with patristic theology as a whole, in the sense that St Bernard and William of St Thierry focused their interest above all on this 'experience' of the individual soul and therefore precisely on those aspects of the dogmas of the Church which were related most intimately to this experience. Cf P. Bonard, 'La Bible,' 24-25: 'cette théologie monastique et celle de S. Bernard plus encore que celle de ses predecesseurs est fortement teintée d'interiorisme et tout orientée vers l'experience religieuse.'

[6]Particularly outstanding are the works of Déchanet, to whom this study is greatly indebted. See above, Preface, n. 2,

for a brief bibliography of his work. Among works by other authors on William of St Thierry, those especially by Père Bouyer and Père Malevez are of considerable interest on this subject; see above, Preface, n. 2.

[7]Among Déchanet's works mentioned above, certain aspects of William's trinitarian doctrine have been treated in isolation. But as there had been no study of his doctrine of the Trinity as a whole, the important question remained as to whether there was any fundamental theme among William's often very varied presentations of the dogma of the Trinity, and how these different ways of approaching the Trinity in his works were related to each other.

[8]Déchanet, *OEuvres choisies*, 253.

[9]Ibid.

[10]See Ep frat, PL 184, 341D: 'ad imaginem et similitudinem ejus conditus est....adhaerere festinat similitudini suae devota imago.' Ibid. 348: 'creati sumus et vivmus ut Deo similes simus, cum ad Dei imaginem creati sumus.' See also Cant, PL 180, 473C: 'ad imaginem et similitudinem tuam creasti nos,'; Aenig PL 180, 399B: 'similitudo ista est....secundum imaginem ejus qui creavit eum.' This distinction originates at least with St Irenaeus. Cf H. Crouzel, *La théologie de l'image de Dieu chez Origène* (Toulouse, 1955) p. 65 and the bibliography for this theme among the Fathers. It is present in St Clement (A. Mayer, *Das Gottesbild im Menschen nach Clemens von Alexandrien*. Studia Anselmiana 15 [Rome, 1942] 5-21). Cf Crouzel, 217-245 for this theme in Origen; see also St Augustine, *De trinitate* (PL 42, 1055), Erigena, *De divisione naturae* (PL 122, 585A), St Bernard, Gra (PL 182, 1016B).

[11]Nat corp, 722AB: 'Sicut nihil sine creatore Deo, ipsa scilicet sancta Trinitate existit, ita nihil omnino esse potest, quod non et unum sit et trifariam consistit.'

[12]See M. Schmaus, *Die psychologische Trinitätslehre des heiligen Augustinus*, (Münster, 1927) 201 ff., where he shows the ascending hierarchy of images from the 'outer' to the 'inner' man.

[13]Nat am, 382CD: See also Nat corp, 721BC, a similar text showing the same image as an illustration of Trinity in unity, but without showing the order of the processions. The direct source for the text from Nat corp is Claude Mamert, *De statu animae*, PL 53, 734CD; see Déchanet, *OEuvres choisies*, 64-66 and 71 for the table of sources, comparing Nat corp with *De statu animae*,

and showing the corresponding passages. The theme is Augustinian
in origin. See *De trinitate* (PL 42, 1043-1044) for an analysis of
the image of memory, intellect and will and *De trinitate* (PL 42,
1090) for a comparison between the relationship of the Father, the
Son and the Holy Ghost to the faculties of memory, intellect and
will respectively, similar to that of William's text from Nat am
(382CD). See also a similar treatment of the image of faith, hope,
and charity, Spec fide (*Le miroir*, 55-59; 367 C-368B), influenced
perhaps by St Bernard, *Div* (PL 183, 668B) and of the image of faith,
intellect and love, Aenig (433D).

[14]Spec fid, 54-57; 367 CD-368A.

[15]Ibid., 48-55; 365B-367C, and again 58-59; 368C. These
passages both precede and follow the text on the theme of the
'illustration,' thus giving the impression that he was primarily
interested in the image as a means of salvation and union with the
Trinity. See 365B, where this created trinity is described as
'machina illa salutis humanae,' and 367B: 'Quicunque ergo vere
quaerunt Deum Trinitatem, trium virtutum harum affectent in semetipsis habere trinitatem et conformare se studeant ad earum disciplinam.'

[16]Nat corp, 721CD. The source of this text is Claude Mamert, *De statu animae*, PL 53, 735B: 'Formatus es ipse, non for-
mator....accede formatrici formae....' This conception of the
image imprint is a theme of the Greek Father. See St Gregory of
Nyssa, *De hominis opificio* (PG 44, 137BC) referring to the image in
man in terms suggesting an imprint from the creator: τοῦτν καὶ
ἡμέτερον πεποίηται πρόσωπον ὁ τῆσ φύσεωσ πλάστησ. See also *In
Cantica Homily* 2, PG 44, 806D: τῆσ ἀληθινῆσ θεότητοσ ἀποτύπωμα.
See Cyril of Alexandria, In Ioannis Evangelium IX, PG 74, 278D:
τινὰ σφραγῖδα τῆσ ἑαυτοῦ φυαεωσ...κατ' εἰκόνα τοῦ κτίσαντοσ.
This theme was not unknown to St Bernard. See Déchanet, *Aux sources
de la spiritualité* 15, footnote referring to *Sermo 2 de nativitate
Domini* (PL 183, 120CD). Generally, however, St Bernard places the
image in the will. See E. Gilson, *La théologie mystique*, p. 64 ff
and Déchanet, *Aux sources* 14, who contrasts his doctrine in this
respect from that of William.

[17]Cf. PL 180, 722B: 'Haec omnia anima intellectu con-
spiciens, non jam tam delectatur in sua formositate quam in forma
formatrice cui intendendo sumper efficitur formosior.' The imprint
of the Trinity is extended also to the corporeal creation. Ibid:
'Permanat enim a summo quod Deus est; per medium, quod est anima;
ad imum, quod sunt corpora....' Père Déchanet shows how this
theme of an ascending range of imprints of God through creation is

already found in Origen, St Gregory of Nyssa and St Basil. See
Déchanet, *OEuvres choisies*, 56, footnote, referring especially to
St Basil, *Homilia in illud: Attende tibi ipsi* (PG 31, 216-217).

[18] 'Natural' will be considered here in the philosophical
rather than the historical sense of the term. For this distinction cf. Vagaggini, 303ff.

[19] Ep frat, 348CD-349A. Although William does not use the
term, 'natural' here, he is referring implicitly to nature in the
philosophical rather than the historical sense, as is shown by this
conception of the image of God in abstraction from any further action of the will, or the gift of grace. This is evident from the
words, ibid., 348C: 'Est autem Dei similitudo quaedam quam nemo
vivens nisi cum vita exuit, quam omni homini in testimonium amissae melioris et dignirois similitudinis creator hominum relin-
quit; quam habet et volens et nolens....'
    It is of interest to observe the probable influence of
St Gregory the Great on the passage, ibid., 348D: 'Sicut semper
sibi indissimilis Deus indissimiliter dissimilia in creatura operatur; sic anima....in sensibus tamen corporis et in cogitationibus
cordis indissimiliter operatur assidue dissimilia.' See the parallel text, St Gregory, *Homil in Ezech* (PL 76, 990): 'Sibi semper
indissimilis dissimilia disponit....' We shall be referring to
the question of the influence of St Gregory on William's mystical
doctrine later.

[20] Malevez, 'La doctrine de l'image,' p. 263.

[21] Nat am, 382D.

[22] Déchanet, 'La connaissance de soi d'après Guillaume de
Saint-Thierry,' *Vie spirituelle, Supplement* 56-57 (1938) 3-4,
102-122.

[23] This is an idea of platonic and neoplatonic origin.
See H. Crouzel, *Théologie de l'image de Dieu chez Origène*, p. 35:
'La parenté platonicienne est, comme l'image plotinienne ou le
selon-l'image origénien, un concept dynamique: l'image tend d'elle-
même a revenir au contact du modèle.' See Plotinus, *Enn.* VI, 4,
9, where he writes of the impossibility of the separation of the
image from its archetype.

[24] Nat am, 382CD.

[25] This conception is similar to that of St Gregory of Nyssa, *Oratio catechetica* (ed. L. Meridier, Paris 1908, p. 26):

ἀναγκαῖον ἦν ἐγκραθῆναί τι τῇ ἀνθρωπίνη φύσει συγγενὲσ πρὸσ τὸ
θεῖον ὣσ αν διὰ τοῦ καταλλὴλου πρὸσ τὸ οἰκειὸν τὴν ἔφεσιν ἔχοι.
This text is quoted by Déchanet (*OEuvres choisies,* 249) in connection with the image in William.

26Nat am, 382BC.

27PL 180, 725C. Déchanet has traced this text to its
source in the *Enneads* of Plotinus, I, 8, 13. (Déchanet, 'Guillaume et Plotin,' p. 245). But the context of creation (725C) and
eternal punishment (726C) shows how the originally Plotinian theme
has been transformed by the historical order of Christianity. See
p. 58 for a more complete reference to the influence of Plotinus.

28PL 180, 216CD-217A. Déchanet, 'Guillaume et Plotin,'
p. 242. But the transformation of the theme of Plotinus by the
Christian context is even clearer here than in the preceding text
from **Nat corp** (see above note 16). This text from the Med with
its references to Eve and the serpent show that the 'paradise' refers to the earthly paradise and the text treats explicitly of the
expulsion from this paradise into the *regio dissimilitudinis,*
associating the *regio dissimilitudinis* with the historical order
of creation, sin, redemption. Also see Déchanet, 'La connaissance
de soi,' 119, referring to the historical approach of William to
the *nosce teipsum.*

29Nat corp, 722BC.

30L. Malevez, 'La doctrine de l'image,' 258.

31Nat corp, 722D; Nat am, 382D-383A: 'Quae cum prae-
veniente et cooperante gratia, Spiritui ipsi sancto, qui Patris
et Filii amor est et voluntas, bono sui assensus incipit inhaerere.'

32Nat corp, 723A-726C. See above, footnote 27, for the
Plotinian character of this text, transformed by the Christian
historical order.

33Déchanet, *OEuvres choisies,* p. 254.

34There is a similar hierarchical treatment of the image
of the Trinity through the virtues of faith, hope and charity in
terms of a journey in the ascent to God. See Spec fid, 48-50;
365BC: '....a fide enim incipit homo....dum peregrinamur a Domino
....spes....quae consolatur in via....nec tamen fides et spes peribunt, sed in res suas transibunt....charitas vero non tantum erit,

sed perfecta **erit.**'   Cf. the same theme, ibid., **568ABC.**   See also Aenig, PL 180, 433D, for the treatment of the image faith, intellect and love in terms of an evolution: 'fides incipiens operari per dilectionem, incipit etiam ipsa formari in dilectionem, et per dilectionem in intellectum....'

[35]Cant, 503C-504A.

[36]The image of memory, intellect and love from the text of Cant 503C-504A is identical with that of memory, intellect and will, which is explicitly related to the Trinity.   Will in the text from Nat corp is synonymous with love: 'et vult cogitare et meminisse, hoc est amat habere mentem et cogitationem' (PL 180, 721B).   See also Nat am, 383A: 'Nihil aliud est amor quam vehemens in bono voluntas.'

[37]Cant, 503CD.

[38]Ibid., 503D-504A.

[39]Cf. ibid., 505C, where *affectus* is associated with the state of *unitas spiritus:*   'Fit homo Deo affectus, hoc est cum Deo unus spiritus.'   Cf. L. Malevez, 'La doctrine de l'image,' 266-267.

[40]See below, Section III, THE HOLY GHOST AND THE RESTORATION OF RESEMBLANCE....

[41]Cf. Perino, *La dottrina,* p. 23; showing that St Augustine was the basis for the developments of St Anselm: 'Si valse di lui come di una base di partenza.'

[42]Ibid., 204-205.

[43]The trinity in the soul only becomes an image and not merely a trinity where the faculties are directed towards God and the things of eternity: *De trinitate* (PL 42, 1000, 1048).

[44]Perino, 204-210.

[45]Ibid., 191-198.

[46]Ibid., 206.

[47]Cf. L. Bouyer, *La spiritualité,* p. 142:   'La théologie trinitaire de Guillaume....concourt entièrement a dégager le mystère qui place l'être divin absolument à part.'

[48]See above, *The imprint of the Trinity.*

[49]Spec fid, (*Le miroir*) 56-57; 367D; Aenig, 433D. William's acceptance of the trinities based on faith as an image contrasts with St Augustine's refusal to do so on the grounds that faith is bound to time and the image arises from the consideration of eternity. Cf. Schmaus, *Psychologische Trinitätslehre,* p. 300. This indicates that William has an altogether freer conception of what constitutes an image of the Trinity, and therefore is even less likely than St Augustine to interpret the psychological image as a strict analogy of proper proportion.

[50]See above, *The imprint of the Trinity.*

[51]*Monologion* 67, 68, (ed., F. S. Schmitt, *S. Anselmi Opera omnia,* vol. I [1938]). Cf. Perino, *La dottrina trinitaria di S. Anselmo,* 202-203. Perino speaks of the 'valore antropologico o ascetico' which St Anselm occasionally gives to the image, due to the Augustinian element of *sapientia* which remains in his theology and directs his speculation towards contemplation.

[52]Perino, 191-199; and 204-210; he concludes, 211, to the predominantly metaphysical and dialectic character of St Anselm's theology.

[53]See above, note 49; note also the presence of the dynamic approach to the image tending towards resemblance, similar to William's approach, *De trinitate,* PL 42, 105: 'in hac quippe imagine tunc perfecta erit Dei similitudo;' and 1051: 'qua in se imagine Dei tam potens est, ut ei cujus imago est valeat inhaerere.'

[54]Cf., Perino, 31; M.-R. Gagnebet, 'La nature de la théologie spéculative,' *Revue thomiste* 44 (1938) p. 254: 'Saint Augustin et tous ses disciples répugnent à l'idée de la recherche d'un savoir qui serait poursuivi pour lui-même. La fin spéculative de la science telle qui la Grèce l'avait conçue leur semble inacceptable lorsqu'il s'agit des vérités révélées qui nous sont enseignées par Dieu pourque nous fassions notre salut.'

[55]*De trinitate* PL 42, 832: 'Hoc est enim plenum gaudium nostrum, quo amplius non est, frui Trinitate Deo, ad cujus imaginem facti sumus.'

[56]The following texts illustrate this psychological preparation for the contemplation of the Trinity, *De trinitate* (PL 42, 1035): 'Placuit quippe velut gradatim ascendentibus in utraque requirere apud interiorem hominem quamquam sui cujusque generis

trinitatem, sicut prius apud exteriorem quaesivimus; ut ad illam
Trinitatem quae Deus est, pro nostro modulo, si tamen vel hoc possumus, saltem in aenigmate et per speculum contuendam (I Cor 13,
12) exercitatiore in his interioribus mente veniamus.' The idea
is that of a progressive series of created images leading pedagogically to a psychological perception of the uncreated Trinity con-
templated through the medium of created images. See also ibid.,
1088: 'et maxime per rationalem vel intellectualem creaturam,
quae facta est ad imaginem Dei; per quod velut speculum, quantum
possent, cernerent Trinitatem Deum, in nostra memoria, intelligentia, voluntate.' The end is contemplation of the Trinity, but
achieved through psychological reflection.

[57]In the work of M.-D. Chenu, *La théologie au XIIe siècle*,
(Paris, 1957) p. 299, footnote, it is suggested that William abandoned the Augustinian analogy of the Trinity, *mens, notitis, amor*,
as a result of Greek influence. This is an interesting theory, but
difficult to prove conclusively. The Augustinian triad, memory,
intellect, will, though not explicitly related to the Trinity is
still found in Cant, as we have seen, together with the beginning
of the influence of Origen with the three stages, *animalis, rationalis, spiritualis* (PL 180, 477BC). The Augustinian influence is
very strong in the Aenig, one of his latest works and in the theory of the Holy Ghost in his last important work, the Ep frat.
There is no evidence that in the course of the evolution of his
Trinitarian theology he abandoned Augustinian influence in favor
of the Greeks. It is possible that he may have done so on this
particular point, but there is no proof. His reason may well
have been the growing realization that this illustration was not
essential to his doctrine. As we have seen throughout, the heart
of his doctrine does not lie in the Augustinian analogy. In the
Aenig, the further reason for abandoning this analogy would be his
desire to present the bare mystery of the Trinity without any explanation.

[58]See above, *The imprint of the Trinity*.

[59]M. Standaert, 'La doctrine de l'image chez saint Bernard,' *Ephem. theol. Lovan.* 23 (1947) 102.

[60]Ibid.: 'Dieu a créé l'homme dans un état de grandeur, a savoir dans une capacité de grandeur et de bonheur réelle-
ment indestructible. Le péché est venu et a porté atteinte a
cette oeuvre divine, mais toujours il reste dans l'homme, 'quelque
chose', image ou ressemblance divine, peu importe, qui garde
l'homme 'capax Dei' qui permet d'espérer le retour a Dieu et de
voir se réaliser finalement le dessin de Dieu' Cf. Gilson, *La*

théologie mystique, 48-77.

[61]See above, footnote 16.

[62]This conception, through akin to that of St Bernard, can be traced beyond Bernard, to the Greek Fathers. Déchanet has proved the influence of St Gregory of Nyssa on William's Nat corp: See *Aux sources,* 47-59, for this same historical approach to the image.

[63]Div, PL 183, 668B: 'Et haec est trinitas, scilicet fides, spes, charitas, per quam velut per tridentem reduxit de limo profundi ad amissam **beatitudinem** illa incommutabilis et beata trinitas nutabilem, lapsam et miseram trinitatem. Et fides quidem illuminavit rationem, spes erexit memoriam, charitas vero purgavit voluntatem.' The context of this passage (ibid., 667A-669B) these various 'trinities'; cf. ibid., 669AB; there is the Trinity *suggestio, delectatio, consensus,* through which the memory, reason and will falls. Then there is the trinity into which it falls, *impotentia, caecitas, immunditia,* followed by the various **trinities** into which the memory, reason and will fall respectively. The treatment of the subject is throughout much more **artificial** than that of William, but in both cases the underlying theme is that of the history of the soul.

[64]It is true that the faculties of the image, memory, intellect and will, were shown to be connected with the states, animal, rational and spiritual, to which there was an implicit allusion. This is the nearest approach to a suggestion that the three states themselves **constitute** an image of the Trinity. But this is not stated explicitly and in this particular text the **faculties** of memory, intellect and will are not even explicitly stated to be an image of the Trinity.

[65]Cf. Aenig, 414A-415D; Med, 210BCD, 214BCD: these three texts are placed in a trinitarian context. For other examples not directly connected with the Trinity, see Spec fid, 78-80, 372D -373A; 134-137, 386ABCD; 154-155, 390D-391A; Ep frat, 315C, 316B, 340BC, 345CD, 347ABCD, 348ABD, 349A, 352C; Cant, 477BC, 481A-482D, 503CD, 516CD; Exp Rom, 609D-610A; Sacr altar, 344AB, 346B; Nat corp, 713D-714A, 715C, 718B, 720A; Med, 216D-217A. The main divisions in the grouping of the varied terminology in these texts are given in L. Bouyer, *La spiritualité,* 127.

[66]The same characteristics are evident even in those terms which **at first sight** do not seem to have much relevance for this scheme; *obedientia necessitatis* (Ep frat, 345CD, 347ABCD)

implies compulsion from without, suggesting the note of the external. *Ubiquitas* is used to describe the omnipresence of the soul in all its actions through the various senses (Nat corp, PL 180, 713D-714A). *Regnum* is used to express the idea of the soul as master of itself through reason (715C). The same theme of life according to the senses, reason and the spirit is expressed by the Augustinian image, memory, intellect, love. The terminology however is not always consistent. See alternate use of *anima* for both the first and the middle term, and the striking inversion of the usual terminology in the text from the Exp Rom, 609D, where *rationalis* relates to the senses through the sacraments, *spiritualis* to the intermediary rational stage, and *intellectus* to the last stage.

[67]Aenig, 414B. The first lines of this text, 'tribus enim intelligentiae gradibus proficerent fidei ascendendum est ad Deum,' shows signs of the corruption of the original text but the general sense of the text as a whole is very clear with its distinction between the three degrees of faith, understanding of the faith rationally, and finally experience of the faith. See also Med, 210BCD, where the problem of knowledge of the Trinity is seen in terms of three ascending degrees of knowledge, though here the senses and the imagination form together the first degree of knowledge. The connection between the two formulae from the Aenig and the Med can be seen from the relationship of faith to sense knowledge in the Spec fid, 134-135; 386A: 'quae proprie fidei sunt; eas scilicet res quae sensibiliter menti inferuntur per sensus.'

[68]Ep frat, 315C-316B. A comparison between these two texts fully justifies the parallel originally discovered by Déchanet; *Guillaume de Saint-Thierry*, 94, footnote, developed by Bouyer, *La spiritualité*, 139-154.

[69]Aenig, 414C; cf. Sacr altar, 345A.

[70]Ep frat, 317B.

[71]Aenig, 414CD.

[72]Ep frat, 316B.

[73]Aenig, 415C.

[74]Ibid., 415C.

[75]Ibid., 414D.

[76]Ep frat, 316A. *Affectus* here denotes a special mystical form of knowledge associated with the final state of spiritus; cf. Cant, 505C, and L. Malevez, 'La doctrine de l'image,' 266-267.

[77]Ep frat, 316A.

[78]Ep frat, 315C-316B.

[79]Ibid., 430C; 348CD-349A. The existence of a psychological foundation distinct from the spiritual states is evident from the description of *anima* as *res incorporea*, the source of the animal state, *animales constituit homines* (340B).

[80]Ibid., 340C: 'anima....efficitur animus.' The implication is that of the evolution and perfection of already existing capacities rather than of different elements ontologically; cf. 340BC, where *anima* is described as *rationis capax* and *animus* as *rationis princeps*.

[81]Ibid., 352C: 'spiritus et anima et corpus suo modo ordinata, suis locis disposita.'

[82]L. Bouyer, *La spiritualité*, 121: 'La spiritualité de Guillaume se developpera non comme une statique, mais comme une dynamique de l'âme. Elle ne vise pas tant à équilibrer *anima-animus-spiritus* qu'a la faire passer d'*anima* à *animus* et d'*animus* à *spiritus*.'

[83]Cf. St Bernard, *In Cantica*, PL 183, 871D: 'carnalis, rationalis, spiritualis,' and PL 182, 789D: 'dispensativa, aestimativa, speculativa'; cf. Brev comm, PL 184, 407C, referring to the three degrees of love: 'sensualis et animalis,' 'rationalis' and 'spiritualis vel intellectualis'; a passage which is probably the work of both William and Bernard (see J. Hourlier, 'Guillaume de Saint-Thierry et la *Brevis commentatio in Cantica*,' ASOC 12 (1956) 105-114). See also J. Leclercq, 'Etudes sur saint Bernard et le texte de ses écrits,' ASOC 9 (1953) p. 113, for the distinction of the three degrees of love in St Bernard. But the trichotomy as the basis of three degrees of spiritual development is more fully developed by William where it becomes the main theme of the Ep frat, and Ivanka refers to the increasing influence of William on St Bernard: E. Ivanka, 'La structure de l'âme selon saint Bernard,' *S. Bernard théologien*, p. 205.

[84]Med, 214BCD, and Spec fid, 154-155; 390D-391A.

[85]*Senteniae Anselmi*, ed. F. Bliemetzrieder in *Beiträge*

zur Geschichte der Philosophie des Mittelalters 18, (Münster, 1919) p. 153.

[86]Déchanet, *Guillaume de Saint-Thierry*, 10-11.

[87]*De divisione naturae*, PL 122, 579BCD: *intellectus* is identified with *animus* (574B).

[88]The intellectual character of Erigena's third stage of knnwledge lacks the mystical character of William's *spiritus*. See Fliche-Martin, *Histoire de l'Eglise*, vol. 13, (Paris, 1934) p. 27. There is also no evidence in William's theology of any reference to *sensus, ratio* and *intellectus* as an illustration of the Trinity, in contrast to Erigena's explicit comparison of *animus, ratio*, and *sensus* to the Father, the Son and the Holy Ghost respectively (*De divisione nature*, PL 122, 579ABCD).

[89]*Contra Celsum*, PG 11, 1309C.

[90]Περὶ ἀρχῶν, PG 11, 364B-365A; especially 365A.

[91]Ibid., 223B.

[92]Déchanet, *Guillaume de Saint-Thierry*, 116. Despite the evidence for the influence of Origen, the similarity between William's and Origen's trichotomy should not be pressed too closely. The νοῦσ of Origen has a closer association with contemplative experience than the *animus* of William (cf. H. Crouzel, 'L'anthropologie d'Origène,' *RAM* 31 (1955) 373, and the πνεῦμα of Origen has the character of a divine guide, a leader of the soul rather than a state of the soul (Crouzel, 'L'anthropologie' 366-368, and *La theologie de l'image de Dieu chez Origene*, 131).

[93]Erigena, *De divisione naturae*, PL 122, 510C, and Fliche-Martin's apt comment on Erigena's approach to knowledge, vol. 13, p. 12-13; 'La connaissance est toujours une purification....tout le mouvement de la pensée consiste donc dans la recherche d'une intelligence plus haute.'
The psychology of Origen reveals this same dynamic impulse, and is placed in the whole context of the fall of the soul from νοῦσ under the dominion of πνεῦμα into ψυχή and the aspiration to return through the trial of purification to the original state of νοῦσ. A philosophical dichotomy is not incompatible with this dynamic trichotomy, for, as Crouzel says referring to H. de Lubac, *Histoire et esprit*, 157: 'il s'agit plutôt de principes d'action que de principes d'être' (H. Crouzel 'L'anthropologie,' 365 and 384).

[94]The neo-platonic scheme of descent from unity to multiplicity and ascent to the original unity underlies Erigena's thought: see M. Cappuyns, *Jean Scot Erigène, sa vie, son oeuvre, sa pensée* (Louvain, 1933) 307-308.

[95]E. Bréhier, *La philosophie de Plotin* (Paris, 1948), p. 449. This élan is achieved through three levels of the soul, intuitive, discursive, sense operations; ibid., p. 41; H. Crouzel, *La théologie de l'image de Dieu chez Origène*, 43, and F. Copleston, *A History of Philosophy*, vol. I (London, 1946), p. 471.

[96]See the long introduction to the central trinitarian section of Aenig, 397B-407C. In the course of this introduction the incarnation and the whole temporal economy is seen as the necessary preparation to enable man under the dominion of the senses in the animal state to rise to a knowledge of what is eternal (Aenig, 402BC and 403CD).

[97]This forms the subject of the central section of Aenig which we hope to treat fully in another article.

[98]Perino, *La dottrina trinitaria*, 191-210.

[99]Aenig, 426C.

[100]Compare a future article on the speculative aspect of the Aenigma fidei [Chapter 3].

[101]The value of the doctrine of the Trinity as a means of life rather than as a problem to be scrutinized by the reason is suggested in the famous text of St Bernard from Csi, PL 182, 799C: 'Scrutare hoc temeritas est, credere pietas est; nosse vita, et vita aeterna est.' But it was William who was to expand this theme into a fully developed theology.

[102]*De trinitate*, PL 42, 1079, 1087.

[103]Spec fid, 164-165; 393B; cf. contemp, 374D-375A; Med, 224B; Cant, 506C; Ep frat, 349A; Adv Abl, 259C; Exp Rom, 561D.

[104]Nat corp, 722D; Med, 213A; Exp Rom, 667D; Contemp, 376C; Spec fid, 158-159; 391C.

[105]Spec fid, 162-163; 393A: 'Ea vero cognitio quae mutua est Patris et Filii, ipsa est unitas amborum, qui est Spiritus Sanctus.'

[106]See also, ibid. 'notitiam mutuam eorum....'; ibid.,
164-165, 393B: 'ibi mutua cognitio.'

[107]Ibid., 383A: 'communis voluntas est amborum'; 393B:
'mutua charitas.' Even when he speaks of the Holy Ghost simply as
'the will or the love of the Father and the Son,' as in Nat corp,
722D, his general doctrine of the Holy Ghost as whatever is common
to the Father and the Son, implies that it is the mutual reciprocity of charity rather than charity as such which is proper to the
Holy Ghost in William's doctrine. See Malevez, 'La doctrine de
l'image,' 198, on the same question applied to 'mutua cognitio.'

[108]Ep frat, 349B.

[109]Cf. Contemp, 376D-377A, showing the ontological character of this union. Hourlier in his essay on the comparison between St Bernard and William's *Liber de amore* (J. Hourlier, 'S.
Bernard et Guillaume de Saint-Thierry,' *S. Bernard théologien*,
pp. 223-233) comments on the greater emphasis on the union between
God and man in William's doctrine, stressing its more ontological
character (230): 'S'il nous était permis de forcer les positions,
nous dirions qu'au terme de ses recherches S. Bernard situe la
possession de Dieu dans la béatitude de l'amour qui réunit deux
êtres; Guillaume de Saint-Thierry situe la connaissance dans la
béatitude de l'unité en un seul être.' See also his interpretation
of St Bernard's 'sic affici, deificari est' (p. 232): 'Il n'entend
pas par la que nous devenious un seul être avec Dieu, mais que nous
nous transformions complètement en la volonté de Dieu,' implying
that St Bernard's conception of deification is on a more psychological level.

[110]Spec fid, 164-165; 393B: 'In creatore....in creatura
....in propria natura....in gratia....in aeternitatis incommuta-
bilitate....in temporali permutatione.'

[111]M.-M. Davy, *Théologie et mystique de Guillaume de
Saint-Thierry* (Paris, 1954) 166-168, footnote, opposes Déchanet's
interpretation that William's doctrine of resemblance implies an
ontological resemblance with the Holy Ghost on the grounds that
the distinctions made by William between the substantial uncreated
union of the Trinity and the union of resemblance through grace
prove that William was referring only to a created gift. But the
texts imply more than a created gift and show that William intended to convey the idea of a real participation in the life of the
Holy Spirit. Davy impoverishes William's doctrine by stressing
only one of the two antitheses, both of which have been carefully
emphasized by Père Déchanet (*OEuvres choisies*, 158) where he speaks

of an 'identité qui persiste au coeur de la distinction.' The
Holy Spirit is 'plus que donateur de la grâce qui unifie. Il est
cette grâce, il est cette union d'une manière mystérieuse, certes,
mais non moins évidente.'

[112]Spec fid, 164-165; 393B: 'ibi mutua cognitio Patris
et Filii unitas est, hic hominis ad Deum similitudo.' This theme
of the Holy Ghost, the substantial unity of the Father and the Son
as the foundation for our participated unity, is shown also in the
following texts: Nat corp, 722D; Med, 213ABCD, 224BCD, 231A; Cant,
520B; Aenig, 399D; Contemp, 374D, 376BCD.

[113]Spec fid, 164-165; 393C: 'quem in tantum videbit,
sive cognoscet, qui cognoscet vel videbit, in quantum similis ei
erit; in tantum erit ei similis, in quantum eum cognoscet vel ide-
bit. Videre namque ibi seu cognoscere Deum similem est esse Deo,
et similem et esse, videre seu cognoscere eum est.' Cf. Aenig,
399B; Ep frat, 350B.

[114]Cf. Malevez, 'La doctrine de l'image,' 267-268.

[115]Spec fid, 162-163; 392D: 'Cognitio autem haec Dei
alia fidei est, alia amoris vel charitatis.'

[116]Ibid., 154-157 (390D-391A); Med, 213ABC. Cf. Déchanet,
Guillaume de Saint-Thierry, Méditations et prières, (Brussels, 1945)
p. 45; Malevez, 'La doctrine de l'image,' 182 ff.

[117]Spec fid, 154-155; 390D: 'Major tamen et dignior sensus ejus et purior intellectus, amor est; si fuerit ipse purus.'

[118]Ibid., 156-157; 391A: 'in eis vero quae sunt ad Deum
sensus mentis amor est.' Cf. Med, PL 180, 213BC.

[119]Nat am, 393C: 'hoc discere non potest, nisi experien-
do, sic nec communicare potuit inexperto'; Med, 246C: 'nec ratione discuti, nec exponi verbis, nec sensibus potest concipi.'

[120]Med, 246C: 'Divinum quiddam est, et arrha vel pignus
spiritus'; Cant, PL 180, 504C: 'in quemdam spiritualem vel divinum
formatur intellectum.'

[121]Cf. Déchanet, *Méditations et prières,* 50, 62 ff.

[122]Spec fid, 162-163; 392D; 164-165; 393A; Cant, 491D,
499C, 500C, 504C, 505D.

[123]Adv Ab, 252C; Cant, 491D, 499C.

[124]Cf. the criticism made by Déchanet against Gilson (*Me-ditations et prières*, 68, footnote): 'il donne au mot connaissance une acception purement intellectuelle, notionelle, conceptuelle.'

[125]Ibid., 50, footnote. This is the interpretation given by Rousselot which Déchanet rightly answers by saying that 'amor ipse intellectus est' should be translated not as 'l'amour lui-même est intellect,' but 'l'amour est une intellection, une sorte d'entendement.' The opposition of Mlle Davy to Père Déchanet on this point (*Théologie et mystique de Guillaume de Saint-Thierry*, 211-215, footnote) is based on a confusion of this issue, and she discusses the whole problem on the false question of the distinc-tion of the faculties, love and knowledge, a distinction which Déchanet clearly admits.

[126]Cf. Nat am, 393A: 'amor et ratio' with Cant, 504B: 'ratio et amor.' This is a clear assertion of the distinction of the faculties as such and the following, 504C: 'Fiunt que saepe duo isti oculi unus oculus....ratio transit in amorem' implies the interpenetration and union of these faculties in a single act of knowledge rather than the formal identification of these facul-ties as such.

[127]Med, 214C: 'Videant aliquatenus te qui es, quamvis non videant te sicut es; sed tamen medium quid....' this is in context of the direct beatific vision. Cf. 213D-214A, referring to the knowledge of God 'facie ad faciem.' Cf. also Spec fid, (*Le miroir*) 168-169; 394C: 'Hujus boni sensus et suavitas exper-ientiae....quamvis non plena verta tamen est vita, et vere beata; in futura plena et plene beata.'

[128]Ep frat, 353A.

[129]Aenig, 414D.

[130]Contemp, 377.

[131]Aenig, 426C.

[132]Ibid., 399D; Ep frat, 349C.

[133]Rom, 638CD.

[134]Med, 214CD.

[135]Ibid., 214; 'ut sensum intuentis non dividat Trinitas,
non confundat unitas (following Déchanet's correction of the read-
ing from Migne; cf. *Meditations et prières*, p. 120, footnote), non
offendat Trinitas pietatem unum Deum quaerentis, non contristet
substantiae unitas charitatem Patris et Filii dilectione gaudentis.'
The implication may be that the mind no longer moving on a conceptual plane is no longer troubled by the antithesis of two apparently irreconcilable concepts. The same kind of intuitive vision of
Trinity and unity is expressed in the description of the ultimate
beatific vision. Aenig, PL 180, 435C: 'uno simul cernent intuitu
....visio illius contemplationis....non in tres dividetur, nec
collegetur in unum' though even here in the beatific vision he do
does not speak of an elimination of the mystery.

[136]Spec fid, 156-165; 391CD, 392B, 393ABC; Aenig, 399BCD;
Med, 213ABC, 214BCD, 244BC, 246C; Cant, 491D, 495A, 500CD, 506BCD;
Exp Rom, 638CD; Contemp, 376BCD.

[137]Contempt, 376B. The question of the identification
of the virtue of charity with the Holy Ghost was much discussed
among William's contemporaries. See A. M. Landgraf, *Dogmengesch-
ischte der Frühscholastik*, I (Regensburg, 1952) 220-237. This
identification was taught by Peter Lombard, as is shown by the
references of Landgraf to the *sententiae* (pp. 220-221). The opposite view was already held by Abelard (*Epistola ad Romanos*, PL
178, 860) and by Rupert of Deutz (*De officiis*, PL 170, 300), where
he distinguished clearly the Holy Ghost as *substantialiter amor*,
from the participation *accidentali dono*. Lombard's theory was
still upheld by Odo of Ourscamp, but with Peter of Capua, Stephen
Langton, William of Auxerre, John of Treviso and Hugh of St Charo,
the break with Lombard's doctrine was finally effected (Landgraf,
234).
        Despite an apparent similarity between William's doc-
trine and that of Peter Lombard, the question does not seem to
have been treated from the same angle. William may have been influenced by Lombard's doctrine, but his approach to the question
is very different. He does not explicitly consider the problem of
a metaphysical identification of the Holy Ghost and the virtue of
charity. His emphasis on the apparent identification of *amor-
intellectus* with the Holy Ghost is intended to show that *amor-
intellectus* is real participation in the life of the Holy Ghost,
without suggesting a formal identification of the Holy Ghost with
the virtue of charity; see above, *ressemblance*, where 'resemblance'
is shown to be a real participation in the life of the Holy Ghost,
yet through 'grace' and not by 'nature' in the 'creature' and not
in the 'creator.' Moreover the whole force of the argument is
centered on the conception of the participation in the Holy Ghost

as mutual union, rather than primarily as charity.

[138]Spec fid, 164-165; 393A.

[139]Déchanet, *Guillaume de Saint-Thierry*, 64-65.

[140]Spec fid, 158-170; 391D-394C; Ep frat, 348B-350B; Med, 213A-214D.

[141]Aenig, 421BCD, 435CD; Adv Ab, 252CD, 253A; Er Guil, 336D-337A.

[142]PL 180, 439D. This long text is summed up in the words, 439CD: 'Donum enim Dei intantum est Spiritus Sanctus, ut donorum Dei quae nemo omnia habet, qui Spiritum Sanctum non habet, quorum quicumque habet ullum non nisi in Spiritu Sancto habet.'

[143]See above notes 110-111.

[144]Ep frat, 349A.

[145]Spec fid, 164-165, 393B.

[146]Expressions such as *efficit, facit,* without an explicit formulation in terms of causality, tend towards what is now called efficient causality.

[147]Ep frat, 349B. See also Spec fid, 168-169; 394B.

[148]Cf. J. Mahé, 'La sanctification d'après saint Cyrille d'Alexandrie,' *RHE* 10 (1909) 30-40, 469-492, especially 478.

[149]This raises the question of the possibility of a special assimilation to each Person. In addition to the discussion of this question in the article of Mahé quoted above, see especially Vagaggini, *Il senso teologico,* 164-165, for the possibility of a special assimilation to what is proper to the Persons in the order of extrinsic formal causality.

[150]Cf. Ep frat, 349B; Spec fid, 168-169; 394B.

[151]It is through the Persons and in particular through the Holy Ghost that the divine nature is made present, rather than through the divine nature that the Persons are made present. Spec fid, 168-169; 394B: 'In amplexu et osculo Patris et Filii, qui Spiritus Sanctus est, hominem quodammodo invenire se medium, et ipsa caritate [the Holy Ghost] Deo unire, qua Pater et Filius unum

sunt'; see also Ep frat, 349A. Cf. de Régnon, *La sainte Trinité*,
IV, 532: 'Les anciens Grecs, et même les anciens Latins, visaient
toujours les personnes *in recto*. Pour eux, l'inhabitation des
Personnes n'est point le résultat de la presence de la nature divine; mais tout au contraire, la présence de la divinité dans le
juste est le résultat de l'arrivée d'une Personne divine, comme on
pourrait dire: l'homme est dans cette chambre, puisque Pierre y
habite.'

[152]I Jn 3, 2-3; Spec fid, 164-165; 393BC; Aenig, 399A.

[153]See above, *Amor ipse intellectus est*, p. 000.

[154]St Gregory, *Homiliarum in Evangelia 27* (PL 76, 1207A):
'amor ipse notitia est'; cf. also St Gregory, *Moralia*, XXIV, 6, 12
(PL 76, 293A): 'quam tamen praesentiam et sentire possit et explere non possit.' Cf. M. Frickel, *Deus totus ubique simul* (Freiburg im Br., 1956) 12-13, but the mysticism of St Gregory has a
more intellectual character than that of William, and the *amor-
intellectus* of William lacks the constant tension towards a purely
intellectual insight that we find in St Gregory. Frickel, 13:
'Es offenbart sich nämlich in den kontemplativen Texten Gregors
sehr stark ein Suchen nach rationaler Wesenserkenntnis. Die mys-
tische Erfahrung als solche kann die Einsicht der Schau weder ver-
mitteln und noch weniger ersetzen. Der Schau aber ist kern und
Ziel der gregorianischen Mystik, welche fast nirgends die liebende
Einswerdung mit Gott hervorhebt....' William evidently makes higher claims than St Gregory for the value of *amor-intellectus* in
the order of actual knowledge. Frickel, 13, footnote 24: 'Butler,
Western Mysticism 98, und noch weniger Lieblang, *Grundfragen*, werden dem intellektuellen Zug in der Mystik Gregors nicht gerecht.'

[155]Cf. Déchanet, *Meditations et prières*, 49-50, where he
refers to Origen, *In Cantica* (ed. Baehrens, VIII, 91, 29; 100,
28-29; 220, 7-26; 223; 26-29; 233, 9-13), to St Cyril of Alexandria,
In Joannis Evangelium (PG 73, 182A), and also in a general way to
St Gregory of Nyssa, St Augustine, Scotus Erigena. St Augustine
refers to love as a means of knowledge in the *Confessions* VII, 10
(PL 32, 742): 'Qui novit veritatem, novit eam; et qui novit eam,
novit aeternitatem, charitas novit eam.' Cf. Dionysius, *De divinis nominibus* (PG 3, 714AD) and the comment by R. Roques, *L'univers dionysien* (Paris, 1954) p. 125: 'une telle connaissance n'est
pas séparable de l'amour, et c'est en effet l'amour de Dieu qui
l'accomplit.'

[156]Déchanet, 'Guillaume et Plotin,' 241-260, compares William and Plotinus, showing the close parallel between many of the

texts of William including Spec fid 154-157; 390D-391A, and *Enn.*
VI, 7, 34, 35. The whole of the concluding section of Spec fid he
shows to be based closely on the sixth *Ennead*. He shows (256-259)
that William often follows those parts of the *Enneads* which are
least often quoted in the general patristic tradition, comparing
the texts of Plotinus followed by William with those quoted by P.
Henry in his *Etudes plotiniennes, Les états du texte* (Louvain,
1938) 399-408 and 416-423, and *Plotin et l'Occident* (Louvain, 1934)
224-225. Père Déchanet observes that there is no reference to the
sixth *Ennead* in St Augustine and that those parts of the *Enneads*
quoted most closely by William are absent from the general tradition: 'Je veux dire qu'on ne les rencontre chez aucun des anciens
auteurs païens ou chrétiens qui, de Porphyre à Claudien Mamert et
à Boèce, ont cité, copié, ou commenté, ou paraphrasé les divers
traités de Plotin' (256-257). He concludes to a knowledge of Plotinus by William either directly or through an intermediary. This
possibility of a knowledge of Plotinus through an unknown intermediary is supported further by the reference of Malet to the importance of unknown or lost translations as a medium in the transmission of oriental ideas in the twelfth and thirteenth centuries.
See A. Malet, *Personne et amour*, 171. It is possible that the
Plotinian doctrine of the 'one' may have influenced William in the
construction of this whole doctrine in terms of unity, from the
first principle of the Holy Ghost as mutual union to the communication of this intratrinitarian unity through resemblance and knowledge through likeness. Note the emphasis at the end of Spec fid
on the return to unity (*Le miroir*, 177-179; 396C): 'ad unum nos
vocant, ad unum nos mittunt,' a text compared by Déchanet to *Enn.*
VI, 9, 4, ed. E. Bréhier, 176 ('Guillaume et Plotin,' 251).

157St Bernard, *In Cantica*, PL 183, 1181A: 'Charitas illa
visio, illa similitudo est.' See also E. Gilson, *La théologie mystique*, 172-177; J. Chatillon, 'Influence de S. Bernard sur la sco-
lastique,' *S. Bernard theologien*, 274; M. Standaert, 'La spiritualité de saint Bernard," *S. Bernardo, Pubblicazione commemorativa*
(Milan, 1954) p. 47; P. E. Wellens, 'S. Bernard mystique,' ibid.,
87.

158Houlier in his article on the comparison between St
Bernard and William ('S. Bernard et Guillaume de Saint-Thierry,'
S. Bernard théologien, 223-233) writes of this doctrine (220):
'Si l'abbé de Clairvaux admet volontiers l'idée, il ne lui donne
pas, il s'en faut de beaucoup, la même importance dans ses dével-
oppements: il se borne a utiliser, quand l'occasion s'en présente,
une conclusion, dont Guillaume a échafaudé toute la théorie.' A
further difference is the more important place given by William to
the Holy Ghost in *amor-intellectus*. J. Hourlier, 231-232 and

Déchanet, *Aux sources,* 16-17.

[159]C. Butler, *Western Mysticism* (London, 1922) especially
179 ff.

[160]Aenig, 426C, 428D-429A.

[161]Spec fid, 168; 349C.

[162]See especially Spec fid 158; 391D-392D, treating of
this experience in terms of light illumination, and joy (391D):
'transmutetur....in gaudium illuminantis gratiae et sensum illum-
inatae conscientiae.' In the Ep frat (349CD) even though this
knowledge is in this life *speculum* and *aenigma*, it is compared to
a light: 'lumen quoddam vultus Dei ostenditur (sicut lumen clau-
sum in manibus patet et latet ad arbitrium tenentis).' The texts
treating of *amor-intellectus* from Cant refer in a similar way to
the experience of illumination, (PL 180, 500): 'sensibile quiddam fit divini cujusdam gaudii, et illuminantis ac beatificantis
gratiae, quod solus amor illuminatus sentire permittitur; suavitas
quaedam....' See also, ibid, 508C. In this respect his mysticism
has a very different character from that of Ruysbroeck and Eckhart,
Tauler and Suso, who were strongly influenced by the Dionysian
theology of negation, which became a prominent element in Western
contemplative tradition from the twelfth century onwards (cf. Butler, *Western Mysticism,* 181). It is of interest to observe this
difference, in view of the similarity between the trinitarian
character of William's contemplative experience and that of the
Flemish mystics such as Eckhart and Ruysbroeck.

[163]Mt 2, 27. See also Ep frat, 352C, for a reference to
17, 21: 'ut et ipsi in nobis unum sint.'

[164]Jn 14, 20-21.

[165]Cf. L. Reypens, 'Dieu (connaissance mystique),' in
Dictionnaire de spiritualité III, col. 883-929. See col. 888-890
for reference to the mystical knowledge of the Trinity until the
twelfth century. Cf. Origen, *In Numeros* (PG 12, 639-640, 1280B);
St Gregory of Nyssa, *In sanctum Stephanum* (PG 46, 717AB); Haymon,
In II Epistolam ad Corinthios (PL 117, 662D-663A); St Bernard, *In
Cantica* (PL 183, 812AB, 811AC). He mentions also Evagrius, re-
ferred to also in this connection by P. Sherwood OSB, in *The Ear-
lier Ambigua of St Maximus the Confessor.* Studia Anselmiana 36,
(Rome, 1955) p. 125, in relation to the article of I. Hausherr,
'Ignorance infinie,' in *Orientalia christiana periodica* 2 (1936)
351-362, especially 357-358, referring to the knowledge of the

Trinity through the restoration of the image: 'La réceptivité du
νοῦσ par rapport a la contemplation de la Trinité fait tellement
partie de son être qu'elle sert a la definir.'

166Reypens refers explicitly to the influence of William
on Hadewijch (col. 893). He observes that the Rhineland mysticism
is especially characterized by its trinitarian character, and mentions John of Colognes (col. 901), Eckhart (col. 902) as being in
this tradition. See also his reference to the interpretation of
the text of St John: 'ut et ipsi in nobis unum sint,' by Ruysbroeck (col. 909) which gives to this text the same mystical significance as in the interpretation given by William.

There is one point on which this article is misleading.
It is divided into two sections, treating first of mystical knowledge through assimilation by means of love, and secondly of an
intellectual intuition of the divine essence through a trinitarian
mysticism. He mentions the importance of William in both sections,
but it is especially in the second section that he sees him as the
founder of a tradition (col. 892). This tends to overemphasize the
intellectual character of William's mysticism, even referring explicitly to his teaching on a vision of the *id quod* of God (col.
891). This is contrary to the text quoted on this subject by
Déchanet (*Meditations et prières,* 43) Med, 244C: 'similitudinem
autem ipsam Dei conferet nobis visio ejus, quo Deum videbimus,
non quod est, sed sicut est.' This knowledge, as Déchanet points
out (45), is reserved not to a purely intellectual vision, but to
the *sensu illuminati amoris.* Cf. Ep frat, 353A: 'Ipsum vero quod
est ipsum, id quod est cogitari omnino non potest, nisi quantum ad
hoc sensu illuminati amoris attingi potest.' See also C. Kirch-
berger, *Richard of St Victor* (London, 1957) 71-72, for the probable influence of William on Walter Hilton, one of the English
Mystics, referring to Hilton, *The Scale of Perfection,* 34-36.

167J. Hourlier, 'S. Bernard et Guillaume de Saint-Thierry,'
223-233; cf. 225-229. Hourlier is treating specially of the comparison between St Bernard and William in the *Liber de amore* showing the distinction of doctrine and outlook as illustrated in St
Bernard's Dil and the works of William, Contemp and Nat Am, which
have been falsely attributed to St Bernard. For instance on the
question of the primacy of love in St Bernard, he writes (229):
'Dans l'ensemble de son oeuvre S. Bernard s'intéresserait moins à
la conaissance qu'à l'amour, alors que Guillaume se préoccuperait
davantage de lier l'un à l'autre et d'arriver à la pleine connaissance de Dieu.' Although Hourlier is treating especially only of
certain works of these authors, there is no indication that he
thinks that these differences of outlook are less apparent in
their other works, and his conclusions (ibid., 232-233) suggests

a more general comparison.   See also W. P. Delfgauw, 'La nature et
les degres de l'amour selon saint Bernard,' *Saint Bernard théologien,* 234-235, especially 234:   'La doctrine de la charité est la
doctrine centrale de saint Bernard.   Tout le reste conduit à elle
et s'explique par elle.'

[168]J. Hourlier 'S. Bernard et Guillaume,' 227-228, and
231, especially 228:   'Lorsqu'on veut comparer les deux abbés, non
seulement dans les traités qui font l'objet de cet exposé, mais
dans l'ensemble de leurs oeuvres, on reconnait que saint Bernard
fait la part la plus large au Christ, alors que Guillaume insis-
terait plus volontiers sur le Saint-Esprit dans notre sanctification.'

[169]Aenig, 426C, 428D-429A.

[170]M.-D. Chenu, *La théologie au douzieme siècle,* p. 295:
'la *deificatio* des Grecs ne se definit donc pas immédiatement en
liaison avec un episode historique, humain ou divin, et la grâce
se présente sous l'aspect d'une réalité objective plus que comme
une disposition bienveillante du coeur de Dieu, au cours de son
libre rapport personnel avec l'homme.   Elle est alors en nous
comme une nature, selon laquelle l'homme est *imago Dei.*   Suivre
cette nature, c'est s'assimiler à Dieu.   Guillaume de Saint-Thierry,
dont on connaît les perceptions orientales, est un bon temoin de
cette position, lors même qu'il lui superpose l'analyse augustin-
ienne.'   A few lines earlier Chenu describes this Greek conception
of 're-creation' not so much as a *reformation* but as a return to
the original state of paradise.

[171]M. Schmaus, *Die psychologische Trinitätslehre des
hl. Augustinus,* 369 ff.

CHAPTER 3

THE SPECULATIVE DEVELOPMENT
OF THE TRINITARIAN THEOLOGY OF WILLIAM
OF ST THIERRY IN THE *AENIGMA FIDEI**

IN THE STUDY OF the trinitarian aspect of the ascent of the
soul to God, reference was made to the more speculative aspects of
William's doctrine which is found in the second of the theological
stages. Although this development is associated closely with his
polemics against **Peter** Abelard,[1] the character which it assumes
in the *Aenigma fidei* is **sufficiently** distinct from the purely polemical works to justify separate treatment. Moreover the more
mature approach to these questions in the *Aenigma fidei* takes us
to the heart of William's speculative doctrine. Unlike the works
directed ex professo against **Abelard** and de Conchis, William's
aim here is not simply to answer his opponents with a refutation
of their errors, but with a fully developed theology on very
different lines, dominated, as we shall see, by the sense of the
mystery of the Trinity.

I. *Ratio fidei*

1. THE PROBLEM

William's opposition to Abelard on the grounds of rationalism
raised acutely the whole question of the use of reason in theology.
This is apparent in the construction of the *Aenigma fidei*. Two
problems occur. First, this speculative development approaches
the Trinity in a very different manner from his trinitarian theology as studied in the previous article. What is the relationship
between these two contrasting ways of thought? Secondly, William
seems to oscillate between the desire to react against Abelard by
a return to the simple scriptural faith exclusive of any further
development and a recognition of the need to counteract him by a
theology treated on the same speculative plane but from a wholly
different angle.

The problem of the construction of the 'Aenigma fidei.'[2]

An examination of the manuscript, *Charleville 114,* proves conclusively that the manuscript shows signs of having been rewritten[3]
at the end of the introductory section and at the beginning of the
text on the Trinity in Scripture.[4] In itself this discovery tells
us nothing as to which part of the *Aenigma fidei* formed the original treatise. It does however show definitely that additions of
some kind were made to the original structure. The reasons

arising from the nature of the ideas expressed are the only means
of reaching further conclusions.

A study of the construction of the *Aenigma fidei* reveals several distinct sections, each presenting its own particular character. First there is the introductory section treating in a general way of the problem of the knowledge of God, the theme of knowledge through likeness, the restoration of the image, the pedagogic role of the incarnation as a preparation for the Trinity.[5]
This is followed by the section on the return to the simple scriptural faith,[6] followed by an exposition of the evolution of dogma
in the controversies of the Fathers at the time of the heresies of
Arius and Sabellius.[7] Then begins the more technical part of the
work. After a preliminary discussion on the meaning of number and
person in the Trinity,[8] he leads through the passage on the three
degrees of knowledge[9] and the doctrine of *ratio fidei*[10] to the central portion of the work.[11] This consists of an introduction with
the general rules,[12] followed by three distinct divisions, the
essential names,[13] treating of the divine essence, the essential
and relative names,[14] showing God in relation to creatures, and
finally the proper names showing God on his inmost trinitarian
life.[15] Then this treatise on the divine names gradually gives
way through a transition passage[16] to a general conclusion on the
Trinity reminiscent of the earlier text on Sabellius, Arius and
the problem of number.[17] Finally there is the concluding section[18]
based on the trinitarian economy leading from the Father through
the Son in the Holy Spirit. These divisions can be reduced to
three main sections, the introduction,[19] the central and more technical part treating of the Trinity 'quoad se' in the intratrinitarian sphere,[20] and the conclusion,[21] which, despite passages of a
speculative nature, is based primarily on the trinitarian economy
'quoad nos.'

There are several reasons for supposing that the central section on the divine names formed a separate treatise. First of all,
in contrast to the disconnected character of the work as a whole,
it is constructed according to an ordered plan, presenting a complete unity in itself.[22] Secondly there are some notable repeti-
tions. Most significant is the return after the transition passage at the end of the treatise on the divine names to the theme
of Arius and Sabellius and the problem of number,[23] connecting directly with a similar passage prior to the central treatise.[24] It
seems highly probable that the central treatise was written afterwards and then incorporated into the previous structure. It represents a further evolution of thought through a more complete reply to the contemporary rationalistic tendencies represented by
Abelard, Guillaume de Conchis and Gilbert de la Porrée. It is unlikely that William would have first written the development of
his theology and then have returned afterwards to the foundations.

But there is no conclusive evidence for either supposition.

In relation to the problem of *ratio fidei* and the Trinity, the importance of this question of the construction of the *Aenigma fidei* is shown in two ways. There is the contrast between the technical speculative character of the middle sections[25] as opposed to the introduction and the conclusion,[26] and there is the more specific problem of the relationship between theological development, rational speculation and the need to return to the simple faith of Scripture. Both these questions are closely connected and are concerned with the general problem of the justification and the value of speculation on the Trinity.

The relationship of the sections treating of the Trinity quoad se *with those treating of the Trinity* quoad nos.

The question is whether there is an underlying unity which relates the technical sections of the *Aenigma fidei* with the sections treating of the Trinity 'quoad nos' and with his mystical writings on the Trinity, such as some of the closing passages of the *Speculum fidei*[27] and the *Epistola ad fratres de Monte Dei.*[28]

The theme of the three theological stages[29] is very important for this question, uniting the simple scriptural faith with the further stage of *scientia, ratio fidei,* and showing how this *scientia* must tend ultimately towards *sapientia* and the divine mode of knowledge in the Holy Ghost.

The whole speculative section of the *Aenigma fidei* is therefore placed in a wider context, and is seen as an intermediary stage, rooted in faith and passing on to *Sapientia.* But even apart from the text on the three stages there are constant indications throughout which unite the central sections with the introduction and the conclusion, indicating that he never intended the more technical and metaphysical aspects of his theology to be isolated from the basic theme of the evolution of the soul in the return to resemblance. There is for instance the passage in the text on *ratio fidei,* showing that the purpose of *ratio fidei* is to arrive through experience at contemplation 'magis experientia.... ad praemium contemplationis'[30] rather than to indulge in vain disputes. There is the transition passage at the end of the central treatise on the divine names treating of the sanctifying power of the name of God.[31] There is the text on the vivification of faith into intellect and love as an image of the Trinity,[32] followed shortly by an allusion to the union of knowledge and likeness in the beatific vision,[33] recalling the theme of knowledge through likeness in the introduction.[34] Even in the heart of the treatise on the divine names we are told that understanding of the Trinity is reached more through faith and love than through rational investigation.[35]

*The problem of the relationship of rational speculation
to the simple scriptural faith.*

The section in the *Aenigma fidei* on the basic scriptural
faith gives an impression of a strong personal desire to abandon
all the subsequent developments and disputes on the Trinity,[36]
though admitting with reluctance that such developments were necessary in defence against heresy.[37] There appeared to be a conflict
here between two conceptions of theology. This conflict becomes
still more apparent when we compare the technical and metaphysical
character of the central portions of the work with his initial desire to return to the simple scriptural faith. First of all he
disclaimed any desire to ask how the Trinity is three and how it
is one.[38] Yet this is precisely the question which he asks in the
texts treating of the problem of number and person.[39] 'Quid tres,
quid tria?' We had been warned to avoid the subtle disputes of
the doctors, yet the central treatise tells us little of the simple scriptural faith and is introduced as a discussion on those
very questions that concerned the Fathers and doctors: 'Pie ergo
et humiliter in via hac qua ambulamus, praecedentium Patrum vestigia venerantes procedamus.'[40]

2. RATIO FIDEI

The conflict[41] is resolved to a considerable extent through
the concept of *ratio fidei*. This theme is expressed in the following text.

> Idcirco autem dicimus, secundum rationem fidei, quia
> modus hic loquendi de Deo habet quaedam propria verba,
> rationabilia quidem, sed non intelligibilia, nisi in
> ratione fidei, non autem in ratione sensus humani....
> in rebus enim humanis humana ratio parat sibi fidem;
> in divinis vero praecedit fides, deinde ipsa sui gen-
> eris format sibi rationem.[42]

The text shows how the initiative throughout is given to
faith. Faith precedes reason, 'praecedit fides,' and becomes the
very form of reason, 'format sibi rationem.' This transforming
power of faith produces a *ratio sui generis*. The dependence of
reason on faith becomes so complete that although the concepts
formed express in themselves a rational idea, 'rationabilia quidem,' they are unintelligible except in the light of faith: 'non
intelligibilia, nisi in ratione fidei.'

This formative power of faith over human reason is illustrated further with the application of philosophical concepts to God.
Philosophical categories such as substance, accident, relation,

genus, species are, he says in themselves unsuitable for application to revelation.[43] Nevertheless they are not to be rejected entirely, but are to be formed by *ratio fidei*: 'non tam ipsum, quam quid de ipso ratio fidei efficere velit, attendatur.'[44] Faith must never be subjected to these human concepts, but on the contrary they must be subjected to faith.[45] The dominant idea throughout is that of faith acting as if with a creative power transforming reason in its inmost nature so as to make it adaptable to its own purposes.[46]

This leads to one of William's most basic principles that the things of God must be approached from above rather than from below. The following text on faith and reason in relation to the Eucharist helps to illustrate an important aspect of his approach also to the doctrine of the Trinity.

Non enim est hominis rationem habentis, cum tractat divina, pensare ea ex his rebus quae infra Deum sunt, et omnipotentiae immensitatem intra terminos nostrae possibilitatis angustare: eamdemque naturam quodammodo disputando velle informare ad exemplum naturae mutabilis: in qua stant aeternaliter omnes causales formae rerum habentium temporaliter. In hujusmodi enim *de sursum* non *de deorsum* trahenda sunt rationum exempla vel probationum argumenta.[47]

The intimate relationship between faith and reason involving a complete subjection of reason to the light of faith goes far towards a reconciliation of the conflict between trinitarian speculation and the simple scriptural faith. The parallel between the terms 'forma fidei,'[48] the trinitarian faith itself, and the 'forma sanorum in fide verborum,'[49] the reflection on the original faith in the light of *ratio fidei* suggests at once the connection. This is established even more definitely when he tells us that *ratio fidei* has to preserve the very forms and manners of speech of the original revelation as transmitted by the authority of Christ, and the Apostles.[50] It is a form of knowledge which proceeds entirely according to Scripture: 'secundum Evangelium loquantur, qui secundum Evangelium se vivere profitentur.' *Ratio fidei* must avoid all vain disputes and the phrase 'inanium tormenta quaestionum'[51] recalls the 'sine tormentis quaestionum' of the simple scriptural faith.[52]

We can now see how he effects the reconciliation between the return to the bare faith of revelation and the rational speculations on person, number, relation and the processions. *Ratio fidei* is not an independant process of speculation which merely presupposes the faith of Scripture, and then acts entirely according to the initiative of reason. It is an expansion of faith, a

penetration of what in faith is already contained in germ.   Père
Bouyer has made the illuminating comment on the transition from
faith to *scientia* in William's doctrine: 'C'est ainsi que la foi
sera non pas remplacée par la science, la gnose, mais épanouie en
gnose dans notre âme, tout comme la graine s'épanouit en fleurs
et en fruits dans une terre bien préparée.'[53]
     As Père Bouyer shows,[54] this process can only be understood
in the light of the psychological and spiritual foundation in the
transition from the animal to the rational state, from *anima* to
animus on which William bases his theological stages.   Whereas
anima is still dependant on what is external, *animus* is the soul
in a state of rational dominion over itself and over the body.[55]
In a parallel manner in the initial theological stage faith remains a pure acceptance of what comes from without 'quasi aliunde
adventitia,'[56] whereas in the stage of *ratio fidei* there is a penetration of the faith through reflection on its meaning and the
right way of conceiving the dogmas of faith.[57]

3. THE HISTORICAL BACKGROUND

     This very question of the relationship between faith and rea-
son is of great importance in the theology of the twelfth century.
St Anselm in this respect forms the bridge between St Augustine
and St Thomas.   With St Augustine faith is subordinated to reason
without being distinguished from it.   St Anselm follows St Augustine in so far as he does not distinguish theoretically the
spheres of faith and reason, but at the same time he introduces a
practical distinction, so that reason in practice pursues its conclusions independently of faith.   Ultimately St Thomas fixed the
relationship by distinguishing the spheres of faith and reason,
while at the same time subordinating reason to faith.   In the
meantime the conflict continued owing to what Perino calls the
'equilibrio instabile' of St Anselm.[58]
     The practical autonomy of the reason initiated by St Anselm
was continued by Abelard, and William's opposition to this method
is seen in the *Disputatio adversus Abaelardum*.   But whereas this
work is primarily an assertion of tradition in reaction against
Abelard's supposedly unorthodox doctrine, the *Aenigma fidei* shows
a more mature and more personal attempt to evolve a theological
doctrine of the relationship of faith and reason and to establish
his own method on more positive lines.   The hypothesis of the re-
construction of the *Aenigma fidei* indicates the probable sequence
of William's train of thought.   His first reaction was to reassert
the simple faith of Scripture in opposition to Abelard's rationalism.   Afterwards he would have realized that the problem raised
by Abelard demanded a reply from the more speculative angle.
Hence the long metaphysical treatise at the center of the *Aenigma*

fidei. But at the same time it was necessary to show that this speculative treatise proceeded from the opposite standpoint from that of Abelard. The explanation of this contrary method is given in the theory of *ratio fidei*.

Whether or not the hypothesis of the development of the *Aenigma fidei* along these lines is conclusive, William answered Abelard's practical autonomy of reason by reversing the whole trend of the scholastic movement initiated by St Anselm,[59] and placed reason once more in even more complete subjection to faith than in the patristic theology of St Augustine.

Comparison between St Augustine's and William's doctrine
on this point and its influence on their trinitarian doctrine.

In general this doctrine represents a return to St Augustine, in so far as in both cases reason is subordinated to faith practically and theoretically. But William's doctrine is by no means identical with that of St Augustine, and this difference may determine to some extent their respective approaches to the Trinity. William is less of a pure philosopher even than St Augustine, in the sense in which philosophy implies the autonomy of reason. There is nothing parallel in his works to the early writings of St Augustine, which are predominantly purely philosophical in character.[60] But even a comparison with the mature works of St Augustine reveals a difference in outlook. St Augustine's theory of the relation between faith and reason is based on the famous words 'intellige ut credas....crede ut intelligas.'[61] Faith is therefore the indispensable condition for understanding. The understanding of God cannot begin without faith, nor can it end without faith, for all speculation with St Augustine is the quest for beatifying wisdom.[62] But where William carries still further this subordination of reason to faith is precisely in his conception of *ratio fidei*. This means that reason exercised on revelation is without value unless it continually receives the very form of faith, becoming not merely subordinate *to* faith, but a reason *of* faith.[63]

Consequently we find that the exercise of *ratio fidei* gives to William's rational investigation of the Trinity a very different character from that of the *De Trinitate* of St Augustine. His approach is always *de sursum* not *de deorsum*. It is always from the trinitarian faith itself that the whole examination proceeds, precisely because reason is powerless except in the light of faith. Perhaps this is why there is only a suggestion of the Augustinian analogies in the *Aenigma fidei*, whereas the most important contribution of the *intellectus fidei* of St Augustine lies in these psychological analogies from creation. This approach to the Trinity from the trinitarian faith itself gives a character to William's theology which distinguishes it not only from St Augustine's

psychological analogies, but from the subsequent development of
trinitarian theology in St Anselm and Abelard in the light of metaphysics and logic, in which purely human reason has the predominant role.

II. *The Mystery of the Trinity*

1. THE MAIN ISSUES

We have now to study the application of *ratio fidei* to the
mystery of the **Trinity**. As with *ratio fidei* this speculative
treatment of the Trinity is an advance on the *Disputatio adversus
Abaelardum* and *De erroribus Guillelmi de Conchis*. It represents
William's own constructive effort to answer Abelard and de Conchis
not as in the purely polemical works with a mere refutation of
their errors, but with an example of a scientific, speculative
trinitarian theology approached from the opposite principles to
those which he attributed to his opponents, and reaching very different conclusions.

The speculative part of the *Aenigma fidei* is more than a purely polemical work. It shows deep personal reflection. Although it
claims to be strictly traditional, following only the patristic
tradition, 'non de fontibus nostris, sed de fontibus salvatoris,
ex scripturis sanctis, et certissimis auctoritatibus sanctorum Patrum,'[64] the speculative development of the *Aenigma fidei* is in
the direction of a personal synthesis. This originality does not
lie in the novelty of special theories about the Trinity. The polemical motif which underlies his arguments is directed precisely
against such theories on the part of the rising scholasticism and
especially Peter Abelard. If we are looking for this kind of speculation, we shall be disappointed. But this does not mean that the
Aenigma fidei does not offer a contribution of great interest in
the field of trinitarian speculation. To see how this is so, we
have to enter into William's own approach to the subject. In contrast to any attempt to explain the Trinity by showing the 'quomodo' of the processions, 'how' the processions take place, he aims
at showing precisely 'how' the Trinity is a mystery. In this way
the dialectic of *ratio fidei* leads to a conclusion which is intended as the very reverse of the purely philosophical speculations of
human reason alone. This emphasis on the mystery was prominent already in the *Disputatio adversus Abaelardum* and *De erroribus Guillelmi de Conchis,* but it receives a further and more interesting
development in the *Aenigma fidei*.

In the polemical works he simply stated the fact of the mystery with reference to the traditional teaching of Scripture and
the Fathers.[65] In the *Aenigma fidei* he attempts an analysis metaphysically of the Trinity seen from the various angles of the

essential names, the essential and relative names, the problem of Person and the proper names, showing how from every angle the conclusion is ultimately the existence of the mystery. The essential message is to show through this very exercise of reason that reason is ultimately powerless before the mystery. The highest understanding of the Trinity on the rational plane is to understand that it is incomprehensible: 'Nusquam autem in hac vita divinitas melius humano intellectu comprehenditur, quam in eo quo magis incomprehensibilis esse videtur.'[66] The final word lies with the theology of Dionysius.[67]

We shall see how this analysis illustrates the theme of *ratio fidei*. The study of the divine names ultimately reveals no more than the initial scriptural faith. No explanation is proposed. There are only occasional allusions to images illustrating the Trinity and the image of faith, intellect and love,[68] is introduced primarily to recall the general framework of the evolution of the soul through faith into intellect and love. This contrasts with the texts in his other works, where the Augustinian analogies are more fully developed.[69] In one sense he makes no advance on the initial Scriptural faith in which he claimed to find the entire object of his search. Yet in another sense he has given us a new insight. We return always to the *Aenigma fidei*: '....Deum Patrem, Deum Filium, Deum Spiritum sanctum, non tres Deos sed unum Deum,'[70] but with a more exact determination of where the mystery lies. The assertion of the mystery has always been a traditional theme of the Fathers. The novelty of William's emphasis on this theme lies in his application of *ratio fidei* to this single end. The assertion of the mystery is not just one theme among many. It is the whole purpose of the treatise on the divine names.

Historically this unique emphasis is of considerable importance. It shows a scientific and metaphysical theology of the Trinity giving a bare presentation of the mystery in complete contrast to the whole tradition tending towards an explanation of the Trinity. This tradition begins with the psychological illustrations of St Augustine and leads on to the general scholastic tendency to give a demonstration of the 'an sit' or an explanation of the 'quomodo sit' of the Trinity.[71]

The 'Greek' and 'Latin' approach to the Trinity.

The Trinity can be approached from two angles. According to one method the first principle is the distinction of Persons. The problem then is how this initial principle of the distinction of Persons is compatible with one numerically identical nature. Alternatively we can start from the numerical identity of the divine nature. The problem then is how a real distinction of Persons can arise within this unity of nature. These two ways have been

analyzed by de Régnon and summarized in his classic distinction as
the 'Greek' and 'Latin' approach respectively.[72] The criticisms
which have been made against de Régnon are not a denial of these
two ways of approach as such,[73] but against his generalization of
them as 'Greek' and 'Latin.' However, despite these criticisms,
there is good reason for still maintaining this generalization,
provided it is not pressed too closely, and given the further clarification to be made as a result especially of the criticism of de
Régnon by Malet.[74]

Recent studies on William's theology have drawn attention to
the Greek element on his thought. The discovery of the influence
of the *orientale lumen*[75] on the writings of William of St Thierry
is of great value. But the judgment that the *Aenigma fidei* is essentially the expression of the Greek approach[76] to the Trinity
needs further qualification. The general spirit of the speculative part of *Aenigma fidei* with its strong accentuation on the mystery of the Trinity, its bare assertion of the trinitarian faith
as opposed to any particular explanatory theory and its approach
to the mystery through the 'theologia negativa' undoubtedly recalls
the whole ethos of the Greek Fathers. But if we are considering
the distinction between the 'Greek' and 'Latin' view of the Trinity
in the classic sense given by de Régnon, we can hardly say that
William follows primarily the 'Greek' way. The question is much
more complicated. We shall find that the predominance of the
'Greek' and 'Latin' method varies throughout the different parts
of this work, and that in certain sections there is an almost exclusively Latin and Augustinian influence. Moreover in the central
treatise on the divine names, the 'Latin' approach is on the whole
predominant.

The alternation of these two methods is of interest in two
ways. First of all it shows us an attempt to bring together two
distinct traditions. This is an aspect of William's tendency in
the direction of a synthesis of patristic doctrine. Secondly its
effect is to intensify the emphasis on the mystery. Both the
'Greek' and the 'Latin' approach confront us ultimately with the
mystery. The alternation and the interplay of the two ways illustrates the underlying dialectic of William's thought, to approach
the Trinity as far as possible from every angle, and to show invariably how the conclusion is the *Aenigma fidei* of three Persons
in one identical nature.

Principal sources.

William approaches the Fathers as a whole rather than indivi-
dually.[77] His aim is more a general synthesis of catholic tradition than to follow any particular guide. One of the outstanding
sources for his speculation on the intratrinitarian life was

undoubtedly St Augustine. The number of implicit references to St Augustine is very striking. We shall find also that he follows him closely, if with some divergences, on the problem of Person and above all in the predominance of the approach from the unity of nature in the central section on the divine names. In general he draws from St Augustine what is traditional rather than the psychological illustrations which are specific to St Augustine.[78]

In contrast with the array of implicit quotations with verbal similarity to St Augustine, the influence of Erigena is less immediately evident. But it is highly probable that this influence was present.[79] The general spirit and purpose of the speculative part of the *Aenigma fidei* with its emphasis on the transcendance of the Trinity is closer to the 'theologia negativa' of Erigena with its origin in Dionysius than to the *De Trinitate* of St Augustine. He follows Erigena as he follows St Augustine in what is traditional in his general Dionysian teaching on the 'theologia affirmativa,' 'negativa' and 'eminentiae' rather than in Erigena's more personal speculations on the relationship between the Persons of the Trinity and the faculties of *sensus, ratio* and *intellectus*.[80]

The fusion of these elements is peculiar to William. It is curious for instance to find the influence of Erigena with his strong preference for the Greek Fathers,[81] combined with St Augustine's trinitarian theology from the angle of the unity of the nature, in the greater part of the central section of the divine names. The metaphysical character of this part of the *Aenigma fidei* may well have been influenced by the 'intellectualism'[82] of Erigena and his desire for objective truth. But William's *ratio fidei*, which determines his whole treatment of the subject, transforms the intellectualism of Erigena on to a very different plane.[83]

The influence of the Greek Fathers on the specific issue of the approach from the distinction of the Persons is hardly apparent in the earlier part of the central section on the divine names, which is predominantly Augustinian on this question. In the later sections on the proper names the 'Greek' approach becomes more marked than before and the concluding section based on the economy 'ex Patre, per Filium, in Spiritu,' brings the Persons into a position of still greater prominence. Throughout these passages there are traces of the possible influence of St Basil and St Athanasius.

2. AN EXAMINATION OF THE TEXTS

A) *The Divine Names*

*The essential names with reference to the Trinity:
the basic principle*[84]

The whole of this section is in the last analysis based on
the initial principle that whatever is predicated absolutely *ad se*
of the divine nature is predicated substantially. His subsequent
arguments are all deductions from this principle which is stated
in the following text taken directly from St Augustine:

> Quidquid ad se dicitur praestantissima illa et divina
> sublimitas, substantialiter dicitur: quod autem ad
> aliquid non substantialiter, sed relative; tamquamque
> vim esse ejusdem substantiae in Patre et Filio et Spi-
> ritu Sancto, ut quidquid de singulis ad seipsos dici-
> tur, non pluraliter in summa sed singulariter acci-
> piatur.[85]

Further deductions from this principle.

Further conclusions follow in the introductory passage on the
general rules for the application of the **divine** names. 'Ratio fidei' cannot admit the existence of accidents in God, who is 'sine
quantitate magnus, sine qualitate bonus.'[86] It is even strictly
more accurate to speak of the essence of God rather than the 'substance' since substance implies accident.[87] It is impossible to
speak of the Trinity in terms of genus and species, for the Persons are identically the divine essence.[88]

After an analysis of the meaning of 'Ego sum qui sum' in
terms of the metaphysical nature of God,[89] he applies this doctrine
of the divine essence to the Trinity. Since God is being in itself, he is given the name of *essentia*: 'Sic ab eo quod est esse,
essentia.'[90] It is therefore no more possible to speak of three
essences than of three Gods.[91] The conclusion is drawn that the
Father, the Son and the Holy Ghost are identically one single essence.[92]

But whatever is predicated of God *ad se* is **predicated** substantially. Therefore each attribute of God is identically the divine
essence,[93] and each Person of the Trinity is identically each of
the divine attributes, since they are a single unity with the divine **essence.**[94]

This passage is followed by an application of this argument
to a description of the Father, the Son, and the Holy Ghost in
terms of power, wisdom and goodness, clearly referring to Abelard

and de Conchis,[95] showing that just as there can be no division in God between his wisdom, power and goodness as attributes of the divine nature, so there can be no division between his actions ad extra of power, wisdom and goodness.[96]

He admits that Scripture ascribes certain of these attributes more particularly to one Person than to another,[97] but this does not imply separation of the Persons. It is simply a way of giving us some indication of the distinction of Persons: 'fit hoc ad discretionem Personarum ut discernantur, non ut separentur.'[98] If we **always** spoke of the inseparability of the Persons, we should never understand that these Persons constitute a Trinity[99]: 'et tamen non dividat intellectus, quod distinguit auditus.'[100] Although the term 'appropriation' is not used, the doctrine is clearly present.[101]

The approach from the unity of the divine nature.

Throughout this section the approach is undoubtedly from the primacy of the unity of nature.[102] Here as in the polemical works,[103] this may be partly explained by the need to meet his opponents on their own ground. A theory which, according to William's interpretation, bases the distinction of Persons on a qualitative distinction of attributes within the divine nature, could be answered most easily by an analysis proceeding from the divine nature, showing through basic metaphysical principles that any distinction within the divine nature is impossible.

At the conclusion of the whole argument on the essential names, we understand very clearly the unity of the divine essence, and the fundamental principle that everything predicated *ad se* in God is predicated substantially. We accept the conclusions that follow from this principle, the identity of the Persons with the divine essence, and their unity in the operations *ad extra*. The difficulty is rather in seeing how a distinction of Persons can arise from within this absolute unity. This distinction is suggested through the implied doctrine of appropriation: 'insinuetur nobis veritas Trinitatis,'[104] and by the reference to the 'relative names,' the Father, the Son and the Holy Ghost, which, although *ad invicem* are also *propria singula singulorum*.[105] But this distinction remains in obscurity, precisely because the whole argument focusses the attention above all on the unity of the divine essence.

The mystery.

Ultimately we are confronted with the mystery: 'nec singularitas est nec diversitas,'[106] and William introduces one of those suggestions, which occur in the course even of his most metaphys-

ical arguments implying that the answer can only be found in an
intuition which transcends conceptual knowledge: 'difficultas
loquendi cor nostrum ad intelligentiam trahit....vera unitas et
vera Trinitas possit quidem aliquatenus mente sentiri, et si non
possit simul proferri.'[107]   One thing is certain. This mystery
can never be explained by words or rational concepts.

> Haec enim de essentialibus Dei nominibus dicta sint.
> De quibus nihil est quod dicimus, quia nihil ad eum
> est, quidquid de eo dici potest; quoniam non potest
> explicari verbis, quod ineffabile est. Deficiunt
> verba, caligat intellectus.[108]

Despite a final exhortation to pursue the mystery as far as
is possible for the human intellect, this is William's final answer to the problem of the Trinity seen from the angle of the essential names. It is of interest to see how he meets the arguments of Abelard and de Conchis. He places himself on the ground
of his opponents, the essential names, and in particular the attributes of power, wisdom and goodness. But instead of finding
any 'explanation of the Trinity' he reaches the reverse conclusion,
and finds that the examination of the Trinity from this standpoint
leads inevitably to the 'mystery.'

The essential and relative names.
(The Trinity in relation to creation).

This section follows the same principle of the simplicity of
the divine essence. An analysis of the philosophical doctrine on
creation concludes to the immutability of God in the act of creation. The change that takes place in creation can only be on the
part of the creature.[109] Consequently, according to *ratio fidei,*
the name 'creator' is identically the divine essence.[110]
    In the application of this doctrine to the Trinity, he argues
from the principle of the essential names, the 'regula omnium es-
sentialium in Deo nominum'[111] and concludes that the Persons of
the Trinity create as one single creator: 'creator Pater, creator Filius, creator Spiritus Sanctus.'[112]
    The unity of the Persons in creation is therefore a further
·deduction from the unity of the divine essence. Once more we find
that the approach to the Trinity is from the unity of the divine
nature, following closely on the doctrine of St Augustine.[113]
There is no suggestion here of the action of the Persons in creation according to their mutual relation in the economy of *ex Patre,*
per Filium, in Spiritu, in the tradition of Scripture, the Greek
and the pre-Nicene Latin Fathers, such as we shall find in the
closing section of the *Aenigma fidei.* On the contrary the Persons

are seen as acting in creation not according to their personal relationship, but according to their unity in the divine essence.
Nor is there any trace of the later doctrine of St Thomas, who ba-
lances the emphasis on the unity of nature as the *principium quo*
of creation with the conception of the Persons as the *principium
quod,* so that there is *unus creator* but not *unus creans.*[114] As
we shall find again in the problem of Person, the Augustinian doctrine represents what Malet describes as the 'essentialist' approach,[115] with the main stress on the unity of nature. In this
text William is wholly in the Augustinian tradition, as opposed
either to the personalistic economy of Scripture and the Greek
Fathers or to the later thomistic doctrine, which on the metaphysical plane, evolves the trinitarian doctrine of creation in a
more personalistic direction than is found in the doctrine of St
Augustine.

The problem of Person.

In the section treating specifically of the problem of Person,
the unity of the divine essence is once again the fundamental principle from which the whole argument proceeds. The problem is not
to show how the divine nature can be a unity, given the distinction of Persons, but how it is possible for a distinction of Persons to arise from a nature which is numerically one. The first
and immediate principle is the unity of the divine nature.[116]

Number.

The first problem is that of number. The unity of the divine
nature is a numerical unity. William clearly accepts this doctrine
despite his assertion that the unity of God is 'non numero....sed
natura.'[117] *Non numero* is not a denial of what we should call
numerical unity as is shown by the context denying the division of
God into parts.[118] It is in fact an assertion of numerical unity
in the generally accepted sense of the term and William's insistence on a unity in nature and not in number appears from the context to be a denial of the kind of unity which could be given
through the union of a multiplicity of parts. This is accentuated
still further when he contrasts the unity of three men with the
three Persons of the Trinity, who are *verissime unum,*[119] thus
showing that unity in 'nature' certainly does not imply a merely
specific unity.

The problem is therefore how we can speak of number in God.
How is it possible for 'three' to arise within this absolute
unity? 'Quid tres?'[120] He approaches the problem through the
Dionysian tradition mediated through Erigena, using in turn the
way of affirmative and of negative theology. 'Numerus est,'[121]

the affirmative statement that we can in some way predicate number of God, is followed at once by 'numerus non est,'[122] the denial that number exists in God, for this number is a kind of which
we can have no conception. Finally in a text in the section on
the proper names he synthesizes these two ways in the theology of
eminentia.   'Numerus est super numerum, quo **tres** unum sunt, et
unum tres.'[123] We have here all the elements of the thesis, antithesis and synthesis of Erigena, the affirmation, the denial and
the *via eminentiae*,[124] and a close similarity to Erigena's text on
unity and trinity as *plusquam unitas* and *plusquam trinitas*.[125]

But he realizes clearly that this **dialectic** offers no solution to the problem. Human words are ultimately powerless, and
his recourse is to the words of Scripture, illustrating the principle of *ratio fidei* that the Trinity must be approached from
above rather than from below,[126] from the very words of revelation
rather than through human reason reason.   'Deficiunt humana verba,
ad verba verbi confugimus.'[127] These words of revelation tells us
'Ego et Pater unum sumus.'[128] The *unum* expresses **consubstantial-**
ity, *sumus* avoids the error of Sabellius.[129] Once more we return
to the inescapable mystery, which is in no way solved but only accentuated in its rigid simplicity by this appeal to Scripture and
to *ratio fidei*. The interest of Williams mentality is to see how
his analysis of the **problem** ends always in a return to the initial
mystery of the faith. To the question 'quid tres?' the answer is
simply "unum."[130]

The problem of Person ontologically.

The problem of *quid tres* had further implications than the
mystery of number within the Trinity, and led to the fundamental
question of the meaning of Person. What was meant by this traditional term of Person as applied to the Father, the Son and the
Holy Ghost?

This was one of the crucial questions which faced the mediaeval theologians. St Augustine had tackled the problem, but had
found no solution. Basically his difficulty, as Malet has rightly
observed,[131] lay in finding the synthesis between the concepts of
the **relative** and the absolute. He oscillated between two theories.
On the one hand he conceived Person as an absolute[132] rather than
as a **relative** and tended to identify Person with substance; on the
other hand in practice he often conceived of the Persons, Father,
Son and Holy Ghost as pure relations, excluding any idea of sub-
sistance.[133] In either case the result is a logical tendency towards Sabellianism. If Person is identified with substance, there
can be no grounds for distinguishing the Persons from the divine
essence. If on the other hand the Persons are reduced to a pure
esse ad they are devoid of any ontological reality in the order of

absolute being.

St Anselm found no solution to this problem. He conceived the Trinitarian relations not **ontologically**, but as a principle of dialectical opposition.[134] Consequently he was unable to discover the ontological reality of the Persons: 'credat....in trinitatem propter tres nescio quid.'[135] It is the same problem that baffled St Augustine, the synthesis of the absolute and the relative.

Both St Augustine and St Anselm have the greatest difficulty in discovering the ontological reality of the Persons in themselves, and this is one of the consequences of their 'essentialist' approach to the Trinity, conceiving very clearly the unity of the divine essence, but finding great difficulty in understanding how a Trinity of Persons can arise from this absolute unity. Eventually St Thomas discovered the necessary synthesis between the absolute and the relative through his doctrine of the Persons as 'relationes subsistentes.'[136]

This enabled his metaphysics of the Trinity to assume a more personalistic character than that of St Augustine and St Anselm, so as to conceive the processions as acts from subject to subject, the *principium quod* through the medium of the divine nature, the *principium quo*.[137]

William's attempt at a solution of the problem.

If we study the doctrine of William against this background, we shall find that he remains on this point in the 'essentialist' tradition of St Augustine and St Anselm. His initial principle is the unity of the divine essence, and the problem is to discover 'quid tres.' His whole difficulty is to discover what there is ontologically in the Trinity other than the divine essence, and he is reduced to the position of St Augustine, who accepted the term 'Person' simply as a traditional defence against Sabellianism, but not as a satisfactory explanation of the problem. He expresses this standpoint in a text with almost verbal similarity to the text of St Augustine in *De Trinitate*,[138] and he summarizes the whole difficulty with the words 'etsi res sicut est non diceretur, non omnino tamen taceretur.'[139]

But he does not follow St Augustine on his identification of Person with substance. He explicitly rejects the definition of Boethius of person,[140] 'rationalis naturae individua substantia,'[141] on the grounds that in this definition person is identified with substance which would result in the Trinity consisting of one Person. This is a clear rejection of St Augustine's conception of Person as an *absolute* identifiable with substance. He chooses instead the definition 'cujus pro sui forma certa sit agnitio.'[142] This definition, he maintains, is in accordance with the property of the Persons, which is to make themselves known through the acts

of generation and procession, forming 'quaedam personalis agnitio.'143

He follows St Augustine rather in his alternative tendency to
conceive of the Persons as pure relations. They are 'tria propria
relativa.'144 But he is acutely aware that this offers no solution to the problem of what the Persons are ontologically in themselves which is the ultimate object of his search. He wants to
discover the reality of the Persons not in so far as they are *ad
alterutrum* but *in eo quod sunt*,145 and his whole difficulty is to
discover how this reality consists of anything other than the concept of pure relation. The whole problem is that of the synthesis of the absolute and the relative. This is illustrated in his
embarrassment in the application to the Trinity of the principle
that everything which is *relative ad aliquid* is also *aliquid ad
se*.146 The Father, the Son and the Holy Ghost are *ad invicem*.147
They are also *ad se*. But what is this *ad se*? 'Quid tres? Quid
tria?'148 He is then driven back to the impossible conclusion
that if 'there are three Persons *ad se*,' then there are three essences. 'Numquid tres essentiae? Absit!'149

The mystery.

Once more he returns to the mystery of the Trinity, to the
acceptance on faith of this reality of Person, and to the Dionysian doctrine that we can only rise to a knowledge of God through
a recognition of his transcendance over all human concepts. This
conclusion is expressed in a text from a later section of the *Aenigma fidei* on the proper names, which can be quoted here an an
apt summary of his analysis of the problem of Person.

> Cum ergo quaeritur de Patre et Filio et Spiritu Sancto,
> quid sint, qui sint, si tres aliqui, si tria aliqua, ex-
> ceptis relativis, quibus ad invicem sunt, quid dicemus?
> Exceptis enim relativis, cum nulla apud homines nomina
> trium illorum, sive propria, sive communia inveniantur,
> non sine causa hoc esse fides pia intelligit, sed in-
> effabile esse id de quo agitur intelligens, ad cogni-
> tionem divinitatis ex cogitatione humanae ignorantiae
> magis eruditur.150

Further difficulties in the approach from the unity of nature.

This inability to conceive the ontological reality of Person
in the Trinity results in a metaphysics of the Trinity which impoverishes the reality of the Persons, and tends inevitably to
center the attention on the divine essence.151 One of the results
is the doctrine that essence generates essence, as opposed to the

personalistic doctrine that the processions are a result of the
action of the Persons, the *principium quod*, based on the metaphysical principle 'actiones sunt suppositorum.' St Augustine is am-
biguous on this point,[152] and William follows him in his reference
to St Augustine's doctrine of the Son as *sapientia de sapientia,
essentia de essentia*.[153] If it is objected that a passing reference to this formula of St Augustine does not commit him to this
doctrine, there is another text in the *Aenigma fidei* where he refers to generation as 'facientis omnia divinitatis essentia.'[154]
It is difficult to show from such transitory references that he
had formulated a specific doctrine on this subject, but it is evident that he had no clear idea of generation proceeding from the
Person as *principium quod*.

The contemporary background: Gilbert de la Porée.

The question arises as to the existence of another and more
personalistic metaphysics of the Trinity contemporary with William.
Malet has drawn attention to two currents of trinitarian thought
in the middle ages, the Augustinian tradition represented principally by St Augustine, St Anselm and Abelard emphasizing the unity
of the divine essence, and a personalistic tradition inheriting
the doctrine of the Greek Fathers, emphasizing the Persons to the
point of falling into the danger of tritheism.[155] He places the
origin of this last tradition with William's contemporary, Gilbert
de la Porée, and traces the personalistic tendencies through Richard of St Victor, Alexander of Hales and St Bonaventure, showing
St Thomas as representing a synthesis of both traditions.[156]
The interest of this personalistic tradition in relation to
William's doctrine lies principally in the theology of his contemporary, Gilbert de la Porée. Malet interprets the distinction in
the doctrine of Gilbert de la Porée between *subsistens* and *sub-
sistentia* as that between the *id quod* and the *id quo* and maintains
that the aim of his Trinitarian theology was to establish against
the Sabellian tendencies the existence in God of one *id quo* and
three *id quod*.[157] Basically, he maintains, the doctrine of Gilbert de la Porée was on this point very close to that of St Thomas.[158] The interpretation of Malet is interesting,[159] but there
are reasons for a criticism of his case on the grounds of over sim-
plification. It should be noticed that in the thorough examination
of the doctrine of Gilbert de la Porée in the recent work of
Schmidt[160] the author concludes that the emphasis of Gilbert is
primarily on the unity of the divine nature.[161] He argues that
despite Gilbert's opposition to the Augustinian analogies on the
grounds of Sabellianism[162] and his attempt to discover an ontological foundation for Person,[163] he does not succeed in discovering
the answer.[164] Moreover the question of the *principium quod* and

and *quo,* as can be seen also from Häring's study, is more complex
than we are led to believe from the arguments of Malet.[165] Finally there is the possibility that Gilbert's doctrine, like that of
Abelard's, may have to be interpreted more in terms of logical *formulae* than as an insight in the real order into the Trinitarian
life[166] and it is significant that Malet ignores the interpretation
given by Cottiaux to Abelard's doctrine from this point of view.[167]
It is difficult therefore to prove conclusively the existence of a
trinitarian theology contemporary to William, which gives full value to the role of the Persons in the intratrinitarian sphere.

Conclusion on William's doctrine of Person in the Trinity.

It is possible, as has already been suggested in William's
treatment of the numerical distinction, that he emphasized the unity of nature in opposition to the dangers of the doctrine attributed to Gilbert de la Porrée by his contemporaries, such as Geoffrey of Auxerre. The accusation made against Gilbert was that of
introducing a quaternity into the Trinity by separating the Persons
from the substance.[168] The question as to whether the doctrine of
Gilbert de la Porrée correctly interpretated was in fact on the
way to the discovery of a more personalistic intratrinitarian theology than that of William, is difficult to prove conclusively.
Nevertheless even if William is not in positive reaction against
the discoveries which Malet attributes to Gilbert de la Porrée,
he can hardly be said to have advanced the metaphysics of Person
in relation to the Trinity. As regards the pure definition of Person he is even retrogressive. He sees the dangers in the definition of Boethius, but offers no satisfactory alternative,[169] and
ignores the contribution of St Anselm who uses the definition of
Boethius by extracting the note of 'individuality' and 'incommun-
icability.'[170]

The weakness of William's *ratio fidei* is apparent here. In
reaction against the dangers of contemporary scholasticism, he re-
fuses to admit the value of developing a metaphysics in its own
right,[171] which was one of the great contributions of the scholastics, ultimately to be of great service to theology, conditional
on the final subordination of reason to faith.

Despite this lack of a positive solution he shows an acute
realization of the problem, and, as always in his intratrinitarian
theology, his chief contribution lies in his emphasis on the mystery. His conclusion *ineffabile esse id de quo agitur* is still
relevant even after the Thomistic synthesis of *relatio subsistens.*
This synthesis of the relative and the absolute defines the nature
of Person in the Trinity, and offers a personalistic metaphysics
of the Trinity, which is denied to the purely Augustinian tradition, but the mystery still remains and we can never positively

understand the meaning of *relatio subsistens*.

The proper names.

William's treatment of the intratrinitarian life of the processions is marked by his characteristic sense of the transcendance of the Trinity over human concepts. The terms *Pater, Filius, Spiritus Sanctus; gignens et procedens,* are 'divina quaedam instrumenta per homines Dei Deo plenos a Deo nobis transmissa.'[172] But at the same time they are limited by their human connotations, and are therefore incapable of conveying the full divine reality. Their relationship to this divine reality is that of a sign to the thing signified[173] and we should pay attention primarily to what is signified rather than to the sign,[174] accepting the sign in so far as it helps us to understand the Trinity, while rejecting its purely human limitations.[175] This approach recalls Erigena's doctrine that all our concepts of the Trinity are theophanies, *vestigia,* imperfect reflections of a reality which transcends all intellectual concepts.[176] The difference lies in the emphasis given by William to *ratio fidei*[177] and the criterion of the value of these concepts lies in the 'forma hac sanorum fide verborum.'[178] Faith is the formative power in the application to the Trinity of such concepts as 'relation' and 'generation,' rather than any purely metaphysical analysis of the concepts themselves. This subjection of human concepts to the light of faith will be seen to stress principally the dissimilarity rather than the similarity of these human terms to the divine reality.

Relation.

The basis of the problem is the traditional teaching, accepted by William, that relation *ad aliquid* is the principle of plurality as opposed to *ad se* the principle of unity.[179] The difficulty begins with the application of 'relation' to the Trinity in the light of *ratio fidei.*

Relation in God is not an accident,[180] and arises within a substance of absolute unity,[181] whereas the human concept of relation presupposes distinct substances without which we cannot conceive of the relations. The relationship for instance between a master and his servant presupposes two men, two distinct substances, whereas the relationship between the Father and Son in the Trinity arises within a God who is an absolute unity. Relationship in the Trinity is therefore 'extra regulam et ordinem relativorum.'[182]

The special interest of William's treatment of 'relation' lies in his emphasis on the transcendance of 'relation' in the Trinity over the human philosophical concept. This very conception which was used traditionally as a defence of the Trinity

against the charge of absurdity,[183] and which with St Anselm becomes a step in the process of deducing the existence of the Trinity through necessary reasons,[184] is used by William as a means of
emphasizing further the mystery, the incomprehensibility of the
Trinity.[185]

   This approach to the problem was not only of value historically in opposition to a **rationalization** of the mystery, but is of importance even for our contemporary theology. The defence of the
Trinity against absurdity through the concept of relation is always open to the danger of minimizing the mystery. We may easily
think that we have lessened the mystery, when in fact we have only
transposed it into different terms.[186] A relation which arises
within an absolute unity, in William's words 'extra omnem regulam
relativorum,' is no less a mystery than the original statement of
the faith, unity of substance with a distinction of Persons.

The Processions.

   William's treatment of generation is a further example of his
emphasis on the transcendance of the Trinity. An interesting comparison can be made between his approach and that of St Thomas.
In the article from the *Summa* St Thomas proceeds from the analysis of the philosophical concept of generation, illustrating point
by point the similarities between this concept and generation in
the Trinity, in order to demonstrate that the generation of the
Son fulfills all the essential conditions of the philosophical definition: 'origo viventis a principio vivente conjuncto secundum
similitudinem ejusdem naturae.'[187]

   William on the other hand is concerned with demonstrating not
the similarities but the differences between generation in God and
the human concept of generation. The human concept of generation
is not conceived as a definition which is fulfilled in the Trinity
in all its essential notes, as if in demonstration of an analogy
of proper proportion. It is conceived rather as a sign pointing
to an infinitely transcendent reality, but in itself wholly in-
sufficient to convey the full reality of the thing signified.[188]
It is the differences rather than the similarities which are
stressed.

   Generation in the Trinity is neither active nor passive. It
is beyond time or place, excluding any idea of separation within the
divine unity.[189] It is eternal. The Son is always Son, and there
was never a moment when the Father began to be Father, or the Son
began to be Son.[190] Divine generation excludes anything accidental.[191] It is the transcendance which is emphasized, despite the
admission that the term generation can really be predicated of the
Trinity and we are left in obscurity as to how this can be possible.
Ultimately once again we return to the mystery "vera sed divina et

imperscrutabili et inenarrabili nativitate.'192
   The procession of the Holy Ghost, like the generation of the
Son, is eternal.193 William follows St Augustine closely in his
formula for the procession of the Holy Ghost from the Father and
the Son.194 This is a further instance of St Augustine's 'essentialist' approach as opposed to the more personalistic theory of
procession which was developed with Alexander of Hales,195 St Bon-
aventure196 and St Thomas. St Thomas argues that there are 'duo
spiratores' on the grounds, that an act receives its number from
the suppositum.197 This leads to the distinction that there is
'unum principium (principium quo),' but not 'idem principium (principium quod).'198 On this point William remains strictly in the
Augustinian tradition. But this is combined with the Greek emphasis on the Father as the ultimate source of the procession, the
'fons quidam et origo,'199 with a suggestion also of the theory of
the processions in which the nature is conceived as the object of
an act of donation from Person to Person.200

The inseparability of the Persons.

   In the section on the proper names the emphasis on the approach from the unity of nature becomes less pronounced. As the
Aenigma fidei moves towards the conclusion based on the economy of
Persons, there are indications even in the more metaphysical part
of the work of a more personalistic approach to the Trinity.
   The argument for the inseparability of the Persons reflects
the approach both from the unity of nature and from the distinction of Persons. For there are two ways in which we can argue to
the unity of the divine Persons. We can either follow the approach from the unity of nature and prove the unity of the Persons
from the consubstantiality of the essence. This argument places
the divine nature as the first object of attention, arguing that
the Persons are one, *because* the divine nature is one. Alternatively we can argue that the Persons are a consubstantial unity
not from the unity of the divine nature but from the mutual circumincession of the Persons in their relations *ad invicem*. This
argument places the Persons as the first object of attention, arguing that there is consubstantiality, because the Persons are
*ad invicem.*201
   The following text illustrates the interpenetration of these
two methods.

   Nullum ibi nomen sit quo sic nominetur quaelibet Persona, ut non aut tribus naturali unitate conveniat,
   sicut cum dicitur potens, sapiens, bonus et caetera
   hujusmodi; aut alteram ad alteram referri, etiam in
   ipso singularitatis nomine demonstrat, sicut cum

dicitur Pater, Filius, Spiritus Sanctus. In relativis
enim nominibus nequaquam sic una Persona singulariter
dicitus, ut non ad alteram ipso suo nomine referatur.
Relativo quippe vocabulo sic una Persona singulariter
dicitur in se, ut non dicatur ad se. Idcirco relatio
ipsa vocabuli personalis Personas separari vetat, quas
cum simul nominat simul etiam insinuat. Cum enim dicitur Pater intelligitur pariter et Filius, cujus est
Pater; cum dicitur Filius intelligitur et Pater cujus
Filius est. Cum vero Spiritus Sanctus 'donum' dicitur
sicut Verbum Filius ad dicentem, sic et donum ad do-
natem.[202]

In this text we find both arguments. First there is the argument from unity of nature, 'naturali unitate.'[203] Then there
is the argument from the mutual relations. The very concept of
relation implies inseparability: 'relatio ipsa vocabuli personalis Personas separari vetat.' We do not find here the full Greek
scheme of circumincession, when the inseparability of the Persons
is illustrated by the complete scheme 'ex Patre, per Filium, in
Spiritu,' the outgoing movement of expansion, to be brought again
into unity by the return movement 'in spiritu, per Filium ad Patrem.'[204] The unity here is illustrated simply by the opposition
of relations: 'cum enim dicitur Pater intelligitur pariter et
Filius, cujus est Pater; cum dicitur Filius, intelligitur et Pater,
cujus Filius est.' Then follows the corresponding relation of the
Holy Ghost: 'donum ad donantem.' But the principle is the same
as with the Greek circumincession. The inseparability of the Persons is illustrated from the very existence of relative opposition.[205]

The inseparability of the Persons is illustrated further in
relation to creation and to the incarnation. These themes will be
treated with the economy of the Persons *ad extra*. The text on the
action of the Persons in creation,[206] which will later be examined
closely, is an example of the approach from the distinction of Persons according to the economy 'ex Patre, per Filium, in Spiritu,'
occurring within the central speculative section of the *Aenigma
fidei* on the divine names, and suggests a gradual preparation for
the concluding section based on this economy.

B) The Trinitarian Economy.

In the *Epistola ad Romanos* William comments on the Scriptural
presentation of the trinitarian economy 'ex Patre, per Filium, in
Spiritu.'[207] Although he introduces the Augustinian explanation
of the Holy Ghost as the mutual union between the Father and
Son, [208] the general treatment of the subject is on the lines of

a simple commentary on Scripture. In the *Aenigma fidei* this Scriptural scheme is presented from a more technical standpoint, leading to a discussion of the speculative trinitarian problems arising out of this economy. The scheme 'ex Patre, per Filium, in Spiritu' appears towards the end of the central treatise on the divine names showing the action of the Persons in the operations *ad extra*.[209] Finally there is the conclusion of the whole work, based on the whole supernatural economy in the work of redemption.[210] Basically the structure is that of the action of the Persons *quoad nos* rather than in their intratrinitarian life,[211] which gives the conclusion a different character from the central treatise. But within this general structure problems are raised of a speculative nature.

The interest of the conclusion from the speculative point of view does not lie chiefly, as in the central treatise on the divine names, in the intensive analysis of intratrinitarian problems as such. The particular contribution here is that the intratrinitarian life appears as the ultimate foundation for the economy *ad extra*. Seen as the root of the historical economy, the treatment of these speculative questions is influenced by the framework in which they are placed. The Father as the 'fons quidam et origo' of the intratrinitarian life is shown also as the origin of the mission of the Son *ad extra*.[212] The doctrine of appropriation receives the special emphasis that certain attributes are ascribed to the Father on the grounds of his priority of origin.[213] The procession of the Holy Ghost, placed in the context of this emphasis on the Father in his priority of origin,[214] now assumes the character of a chain of principles with the Son as 'principium de principio,'[215] who together with the Father is one single principle, (*unum principium*) of the Holy Ghost.[216] Finally this single principle originating with the Father becomes the origin together with the Son and the Holy Ghost of the whole of creation, 'unum principium....omnis creaturae.'[217] The dominant conception of 'ex Patre' as the source of the trinitarian life first *ad intra*, then *ad extra*, is reflected in all these questions. Again the Augustinian analogy comparing the Word of God to the mental word[218] and the incarnation to its outward vocal expression, is introduced less as an illustration of the Trinity than as an introduction to the economy of 'per Filium,' to the incarnation as the outward manifestation of the eternal Word[219] and the whole pedagogic role of the incarnation in relation to man in the 'animal state.'[220] Finally the doctrine of the procession of the Holy Ghost from the Father and the Son, though 'principaliter a Patre,'[221] and the explanation of the Holy Ghost as the mutual unity and charity of the Father and the Son shows the ultimate roots of the economy 'in Spiritu,'[222] and of the Holy Ghost as the *donum Dei*, the source of charity in us and all gifts throughout creation.[223]

The approach from the distinction of Persons.

Here the problem is the reverse of that which confronted William in the approach from the unity of nature. Although he is no nearer the solution metaphysically of what constitutes Person in the Trinity, which is not the question discussed in these texts, the Persons appear as the first object of attention through the trinitarian economy. The whole problem is now to explain the unity of the divine nature. This is the subject of the following text which occurs towards the end of the central treatise and anticipates the economy of the concluding section:

> Ubi cum a Patre per Filium in Spiritu Sancto condita
> omnia commemorari videantur, tamen in diversis prae-
> positionum appositionibus nulla intelligenda est di-
> versitas operationis, sed simplex cooperatio. Aeque
> enim ex Patre et ex Spiritu Sancto sunt omnia, sicut
> ex natura omnium creatrice, aeque per Patrem et per
> Filium et per Spiritum Sanctum, sicut per Deum om-
> nium opificem; aeque in Patre et Filio et Spiritu
> Sancto sicut in Deo omnia continente.[224]

The contrast is evident between this text and the text treating of the relative names, showing God in relation to creation. There the trinitarian action on creation was seen as proceding from the divine essence, with no suggestion of the trinitarian economy. Here the creative act is seen primarily from the standpoint of the Persons rather than the nature. Each Person intervenes in creation in a manner that is proper to that Person, the Father as *ex quo,* the Son as *per quem,* the Holy Spirit as *in quo,* as is emphasized in a further explanation.

> Quae tamen singula singulis distribuuntur, cum ex
> Patre dicuntur esse omnia, ex quo principaliter est
> omnis creatura; et per Verbum quo ipse dixit et om-
> nia facta sunt; et in Spiritu Sancto, qui Patris et
> Filii bonitas est, continens omnia.[225]

The problem here is how to explain the unity of the divine nature in the act of creation. The distinction of the Persons is evident. He attempts to safeguard this unity by saying that it is equally true to say that creation is 'ex Spiritu Santo,' or 'per Patrem,' or 'in Patre et Filio.'[226] This suggests that each Person intervenes specially according to the order of the Persons *ex, per, in* but none of the Persons act exclusively as either *ex, per* or *in.* Something is proper to each Person in the act of creation, but not to the exclusion of the other Persons. There is a

'personalis adnotatio Trinitatis,'[227] but at the same time a re-
collection into unity: 'sic tamen ut omnia recolligantur ad in-
telligendam in Trinitate veritatem divinae unitatis.'[228]

This emphasis on the distinction of Persons forms the main
structure of the concluding section of the *Aenigma fidei*, showing
each of the Persons in their respective roles of *ex*, *per*, *in*.
The Father is the source of the whole trinitarian action *ad intra*
and *ad extra*, from whom the other Persons proceed as if in a single chain. This activity proceeds first throughout the intratrinitarian life, then into the whole economy *ad extra*, showing the Son
in the role of the incarnation, and finally the Holy Spirit, in
whom every gift of creation is received.[229] At the same time as
if in correction to this initial emphasis on the Persons, he refers constantly to the inseparability of the Persons and to the
unity of their action *ad extra*, as for instance in the classic
formula of trinitarian prayer which **summarizes** this economy.

Oramus etiam Deum Patrem et adoramus, et gratias ei
agimus non sine Filio et Spiritu Sancto; et tamen per
Filium sicut per mediatorem Dei et hominum Dominum
nostrum Jesum Christum, in Spiritu Sancto Paracleto
nostro, et advocato orationum nostrarum apud Deum.[230]

This text is followed by the necessary correction to any danger that this distinction of the Persons might imply separation.

Cum autem oramus Patrem per Filium in Sancto Spiritu,
sicut alium per alium in alio, nonnisi unum Deum oramus in nullo differentem a Deo.[231]

The difference in approach of this concluding section is at
once evident. The presentation of the Trinity within the framework of the economy *quoad nos* contrasts with the emphasis on the
problems of the Trinity *quoad se* in the central treatise. The
'Greek'[232] way of emphasizing first of all the Persons gives a
different perspective from the greater part of the central treatise with its 'Latin' character. But the emphasis on the incomprehensibility of the mystery continues. Generation is 'vera sed divina et imperscrutabili et inenarrabili nativitate.'[233] The Son
is 'ineffabilis de Patre sine initio natus.'[234] The comparison
between the Word of God and the human word is 'magno occultoque
mysterio.'[235] The 'Greek' and the 'Latin' methods are simply
different ways by which we are led to the inevitable conclusion,
the 'aenigma fidei.'

CONCLUSION

In the article on *The Trinitarian Aspect of the Ascent of the Soul* the Trinity was seen *quoad nos* in intimate relationship with the spiritual life. Here the approach is primarily through the objective speculative problems arising from within the Trinity itself *quoad se*. Yet although the spiritual life is now no longer the immediate object of attention, the whole speculative development of the *Aenigma fidei* is constructed against this background. The framework is given in three stages of theological knowledge, which are reflections on the theological plane of the three spiritual states, *animalis, rationalis, spiritualis*. The last of the theological stages is identifiable with the last of the spiritual states. 'Ratio fidei,' the speculative development, the second theological stage, is therefore not treated as an end in itself but is directed ultimately towards the final stage of Spiritus, resemblance, the experimental knowledge of the Trinity through participation in the life of the Holy Ghost.

The *Aenigma fidei* is unique among William's works as being *ex professo* a study of the Trinity. Nowhere else does he treat so scientifically and so profoundly the metaphysical problems arising from this dogma. For this reason there might be a tendency to consider the *Aenigma fidei* in its more technical passages as a complete expression of his trinitarian theology. This would be misleading. As has been shown already, the trinitarian theme which penetrates most deeply into his theological writings is that of the relationship between the Augustinian theory of the Holy Ghost and the mystical experience of the Trinity in fact everything which is associated with the final stage of 'Spiritus.' This, rather than the speculative development of the *Aenigma fidei*, is the most personal, the most original aspect of his trinitarian theology, and the most widely diffused throughout his works. Only in this perspective can the speculative problems of the *Aenigma fidei* be seen in true proportion. They are not the whole of William's trinitarian theology, nor even his most important contribution. They represent a particular development incorporated within his more deeply rooted theology of the Trinity in relation to the spiritual life.

The tendency towards a synthesis of patristic tradition.

William's treatment of these speculative questions is based on a "recapitulation" of the teaching of the Fathers. His aim is not to dwell on the specific theories of any of the Fathers in particular, but to present as far as possible the general catholic tradition of patristic trinitarian doctrine. In these more complex metaphysical problems he has not achieved so successful a

synthesis as in his theology of the Holy Spirit in relation to
the mystical experience of the Trinity. There he blends several
traditional elements into a finely constructed unity to form a
creative theology of considerable originality. Here the elements
are frequently more juxtaposed than united. Examples of this tendency are the 'Latin' and Augustinian central section of the *Aenigma fidei* followed by the more 'Greek' and scriptural 'economy' of
the concluding section, or the attempt to fuse the traditional
trinitarian 'economy' with the Augustinian doctrine of the Holy
Ghost, 'in Spiritu' being the point of contact between the two
schemes. Yet this is never a mere reproduction of traditional
themes without any underlying unity of purpose. The selection and
combination of his sources serves to accentuate the dominant theme
of the 'mystery.'

The 'Greek' and 'Latin' approach.

A distinction must be made between the 'Greek' and 'Latin'
approach in the precise sense given by de Régnon to these terms
and the Greek and Latin influence on the general ethos of his trinitarian doctrine. If this distinction is interpreted in the sense
given by de Régnon, we can reach the following conclusion. There
is a general though not exclusive tendency for William to follow
the 'Greek' approach when showing the Trinity in relation to us
quoad nos[236] and the 'Latin' approach when treating of the speculative intratrinitarian problems of the Trinity *quoad se*. The concluding section presenting the Trinity primarily *ad extra quoad
nos* is predominantly 'Greek,' whereas in the central treatise of
the *Aenigma fidei* on the problems of the intratrinitarian life the
approach is predominantly 'Latin.' If on the other hand it is a
question of the 'Greek' and 'Latin' influence in the sense of the
general mentality underlying these speculations, then William is
throughout more in line with the 'Greek' tradition.[237] The emphasis on the bare mystery and the expression of this mystery in the
Dionysian *theologia negativa* reflects one of the most characteristic elements in the doctrine of the Greek Fathers. In contrast to
the Western 'Latin' development beginning with St Augustine, the
speculations of the *Aenigma fidei* contain only occasional and
transient references to the 'psychological' analogy. Despite a
chain of quotations from St Augustine, William seems to have re-
frained deliberately from any extensive use of his images and illustrations from creation. Nor is there the slightest evidence of
any attempt to give a metaphysical explanation on the basis of this
psychological analogy, as is found in the scholastic speculations
from St Anselm onwards.

'Ratio fidei' *and the mystery of the Trinity.*

William's answer on the speculative plane to rationalistic
tendencies lay in the concept of 'ratio fidei.' The problem of
the construction of the *Aenigma fidei* revealed a tension between
the desire to counteract Abelard by a return to the simple scriptural faith and the need to give some reply to the problems raised by this faith. This conflict is largely resolved by 'ratio
fidei.' As opposed to any conception of speculative theology
which might imply the practical autonomy of reason, 'ratio fidei'
subjects reason so completely to the formative influence of faith
that it is on the contrary simply an expansion, a penetration of
what is present in germ in the initial faith.

His method and its application to trinitarian problems has exactly the opposite advantages and dangers from those of the rising
scholasticism. Its weakness lies in a theological method which
had not yet recognized the need for metaphysics to develop first
of all according to its own laws before it could be placed effectively at the service of faith. This was ultimately to be one of
the great contributions of scholasticism.[238] But despite the value of the true philosophical concepts of person and relation applied to the Trinity there is always the danger of thinking that we
have in this way understood the mystery, when in fact we have only
stated the initial mystery of 'three' and 'one' in different terms.
Here is the strength of William's approach. The whole dialectic
of "ratio fidei" is directed to showing that once such terms as
person, relation and generation have been subjected to faith and
received the "form" of faith, they transcend their purely human
limitations and are therefore inaccessible to human reason. William helps us to see that, even in the light of the later metaphysical development of these concepts, we do not positively understand the mystery in their application to the Trinity.

He approaches the Trinity from every angle and in each case
confronts us with the 'mystery,' the *Aenigma fidei.* At every turn
we are driven back against the initial faith, yet seeing with each
further attempt one more example of where the mystery lies, till
paradoxically we know that we have only understood it to the limits
of our powers when we have seen how it is beyond our understanding.
At this point the impetus of William's thought leads on to the final stage of the mystical experience of the Trinity. The mystery
will always remain, but on another plane an insight is given of a
very different kind, when the *problems* of 'ratio fidei' recede before the *experience* of 'amor ipse intellectus est.'

NOTES

*Published in RTAM 27 (1960) 193-211, and RTAM 28 (1961) 26-58.

[1]The value of these polemics should be judged in the light of the persuasive defence of the orthodoxy of Abelard by J. Cottiaux: 'La conception de la théologie chez Abelard,' RHE 28 (1932) 247-295, 533-551, 787-828. Cottiaux's defence is based on a close analysis of the texts, showing how many of the passages in Abelard's writings had been interpreted as heretical on the assumption that they referred to the ontological plane of reality, whereas in fact they were intended as a defence of the formulae of the Trinity on the purely logical plane of verbal propositions.

The question has been raised of the likelihood that the opposition to Abelard by St Bernard and William was based partly on unpublished writings of Abelard and an oral tradition handed on to his pupils from his lectures. Cf. A. M. Landgraf, 'Probleme um den hl. Bernhard von Clairvaux,' extract from *Cistercienser Chronik* (May, 1954) 1-3. Landgraf refers to Ostlender for this theory of an oral tradition; H. Ostlender, 'Die *Theologia Scholarium* des Peter Abaelard,' *Aus der Geisteswelt des Mittelalters,* I (Münster, 1935) 263-281. He mentions also the existence in the twelfth century of a collection of theological doctrines made by pupils from the oral teachings of their professors in the cases of Anselm of Laon, William of Champeaux and Gilbert of Poitiers. There was also the practice of distinguishing between the doctrines of theologians as given by this oral tradition and the doctrines of their published works, as for instance Odo of Ourscamp on the teaching of Abelard: 'Sic audivi illum docentem.' It is therefore quite possible that some of the more dangerous expressions of Abelard have an origin of this kind. But if Cottiaux's interpretation of Abelard's doctrine as a whole is accepted, showing that the whole mentality of Abelard was directed towards the problems of logic rather than ontological reality, it is unlikely that his oral teaching would have developed on different lines. At least we can say that such teaching should be interpreted in line with the conclusions formed as to his theological method from his published doctrine and the general character of his theology as a whole.

However even if Abelard is vindicated against the charge of heresy, there were inherent dangers in his doctrine. His expressions were often ambiguous, as Cottiaux admits, p. 826, and his disciples tended to misunderstand his doctrine. William's writings were an opportune warning. Furthermore, William's opposition is a protest against a theology dominated by an almost exclusive preoccupation with logical and grammatical formulae, and touches precisely on the need for theology to include those elements which relate more closely to the spiritual life of man and his eternal salvation.

[2]This problem was discovered by Père Déchanet, who has not yet published his conclusions. What now follows on this question of the construction of the Aenig is based on these discoveries, though the conclusions, especially in what relates to the underlying unity of the work, are not identical with those of Déchanet.

[3]J.-M Déchanet, 'Les manuscrits de la lettre aux Frères du Mont-Dieu de Guillaume de Saint-Thierry et le problème de la Préface dans Charleville 114,' *Scriptorium* 8 (1954) 259-271.

[4]Aenig, 407C.

[5]Ibid., 397B-407C.

[6]Ibid., 407C-409B.

[7]Ibid., 409B-410B.

[8]Ibid., 410C-414B.

[9]Ibid., 414B-415D.

[10]Ibid., 416B-417C.

[11]Ibid., 417D-432C.

[12]Ibid., 417D-420B.

[13]Ibid., 420B-423A.

[14]Ibid., 423A-425D.

[15]Ibid., 426A-432C.

[16]Ibid., 432D-434A.

[17]Ibid., 434B-435A.

[18]Ibid., 435D-440D.

[19]Ibid., 397B-407C.

[20]Ibid., 417D-432C.

[21]Ibid., 435D-440D. Note however the different character of the two sections treating of the Trinity 'quoad nos.'

[22]See above, p. 195.

[23]Aenig 434B-435A.

[24]Ibid., 410B-C; see also the parallel between the texts comparing relation in the Trinity and in creatures, 428C-D and 411B-C.

[25]It must not be supposed that the speculative sections of the work are limited to the treatise on the divine names. Already in an earlier section he had introduced questions of this nature: 410-414B, treating of the problem of number and person, the problem of number being resumed again after the end of the treatise on the divine names (435A) but the treatise on the divine names develops considerably these speculative trinitarian problems. It is possible that William first of all introduced the section on number and person into a work of a less technical nature and then developed further this aspect of the Trinity with the treatise on the divine names. Déchanet speaks of the original manuscript having been rewritten several times: 'Guillaume a augmenté son texte, Guillaume a corrigé son texte, et cela même a plusieurs reprises.' (cf. J.-M. Déchanet, 'Les manuscrits,' 270.

[26]The concluding section also contains passages of a more speculative nature but these questions arise out of the structure of the trinitarian economy 'quoad nos.'

[27]Spec fid, 158-169; 391D-394C.

[28]Ep frat, 349A-B.

[29]Aenig, 414B-415D.

[30]Aenig, 417C.

[31]Ibid., 432D-433C.

[32]Ibid., 433C-434A.

[33]Ibid., 435B: 'similes ei erimus; quoniam videbimus eum sicuti est.'

[34]Ibid., 399A-D.

[35]Ibid., 427A: 'Non tam disciplinae alicujus studio quam fidei pietate et fervore amoris ad intellectum et **sensum** rerum aliquem primo ambiendum est.'

[36]Ibid., 407C-D.

[37]Ibid., 409C.

[38]Ibid., 409A.

[39]Ibid., 411C. See also 415C-416A stressing that the pursuit of *scientia* is a moral obligation, and 417 showing that the creation of man in the image of God implants a natural desire for the knowledge of God.

[40]Ibid., 416B.

[41]This conflict is reflected also in the *Speculum fidei* 84-85; 374C, where he distinguishes animal and spiritual reason, condemning only 'animal reason.' There is no condemnation of reason as such (79) in praise of the understanding and defence of the faith and the only question is whether the rational stage is a strictly necessary element in the evolution of the soul. See 103-104 (378D), referring to the 'simplices filios Dei' who receive knowledge of the things of faith directly from the Holy Ghost without the mediation of rational investigation: 'absque omni verborum sive cogitationum disceptantium strepitu a sancto Spiritu discentes,' (104); compare Aenig, 408C referring to the 'strepitu disputationum.'

[42]Aenig, 417B.

[43]Ibid., 418B. This question of the application to God of the ten categories was a recognized problem in the theology of the Middle Ages. N. M. Haring, 'The Case of Gilbert de la Porrée,' *Mediaeval Studies* 13 (1951) 1-40. See p. 17, where he refers to the agreement of Gilbert de la Porrée with Boethius, that if properly explained, we can speak of God in terms of these categories, referring to the reserve of William of St Thierry on this subject, who accepted them only on condition that they were subjected to the light of *ratio fidei*.

[44]Ibid., 419C; cf. 418B-C: 'Ratio tamen fidei quasi morem gerens humanae rationi illata sibi ab hominibus non respuit omnino vel abjicit; sed assumit ea sibi, et conformando singula suis regulis et coaptando, in obsequium fidei ac servitutem captivatum quodammodo rediget eorum intellectum.'

[45]Ibid., 419C: 'nec rationibus seu ratiocinationibus hominum subjiciamus causam fidei nostrae, sed omnia illi.'

[46]Note the continual use in the texts quoted of such phrases as *formare, conformando, assumere, efficere,* in relation to this transforming power of faith over reason. Déchanet describes very well this *exstasis* of the reason under the influence of faith, when he speaks of the incapacity of the intellect to reach its end 'si elle ne sort pas d'elle même' (*Guillaume de Saint-Thierry,* 94). There is an ambiguity as to the exact sense of this exstasis. In the Err Guil, *ratio fidei* is closely connected with a text suggesting the divine mode of knowledge associated with the stage of *spiritus;* See Err Guil (PL 180, 334B-C). See also Med (PL 180, 214B-D) where the expression *ratio sui generis* used explicitly in the Aenig to describe *ratio fidei* (417B) is related to an eschatological anticipation of the knowledge of God as he is and to a special mode of knowledge in the Holy Ghost. In the Aenig *ratio fidei* is explicitly associated, not with this final stage of *spiritus* but with the intermediary stage of rational knowledge (Aenig, 414C-D). The association of *ratio fidei* with the more advanced state of *spiritus* in the other texts may be due to an uncertainty of terminology. Alternatively it may signify the interpenetration of the degrees of theological knowledge showing that *ratio fidei* already contains within itself a tension towards the more advanced mystical knowledge in the Holy Spirit. If this is so, there is a further reason for showing the connection between the metaphysical sections of the Aenig and the spiritual and psychological theme of the movement towards 'ressemblance.'

[47]Sacr alt, 345B-C.

[48]Aenig, 416D.

[49]Ibid., 417A, referring to II Tim I, 13.

[50]Ibid., 417A: 'Forma vero sanorum in fide verborum est proprius quidam modus loquendi de Deo, secundum haec ipsa quae ex auctoritate Christi Domini et apostolorum et apostolicorum doctorum, jam olim usus Christianae pietatis obtinuit circa nomina divina.' And again 417C: 'non verbis praecipitationis et alienis, sed ipsis quibus semetipsum et Patrem et Spiritum sanctum manifestavit mundo Verbum Dei ipso locutionis charactere, quo fidem Trinitatis propagaverunt in mundo homines Dei.' This is in complete accord with the demand for the 'proprium illum stylum spiritus sancti tui' of the scriptural section (407C-D).

[51]Ibid., 417C.

[52]Ibid., 408C.

[53]Bouyer, *La spiritualité*, 130-131. Gilbert of Holland [Hoyland/Swineshead] conceives the relationship of faith and reason in a way similar to William: *In Cantica* (PL 184, 26D-27A): 'Intelligentia quidem, etsi fidem excedit, non tamen aliud contuetur quam quod fide continetur....Ratio inter fidem intelligentiamque discurrens, ad illam se erigit, sed ista se regit....Ratio supra fidem conatur, fide tamen nititur, fide cohibetur....mens rationis ductu pervestigando procedit, sed a fide non recedit, instructa a fide, et restricta ad fidem.' Gilbert died in 1172, about twenty years after the death of William. Some mutual influence may be possible here. For this doctrine of Gilbert of Holland, see also Gilson, *La théologie mystique*, 84-85.

[54]See Bouyer, *La Spiritualité*, 122-123: 'Le second stade résultera de la transformation de l'*anima* en *animus*....par la même sa foi ne lui restera plus exterieure en quelque manière, mais l'âme y pénétrera.'

[55]See 'The Trinitarian Aspect of the Ascent of the Soul:' *The Psychological Roots*.

[56]See Spec fid, 134; 386B.

[57]See Davy, 'La connaissance de Dieu d'aprés Guillaume de Saint-Thierry,' in *R sc rel* 28 (1938) 440-456.

[58]Perino gives a good analysis of this development in *La dottrina trinitaria de Sant' Anselmo*, 14-51.

[59]Even Richard of St Victor, who returned in some measure to the Augustinian *sapientia*, shows a very different conception of the relationship of faith and reason from that of William. See A.-M. Ethier, *Le De Trinitate de Richard de Saint-Victor*, (Paris-Ottawa, 1939) p. 54: 'La foi n'est pas précisément la lumière qui va éclairer le sillage ardu par où s'avance l'esprit. Elle indique, mais n'illumine pas.'

[60]Déchanet, *OEuvres choisies*, p. 18.

[61]*Sermo* 43, PL 38, 253.

[62]See E. Gilson, *Introduction à l'étude de saint Augustin* (Paris, 1943) p. 41; cf. 43.

63This conception of the impotence of reason in theology
except when transformed by faith contrasts with the description
given by Gilson of faith and reason in St Augustine, maintaining
that reason with St Augustine has the power of itself to gain some
understanding of every truth of revelation. See Gilson, *Introduction*, 41: 'Il n'en est pas une seule dont notre raison ne puisse
gagner quelque intelligence pourvu qu'elle s'y applique, et ce
faisant, c'est bien comme raison que la pensée fonctionne, puisque
la foi n'y intervient pas a titre de preuve, mais seulement a titre d'objet.'

64Aenig, 432C.

65See Adv Abl, 258C.

66Aenig, 426C.

67See *De divinis nominibus* VII (PG 3, 871). The immediate
source here may be St Gregory, *Moralia* V, 36 (PL 75, 716A): 'Tun
verum est quod de Deo cognoscimus, cum plene nos aliquid de illo
cognoscere non posse sentimus.' See Erigena, *De divisione naturae*
I, 16 (PL 122-522C): 'Sancta Trinitas, cum sit super omnia quae
de se dicuntur,' and ibid., 510C: 'qui melius nesciendo scitur.'

68Aenig, 433D.

69Nowhere throughout his works is there any ground for
giving to these illustrations the value of a metaphysical 'explanation' according to an analogy of proper proportion.

70Aenig, 426C-D.

71It is interesting to notice that Gilbert of Poitiers
among William's contemporaries also refused to attempt any reconciliation to the trinity and unity in God. See M. A. Schmidt,
*Gottheit und Trinität nach dem Kommentar des Gilbert Porreta zu
Boethius' De Trinitate* (Basel, 1956) 164-169, esp. 167: 'Die Dreiheit lässt sich aus der Einheit nicht entwickeln, sondern nur sich
ihr gegenüberstellen, die Einheit sich nicht zur Dreiheit philoso-
phisch-theologisch entfalten, sondern nur in der natürlichen Betra-
chtungsweise durchbrechen. Damit aber verzichet Gilbert, der doch
sonst in seinem Kommentar vielfach über Boethius hinausführt, auf
die Möglichkeit der gängigen Trinitätsspekulation.' Nevertheless
the character of Gilbert's theology is of a much more independent
and speculative nature than the *ratio fidei* of William, as can be
seen from his speculations on the *quod est* and the *quo est*. Nor
does Gilbert's theology belong primarily to *theologia negativa*.

St Bernard on a much smaller scale treats the intratrinitarian problem with a similar emphasis on the bare mystery in *Csi*, PL 182, 797A-800A. See especially 799B: 'Quaerit quis quomodo illud quod catholicum esse dicimus, possit esse. Sufficit ei tenere sic esse.'

[72]de Régnon, *Etudes de théologie positive sur la sainte Trinité*, 4 vols. (Paris, 1892).

[73]See A. Malet, *Personne et amour dans la théologie trinitaire de saint Thomas d'Aquin* (Paris, 1956). Even though a strong critic of de Régnon, the author bases the whole structure of his book on these two ways, the existence of which is indisputable.

[74]The weakness of Malet's case is that he has not emphasized the primacy throughout the Greek Fathers of the trinitarian scheme *ex Patre, per Filium, in Spiritu.* It is precisely this structure which makes the Persons appear so strongly as the first object of attention. First of all in the intratrinitarian life, the processions appear in this way as donations of the divine nature from one Person to another as in a successive chain of transmission. Then this life is reflected in the economy *ad extra,* which follows the same structure, *ex Patre, per Filium, in Spiritu,* making present first of all the Persons and then leading us to the divine nature through the unique role of each of the Persons. This scheme, *ex, per, in,* is basically scriptural and liturgical. The specific contribution of the Greek Fathers was to transfer the scriptural scheme, describing the economy *ad extra* to the order of the Processions *ad intra,* while retaining also the scriptural economy *ad extra.* The metaphysical deficiencies of the Greek Fathers in their concept of Person and its role in the intratrinitarian life, to which Malet as drawn attention, do not obscure essentially the primacy of this personalistic presentation.

On the other hand, in the Latin tradition there is, as Malet admits, a trend of thought which makes the unity of the divine nature the starting point for its speculations. St Augustine, St Anselm and Peter Abelard are notable examples. Malet rightly draws attention to the great contribution of St Thomas to the metaphysics of Person in the Trinity, imparting a personalistic character to the processions, especially through the conception of *relatio subsistens* and the distinctions between the *principium quod,* the Persons, and the *principium quo,* the nature, but in comparison with the Greek Fathers, it still be maintained that the 'Latin' and scholastic tradition approaches the Trinity more from the angle of the unity of nature. This conclusion can be justified in several ways. First, the strongly 'essentialist' trend in the

Latin tradition as shown in such leading theologians as St Augustine and St Thomas centers on the metaphysics of the intratrinitarian life, with comparatively little emphasis on the *ex, per, in* economy, which is the principle means of focussing attention on the Persons. Finally the psychological explanation of the processions, by way of intellect and love, shows the faculties of divine nature as the 'principium formale quo principium formale quo proximum' of the processions, even though the Persons are the 'principium quod' in St Thomas' theology.

De Régnon's distinction is true as a generalization. But it should not be pressed too closely. Apart from Malet's main point on St Thomas' clarification of the role of the Persons metaphysically in the intratrinitarian life, there are further qualifications which must be made. The approach from the Persons cannot be described as exclusively 'Greek.' As we have said, it is also the emphasis of Scripture and the liturgy. Moreover some of the pre-Nicene Latin Fathers follow the Greek scheme: Tertullian, *Adv. Prax.* (PL 2, 159B); and some of the Greeks after Nicaea in opposition to Arianism follow the Latin method: St Athanasius, *Ep 3 ad Serap.* (PG 26, 634). Even after Nicaea the Greek approach is occasionally found in Latin authors: See I. Chevalier, *S. Augustin et la pensée grecque, les relations trinitaires* (Fribourg, 1940) 167-168, and M. Schmaus, *Die psychologische Trinitätslehre des heiligen Augustinus,* p. 153.

75See 'The Trinitarian Aspect,' [Chapter 2] on *Image-resemblance.*

76See Déchanet, *Guillaume de Saint-Thierry,* 109, and Bouyer, *La spiritualité,* 143.

77Note the references to 'the Fathers' in general. Aenig, 432C, 416B, 434A; Err Guil, 334B; Prologue to Nat corp, 695-696. Déchanet rightly remarks (*Guillaume de Saint-Thierry,* 162): 'Il s'honore de suivre les traces non de tel docteur de l'Eglise en particulier, mais des Pères en général.'

78Déchanet, *Guillaume de Saint-Thierry,* 110, footnote. The emphasis on the unity of nature which is the main aspect of St Augustine followed by William in the Aenig is the more traditional aspect of St Augustine's teaching. See M. Schmaus, *Die psychologische Trinitätslehre,* p. 7, where the specifically Augustinian elements are distinguished from the traditional elements, and 101-102 where he refers to the traditional character of St Augustine's emphasis on the unity of the divine nature: 'Deutlich steht er sich in die Reihe jener Theologen, die den Hauptton auf die Einheit des göttlichen Wesens legen.'

[79]Erigena was without doubt the intermediary in William's knowledge of St Gregory of Nyssa in Nat Corp. See Déchanet, *Aux sources*, 55-56. So there is at least a probability that his influence appears in his other works.

[80]See *De divisione naturae* II, 24 (PL 122, 579). The influence of St Gregory the Great is also probable. The general character of this central section of the Aenig, presenting the bare mystery of the Trinity with only a passing reference to the psychological illustration of St Augustine, can be compared with the almost complete neglect of this Augustinian doctrine in St Gregory. See M. Frickel, *Deus totus ubique simul*, p. 23, footnote 89: 'von der psychologischen Trinitätslehre ist bei Gregor jedoch kaum eine Spur zu finden.' There is also the emphasis in St Gregory on *theologia negativa*; see pp. 11 and 28, 44, 64.

[81]See Ethier, *Le De Trinitate de Richard de Saint-Victor*, p. 12.

[82]See *De divisione naturae* III, 10 (PL 122, 650A): 'Nulla enim pejor mors est quam veritatis ignorantis.' This desire for objective truth is evident throughout this section of the Aenig and is expressed (424D): 'Ratio non est ratio, si non continuo abjecta cura verborum, veritati acquiescit.' The introductory section already suggests the influence of Erigena. Compare the prayer for truth (Aenig, 400D-401A) with Erigena, *De divisione naturae* III, 10 (PL 122, 649D-650B); the reference to the 'spinas' and 'tribulos' (Aenig, 406A) hindering the search for scriptural knowledge with *De divisione* IV, 2 (PL 122, 744B); and the text on the limitation of the knowledge of God to 'that he is' (Aenig, 397) with *De divisione* II, 27 (PL 122, 585B).

[83]Erigena's doctrine of the relationship between reason and authority gives a certain priority to reason. This applies especially to the authority of the Fathers: *De divisione naturae* IV, 15 (PL 122, 810C, 781C-D). M. Cappuyns, commenting on these texts, *Jean Scot Erigène, sa vie, son oeuvre, sa pensée*, admits that Erigena does not carry his principles to their extreme consequences, and that reason becomes a criterion of authority only in the case of dispute among the Fathers, referring to *De divisione naturae* II, 16 (PL 122, 548D-549A). But certainly his principle is very different from William's claim to follow only the authority of the Fathers. See Aenig, 432C. A. Forest (A. Fliche-V. Martin, *Histoire de l'Eglise*, XIII [Paris, 1951] p. 113) maintains that Erigena did not explicitly consider the relationship between faith and reason. But William's marked faith and sense of the submission of reason to faith through *ratio fidei* gives his 'intellectualism' a very

different tone from that of Erigena, one of the characteristics of *ratio fidei* being complete fidelity to the authority of the Fathers; see Err Guil, 334B-C.

[84]This is the first section of the central treatise on the divine names, Aenig, 418A-432D. In the course of this analysis of the trinitarian theology of the divine names references will be made also to the passages preceding and following this treatise, approaching the Trinity from the same speculative angle (cf. 410-414C, 434B-435A). The purpose of this grouping of the texts is to show the special character of this speculative development in the Aenig. This development offers a treatment of trinitarian problems from an angle which is primarily metaphysical, approaching the Trinity *quoad se*, rather than *quoad nos* and showing an advance on his purely polemical works. In this way an examination of the texts themselves will illustrate in greater detail the general principles underlying William's thought which have been outlined in the previous chapter.

[85]Aenig, 419D-420A. Cf. the source in St Augustine, *De trinitate* (PL 42, 916, 917): 'quidquid ad se dicitur praestantissima illa et divina sublimitas, substantialiter dici; quod enim ad aliquid, non substantialiter, sed relative: tantamque vim esse ejusdem substantiae in Patre et Filio et Spiritu Sancto, ut quidquid de singulis ad seipos dicitur, non pluraliter in summa, sed singulariter accipiatur.'

[86]Aenig, 418C. Cf. Erigena, *De divisione naturae* I, 15 (PL 122, 464A-B): 'non est quantitas, quia plus quam quantitas est. Caret igitur quantitate.' There is the same conception of the transcendance of God over human categories.

[87]Aenig, 418C-D: 'ubi accidens non est, neque substantia est....melius ergo essentia dicitur quam substantia.' Cf. the source St Augustine, *De Trinitate* VII, 5 (PL 42, 942): 'Essentia proprie dicitur....sive substantia quod abusive.'

[88]Aenig, 419B: 'neque secundum genus et speciem intelligenda aliquando est Trinitas Deus....essentiam ipsam nihil aliud esse quam tres personas et tres personas ipsam esse essentiam.' See **Erigena**, *De divisione naturae* I, 15 (PL 122, 463C): 'Deus autem nec genus nec species, nec accidens est.' William is here implicitly attacking Abelard's doctrine of generation in terms of genus and species: See Adv Abl, 255, 256A-D.

[89]Aenig, 420B-D.

[90]Ibid., 420C.

[91]Ibid., 420D: 'Tres tamen ibi essentias dicere non minus devitamus, quam tres Deos; cum non sit ibi aliud esse, aliud
Deum esse, sed idem est.'   Cf. the source in St Augustine, *De trinitate* VII, 3 (PL 42, 939):   'nec aliud est ibi esse quam Deum
esse.'   This may be a simple quotation from St Augustine or may
imply also an attack on the doctrine of Gilbert of Poitiers, who
was accused of distinguishing God and the divine essence by a real
distinction.   See A. Fliche-V. Martin, *Histoire de l'Eglise*, t.
XIII, 81; Ethier, *Le* De Trinitate, 25.   For this question of apologetics against Gilbert see Déchanet, *Guillaume de Saint-Thierry*,
79-80.   C. Oudin read the lost manuscript of William's *Sententiae
fidei*, written as a prolongation of the dispute against Abelard as
a basis for the Aenig, and held the theory that the *Sententiae*
were directed against Gilbert of Poitiers.   Yet it was only in
1146, after the letter in which William mentions the *Sententiae*,
that the doctrines of Gilbert of Poitiers were beginning to arouse
suspicion.   On the other hand, a treatise on the divine relations
against Gilbert of Poitiers has been attributed to William on the
faith of a manuscript of Clermont.   This treatise is only a docu-
mented account of a discussion at Rheims on the doctrines of Gilbert of Poitiers.   But it is probably written by Geoffrey of Auxerre and is published by Mabillon under the title of *Ejusdem Gau-
fridi contra capitula Gilberti Pictaviensis Episcopi* (PL 185, 595-
618).

[92]Aenig, 420D: 'Essentiam Patrem, essentiam Filium, essentiam Spiritum Sanctum.'

[93]Ibid., 421A: 'Haec autem omnia nomina....sicut tres
ibi sunt, et unum tres, sic ipsa omnia sunt unum, et unum omnia
....Hoc enim ibi est posse, quod velle, quod sapere, quod nosse,
et quod caetera omnia; quae, ut dictum est, essentialiter et ad
se de Deo praedicantur.'

[94]Ibid., 421B: 'Non minus est in singulis quam in omnibus, sed totum in singulis est, et in omnibus unum.   Alioquin non
simplex esset Deus noster, sed multiplex.   Non solum autem, sed et
omnia haec simul sunt singularum in Trinitate personarum; ut sicut
in Deo unum sunt haec omnia, sic haec omnia sit quaelibet
in Trinitate persona.'   See the source in St Augustine, *De trinitate* VII, 10 (PL 42, 932).   'Summa Trinitate tantum est una quam
tres....ita et singula sunt in singulis, et omnia in singulis, et
singula in omnibus, et omnia in omnibus et unum omnia.'

[95]See Adv Abl, 250A-B; Abelard, *De unitate et trinitate*

divina (ed. R. Stolzle [Fribourg, 1891] pp. 2-4, 60-62). See also Err Guil, 333C, a text quoted from *De philosophia mundi*, now attributed to de Conchis (PL 172, 44D-45A).

[96]Aenig, 421C: 'Sicut enim non aliter potens est Deus, aliter sapiens, aliter bonus; sic nec, quantum in ipso est, aliter agit quae sunt potentiae, aliter quae sunt sapientiae, aliter quae bonitatis.' See St Augustine's doctrine, *De trinitate* I, 12 (PL 42, 838): 'etiam de singulis dici quod omnium est, propter inseparabilem operationem unis ejusdemque substantiae.' See also, Ibid., IV, 21 (909); Schmaus, *Trinitätslehre*, p. 152.

[97]Aenig, 422C.

[98]Ibid., 421D.

[99]Ibid., 422C-D: 'Quae cum sit inseparabilis, numquam intelligeretur Trinitas, si simper inseparabilis diceretur.'

[100]Ibid., 422C.

[101]This shows the influence of St Augustine. See Schmaus, *Trinitätslehre*, 390-391, 415, showing that the concept though not the term is present in St Augustine. The doctrine is explicitly formulated in St Thomas, I[a], q. 39, a. 7-8.

[102]There is only one transient suggestion of the approach from the distinction of Persons, whereby the inseparability of the Persons is seen as following not from the unity of essence, but from the very nature of the personal relations themselves in so far as they are *ad invicem*. Cf. Aenig, 420B: 'haec autem in eo quod singulorum propria sunt singula, Trinitatis veritatem: in eo autem quod ad invicem sunt et se alterum ad alterum ipso singularitatis suae nomine referri ostendunt, substantiae unitatem.' This is immediately preceeded by the approach from the unity of nature: 'in eo quod in summa semper unum sunt, consubstantialem unitatem.' This is an example of the blend of the two approaches, which we shall find more marked in the section on proper names, where the contrast between these two approaches is explained and illustrated more completely.

[103]See the whole of the second chapter of Adv Abl, 250A-254C and 256A-D, 258D-259B).

[104]Aenig, 422C. In itself this doctrine does not imply the approach from the unity of nature, as it is evident from its presence in Scripture, which presents the Trinity primarily through the distinctions of Persons. Cf. Eph 1, 3, 4, 6; I Petr

1, 3. But in the present context, the primacy of the argument
from the unity of nature is always apparent. The purpose of the
argument is to emphasize the unity of divine essence, the identity
of the Persons with the divine essence, and consequently the impossibility of founding a distinction of Persons on a distinction
of divine attributes. The question of appropriation is introduced
as if in a fictitious objection to the preceeding argument. The
objection is shown to be invalid, as he shows from the meaning of
'Sapientia quippe Patris Filius est,' of *De trinitate* VII, I (PL
42, 935, 936). He shows according to St Augustine's argument that
the meaning of this expression is not that the Father is wise
through the Son, as if the Father were not himself Wisdom, but that
the wisdom of the Son comes from the Father as from its origin.
See Aenig, 422A: 'Sapientia de Sapientia.'

[105]Ibid., 421D.

[106]Ibid., 422D.

[107]Ibid. See the source in St Leo, *Sermon 76* (PL 54, 405B):
'Bene ergo ipsa difficultas loquendi cor nostrum ad intelligentiam
trahit....'

[108]Ibid., 422D. This conception of the transcendence of
the divine names reflects the theology of Erigena, *De divisione
naturae* II, 28 (PL 122, 589C): 'hoc vere est mirabile nomen, quod
est super omne nomen. See also 510C: 'super omnem essentiam et
intelligentiam.' William was also influenced by St Augustine on
this question. Cf. Aenig, 411C; Spec fid, (*Le miroir*) 168, 394C:
'Interim etenim etsi non potest Deus videri, vel cognosci sicut
est, non parum proficit proficiens, si nil pro Deo suscipit quod
ipse non est.' This shows a verbal similarity to *De trinitate*
VIII, 2 (PL 42, 948): 'non enim parvae notitiae pars est....si
antequam scire possimus quid sit Deus, possumus jam scire quid non
sit.' But the text under discussion with its reference to the divine names suggests rather the influence of Erigena's 'super omne
nomen,' especially in view of the Dionysian character of the Aenig,
emphasizing above all the transcendance of the Trinity.

[109]Aenig, 423-425D. Cf. St Augustine, *De trinitate* V, 15
(PL 42, 922-924).

[110]Aenig, 425C-D: 'Nomina tamen creatoris ad creaturam
non relative accidentia, sed principalem in Deo essentiam creaturae
significantia intelligantur.' The importance given to the relationship between God and creatures can be explained by the implied attack on Abelard's doctrine of the Holy Ghost as an extension of God

ad extra towards creation. See Adv Abl, 261A-C.

[111]Aenig, 425D. This refers to 410D-411A, where this rule
is shown to be the principle that whatever is predicated on of the
Persons *ad se* is predicated substantially. See also 419D-420A.

[112]Ibid., 425D.

[113]See *De trinitate* V, 13 (PL 42, 920): 'Pater et Filius
simul ad creaturam unum principium est, sicut unus creator, sicut
unus Deus....non possumus negare etiam Spiritum Sanctum recte dici
principium, quia non eum separamus ab appellatione creatoris.'

[114]*Comm. in Sent.* I, d. 11, q. 1, a. 4 *ad* 2. See A. Malet,
Personne et amour, pp. 85-86.

[115]In relation to St Augustine and St Anselm, see Malet,
24-57.

[116]The guiding principle is once again that of the unity
of the Persons in whatever is predicated *ad se*. See Aenig, 411A:
'quidquid de singulis ad seipsos dictur non pluraliter in summa,
sed singulariter accipiatur.'

[117]Ibid., 412A. He adds (412B) that whenever Scripture
writes 'one' without further qualification, it implies unity of
nature. See St Augustine, *De trinitate* VI, 3 (PL 42, 926).

[118]Aenig, 412B: 'non habens partes, sed in omni quod est
vel habet, habens integrum totum suum; si tamen omne, vel totum,
vel integrum dici potest, ubi partes nullae sunt.'

[119]Ibid., 412B-C.

[120]Ibid., 412C. This problem of number was the subject of
discussion amongst theologians of the period. Haring, 'The Case
of Gilbert de la Porrée,' p. 25, refers to this problem in relation
to Gilbert de la Porrée, explaining that Gilbert 'stressed the numerical plurality of the trinitarian Persons against the actual
dangers of veiled Sabellianism apparent in a widespread opposition
to a numerical distinction,' but 'warned that it is not a number
in the ordinary sense.' He refers to *De trinitate* (PL 64, 126B)
and to the same problem in St Bernard, *Csi* V, 7 (PL 182, 798C) and
also to the text of William of St Thierry, *Aenigma fidei*, 410C.
Haring remarks that the criticism of the use of the term number is
to be explained by 'the then widely accepted opinion that numerical
distinction is due to accidents and thereby not applicable to the

trinitarian distinctions.'

The question of William's argument being directed against
Gilbert of Poitiers is disputable. However that may be, the texts
of William on number in the Trinity reflect one of the problems of
the period, and his strong emphasis on the identity of the Persons
with the divine nature contrasts with the doctrine of a substance
distinct from the three Persons which had been **attributed** to Gilbert. We are reminded of the text of St Bernard in *Csi* V, 7-8
(PL 182, 797A-800A), where the unity of the divine nature is
strongly emphasized with a distinctly polemical tone in opposition
to the doctrine attributed to Gilbert of Poitiers. The date of
the text of St Bernard is 1152-1153, after William's death.

At the same time William was aware of the difficulty in
the approach from the unity of the nature as is shown in his problem of discovering how number can arise from this unity and later
in the question of the ontological foundation of the Persons.

[121]Aenig, 410D.

[122]Ibid., 410D. Cf. Med, 210B: 'extra omnem numerum.'

[123]Aenig, 435A.

[124]See Erigena, *De divisione naturae*, I, 14 (PL 122, 462C):
'Essentia est, affirmatio; essentia non est, abdicatio; superes-
sentialis est, affirmatio simul et abdicatio.' See F. Copleston,
A History of Philosophy, vol. II, p. 119, showing this dialectic
of thesis, antithesis, synthesis.

[125]*De divisione naturae* II, 35 (PL 122, 614C); see I, 13
(456A). Erigena is here the medium of the doctrine of Dionysius,
De divinis nominibus XIII, 3 (PG 3, 980).

[126]See the polemics against Abelard: Adv Abl 3, 255D-260C.

[127]Aenig, 411D.

[128]Ibid., 411D, referring to Jn 10 30.

[129]Ibid., 412C: 'Cum ergo quaeritur de Patre, et Filio,
et Spiritu Sancto si tres, quid tres? ex **auctoritate** Domini, et
secundum rationem fidei, nil melius, seu convenientius veritati
respondetur, quam unum.'   In this sense of the mystery underlying
this problem he is influenced by St Augustine. The text 411C:
'Excedit vero supereminentia divinitatis omnem communis eloquii
facultatem,' is from *De trinitate* VII, 4 (PL 42, 939), where St
Augustine writes treating of the same problem: 'quid tres?....

excedit supereminentia divinitatis usitati eloquii facultatem.'

[130]Ibid., 412A.

[131]See Malet, *Personne et amour*, pp. 22-24.

[132]See *De trinitate* (PL 42, 943): 'neque in hac Trinitate cum dicimus personam Patris aliud dicimus quam substantiam Patris.' See I. Chevalier, *S. Augustin et la pensée grecque. Les relations trinitaires*, p. 48, showing that although the two concepts of Person and substance are not absolutely synonymous there is no real distinction. See also A. Malet, 22.

[133]See, *In Psalmum 68* (PL 36, 845): 'Pater non ad se sed ad Filium dicitur; ad se autem Deus dicitur.' See Malet, 23 and Chevalier, 69-73.

[134]See *Monologion 38* (ed. F. S. Schmitt I, 56), and Perino, *La dottrina trinitaria de Sant' Anselmo*, p. 171.

[135]*Monologion 79* (Schmitt I, 85). The same difficulty is illustrated in chapter 38 of the *Monologion* (I, 59), v. 27; 'sic est idipsum quod est et Pater et Filius ut non intelligam quid duos dixerim.' For this problem in St Anselm see R. Perino, 173: 'Finchè la relazione **trinitaria** rimane principio dialettico e non è considerata *entitativamente*, per contraccolpo la natura (il *quid sit*) delle persone divine rimane **preclusa in** modo assoluto a qualsiasi grado di conescenza.' See also Malet, 56-57.

[136]*Comm. in Sent.* I, d. 23, a. 3, *in fine corp.*

[137]See I^a, *q*. 41, *a*. 5, *ad* I: 'dicimus quod essentia divina est principium quo generans generat.' Malet demonstrates this doctrine of St Thomas with a close examination of the texts (pp. 72-78), and he summarizes this Thomistic theme with a description of generation (pp. 117-118): 'La génération va d'un sujet à un sujet à travers la nature.'

[138]Aenig, 412D-413A. The whole text beginning 'timuit catholica pietas dicere tres essentias....' follows closely St Augustine *De trinitate* VII, 4 (PL 42, 941-942): '**timuit** dicere tres essentias....' See the explanation of the use of the term Person for apologetic reasons, Aenig, 412C: 'Placuit tamen Patribus propter disputandi necessitatem' and St Augustine *De trinitate* V, 9 (918).

[139]Aenig, 413A; St Augustine, *De trinitate* V, 9 (918).

140Aenig, 413B-C. Abelard also rejected this definition:
Tractatus (ed. Stolzle, p. 95); *Theologia christiana* III (PL 178,
1258C).

141*Liber de persona et duabus naturis* 3 (PL 64, 1343C).
In *De trinitate* XV, 7 (PL 42, 1065) St Augustine virtually accepts
all the elements of this definition: 'una persona, id est singu-
lus quisque homo....id est substantia rationalis constans ex anima et corpore.' See Chevalier, p. 53. The definition of 'person'
in absolute terms had already aroused suspicion in the early Middle Ages. See Haring, 'The case of Gilbert de la Porrée, p. 19.
Haring refers to the opposition to Gilbert in his definition of
person as *per se una* and **mentions** that Hincmar of Rheims rejected
Godescalc's description of person as *per se una* on the grounds that
it overstressed the idea of individual substance (PL 125, 581A,
586A, 587C).

142Aenig, 413C-D. Déchanet suggests the possible influence
of St Basil on this text: *Guillaume de Saint-Thierry*, p. 97, footnote referring to St Basil *Ep* 236, 6 (PG 32, 883) where ὑπόστασισ
is opposed to οὐσία and ὑπόστασισ is seen as a means of our knowledge, ἔννοια, of the Persons. The ἔννοια of St Basil can be compared with the *agnitio* of William. William's 'tres personae com-
muni nomine' (Aenig, 413C) can be compared with St Basil's contrast between ὑπόστασισ and οὐσια as the individual to the common
element (see PG 32, 884). It is very probably that the preceding
epistle of St Basil, 235 (PG 32, 872) influenced William in the
text comparing the growth of *ratio fidei* to the **formation** of the
letters of the alphabet (Aenig, 416C-D; see Déchanet, *Guillaume de
Saint-Thierry*, 95). William also shows a knowledge of the Greek
terminology in the context of the passage on the definition of Person; Aenig, 414A: 'Personas sive, ut Graeci dicunt, hypostases,
hoc est subsistentias.' See also the context on the Greek theme
of the Persons as relations of origin. It is therefore possible
that he may have been influenced by St Basil in this definition of
person, but no definite conclusion can be drawn.

This definition occurs also in the anonymous *De diversi-
tate naturae et personae*, quoted by J. de Ghellinck, 'L'histoire
de persona,' *Revue néoscolastique de philosophie* 36 (1934) 115.
See Haring, 'The case of Gilbert de la Porrée,' p. 20.

143Aenig, 413D; also 429D-430A. On this point he is in the
tradition of the Greek Fathers, who conceived the persons in terms
of relations of origin. See Malet, p. 13.

144Aenig, 413D; also 428A: 'trium personarum, seu mutu-
arum ad invicem relationum.'

145Ibid., 411B.

146Ibid., 411B: 'omne quod relative ad aliquid dicitur, est etiam aliquid ad se, praeter id quod relative ad aliquid dicitur.'

147Ibid., 411C: 'Tria ergo aliqua, seu tres aliqui ad se sunt; qui Pater, et Filius, et Spiritus Sanctus ad invicem sunt.'

148Ibid.

149Ibid. See a similar passage in St Bernard, *Csi* V, 7 (PL 182, 799A). St Bernard, starting also from the initial assumption of the unity of nature, is unable to discover how a plurality of Persons can arise within this nature: 'Quid numerasti? Natura? Una est. Essentia? Una est....'

150Aenig, 428D-429A.

151The reference to the Greek Terminology 'hypostases' (*hoc est subsistentias*) does not alter this strongly essentialist trend. The significance is purely terminological as is shown by William's dilemma in finding the ontological foundation of Person, unable to find a *tertium quid* between 'essence' and 'relation.' The reference is to a text falsely attributed to St Jerome: 'personas sive, ut Graeci exprimunt, hypostases.' **See Err Guil, 336B,** explicitly referring to St Jerome. The use of this terminology is resumed again by Peter Lombard *I Sent.* (PL 192, 589). There is a further suggestion of Peter Lombard's doctrine on the Persons as excluding *solitudo* in the Trinity. See Aenig, 434D: 'Solitudinem non recipiat Patris et Filii et Spiritus Sancti Trinitas,' and Peter Lombard *I Sent.* (PL 192, 589). See Malet, 64-65, for Peter Lombard's doctrine of Person. Some mutual influence of William and Peter Lombard is possible. Peter Lombard held the chair of theology at Notre Dame 1135-1150, contemporary with William's principle works.

152*De trinitate* VII, 2 (PL 42, 936): 'Sapientia de sapientia, sicut essentia de essentia,' is an example of St Augustine's apparent acceptance of the doctrine that generation follows from the essence. Chapter 7 of book XV *De trinitate* (1065-1067) affirms both the doctrine of Person generating Person, and essence generating essence. See Malet, p. 24.

153Aenig, 422A: 'Sapientia de sapientia....essentia de essentia.' The source is *De trinitate* VII, 2 (PL 42, 936).

154Aenig, 432B.

155Malet, p. 31.   This work gives an appendix on the sources of the Greek Fathers which were available to the mediaeval
theologians (see pp. 161-187) and suggests (31) that the more personalistic trend in the middle ages was influenced by the Greek
Fathers.   But he was against an over-simplification of this question.   He refers to Abelard's knowledge of the Greek Fathers together with his modalistic trinitarian theology, and to Richard of
St Victor's Augustinian inspiration together with his emphasis on
the Persons.

156Ibid., 31-53.

157Ibid., 31-34.

158Ibid., he refers to M. E. Williams, *The Teaching of Gil-*
bert Porreta on the Trinity as Found in His Commentaries on Boeth-
ius (Rome, 1951), and to Haring, 'The Case of Gilbert de la Porrée,' whose interpretations are on the same lines as William's
(Malet, 32-33, footnote 3).   Malet refers (p. 35) to the conclusion of William's (p. 104):   'Williams pense à juste titre que,
sur la question des rapports de la personne et de la nature, on ne
peut pas prouver que la position de Gilbert soit très différente
de celle de saint Thomas.'

159Chenu, *La théologie au XIIe siècle*, p. 308, appears to
support Malet by his reference to Gilbert's development of a personalistic trinitarian theology.

160M. A. Schmidt, *Gottheit und Trinität nach dem Kommentar*
des Gilbert Porreta zu Boethius De Trinitate (Basel, 1956).

161Ibid., 21, 164, 168, especially 164:   'daruber hinaus
aber ist Gilbert der göttlichen Seinseinheit so verhaftet, dass
er noch viel weniger als Augustin zu einer Darlegung dessen kommt
was die drei Personen eigentlich seien.'

162Ibid., 13, 14, 164, and especially, 110-111, footnotes
287 and 288, where he refers to the text of Gilbert's commentary
In librum De Trinitate (see PL 64, 1279C):   'ut Sabelliani....vel-
utius animae mentem, notitiam, amorem....'

163Ibid., 168:   'über Augustine und Boethius hinaus ver-
sucht er dann wieder, das Wort 'Person' in der Trinität....aus einem Verlegenheitswort zu einem inhaltlich gefüllten Analogiebegriff
zu machen.'

[164]Ibid.: 'Dieser Versuch konnte nur in sehr bescheidenem Masse gelingen'; p. 113, footnote 193: 'faktisch doch nicht sehr viel weiter kommen als Augustin und Boethius.' See also p. 164.

[165]Admittedly, Schmidt (p. 157) associates the *quod est* primarily with Person, and the *quo est* with nature, but the nature is also associated with *quod est* ('dass neben dem dreifachen *quod* noch ein einfaches *quod* gibt....') and the Persons also with the *quo* ('Die Zahlbarkeit....muss ihr eigenes *quo est* haben....' and again, 158: 'also müssen hier drei verschieden *quo est* angenommen werden, die als die Relationen der drei Personen bezeichnet werden'). Haring, 'The Case of Gilbert de la Porrée, 15-16 and 18 referring to the text of Otto of Freising, *Gesta Friderici,* I, 52 (MGH SS, xx, 379): 'Patrem alio esse esse Deum.' See the article of Haring p. 16) explaining that the meaning is 'the Father as God has another *quo* than the Father as the Father.'

[166]J. Cottiaux, 'La conception de la théologie chez Abélard,' RHE 28 (1932) 813-814: 'Cette manière d'isoler les mots de leur contenu est déconcertante mais non pas singulière à l'époque d'Abelard. Gilbert de la Porrée agit de la même façon quand il raisonne sur la divinité en la distinguant de la nature divine.' See Haring, 'The Case of Gilbert de la Porrée,' p. 18 'his differentiation between God and **Divinity** is basically one of grammar formally one of logic and not of **metaphysics**,' and again, p. 40: 'Gilbert's use of *id quo* and *quod* in its numerous applications is first of all an application of a grammatical and logical rule of speech.'

[167]See the treatment of Abelard's trinitarian theology by Malet, pp. 60-62, repeating the accusations of Sabellianism without even a reference to Cottiaux or an attempt to answer his arguments based on a close study of the texts of Abelard; J. Cottiaux, 'Théologie chez Abélard,' 247-295, 533-551, 787-828.

[168]Haring, 'The Case of Gilbert de la Porrée,' especially pp. 18-26. See p. 20 referring to Geoffrey's assertion *Contra Gilbertum* (PL 185, 609C-D) that Gilbert taught that 'the personal *proprietates* are as he [Gilbert] affirms, numerically so distinct, that the divine Substance is one *unum* and each *proprietas* another *unum*.'

[169]The definition 'cujus pro sui forma certa sit agnitio' does not offer a satisfactory metaphysical solution. It does not offer a definition of Person in its ultimate ontological reality, but defines Person simply as a means of manifesting to us the distinction of the opposing relations.

[170]Perino, *La dottrina trinitaria*, pp. 179, 182.

[171]His approach to the problem of Person is based on this conception of *ratio fidei* and is a resumption of traditional doctrine rather than an attempt towards further progress through metaphysical reflection on the meaning of Person. See Aenig, 413D: 'Haec de nomine personae, quod in causa et ratione fidei a sanctis Patribus appositum est.'

[172]Aenig, 427A.

[173]Ibid.:   'rerum notitiam, quarum signa sunt, minime impleta.'

[174]Ibid., 409C-D: In the general rules for the evolution of dogma, 'non tam signa ipsa nominum vel verborum attendenda sunt, quam id quod per signa ipsa designatur.'

[175]Ibid., 427A: 'quantum nos verba adjuvare possunt, veneranda et amplectenda nobis sunt; ubi vero deficiunt verba, sicut verba, cum gratia ejus qui nominatur et benedictione, pertranseunda sunt.'

[176]See *De divisione naturae* II, 35 (PL 122, 614C): quaecumque de simplicissimae bonitatis Trinitate dicuntur, seu cogitantur, seu intelliguntur, vestigia quaedam sunt atque theophaniae veritatis, non autem ipsa veritas, quae superat omnem theoriam non solum rationalis, verum etiam intellectualis creaturae.' See also *De praedestinatione* IX, 2(390C).

[177]Forest writes of Erigena (Fliche-Martin, *Histoire de l'Eglise*, t. XIII, p. 11):   'Il ne faut songer à aucun type de connaissance qui ne procéderait pas d'une influence surnaturelle ....la raison est en elle-même l'instrument d'une connaissance religieuse,' but there is not the same explicit insistence on faith which we find in William's unique concept of *ratio fidei*.

[178]Aenig, 428A: 'rerum enim divinarum intellectus, quarum haec signa videntur esse, non tam per haec datur, quam ad intelligendum de Deo quod cupimus, forma hac sanorum in fide verborum informamur et nutrimur.' See also 427A. This whole passage on the limitations of human words and concepts reflects his apologetics against Abelard.

[179]Ibid., 430B-C: 'altera se habeat circa ea quae ad se sunt, servando ubique unitatem; altera circa id quod ad invicem sunt, praedicando Trinitatem.' See also 420A. 'Ad invicem' is

specifically stated to be 'relation'; see 428A: 'ad invicem tres Personae relative.' The texts contrasting 'ad aliquid' with 'secundum substantiam' (418B, 419A) illustrate the Aristotelian and Augustinian concept of relation in opposition to substance as opposed to the neoplatonic tendency in the Greek Fathers, showing relation in terms of the bond uniting the processions in their dynamic movement proceeding from and returning to the principle of the Father. For this theme see Chevalier, *S. Augustin et la pensée grecque*, 167-179.

[180]Aenig, 428A: 'tres personae relative....non secundum accidens.'

[181]Ibid., 428C-D: 'omnis essentia quae relative dicitur est etiam aliquid, excepto relativo suo, sicut homo dominus.... sed homo dominus et homo servus, cum ad invicem dicuntur duo homines sunt. Deus autem Pater et Deus Filius, non duo dii sed unus Deus sunt.' See St Augustine, *De trinitate* VII (PL 42, 934-935). This is an interesting example of William's choice of a text from the Fathers, adapting it to illustrate a different theme from its original purpose. St Augustine uses this argument to prove that the Father cannot be wise only through the wisdom of the Son, whereas William uses it to show the transcendance of 'relation' in the Trinity.

[182]Aenig, 428A. This principle is summarized very clearly in 419C: 'extra omnem regulam relativorum una substantia suam verissimam ac solidissiman teneat unitatem.' Cf. similar emphasis in Erigena on the transcendance of relation; *De divisione naturae* I, 16 (PL 122-465B): 'ut enim, ni fallor, quem ad modum superat omnem essentiam, sapientiam, virtutem, ita etiam et omnem habitudinem ineffabiliter supergraditur. Quid enim crediderit, talem habitudinem inter Patrem et Verbum suum esse qualem inter Abraham et Isaac potest cogitare.'

[183]Cf. DThC XIII, 2136; Michel 'Relations divines,' 66-67; Chevalier, *S. Augustin et la pensée grecque*, 29-36.

[184]Cf. Perino, *La dottrina trinitaria*, p. 171.

[185]The apologetic purpose of the concept of relation is present but is wholly subsidiary to the theme of the mystery; cf. the transient reference to the apologetic argument. Aenig, 430C: 'relatio tres personas relative se habentes ad invicum dicit, sed tres Deos dici omnino contradicit.'

[186]Cf. M. T.-L. Penido, *Le rôle de l'analogie en théologie*

dogmatique (Paris, 1931). His analysis of subsisting relations according to the concept of an analogy of proper proportion is an example of a recent work, which expounds the problem with great skill, but not sufficiently stressing that the mystery is in no way lessened through being stated in terms of relation. See p. 312, on the role of analogy: 'son rôle qui consiste non point à demontrer le *an sit* ou le *quid sit*, mais à expliquer le *quomodo sit.*' His conclusion, p. 322-323, is: 'Nous soupçonnons enfin que Dieu doit être aussi nécessairement trine qu'il est un. Pourquoi? Nous ne saurions le dire, mais n'est-ce point beaucoup que l'analogie, en nous montrant la sureminence ineffable et féconde, nous ait montré le pourquoi de cette nuit?'

[187]I[a], *q.* 27, *a.* 2, c.

[188]Cf. Aenig 427A-B; such terms as 'gignens' and 'procedens' are 'divina quaedam instrumenta....sed tamen rerum notitiam, quarum signa sunt, minime impleta.' See the whole context from 426D contrasting the different methods in the knowledge of human and divine things 'quibus significandis nulla prosus verba idonea sunt.'

[189]Ibid., 427B.

[190]Ibid., 427B-C. Compare 'non ita esse semper, quasi ex quo natus est Filius....sed ex eo quod semper natus est Filius' with the source in St Augustine *De trinitate* V, 5 (PL 42, 914).

[191]Aenig, 428B.

[192]Ibid., 436D.

[193]Ibid., 427D.

[194]Ibid., 430D: 'Unum enim sunt principium Spiritus Sancti, Pater et Filius, sed principaliter Pater, quoniam et hoc Filius a Patre nascendo accepit, ut cum Patre unum et ipse principium Spiritus Sancti sit.' Cf. 435D-436A. See St Augustine *De trinitate* XV, 17, 26; V, 14 (PL 42, 1081, 1094, 921): 'non duo principia....sic relative ad Spiritum Sanctum unum principium.'

[195]*Summa, Pars* I, *inq.* 2, *tract. un, q.* I, *tit.* 2, *c.* 1 et 5 (ed. Quaracchi 1924, t. I, n⁰ 304, 311).

[196]*I Sent. d.* 29, *a.* 2, *q.* 2 (ed. Quaracchi 1882, t. I, p. 515).

[197]*I Sent.*, *d.* 11, *q.* i, *a.* 4.

[198]See *I Sent.*, *d.* 29, *q.* I, *a.* 4, *ad* 3, and *Summa theol.*
I^a, *q.* 36, *a.* 4, *ad* 6. See Malet, *Personne et amour*, pp. 143, 145,
and 48-53 for this doctrine in Alexander of Hales and St Bonaventure.

[199]See Aenig, 435D, where this doctrine of the procession
of the Holy Ghost coincides with his introduction of the presentation of the Persons *quod nos:* 'ex patre, per Filium, in Spiritu
ad Patrem' (see 436AB and 430D-431A).

[200]431A: 'Pater enim ex nullo originem ducens, origo divinitatis est. De ipso vero habet Filius quod nascendo ab eo accepit, ut naturali essentia unum cum ipso est.' See Régnon, *La
sainte Trinité*, vol. I, c. 2, pp. 341, 342, 343.

[201]See Régnon, p. 410ff., especially p. 410, distinguishing the two methods: 'Les personnes sont l'une dans l'autre parce
qu'elles sont consubstantielles....Les personnes sont consubstantielles parce qu'elles sont l'une dans l'autre.'

[202]Aenig, 429C-D.

[203]See also 427C for the same argument: 'veritate unius
divinae essentiae.'

[204]See St John Damascen, *De fide orthodoxa* I, 8 (PG 94,
829).

[205]Régnon, p. 409ff. This passage may have been influenced
by St Athanasius: See *Epistola I ad Serapionem* 14 (PG 26, 565,
A-B). See the similarity between PG 26, 565 A-B: καὶ λεγομένου
τοῦ Πατρὸσ, πρόσεστι καὶ ο τούτου λόγοσ.....and Aenig, 429D: 'cum
enim dicitur Pater intelligitur pariter et Filius....' This is the
source suggested by Déchanet, *Guillaume de Saint-Thierry*, p. 203.
There is the possibility also of the influence of St Hilary on his
argument to unity through opposing relations; compare St Hilary
De trinitate VII, 32 (PL 10, 227A): 'nec non unum sunt qui invicem sunt. Invicem autem sunt cum unus ex uno est,' and Aenig,
429D: 'id circo relatio ipsa vocabuli Personas separari vetat,
quas cum simul nominat, simul etiam insinuat.'

[206]Aenig, 431C-432B.

[207]Exp Rom, 590C, 592C.

208Aenig, 431C-432A.

209Ibid., 591D.

210Ibid., 435D-440D.

211The trinitarian life *quoad nos* is usually related in William's theology to the inward development of the soul. This contrasts with the more objective historical presentation of the works of the Trinity *ad extra* in the *De trinitate* of Rupert of Deutz. These concluding passages of the Aenig are exceptions to this general rule. The wide historical trinitarian scheme revealing in turn the works of the Father, the Son and the Holy Ghost recalls the approach to the Trinity of Rupert of Deutz. Some influence from Rupert is possible, especially when it is recalled that William's treatise *De sacramento altaris* was an epistle to Rupert showing a familiarity with Rupert's doctrine. See 341A: 'Lego et relego, charissime, opus vestrum de officiis....' But the similarity of the treatment of the trinitarian economy in the Aenig and that of the *De trinitate* of Rupert of Deutz is not sufficiently close to prove with certainty any direct influence. The specific character of Rupert's doctrine is absent. See the prologue to the *De trinitate* of Rupert (PL 167, 197-200). This particular interpretation of the trinitarian economy is based on a triple division of history, from creation to the fall, from the fall to the passion of Christ, from the resurrection to the end of the world. These three phases are seen as the special works of the Father, the Son and the Holy Ghost respectively. See ibid., 199A-B: 'Et primum quidem Patris, secundum autem Filii, tertium vero Spiritus Sancti proprium opus est.' In this way we are able to see the glory of the Trinity reflected in the works of creation and redemption. See ibid., 247A-B: 'quid enim propositum est nisi sanctae Trinitatis gloriam per opera ipsius quasi per speculum contemplari,' and also 198D.

212Aenig, 435D and 437C-D.

213Ibid., 435D: 'principaliter Pater, non principaliter quasi praecipue, vel principaliter aliqua seu temporis seu dignitatis sed originis.'

214Ibid., 435D.

215Ibid., 436A.

216Ibid. The source is St Augustine. See note 194 above.

[217] Ibid.

[218] Ibid., 436D-437A.

[219] Ibid., 437A: 'Sic Verbum caro factum est assumendo eam in qua manifestaretur hominibus.' Cf. Augustine, *De trinitate* X, 11 (PL 42, 1072): 'Sicut Verbum Dei caro factum est, assumendo eam in qua et ipsum manifestaretur sensibus hominum.' For this theme see also St Irenaeus, *Adv. haereses* IV, 6, 5 (PG 7, 989) and Origen, Περὶ ἀρχῶν I, 2, 8 (PG 11, 136).

[220] Aenig, 437A-B, with the reference in 437B to the 'animal state': 'docuit enim carnales homines sensibus carnis deditos,' recalling the introductory section of the Aenig, treating of this theme (402B-403D).

[221] Aenig, 439B.

[222] Ibid., 439C.

[223] Ibid., 439C-440D. In this concluding passage there is a reference clearly to St Augustine. Compare 440C 'perfundens omnia....' with *De trinitate* VII, 10 (PL 42, 932); 439D 'donorum Dei....' suggests Didymus, *De Spiritu Sancto* 8 (PG 39, 1040C), and expressions such as: 'disponens utilia....divisiones gratiarum' can be compared with Erigena's conception of the Holy Ghost distributing gifts throughout creation (*De divisione naturae* II, 22 PL 122, 563B: 'distributionem Spiritui Sancto,' and 563D: 'per differentias....distribueret atque ordinaret....').

[224] Aenig, 431C-D.

[225] Aenig, 431D. For this conception in the Greek Fathers, see Régnon, *La sainte Trinite*, vol. I, p. 346-365.

[226] This text shows a similarity with St Basil, *De Spiritu Sancto* 2, PG 32, 73, especially where St Basil refers to the interchange of the particles *ex-per-in* among the Persons. Cf. Ibid. 5 (81B-C): τὸ ἐξ οὗ τῷ Τίῳ προσαρμόζον...τὴν δι' οὗ φωνὴν τῷ Θεῷ πρέπειν...: Ibid. 84C: ἐν...ὅτι καὶ ἐπὶ τοῦ Θεοῦ καὶ Πατρὸσ; cf. Aenig, 432A: 'videre enim Filio Patrem hoc est esse, quod ille est; videre operantem, cooperari est....,' and 430A: 'sicut nulla potest esse separabilitas operis, ita naturaliter manet unitas incommutabilis.' The inseparability of the operations of the Persons suggests Basil, *Epistle* 139 (PG 32, 693A): Ἐὰν δὲ μίαν νοήσωμεν τὴν ἐνέργειαν Πατρόσ τε καὶ Τίοῦ καὶ Πνεύματοσ ἁγίου, ἐν μηδενὶ διαφέρουσάν τι ἢ παραλλάσσουσαν· ἀνάγκη τῇ ταυτότητι τῆσ ἐνεργείασ

τό ἡνωμένον τῆσ φύσεωσ συλλογίζεσθαι. This similarity has
been observed by Déchanet (*Guillaume de Saint-Thierry*, p. 105,
footnote). The influence of St Basil is not improbable, especially in view of the possibility of Latin translations of *De Spiritu
Sancto* in the Middle Ages. See Malet, *Personne et amour*, p. 164,
referring to the testimony of Fortunatus that the Merovingian period had access to translations of St Basil (cf. PL 88, 263).

[227]Aenig, 431D.

[228]Ibid. Cf. the doctrine of the Greek Fathers on the illustration of unity in the Trinity through the movement of recol-
lection *in-per-ad*, which brings back the expanding movement *ex-per-
in* into unity. Cf. Pope Dionysius (H. Denzinger 48): ἤδη καὶ τὴν
θείαν τριάδα εἰσ ἕνα, ὥσπερ εἰσ κόρυφήν τινα, τὸν Θεὸν τῶν ὅλων
τὸν πολυκράτορα λέγω, συγκεφαλαιοῦσθαί τε καὶ συνάγεσθαι πᾶσα
ἀνάγκη.

[229]Aenig, 435D-440D.

[230]Ibid., 436A. Cf. the test in the central treatise,
426C, where there is a suggestion of the trinitarian economy with
a similar emphasis on Christ as mediator. In this text Christ is
seen as mediator praying to the Father and manifesting him, while
continuing this role through communicating the gift of the Holy
Spirit.

[231]Ibid., 436B. Note also the care to avoid this danger
throughout the concluding section (437C): 'Ne missio Filii a Patre quasi separabilis intelligatur'; 437D: 'servilem enim formam
quam unigenitus Deus assumpsit, tota Trinitas fecit'; 438B: 'sicut inseparabilis in natura divinitatis necesse est credere tres
Personas.'

[232]The concluding section follows the 'Greek' way more in
what is traditional, scriptural and liturgical, rather than in
what is specific to the Greek Fathers, i.e. in presenting the *ex*,
per, *in* scheme according to the economy *ad extra* rather than in the
intratrinitarian life. For this distinction see Vagaggini, *Il senso teologico*, p. 169. This illustrates William's tendency to follow the Fathers more in the traditional aspect of their doctrine
than in their particular theories as in his choice, at least in
the Aenig, of the more traditional elements in St Augustine's theology rather than of the theories more specific to St Augustine.
Yet these traditional doctrines are adapted to the perspective of
William's own theological structure. In this example of the economy *ex*, *per*, *in* the sense of *per Filium*; and *in Spiritu* cannot be

simply identified with the sense given to that formula by the Greek Fathers or even with its presentation in Scripture and liturgy. *Per Filium* and *in Spiritu* in this concluding section of the Aenig cannot be understood without the implicit allusion to the journey of the soul through the spiritual states *animalis, rationalis, spiritualis*, cf. Aenig, 437B on the purpose of the incarnation 'docuit enim carnales homines...;' and 439C-440D on the Holy Spirit, where the reference to the Holy Spirit as the charity and unity of the Father and the Son, in the context of the communication of this charity to us, implies William's whole doctrine of the Holy Ghost in relation to the state of *spiritus, resemblance*. For this question of the incarnation and the Holy Spirit in relation to the spiritual development of the Soul, see the Chapter on the Trinitarian Aspect of the Ascent of the Soul. In this ascent of the soul one of the most marked characteristics is the relationship of the Word primarily with the initial stage of purification from the *status animalis* through the Incarnation, whereas the Holy Spirit is almost exclusively associated with the final state of *Spiritus*; see the interesting comparison between William and St Bernard made by Hourlier, 'S. Bernard et Guillaume de Saint-Thierry,' pp. 223-233; see p. 228: 'pour conclure d'une façon un peu sommaire, nous dirons que S. Bernard présenterait le Saint-Esprit comme le complément du Verbe, alors que Guillaume présenterait le Verbe comme la condition du Saint-Esprit.'

A comparison of this relationship with the traditional trinitarian economy reveals a difference in interpretation. Whereas with William the initial stage is *per Filium* leading to *in Spiritu*, in the traditional economy *in Spiritu* is the first point of contact with the Trinity in the ascending movement leading us *per Filium ad Patrem*. Moreover the very sense of 'priority' is not the same in both cases. With William it is a priority of stages in the journey of the soul. In the traditional scheme it is the logical priority of contact with the Persons in the descending and ascending trinitarian movement. William has presented the traditional formula, but he has given it a different meaning. Ultimately we can feel here a certain tension in William's attempt to fuse the traditional economy 'ex Patre, per Filium, in Spiritu' with the Augustinian theory of the Holy Ghost as the mutual union of the Father and the Son.

Despite the connection between 'per Filium' and 'in Spiritu' in the economy at the end of the Aenig, William offers no developed theology of an explicitly trinitarian relationship of this economy as such with the ascent of the soul to resemblance. On this question the Augustinian theory of the Holy Ghost as the mutual unity of the Father and the Son is undoubtedly the leading theme. See 'The Trinitarian Ascent of the Soul,' above, pp. 30, 30-7.

233Aenig, 436D.

234Ibid., 438C.

235Ibid., 436D.

236This is true despite the primacy of the Augustinian doctrine of the Holy Ghost, for in his adaptation of St Augustine, William emphasizes strongly the realistic and personal role of the Holy Ghost *ad extra*.

237See above, p. 35-36, for the influence of the general Greek mentality in William's approach to the image-resemblance question.

238This comparison is well illustrated in the whole question of the search for the meaning of Person in the Trinity.

CHAPTER 4

FAITH AND MYSTICAL EXPERIENCE IN
WILLIAM OF ST THIERRY*

A CONTEMPORARY THEOLOGIAN has said that theologians of the
past should be studied not only for historical research, nor simply to justify current positions, but to shape future development.[1]
Frequently recent theological development is based on a return beyond the Counter-Reformation to an older tradition rooted in the
teaching of St Thomas, the Fathers and the Bible, and nowhere perhaps is this more apparent than in the treatise on faith. The tendency now is to draw attention to the more intuitive aspect of the
act of faith and even to suggest that the intuition in the judgement by connaturality, made by all believers in the initial act of
faith, may be a remote basis for a development towards mystical experience. Although this opinion might be suspected by the more
conservative theologians as open to the dangers of illuminism, it
has a strong foundation in the older theological tradition prior
to the Reformation.[2] Those who wish to pursue this line of thought
should investigate more thoroughly St Thomas's doctrine of the *interior instinctus*[3] which induces us to make the act of faith, together with the doctrine among the Fathers[4] and the medieval monastic theologians which sees faith as orientated towards contemplative experience.

CREDO UT EXPERIAR[5]

FAITH AS AN ASCENT TO GOD

Credo ut experiar. What has been said of St Bernard[6] should
be said also of his intimate friend William of St Thierry. These
masters of the twelfth-century monastic theology, with their
sources deep in the tradition both of the Latin and of the Greek
fathers, assimilated the patristic teaching through the ethos of
the monastic culture. This led to a theology of the ascent of the
soul to God which is exemplified in the writings of William of St
Thierry. His *Speculum fidei* is one of the first attempts towards
an integral theology of faith and his insight into the structure
of the act of faith is an historical landmark.[7] But his contribution for us is not principally in his metaphysical analysis of the
act of faith but in his vision of faith in union with hope and charity as the *machina salutis*[8] which sets in motion the ascent to God.
He sees faith dynamically rather than statically, not as the unchanging metaphysical essence of the act of faith but as an initiation into the life of God. Faith for William of St Thierry is what
Dom Vonier has described as a 'kind of psychic link'[9] that leads

through progressive gradations of insight to the mystical experience of the Trinity in this life and to the immediate vision of
God in the future life.

In this ascent from faith to mystical experience two main divisions can be discerned. The less advanced experience is that of
faith itself. The more advanced experience is that to which faith
tends for its ultimate end in this life.

EX FIDE IN FIDEM[10]

The first kind of experience is faith itself at a deeper level.[11] These two levels of faith are explicitly contrasted as
faith received externally, and as faith penetrated inwardly.
Faith received externally is faith revealed by flesh and blood.
It is the *forma fidei*, teaching us what is to be believed. Faith
penetrated inwardly is faith revealed by the Father, an *intellectus fidei*, an understanding of what is believed, in the literal
sense of an *intus-legere* and this *intus-legere* is given in the
affectus cordis, not to all men but only to those who have received illumination.[12]

The *intus-legere* is *intellectus fidei* but it is not *ratio fidei*. The distinction is clear from the description of the *simplices filii Dei* who, through the teaching of the Holy Spirit, can
ascend directly without the mediation of discursive reason to the
intellectus fidei given in the faith revealed by the Father.[13]
The *intellectus fidei* of the *simplices filii Dei* gives an insight
into faith without the clear communicable understanding of faith
given by the discursive reason, *sapit sed non lucet*,[14] for, inseparable from the *sensus amoris*,[15] this *intellectus* transcends
ratio and it can only be attained through the illuminating grace
of the Holy Spirit.[16] The metaphorical terms *sentire* and *sapere*
borrowed from sense-experience suggest a more immediate kind of
understanding than that given by *ratio*.[17] Whether or not this
description given by William would satisfy the more exacting cri-
teria for mystical experience, there can be no doubt that the
faith revealed by the Father, and taught by the illuminating grace
of the Holy Spirit, initiates us into an *intellectus fidei* that
transcends both the bare assent of faith and the discursive reasoning of *ratio fidei*.

The theology of faith, as Père Aubert has observed, oscillates
between two positions. Is faith an assent to truths imposed by authority from without, or is it a more direct and more inward contact with God?[18] For William faith in its initial stage is an assent to authority and in its mature development it is a more direct contact with God[19] through the *affectus fidei* and the illuminating grace given by the direct action of the Holy Spirit.[20]

The division of faith into two successive stages raises a

problem. Is faith on authority abandoned for a gnosis beyond authority? The problem confronts us most acutely in the parallel between faith on authority and the pedagogic action of the law in the Old Testament. As the law was a preparation for the Gospel, so the authority of the Gospel is a preparation for illumination from the Holy Spirit, and as the pedagogy of the law gives way to the authority of the Gospel, so the authority of the Gospel gives way to illumination from the Holy Spirit.[21] The danger here that faith on authority might be conceived as a temporary stage, to be totally abandoned in the more advanced stage of illumination from the Holy Spirit, is corrected by the statement elsewhere that faith is ruled by authority in the whole 'interim' period of this present life.[22] How are these two points of view to be reconciled? First William divides the life of faith into the two stages of authority and illumination by the Holy Spirit. Both these stages belong to this present life and they are presented in succession to each other. Secondly he says that the present life is ruled throughout by faith on authority. No explicit indication is given as to the solution. But the two apparently conflicting statements are not necessarily in contradiction. For faith can be ruled by authority under one aspect and by interior illumination under another aspect. In so far as all knowledge of God in this life is, as William says, *per speculum* and *in aenigmate*,[23] the believer is ruled by authority at least with regard to what he does not see clearly. But in so far as the Holy Spirit gives a more direct contact with God, the believer is no longer ruled by authority alone. William's division of faith into these two stages can be explained by his conception of faith as a progressive movement from an external to an inward faith, from faith as an assent on authority to faith as experienced through the illumination of the Holy Spirit. The role of external authority decreases in proportion to this inward illumination, but it is never wholly abandoned in this life where God is seen only *per speculum* and *in aenigmate*.

A FIDE AD SPECIEM

Whereas the experience of faith under the illumination of grace and of the Holy Spirit is faith itself penetrated at a deeper level, the more advanced *cognitio amoris* or *cognitio caritatis* of the trinitarian experience is a transition from faith towards vision. The first experience is *ex fide in fidem*, the second is *a fide ad speciem*.

The *cognitio amoris* in the experience of the Trinity is explicitly distinguished from *cognitio fidei*,[24] as knowledge of God through the medium of faith is distinguished from the more immediate knowledge of God as he is in himself. In the *cognitio fidei* God is known through the medium of the *affectus pietatis* in the

experience of faith. In the *cognitio amoris* God is known as he
knows himself.[25] *Cognitio fidei* is of this life. *Cognitio amoris*
is a transition from faith to vision.[26]

Although *cognitio amoris* is contrasted with *cognitio fidei*,
the *cognitio amoris* is not a superstructure extrinsic to the life
of faith, but an experience to which faith is intrinsically orientated. It grows **organically** from the life of faith. In William's
view of living faith as inseparable from love[27] faith is directed
towards *cognitio amoris*, the knowledge through love which is the
experience of the trinitarian life. According to William's strict
equation of knowledge and likeness, we not only become like God
through our knowledge of him, but we know him through our likeness
to him,[28] and this likeness to the Trinity, the *similitudo*, the
perfection of the image of the Trinity, is given through love.[29]
Therefore it is through love that we know God as he knows himself.
God's knowledge of himself is identically the Holy Spirit as the
mutual union, the mutual knowledge and love of the Father and the
Son.[30] To know God as he knows himself is to participate through
the *similitudo* in the Holy Spirit as that mutual union, knowledge
and love.[31] Living faith, the faith which is united with love, is
therefore impelled through the exigence of love towards this experience of communion with the Persons of the Trinity and it is
given its ultimate meaning in this experience.

THE PENETRATION OF THE *SACRAMENTUM* THROUGH FAITH

As a preparation for these two kinds of experience faith penetrates the *sacramentum*. According to the traditional patristic
doctrine[32] inherited by William and shaped more specifically to
his own theological vision, the *sacramentum* is the whole structure
of the temporal economy, centered on Christ the Mediator, whereby
exterior, visible, temporal signs evoke and communicate God's inward, invisible, eternal life.[33] This sacramental structure is the
point of contact with man in the situation of sin, enslaved under
the dominion of the senses,[34] and through that point of contact man
is led from the things of time to the things of eternity,[35] from
Christ known according to the flesh to Christ known according to
the spirit.[36]

But the *sacramentum*, rooted in the life of the senses, is extraneous to the life of the mind until it is penetrated by faith.[37]
Faith associated specifically with the temporal economy[38] breaks
through the external *sacramentum* into the inner life of the Holy
Spirit, the *Sacramentum Sacramentorum*,[39] in a movement **towards** the
total transcendence of the external *sacramentum* in the future life.[40]
This insight into the inward *sacramentum* is simultaneously an advance in the development of faith, and through the pedagogic action of the sacramental economy *fidei assensus* is transmuted into

amoris sensus.[41]   The **structure** of the *sacramentum* and the structure of the development of faith interact in a reciprocal causality.

CREDO UT INTELLIGAM[42]

The orientation of faith towards mystical experience is the
specific note of William's theology of faith. But to explain his
theology exclusively in this light would be to ignore the complexity of his doctrine. The *Aenigma fidei* opens significantly with
the question whether the essence or nature of God can be understood by the human mind,[43] and the problem as to how far we can
know God through the *lumen in fide, per speculum et in aenigmate,*
follows directly from that initial question.[44] A new element has
been introduced. *Credo ut experiar* has shifted to *credo ut intelligam.* Faith as **orientated** towards mystical experience is predominantly the theme of the *Speculum fidei.* Faith as a response to
the desire of the human mind to understand the essence of God is
predominantly the theme of the *Aenigma fidei.*
The ascent of the mind towards the understanding of God's nature, foreshadowed in the final pages of the *Speculum fidei,*[45]
is the dominant theme of the *Aenigma fidei,* where the central section on *ratio fidei,*[46] possibly composed originally as a distinct
treatise on the divine names under the influence of Scotus Erigena,[47] is almost exclusively on the metaphysical plane. The
Speculum fidei described the ascent of faith through love to the
cognitio amoris in the trinitarian experience. The central treatise of the *Aenigma fidei* describes the ascent of faith towards a
metaphysical understanding of the Trinity. In this intellectual
ascent the mind of man is raised to a new level. The philosophical concepts of person, number, relation, generation are compelled
to abandon their purely human connotations and are formed by *ratio
fidei* in the new light of the trinitarian mystery,[48] so that ultimately the mind ascends to an understanding of the Trinity only at
the moment of its recognition that the Trinity is beyond its understanding.[49] It would be difficult to find a treatise on the Trinity more impregnated with the Dionysian *theologia negativa.* *Ratio fidei* approaches the Trinity both from the 'Greek' and from
the 'Latin' perspective only to find that it is infallibly driven
back against the distinction within identity which is the initial
mystery of faith. But through this dialectic faith has gained a
deeper insight. From *fides* it has advanced to *ratio fidei.* From
the bare statement of the trinitarian mystery in the initial act
of faith it has advanced not to a positive understanding of the
mystery of the Trinity, but to an insight as to how the mystery
transcends our understanding.

TOWARDS A SYNTHESIS

Through *ratio fidei* human reason transcends its limitations and understands not by philosophical concepts alone but by philosophical concepts purified and transformed by faith. But this advance opens up a new perspective. For *ratio fidei* is limited to thinking about God without knowing God as he knows himself.[50] *Amor illuminatus*, not *ratio fidei*, leads us into God himself[51] and the treatise on *ratio fidei* leads significantly into the union of faith with *intellectus* and *dilectio* fused in an inseparable unity as an image of the Trinity.[52]

William is groping towards the synthesis of *credo ut experiar* and *credo ut intelligam*. This attempt, initiated in the *Speculum fidei*,[53] finds its most complete expression in the three stages of faith in the *Aenigma fidei*. *Credo ut experiar* was the ascent from faith to mystical experience without the intervening stage of *ratio fidei*. *Credo ut intelligam* was the ascent of the mind through *ratio fidei* towards a metaphysical insight into the Trinity. The three stages are an attempt to integrate these two movements into one movement, in an ascent from faith through *ratio fidei* into mystical experience.[54] The synthesis is never completely achieved. The three stages of faith in the *Aenigma fidei*, despite allusions in the final stage to knowledge through love,[55] and to our participation in God's knowledge of himself,[56] contain no explicit reference to the trinitarian experience, still less an analysis of this experience comparable to that of the *Speculum fidei*. The central treatise in the *Aenigma fidei* remains predominantly the ascent of the mind towards an insight into the Trinity on the metaphysical plane. *Ratio fidei* is closely related to the ascent from faith to mystical experience but never wholly integrated with it.

CONCLUSION

Faith initiates us into mystical experience. The various aspects of William of St Thierry's theology of faith converge on this central theme. This experience is not an extrinsic structure superimposed on faith. It develops organically from the life of faith. Implicitly William sees an intrinsic relationship of faith to mystical experience. The further question remains as to whether the intuitive aspect of faith in the judgment by connaturality, discerned by many theologians in the initial act of faith, can give a sufficient metaphysical basis for William's intuition. Here is a question which should engage our attention more deeply.

NOTES

*Published in *The Downside Review* (1964) 93-102.

[1]Karl Rahner, *Theological Investigations*, I (London, 1961) 9-10.

[2]See R. Aubert, *Le problème de l'acte de foi* (Louvain, 1958) 58-62, 587-600, 723, and I. Trethowan, *Certainty* (London, 1948) 113-29.

[3]II. II, *Q*. 2, *art*. 9 *ad* 3: 'Ille qui credit habet sufficiens inductivum ad credendum; inducitur enim auctoritate divinae doctrinae miraculis confirmatae, et quod plus est, interiori instinctu Dei invitantis.'

[4]See Aubert, p. 16.

[5]*Credo ut experiar* is not a contrast of faith and experience as if faith and experience were mutually exclusive. It is faith orientated towards mystical experience in contrast with faith orientated towards a speculative scientific understanding of God.

[6]Leclercq, *L'amour des lettres*, 202.

[7]See Déchanet, *Le miroir*, 38.

[8]Ibid., 48-49; 365B.

[9]A. Vonier, *A Key to the Doctrine of the Holy Eucharist*, 2nd ed (London, 1931) 4-6.

[10]Spec fid, p. 128-9; 384D: 'Ipse ex fide in fidem revelat fidelibus Dei justitiam; cum pro gratia dat gratiam; pro fide auditus fidem illuminatam.'

[11]Ibid., 102-03; 378C: 'Altera; et non altera. Eadem fides; sed alter effectus.'

[12]Ibid., 'Ista fidei suum suggerit intellectum....cum qui credit intus in affectu cordis legit quod credit.'

[13]Ibid., 102-05; 378C-D: '....et absque omni verborum sive cogitationum disceptantium strepitu a Sancto Spiritu discentes; ad quod docendum, si non assit ipse Spiritus et docenti et discenti, deficiunt perstrepentes rationum ratiocinationes.'

14Ibid., 106-07; 379C.

15Ibid., 104-05; 379A.

16Ibid., 378D; 379A.

17Ibid.

18Aubert, 703.

19Origen, whose influence on William of St Thierry is now generally recognized, also distinguishes the faith of beginners, as an indirect contract with God through authority, from the faith which develops through knowledge into a more direct contact with God. See H. Crouzel, *La théologie mystique d'Origène*, 444-50.

20Déchanet, *Le miroir*, pp. 82-83; 373D-374A: 'quamvis noniam tam cogitatur quam agitur; quia quidquid fidei est Spiritus Sanctus in anima illa actualiter quodammodo operatur; cum affectus fidei fervet in conscientia, in intellectu vero fulget illuminans gratia.'

21Ibid., 78-81; 373A-373B: 'Sit ergo interim auctoritas paedagogus noster cum enim venerit illuminans gratia, iam non sumus sub paedagogo....' See 82-83; 373D: 'Nulli melius animus regendum se credit et committit, quam divinae auctoritate....donec per operationem Sancti Spiritus, ipsa sicut dicit Propheta experientia intellectum incipiat dare auditui.'

22Ibid., 168-9, 394D: 'Sed regat interim auctoritas fidem.'

23Aenig, 397D; 399D.

24Spec fid, 162-63; 392D: 'Cognitio autem haec Dei, alia fidei est; alia amoris vel caritatis.'

25Ibid., 392D-393A.

26Ibid., 392D: Quae fidei est hujus vitae est; quae vero caritatis, vitae aeternae,' and Aenig, PL 180, 414D: 'finiens fidem, seu potius beatificans in amorem, a fide ad speciem transmittens, inchoando cognitionem non eam quae fidei est....' This conception of a stage of transition from faith to vision is based on William's doctrine that there can be an anticipation *per speculum* and *in aenigmate* of the future vision. See Déchanet, 166-7, 393CD, and Aenig, 399D-400A.

[27]Spec fide, 48-58; 365B-368B. See especially 367C:
'Tres autem cardinales istae virtutes ubi sunt, ad aliquam similitudinem Trinitatis Dei, sic sibi invicem conesae et coniunctae,
ut sint singulae in omnibus, et omnes in singulis,' and 368B: 'fides et spes, nonnunquam non tam caritati conformantur, quam uniun-
tur....saepe tamen in tribus nonnisi una sit seu appareat facies
caritatis.'

[28]Ibid., 164-5; 393C: 'quem in tantum videvit, sive cognoscet, qui cognoscet vel videvit, in quantum similie si erit.'

[29]Ibid., 154-8, 390D-391D.

[30]Ibid., 162-5, 393A; 393B. The Augustinian doctrine of
the Holy Ghost as mutual love (*De trinitate*, PL 42, 1079; 1087) is
interpreted here through William's doctrine of 'cognitio amoris'
or 'amor-intellectus' as mutual union not only of love but also of
knowledge.

[31]Ibid., 164-5, 393A: 'Quibus ergo revelat Pater et Filius, hii cognoscunt, sicut Pater et Filius se cognoscunt; quia habent in semetipsis notitiam mutuam eorum; quia habent in semetipsis unitatem eorum et voluntatem vel amorem; quod totum Spiritus
Sanctus est,' and 393B: 'aliter in propria natura, aliter in gra-
tis....ibi mutua cognitio Patris et Filii, unitas est; hic hominis
ad Deum similitudo.'

[32]See Vagaggini, *Il senso teologico*, 36-38, 42-47, 473-4.
This traditional doctrine is also developed by E. H. Schillebeeckx
OP, *Le Christ, sacrement de la rencontre de Dieu* (Paris, 1960).

[33]Spec fid, 381D-384A.

[34]Aenig, 402BCD.

[35]Spec fid, 120-1; 382D-383A: 'Quod potissimum in persona
mediatoris elucet nobis qui in seipso manens Deus aeternus, in tempore est homo factus; ut per temporalem et aeternum; a temporalibus ad aeterna transeamus.'

[36]Ibid., 136-7; 386D; and Ep frat, 336BC.

[37]Ibid., 134-5; 386B; 136-7; 386C: 'quasi adventitia aliunde per sensus inferuntur; non ea facilitate adhaerent menti; donec fide perficiente, et gratia illuminante, scientia temporalium
transformetur in sapientiam aeternorum.'

[38]Ibid., 124-5; 383D: 'Fides autem maxime est rerum temporaliter pro nobis gestarum: per quam corda nostra mundantur, ut
ad aeterna non credenda, sed intelligenda idonea inveniantur.'
Compare St Augustine, *De doctrina christiana*, II, xii, 17.

[39]Ibid., 96-97, 382A.

[40]Ibid., 383C: 'Qui ad Sacramentum cognoscendum internae
Dei voluntatis jam non habeat opus exterioribus sacramentis. Quorum tamen sacrosancta religione quandiu hic vivitur, religantur ex-
teriora nostra....'

[41]Ibid., 383ABC: 'sic enim quibusdam Christianae pietatis
rudimentis paulatim erudiendus erat fidei nostrae assensus....cum
illuminante gratia intellectum rationis fidei assensus efficietur
amoris sensus.'

[42]The antithesis of *credo ut experiar* and *credo ut intelligam* is to be understood as follows: *credo ut experiar* led to an
intellectus fidei in a non-conceptual understanding on the mystical plane; *credo ut intelligam* leads to an *intellectus fidei* in a
conceptual understanding on the metaphysical plane.

[43]Aenig, 397A: 'Humanae infirmitatis religiosa confessio
est, de Deo hoc solum nosse, quod Deus est. Caeterum essentiam
ejus vel naturam, et secreta illa imperscrutabilis judicii ejus decreta investigare quidem et perscrutari pium est: quae tamen cum
mens terrena non penetret, inscrutabilia et investigabilia esse
confitendum est.'

[44]Ibid., 397D: 'Sed in quantum ratio coelestis se permit-
tit intelligi, in tantum expetenda est;....Habemus enim interim hic
promissorum bonorum lumen in fidei: in qua tanquam per speculum et
in aenigmate felicium rerum et futurorum bonorum imaginem intuemur.'

[45]Spec fid, 168-78; 394C-398A.

[46]Aenig, 417D-431C.

[47]See my article 'The Speculative Development of the Trinitarian Theology of William of St Thierry in the *Aenigma Fidei*,'
[Chapter 3 of this volume].

[48]Aenig, 418BC; 419C.

[49]Ibid., 426C.

[50]Spec fid, 170-1; 394D: 'Ipsum dico; non de ipso. De
ipso enim multi cogitant qui non amant. Ipsum autem nemo cogitat,
et non amat.' See also Aenig, 415A: 'Duae enim istae cognitiones
tantum ab invicem sunt differentes, quantum differt a Deo in eo
quod ipse in semetipso est, quidquid homo secundum hominem de Deo
seu cogitando seu loquendo sentire potest.'

[51]Ibid., 172-3; 395C: 'De ipso ergo multa multis edicere
fas est; ipsum autem cui praeter ipsum? Amor tamen, amor illuminatus, qui intus Deo loquitur, melius hoc agit.'

[52]Aenig, 433D: 'Hoc autem fit cum fides incipiens operari per dilectionem, incipit etiam ipso formari in dilectionem,
et per dilectionem in intellectum, et per intellectum in dilectionem, seu in intellectum simul et dilectionem. Difficile enim est
homini sic affecto discernere quid de quo, cum jam in corde credentis et intelligentis et amantis tria haec unum sunt, ad similitudinem quandam summae Trinitatis.'

[53]Spec fid, 106-07; 379C.

[54]Aenig, 414D. See especially 414BCD: 'Primus gradus
est diligenter investigatum habere, quid sibi de Domino Deo suo
sit credendum; secundus, quomodo de eo quod recte creditur, recte
nihilominus cogitandum sit et loquendum; tertis, ipsa jam rerum
experientia est....primus gradus in auctoritate fundatus fidei est
....secundus rationis est, non rationis humanae, sed ejus quae propria fidei est....tertius jam gratiae illuminantis et beatificantis est, finiens fidem, seu potius beatificans in amorem, a fide ad
speciem transmittens....' The three theological stages have their
spiritual and psychological counterpart in the three spiritual
states: *animalis....rationalis....spiritualis* (Ep frat, PL 184,
315C) and in the psychology *anima....animus....spiritus* (Ibid.,
340BC). See the source of this psychology in Origen, περὶ ἀρχῶν
(PG 11, 364B-365A and 223B).

[55]Aenig, 414D.

[56]Ibid., 415A.

134

CHAPTER 5

WILLIAM OF ST THIERRY'S DOCTRINE OF THE
ASCENT TO GOD BY FAITH*

INTRODUCTION: FAITH AS AN ASCENT TO GOD.

THE THEOLOGY OF FAITH can be studied in two ways. It can be
analyzed in its metaphysical causes so as to explain all that belongs essentially to the very structure of the act of faith.   This
aspect of the theology of faith is of the greatest importance.
Faith is supernatural, free, certain and reasonable. How to recon-
cile these apparently conflicting elements is a major metaphysical
problem and the answer can be given only through the exact determination of these various aspects of the act of faith according to
the different orders of causality.
    To insist on the necessity and even on the primacy of this
question for the theological treatise on faith should not obscure
the need for another approach. An integral theology demands not
only this analysis of faith in its metaphysical **causes**. It demands also the description as to how faith is lived in the individual believer including much that lies outside those metaphysical causes. This investigation of the lived experience of faith
reveals to the fullest its dynamic aspect. For although this dynamic aspect belongs to faith in its very nature[1] it is still more
apparent in the description of faith in the life of the believer.
It is not possible for the act of faith metaphysically to be more
or less an act of faith. What belongs to the essence of an act
belongs to it necessarily and **invariably**. But it is possible for
the believer to live the life of faith more perfectly or less perfectly. For in the description of faith in the life of the believer there is much that is not limited to the essential elements
in the act of faith.[2] From this angle faith can be studied gene-
tically as developing progressively towards perfection in a movement towards the final transition from faith to vision. It is precisely in this sense that the study of the growth of faith throughout the life of the believer is the more dynamic **approach** and the
metaphysical analysis of the essential elements in the act of faith
is the more static approach, and it is for this reason that William's approach to faith is essentially dynamic. His attention is
directed not primarily to what faith is in itself but to what it
is for. The act, the virtue, the material object, the understanding, and the life of faith all receive the impress of this unifying vision of faith as an ascent that leads us by progressive
stages into the depths of God's life, and finally to the vision of
God.[3]
    In this ascent faith is orientated towards an experimental

contact with God. 'Credo ut intelligam' becomes for William as
for St Bernard 'Credo ut experiar.'[4] The tendency in the Fathers
to see faith as an initiation into the life of God leading to contemplative experience[5] is accentuated more acutely with the further interiorization given by the twelfth century Cistercian monastic theology to the patristic *sapientia* or *gnosis*[6] and for William
this experience is ultimately to be the experience of the Trinity.[7]

In this light the 'supernaturalism' of William's theology of
faith is given its true meaning. Grace is of primary importance
in his analysis of the act of faith. But his supernaturalism is
not simply the grace needed for the act of faith. It is the *machina salutis* setting in motion the ascent to God.[8] Faith is supernatural not only in the sense of the grace needed to assent to
a truth beyond our natural powers but in the sense of what Dom
Vonier has called a 'psychic link'[9] and through this link we are
initiated ultimately into the trinitarian life of the Holy Spirit
as the mutual union of the Father and the Son.

This movement demands a continual dépassement from lower to
higher gradations of insight,[10] for the insight given indirectly
in the *speculum* and in the *aenigma*[11] of faith tends of its nature
towards direct perception.[12] There are three different aspects of
this ascending movement. First there is the ascent through faith
to the experience in the Holy Spirit and to the vision of God.
This is predominantly the approach of the *Speculum fidei*. Then
there is the ascent of the intellect in its attempt to attain
through faith to the speculative understanding of the nature of
God. This is predominantly the approach of the central section
of the *Aenigma fidei*. Finally there is the tendency towards a
synthesis which finds its most complete expression in the outline
of the three theological stages in the *Aenigma fidei*, faith, 'ratio fidei,' and the experience in the Holy Spirit that initiates
the transition from faith to vision.[13] The question that underlies this development is whether the ascent to God by faith is to
be made with or without the mediation of speculation by the intellect as to the nature of God.[14] This study of William's theology
of faith is an attempt to trace this pattern.

After a study of the structure of the act of faith and of
faith as a reasonable act, both of which are seen by William in
the light of the ascent to God, these two articles will describe
first the movement from faith to experience and to the vision of
God, then the ascent of the intellect through faith to the speculative understanding of God's nature and finally the attempt at a
synthesis of these two ways.

THE STRUCTURE OF THE ACT OF FAITH.

Faith is an assent of the mind.[15] It is a certain assent,[16] and, in opposition to Abelard, not merely a probable opinion.[17] But the certainty of the assent in faith is not the certainty that is given in knowledge.[18] Moreover, it is the will which draws the reason and not the reason which draws the will to make the act of faith.[19] Faith is a meritorious act[20] and it is a supernatural act.[21] It is also an act which is fundamentally reasonable.[22]

But the dominant element in William's analysis is that faith is supernatural. The act of faith depends on the will making or not making the decision to believe. To will to believe is to believe. 'Si vis credis.'[23] But this act of the will is not made except under the impulse of grace.[24] The total dependence of the will on grace does not mean that grace forces the will against its freedom. On the contrary it is grace that frees the will from captivity to sin and gives it the power to use its freedom rightly.[25] The act of faith is therefore a free act with a freedom that is wholly dependent on grace and ultimately the act of faith is the result of predestination. William's thought is based on uncompromising logic. The reason is drawn by the will to make the assent of faith. The will depends on the attraction of grace and this grace is the result of predestination. The recognition of the primacy of grace is finely expressed in the following text deeply reminiscent of St Augustine:

> Non ergo volentis, neque currentis, sed miserentis est Dei, et quod bene vis, o homo, et quod credis. Equidem si non vis credere, non credis; credis autem, si vis: sed non vis, nisi a gratia praeveniaris: quia nemo venit ad Filium, nisi Pater traxerit eum. Quomodo utique creando in eo et inspirando ei liberam voluntatem, qua libere vult id quod vult, hoc est ut voluntatis ejus sit, quod bene vult. Deo enim inspirante fit in nobis voluntarius mentis assensus in his quae de ipso sunt, ut corde creditur ad justitiam, ore autem confessio fit ad salutem; et ipsa est fides. Sic ergo dictum est: si vis credis, sed non vis, nisi a Patre traharis: et si vis, ideo utique vis, quia a Patre traharis.[26]

The relevance of this structure for the conflict of faith and doubt.

William sees clearly the essential elements in the act of faith. But his purpose is not primarily to analyze them entitatively, still less to explain how they are mutually compatible.

His purpose is to show their relevance for the actual situation
in which his readers are involved. This situation is that of a
conflict of faith and doubt. The preface to the *Epistola ad fra-*
tres de Monte Dei,[27] written for Carthusian solitaries, explains
how the *Speculum fidei* and the *Aenigma fidei* were written to con-
sole and to encourage those monks of the Cistercians at Signy who
were assailed by doubts against faith. The slightest carnal temptation gives them the impression that their faith is impaired.
This experience, William says, is the effect of a sudden transition from the darkness of the world into the light of a higher
kind of life. They are at first blinded by the light of faith as
a sudden light blinds those long accustomed to darkness. The
Speculum fidei is to point out the way to advance on the journey
and the *Aenigma fidei* is to give warning that the advance should
be made with prudence.[28] However, it can scarcely be doubted,
despite William's caution in the preface to the *Epistola ad fra-*
tres de Monte Dei, that these works were intended not only for the
more simple novices, but also for those who had come under the influence of the theories of Abelard and his disciples.[29]

The argument is not intended for those who do not believe but
for those who do already believe and yet are **attacked** by the temptation to doubt. These temptations are compatible with the existence simultaneously of true faith. For William explains with a
subtlety of psychology and an awareness of the more subjective,
experimental aspect of faith, suggestive of contemporary rather
than of mediaeval thought,[30] how the anxiety caused by these doubts
is a sign of the presence rather than of the absence of faith.

Non sentit hoc, nisi qui pugnat....quid autem timet in
hujusmodi, quid anxiatur, quid dolet nisi fides? Statuit
ergo se contra se homo Dei.[31]

The tension is the division of man against himself and William shows how this division is rooted in the very nature of the
act of faith and more particularly in the nature of the assent of
the intellect that is given in faith. For the will is pure.[32]
Assent is given in the outward confession of faith.[33] Inwardly
the works of faith are there even to the point, if necessary, of
martyrdom and death.[34] The difficulty is in the intellectual aspect of faith. This division in man is ultimately the division of
the mind against itself.[35] The crucial point is that, although
the assent of faith is certain and not merely probable,[36] the certainty of assent has not the **certainty** of knowledge.[37] The intellect seeks knowledge and rebels against the surrender of its autonomy through grace to authority.[38] The *via naturae* has to give way
to the *via gratiae*[39] and the mind is led *per aliam viam*.[40] More
bewildering still, this strange path invades the unique territory

of the mind *in regionem suam*.[41] Even after the surrender has been
made the conflict still persists. For this abdication of the autonomy of reason does not release the intellect from the demands
of its intrinsic nature, which searches for truth as its end and
which searches for truth through its own specific power of reasoning. The dichotomy is admirably expressed in the following text.

> Licet enim simpliciter ire quo jubetur assentit; tamen
> rationem respiciens quasi consuetam sibi viam requirit.
> Nam et si possibile est rationi, in cogitando de fide,
> libramine judicii omnia subdere auctoritati, tamen ra-
> tionalitati eripi non potest vis vel motus naturalis
> ratiocinandi. Menti siquidem ad inquisitionem veri-
> tatis naturaliter semper tendenti, sicut finis solet
> esse quaerendi, inventio ipsa veritatis, ad quam tend-
> itur; sic via ad inveniendum solet esse ratiocinatio,
> qua veritas invenitur.[42]

At this point William, abandoning the attempt to find a solution from within the mind itself, introduces the will as the decisive factor. For it is not the reason which impels the will but
it is the will which impels the reason to the act of faith.[43] But
the motive power behind the will, as is evident from his whole
analysis both of the structure of the act of faith and of the psychological conflict of faith and doubt, is the power of grace.[44]

In the last analysis, there is not a deposition of the reason
as such,[45] but only of the 'ratio animalis.'[46] For it is the 'ratio animalis' which hesitates to accept on belief what it has not
itself experienced.[47] The 'ratio spiritualis' on the contrary,
through its power of spiritual judgement, surrenders to authority.[48]
The apparent deposition of the reason is in reality an ascent to a
higher kind of reason and an advance from the human to the divine
perspective.[49]

REASONS FOR BELIEF.

William's approach to this question is in view of a particular situation. First of all he is not writing for those who do
not believe but for those who do believe and yet are tormented by
temptations to doubt. Although he recognizes that faith is reasonable,[50] his principal aim is not to convince his readers of the
reasons in defence of faith but rather to strengthen them against
the assaults of the destructive reason that is in conflict with
faith.[51] He is writing a polemic for grace rather than for reason[52]
against a danger of rationalism from Abelard and his disciples.[53]

Therefore this question is not discussed directly from the
angle of purely theoretical apologetics but from that of the

particular situation of his readers. Even so he leaves us unsat-
isfied as to how faith is a strictly reasonable act.
  The searching problem for our modern mentality is that of
certainty as to the fact of Revelation. Faced with this problem
William is at a loss to find a satisfying answer. The most powerful reason, he says, is that of the authority of the Gospels.[54]
To the post-Reformation mentality this argument, though often used
by mediaeval theologians,[55] evades rather than solves the problem.
If God has revealed himself then all would admit that it is reasonable to make the act of faith. But the question for debate is
whether God has revealed himself.[56] The main problem is not to
show that it is reasonable to accept the word of a trustworthy authority, but to show that we have sufficient reason for knowing
that this authority has spoken. In fact despite the value which
he gives to the argument from authority William is aware that it
will not of itself convince the faithless and the hesitant.

> Deum quippe facere vel potuisse, vel debuisse quae
> fecisse eum astruit evangelica praedicatio praesto
> sunt multae et multiplices, et ipsi causae dignis-
> simae rationes; fecisse vere extra autoritatem evan-
> gelicam apud pias quidem aures et mentes gravissimam
> et reverendissimam, apud infideles sive hesitantes,
> quas afferimus rationes?[57]

  When he searches here for an argument that will be valid for
the *infideles* or the *hesitantes* he is still unable to find a com-
pelling reason. The experimental insight given by the further advance into the life of faith[58] is not invoked as a motive for belief. For such motives he appeals to the external apologetic arguments from miracles. But the faithless today have not seen the
miracles of Christ[59] nor those of his apostles, and the miracles today are performed not for the hesitant nor for the credulous but
to strengthen in their faith those who already believe, 'non ut
credant, sed quia credunt.'[60]
  Those who do not believe are attached by their will to error,
'errare amant increduli,'[61] and are held captive by their carnal
affections, incapable of understanding spiritual things and still
less of understanding the economy of the Incarnation.[62] Evidently
William is not concerned directly with miracles as valid motives
of credibility on the purely theoretical plane. The question is
how far such miracles will influence the particular situation of
those who are subject to doubt or to a total lack of faith. This
situation will only be effectively changed through a change of
will and through a transition from a carnal to a spiritual state.[63]
  This approach to the reasons for belief, even though it does
not give a convincing theoretical explanation as to how faith is a

reasonable act, should recall to us a principle that is too easily
forgotten. The problem of the theoretical and impersonal demonstration as to how the act of faith is reasonable should be distinguished from the problem as to how the individual person sees
that the act of faith is reasonable for him here and now. In this
last problem the general disposition of the person in question is
of great importance.[64] Scientific apologetic reasons, although as
arguments they are conclusive, lead at the most to the 'judicium
speculative practicum,' that in general all men can and should
reasonably believe.[65] They do not lead to the final 'judicium
practice practicum,' that the individual person with all his particular dispositions can and should reasonably believe here and
now. This ultimate disposing cause can only be given through a
connatural judgement made under the influence of grace, the 'interiori instinctu Dei invitantis' to which St Thomas refers.[66]
The degree of intensity of this impulse depends on the whole disposition of man orientated by grace towards the act of faith. William's insistance on this right disposition and on the need to ascend from the dominion of carnal instincts to the dominion of the
spirit is not irrelevant.

CREDO UT EXPERIAR:
FROM FAITH ON AUTHORITY
TO FAITH THROUGH EXPERIENCE IN THE HOLY SPIRIT.

The theology of faith has oscillated between two positions.
How far is faith an assent to truths imposed by authority from
without and how far is it an inward supernatural experience of
these truths?[67] For William of St Thierry faith in its initial
stage is an assent to authority and in its more mature development
it is a supernatural experience. This supernatural experience is
a deeper and more inward penetration of faith given by illumination from the Holy Spirit.

> Nulli melius animus regendum se credit et committit,
> quam divinae auctoritati;....donec per operationem
> Sancti Spiritus, ipsa sicut dicit Propheta exper-
> ientia intellectum incipiat dare auditui; donec ob-
> tineat fides, ut res cuius praecessit fides creden-
> tis illucescat affectui....Etenim tunc iam bene
> creditur, tunc de fide digne fidei cogitatur; quam-
> vis non iam tam cogitatur quam agitur; quia quid-
> quid fidei est Spiritus Sanctus in anima illa act-
> ualiter quodammodo operetur; cum affectus fidei
> fervet in conscientia, in intellectu vero fulget
> illuminans gratia.[68]

Submission to divine authority is seen here as a preliminary stage[69] until the Holy Spirit takes charge and communicates experimentally the faith that comes from illuminating grace. 'Donec per operationem Sancti Spiritus....' Although the 'res cuius praecessit fides' might imply that faith as such, and not simply faith through authority, is a stage prior to illumination from the Holy Spirit, that illumination is nevertheless seen in terms of faith. It is an 'affectus fidei' and the Holy Spirit actuates 'quidquid fidei est.' But it is a different kind of faith from that of assent to authority. Both faith on authority and faith through the illumination of the Holy Spirit give a supernatural insight.[70] But they give a different kind of supernatural insight. That given by authority is not experienced by ourselves but is believed on the authority of another.[71] That given through the illumination of the Holy Spirit leads to an experience of what we have believed on authority. "Experientia intellectum incipiat dare auditui.'[72] This insight given by the Holy Spirit is described as 'affectus,'[73] 'illuminans gratia,'[74] and it is communicated through the direct action of the Holy Spirit. 'Non tam cogitatur quam agitur; quia quidquid fidei est Spiritus Sanctus in anima illa actualiter quodammodo operatur.'[75]

In his vision of faith as an ascent to God William sees faith on authority simultaneously as a *terminus ad quem* and as a *terminus a quo*. It is the *terminus ad quem* of the whole struggle against doubt, leading to the capitulation of the 'ratio animalis' the reason that is destructive of the values of faith, and culminating in the surrender to the 'ratio spiritualis' that accepts divine authority.[76] It is the *terminus a quo* of a further ascent that leads from an acceptance of divine Revelation from external authority to an inward experience of that Revelation.

This sequence of 'authority' and 'experience' in what are apparently two successive stages raises a problem. Does William suggest that in the later stage faith on authority is abandoned for a Gnosis beyond authority? This problem confronts us still more acutely in the text where he compares faith on authority with the pedagogic action of the law in the Old Testament. As the law was a preparation for the Gospel, so the authority of the Gospel is a preparation for illumination from the Holy Spirit, and as the pedagogy of the law gives way to the authority of the Gospel, so the authority of the Gospel gives way to illumination from the Holy Spirit.

> Sicut enim olim priusquam veniret fides, sub lege
> custodiebamur conclusi in eam fidem quae revelanda
> erat, et lex paedagogus noster fuit in Christo Jesu,
> ut ex fide justificaremur; ut ibi venit fides, iam
> non sumus sub paedagogo....sic etiam in ipso tempore

gratiae, priusquam splendescere incipiat in cordibus
nostris illuminatio Evangelii gloriae Christi, custodiri et concludi habemus sub auctoritate eiusdem
Evangelii, in gratiam revelandus nobis tempore illuminantis nos misericordiae Dei. Sit ergo interim
paedagogus noster in Christo Jesu; ut per humilita-
tem credendi, a gratia mereamur illuminari. Cum e-
nim venerit illuminans gratia, iam non sumus sub
paedagogo, quia ubi fuerit Spiritus Domini, ibi
libertas. Accepto enim Spiritu Filii Dei, effici-
mur et ipsi filii Dei et intelligentes, et sentien-
tes, nos Patrem habere Deum, cum omni iam fiducia
renuntiantes auctoritati, dicimus ei quod mulieri
illi Samaritanae dicebant concives sui: quia jam
non propter tuam loquelam credimus; ipsi enim au-
divimus et scimus, quia hic est vere Salvator mundi.[77]

In this text the parallel of the Old Testament law and faith
on authority is followed very closely. The words 'custodiri' and
'concludi' are used for both the law and faith on authority, suggesting that each phase restricts and encloses us while we await
the further phase that brings release. The word 'interim' suggests
that the rule of authority is temporary and 'renuntiantes auctoritati' that it is even abandoned through the presence of illuminating grace. Yet William explicitly states in another text from the
Speculum fidei, that 'interim' refers to the whole of this present
life as contrasted with the vision of God 'sicuti est' in the future life, and that in this whole 'interim' period our faith is
ruled by authority. 'Sed regat interim auctoritas fidem.'[78]
Here then is the problem. First William shows a strong tendency to divide the life of faith into two stages, with the initial
stage ruled by authority and the later stage ruled by illuminating
grace and the direct action of the Holy Spirit. Both these stages
concern this present life and they are presented in succession one
to the other. Secondly he says that this present life in its en-
tirety is ruled by faith on authority. How are these conflicting
views to be reconciled? William neither explicitly states nor answers this problem. But a solution can be suggested which is in
accord with his doctrine. The apparently conflicting views are
not contradictory. For it is possible that the life of faith
should be ruled by authority under one aspect and by the experience
of illuminating grace under another aspect.[79] In so far as there
is a direct contact with God given by illuminating grace and the
action of the Holy Spirit the believer is no longer ruled simply
by authority. But in so far as all knowledge of God in this life
is, as William explicitly says *per speculum* and *in aenigmate*,[80]
the believer is ruled by authority and not by this experience.

The difficulty remains that William refers to successive phases
rather than to distinct aspects in the life of faith. The phase
of experience and illumination succeeds the phase of authority as
one phase succeeds another in the history of **Salvation** and the
warning not to abandon **authority** at the beginning of the life of
faith suggests the abandonment of authority at a later stage. But
this can be explained by William's general doctrine that the life
is a progressive ascent to God from the more indirect contact with
God from without towards an increasingly direct perception of the
things of God from within.[81] Therefore, although the believer is
always to some extent ruled by authority, the life of faith **can** be
seen as a progress from an initial phase when contact with God is
given indirectly through the acceptance of truths on divine authority from without to a later phase when there is a more direct contact with God through illuminating grace and the immediate action
of the Holy Spirit from within.

FROM FAITH REVEALED BY FLESH AND BLOOD
TO FAITH REVEALED BY THE FATHER.

The antithesis of these two kinds of faith is closely related
to the previous antithesis of faith on authority[82] as distinct
from faith through experience, illuminating grace and the action
of the Holy Spirit. In each case there are two successive stages,
of which the first is a pedagogic preparation for the second.[83]
In each case there is the transition from the acceptance of faith
received from without to the penetration of faith from within and
this inward penetration is 'affectus,' 'illuminatio.'[84] But the
opposition of the faith revealed by flesh and blood to the faith
revealed by the Father throws **further** light on the meaning of this
inward penetration. The faith revealed by flesh and blood, although closely related to faith on authority, approaches faith
more directly from the angle of the object of belief than from that
of the motive for belief. It is an external **acceptance** of faith
less through its reception on external authority than through its
reception as an external form of faith. It teaches 'quid sit credendum'[85] giving the 'forma veritatis' which is offered to all
men.[86] The faith revealed by the Father is on the contrary given
only to those who are more spiritual.[87] Moreover it does not simply teach what is to be believed. It gives an inward penetration
of what is believed. This inward penetration, an intus-legere,
is not a purely intellectual insight but an 'affectus cordis'[88]
through an illumination.[89] The main points in this doctrine are
contained in the following text.

Altera siquidem est fides quam revelat caro et sanguis;
altera quam revelat Pater qui est in caelis. Altera;

et non altera. Eadem fides; sed alter effectus.
Illa docet quid sit credendum; ista fidei suum
suggerit intellectum, et plenam intellectus ethimologiam; cum qui credit, intus in affectu cordis
legit quod credit. Illa paedagogus est, tutor
vel auctor humanae infirmitatis; ista vero ipsa
est haereditas, et perfectio libertatis. Illa
vero tolerat negligentes, nec excludit hebetes,
formam omnibus praeferens veritatis; ista non
suscepit nisi spiritu ferventes, Domino servientes,
habentes illuminatos oculos cordis.[90]

THE SIMPLICES FILII DEI.

Simplicity in William's theology of faith can be the mark
both of the initial assent to faith on authority[91] and also of
the more advanced teaching from the Holy Spirit. It is here that
William states explicitly that it is possible for these 'simplices
filii Dei' to ascent directly to an experience given through the
Holy Spirit without the intervention of rational argument.[92]
Those who receive this special grace are the 'simplices filii
Dei.'[93]   They are deliberately contrasted with the 'hebetes' for
they receive not only the faith that is revealed by flesh and
blood but also that which is revealed by the Father.

Non autem hebetes hos dicimus, simplices filios Dei,
cum quibus eius sermocinatio fit; quorum proprium
est meritum, et singularis gratia, qui fidem acci-
pere merentur revelante Deo; non eam solam quam
revelat caro et sanguis, sed illam etiam quam revelat Pater qui est in caelis; docibiles Dei, et absque omni verborum sive cogitationum disceptantium
strepitu a Sancto Spiritu discentes; ad quod docendum, si non adsit ipse Spiritus et docenti et discenti, deficiunt perstrepentes rationum ratiocinationes.[94]

We find again the recurring characteristics of the affective,
experimental faith through the illuminating grace of the Holy
Spirit as described in the movement from faith on authority to
faith through experience and from the faith revealed by flesh and
blood to the faith revealed by the Father. But here the experience
is described in explicit contrast to all that can be known about
faith through reason. These 'simplices filii Dei' do not themselves make judgments on questions of faith. They surrender their
judgement to the illumination of the Holy Spirit.[95] Without the
work of discursive reason they become 'sapientes'[96] and experience

the things of faith through the 'sensus amoris.'[97]

The value of William's theology of faith is its dynamic conception of faith as an ascent to God. All the themes discussed in this article illustrate this point. His treatment of the structure of the act of faith is of importance historically as one of the first attempts towards a synthesis of its various elements.[98] But from the speculative standpoint the question demands a more thorough analysis through metaphysical causes, and this aspect of William's thought does not deeply engage our interest. His contribution for us lies in his application of that structure to explain the psychological tension of faith and doubt and to resolve that tension through the deposition of the 'ratio animalis' in the ascent to the 'ratio spiritualis.'

Again his attitude towards faith as an act scientifically demonstrated as reasonable is of interest historically for the light thrown on the attitude towards this question at that period. But speculatively his arguments are of little importance. His contribution is in his recognition that, whatever may be the value of speculative reasons for belief, the situation here and now of the believer is determined largely by his whole disposition and that the right disposition is given by an ascent from the 'carnal' to the 'spiritual' man.

Finally, and it is here that his doctrine is most relevant for our theology of faith, William sees faith as orientated towards a supernatural experience. The antithesis in the growth from faith on authority to faith from experience and from the faith revealed by flesh and blood to the faith revealed by the Father is a growth from faith received on external **authority** and expressed in external formulations to an inward penetration of faith through illumination, 'affectus,' and the direct teaching of the Holy Spirit. This inward penetration of faith, as described until now, is not simply an experience to which faith leads. It is an experienced faith.[99]

The interest of William's theology of faith and experience arises from two important questions. First there is the question as to whether there may not be an experience by connaturality in every act of faith,[100] this experience being intensified in the believer in the measure in which he lives his faith. Secondly there is the further question as to whether this experience by connaturality, to be found in some degree in every act of faith, may not be the seed from which the experience of the mystics develops.[101] William neither explicitly asks nor answers these questions. But his testimony as a great mystical theologian is of no little importance. For he states clearly that faith at least in a more advanced stage becomes an illuminated faith, an 'affectus fidei,' an experienced faith communicated by the Holy Spirit, and that faith on authority and faith revealed by flesh and blood leads us pedagogically to this experienced faith. Moreover, as we shall **see in**

a later article, William's trinitarian mystical experience appears
as a development from the life of faith and as an anticipation of
the final vision to which faith ultimately tends. The whole logic
of William's thought is therefore towards an intrinsic connection
between faith and mystical experience so as to see that experience
as developing progressively from the initial act of faith.

   In his use of sources William combines, as throughout his
theology the Latin and the Greek traditions. In his doctrine of
faith as given so far in this article the principal influences
are those of St Augustine and Origen. In general St Augustine is
the principal influence on William's teaching on the role of grace
in the structure of the act of faith and Origen is the principal
influence in the theme of the ascent from the 'carnal' to the
'spiritual' man.

NOTES

*Published in RTAM 30 (1963) 181-204.

¹This is a leading theme in the doctrine of St Thomas.
For the radical orientation of the theological virtues towards
supernatural beatitude cf. *Iᵃ IIᵃᵉ*, *q*. 62, *a*. 3: 'Virtutes theologicae hoc modo ordinant hominem ad beatitudinem supernaturalem,
sicut per naturalem inclinationem ordinatur homo in finem sibi
connaturalem.' More specifically for the virtue of faith cf. *IIᵃ*
IIᵃᵉ, *q*. 4, *a*. I: 'Dicitur fides esse "substantia rerum sperandarum;" quia scilicet prima inchoatio rerum sperandarum in nobis
est per assensum fidei, quae virtute continet omnes res sperandas.
In hoc enim speramus beatificari, quod videbimus aperta visione
veritatem cui per fidem adhaeremus....' Cf. *De verit.*, *q*. 14, *a*.
2. Cf. R. Aubert, *Le problème de l'acte de foi* (Louvain, 1958)
p. 47-48, who refers to A. Stolz, *Glaubensnade und Glaubenslicht
nach Thomas von Aquin* (Rome, 1933) a theologian who has given
special attention to this theme.

²A comparison could be made with the two different approaches to the meaning of person. Metaphysically it is not possible to be more or less perfectly a person. On the metaphysical
plane there either is or there is not what is demanded by the definition 'subsistens distinctum in natura intellectuali.' A definition gives what necessarily and invariably belongs to the
thing defined. But in the description concretely of the life of
a person it is legitimate to speak of a progress from a less perfect to a more perfect person. For in such a description there
are many things that do not enter into the strict definition of
person.

³In *De contemplando Deo*, William extends this progress
even into the vision of God. See *Contemp* 6, 40-65 (ed. J. Hourlier, *La contemplation de Dieu*, *L'oraison de Dom Guillaume*. Sources
chrétiennes 61 (Paris, 1959) p. 80-83; see 6, 60: 'Haec affectio:
haec est perfectio, sic semper ire: hoc est pervenire.' This
doctrine is prominent in the writings of St Gregory of Nyssa. See
J. Daniélou, *Platonisme et théologie mystique* (Paris, 1954) p. 291.
Hourlier remarks how William uses the text of St Paul, Phil. 3, 13,
'quae retro sunt obliviscens, ad ea vero quae sunt priora exten-
dens me,' to illustrate this doctrine in Contemp 6, 60-65 (Hourlier, p. 82-83). See also the use of this text in this sense by
St Gregory of Nyssa (Daniélou, p. 291). In his later writings
William, probably under the influence of St Augustine (*De trinitate* IX, 1, 1), restricts the application of this text to perfection in this life. See its use directly to illustrate the

conception of faith as a pilgrimage, a journey towards the vision
and the contemplation of God (Aenig; PL 180, 407B and 416B). In
this last text the state of *viatores* is contrasted with that of
perventores, unlike the *semper ire hoc est pervenire* of Contemp
Deo and the state of *viator* is that of the journey by faith. 'Et
in via fidei strenuum esse viatorem, perfectio vitae hujus est.
Perventio autem, alterius vitae est.' This theme of a journey or
pilgrimage constantly recurs in William's writings on faith. See
Spec fid, p. 48, 365B; p. 57, 368ABC; p. 60, 369AB, Aenig, 407BC,
416B. See Leclercq, *L'amour des lettres,* p. 55-69 for the theme
of the desire for heaven in monastic literature.

[4]See Leclercq, *L'amour,* p. 202.

[5]The *gnosis* or *sapientia* of the Fathers is illustrated
by their approach towards faith and this aspect of their thought
is well brought out in Aubert's work, p. 15-16: 'mais cela explique aussi la tendance de certains Pères grecs à présenter la foi,
non seulement comme une acquisition de connaissance, mais comme
une participation réelle de l'âme à la vie divino-humaine du Verbe
fait chair avec, comme conséquence, une illumination de l'intelligence qui permet de contempler, bien que d'une manière encore
voilée, les Biens divins qui feront un jour l'objet de la vision
béatifique,' referring to the works A. Lieske, *Die Theologie der
Logosmystik bei Origenes,* Münsterische Beiträge zur Theologie 22
(Münster, 1938) p. 39-45, 113-140; and 'Zur Theologie der Christus-
mystik bei Gregor von Nyssa,' *Scholastik* 14 (1939) p. 499-501.
See Aubert's comments on the meaning of *credo ut intelligam* in St
Augustine, p. 22-23.

[6]See *'The Trinitarian Aspect of the Ascent of the Soul
to God, in the Theology of William of St Thierry,'* [Chapter 2 of
this volume].

[7]These articles on faith will show how his theology of
faith no less than his theology of the Trinity converges on this
center.

[8]Spec fid *(Le miroir),* p. 48-49; 365B. The image of the
Trinity, faith, hope and charity, is the *machina salutis* and the
starting point in the journey is faith. 'A fide enim incipit
homo.' See Ibid., p. 94, 376CD; p. 58, 368B. St Augustine also
conceives of faith as an initiation (*Sermo* 43, 1 and 158, 6: 'incipit homo a fide....'). The end of the journey by faith is the
vision and the contemplation of God; Aenig, 407BC: 'Sic autem
sunt, qui per fidem ambulantes, et si perfecti sunt viatores, non-
dum tamen sunt perventores....jam olim aggressus viam ad te per

fidem ambulandi ad recte vivendum, et disciplinam cordis mundandi
ad videndum te et contemplandum.' This conception of faith as an
initiation into a knowledge that culminates in the Beatific Vision
is to be found in St Augustine; cf. *De trinitate* IX, 1: 'Sed ea
recta intentio est quae proficiscitur a fide. Certa enim fides
inchoat cognitionem: cognitio vero certa non perficietur, nisi
post hanc vitam, cum videbimus facie ad faciem.' Note also the
probable influence of *De trinitate* IX, 1 on the Aenig, 416AB.

[9]See A. Vonier, *A Key to the Doctrine of the Holy Eucharist*, 2nd ed. (London, 1931) 4-6: 'This is a favourite idea of
St Thomas that faith is truly a contact with Christ, a real psychological contact, which if once established, may lead man into
the innermost glories of Christ's life. I feel we are less habit-
uated in our times to think of faith as a kind of psychic link
between the soul and Christ, yet such is the traditional concept
of that wonderful gift.'

[10]The importance of Origen as an influence on William of
St Thierry is now widely recognized. See especially Déchanet,
Guillaume de Saint-Thierry, p. 116, and *Lettre d'or aux Frères
du Mont-Dieu* (Paris, 1956) 7-28. One of the points of resemblance
is this theme of 'dépassement'; see Origen, *In Num. Hom.* 17, 4
(PG 11, 707B): 'eorum vero qui sapientiae et scientiae operam
dant, quoniam finis nullus est (quis enim terminus Dei sapientiae
erit? ubi quanto amplius quis accesserit, tanto profundiora in-
veniet, et quanto magis scrutatus fuerit, tanto ea ineffabiliora
et incomprehensibiliora deprehendet, incomprehensibilis enim et
inaestimabilis est Dei sapientia), id circo....semper proficiunt,
et quanto magis proficiunt, tanto eis proficiendi via augetur,
et immensum tenditur.'

[11]Aenig, 397D: 'Habemus enim interim hic promissorum
bonorum lumen in fide: in qua tamquam per speculum et in aenigmate felicium rerum, et futurorum bonorum imaginem intuemur,' and
399D.

[12]A similar tendency is to be found in Origen who shows
that knowledge in virtue of the directness of its perception is an
advance beyond faith; see H. Crouzel, *Origène et la connaissance
mystique* (Toulouse, 1960) p. 450: 'En quoi consiste donc la connaissance et en quoi est-elle un progrès sur la foi? Dans une
évidence plus grande, dans la perception directe des réalités mys-
térieuses par les sens spirituels.'

[13]I find now that my previous articles on William's doctrine of the Trinity have presented his theology too exclusively

in the light of this attempt at a synthesis of the three stages
with a consequent neglect of this more complex structure.

[14]The polemical note can be detected here. For in Abelard's theology there was not only the danger of a rationalization
of the mystery but there was also the tendency in his *Theologia*
to conceive mystical experience as a prolongation of speculation.
See J. Cottiaux, 'La conception de la théologie chez Abélard,'
541-542. William's integration of speculative theology into the
movement towards mystical experience, is not a prolongation of
speculation but an initiation beyond speculation into a higher
mode of knowledge which wholly transcends scientific reason; see
especially Aenig, 414B-415D.

[15]Spec fid, (*Le miroir*), p. 88; 375B: 'Fides voluntari-
us est assensus mentis in eis quae fidei sunt; credere vero cum
assensus de eis cogitare.' See St Augustine, *De praedestinatione
sanctorum* 2, no 5 (PL 14, 963): 'Quanquam et ipsum credere nihil
aliud est, quam cum assensione cogitare.'

[16]Spec fid, p. 56, 367D; p. 74, 372A; p. 92, 376B, Cant,
535A; Adv Abl, 249AB, quoting St Augustine in opposition to Abelard: 'Fides enim, ait, non conjectando vel opinando habetur in
corde in quo est, ab eo cujus est, sed certa scientia acclamante
conscientia.' See *De trinitate* XIII, 3 (PL 42, 1017).

[17]Adv Abl, 249A: 'in primo limine theologiae suae fidem
diffinivit aestimationem rerum non apparentium.' For the question
as to whether William gives a correct interpretation of Abelard's
thought, see M.-D. Chenu, 'La psychologie de la foi dans la théologie du XIIIe siècle,' *Etudes d'histoire littéraire et doctrinale
du XIIIe siecle* 2 (1932) 163-187. Chenu argues that Abelard used
the term *existimatio* not to distinguish opinion from certitude,
but to distinguish *fides* from *scientia*; so as to show that faith
is of what is not seen. He refers also to the generic use of *existimatio* even as late as the thirteenth century when it was not
yet restricted to mean 'opinion,'(pp. 167-169). See J. Cottiaux,
La conception de la théologie, p. 291: 'Par l'expression *aestimatio
non apparentium* il ne définit donc pas la foi, mais la rapproche
d'un acte de connaissance, *aestimatio*, dont l'objet se présente à
l'esprit dans les mêmes conditions;....Abélard ne minimise donc
pas la certitude de la foi.' For the formulation that defines
clearly both aspects of faith, see Hugh of St Victor, *De sacramentis* I, 10, 2 (PL 176, 330C): 'Fides est certitudo quaedam animi
de rebus absentibus supra opinionem et infra scientiam constitu-
tam.'

[18]Spec fid (*Le miroir*), p. 92; 376B: 'cum in fide etiam certa, sicut certa esse potest fides, quamdiu fides est, non possit esse cognitio certa.'

[19]Ibid., p. 90; 376A: 'non tam ratio volumtatem, quam voluntas trahere videtur rationem ad fidem.'

[20]Nat corp, 718B: 'Licet enim fides non habeat meritum, cui humana ratio praebet experimentum.' See St Gregory, *Hom. in Evang.* 26, 1 (PL 76, 1197C).

[21]See the following section on the relevance of this structure.

[22]Nat corp, 718BC: 'quia in rationalitate fundatur quasi naturaliter semper solet esse avida rationis; quia vix ei fit credibile, quod vel congrua auctoritas, vel ipsa ratio non demonstrat aliquo modo esse rationabile.'

[23]Spec fid, p. 68; 370D.

[24]Ibid., 370CD.

[25]Ibid., p. 62; 369B: 'Est autem fides res liberi arbitrii, sed liberati a gratia....ad peccatum tantum per se liberum est.' See Ep frat, 340D: 'in poenam peccati et testimonium amissae dignitatis naturalis, positum est in signum ei arbitrium sed captivum.' The *arbitrium* remains after sin, but the liberty to act rightly is held captive. Déchanet comments on the influence of St Augustine on this doctrine (*Le miroir*, p. 19). For St Augustine's doctrine, see Gilson, *Introduction à l'étude de saint Augustin.* See St Augustine, *Opus imperf. contra Jul.* VI, 11 (PL 45, 1520), for the distinction between *libertas* and *liberum arbitrium.* In line with William's whole approach to faith this more speculative analysis of faith in the light of predestination, grace and free will is in the context of the ascent of the soul; the immediate context, Spec fid, p. 60; 369AB: 'in quo hic proficere, per fidem ambulare est. In quo quicumque proficiens invenietur exiens de hac vita; indubitanter de eo credendum est et sperandum, perficiendum eum in futura vita.' Note the dynamic aspect of grace, p. 70-72; 371D: 'voluntas vero in hoc, filia gratiae est. Gratia eam generat; gratia lactat; gratia nutrit, ac provenit; et ad perfectum usque perducit.'

[26]Spec fid, p. 68; 370CD. For St Augustine's doctrine, see *Tract. in Ioann.* XXVI, 2-7 (CC 36, 260-263). St Augustine's doctrine in opposition to semi-pelagianism was effectively used by

William for his opposition to what appeared to be Abelard's rationalism. The text from the Spec fid quoted above is the culmination of the argument that faith is the result of predestination and is not given to all men; 369CD: 'Nam sicut dicit Apostolus: Non omnium est fides....Quicumque enim ab aeterno in praescientia Dei sunt praecogniti, ipsi sunt qui crediderunt, qui credunt, qui sunt credituri....ipsi sunt vere credentes....praedestinati.... vocati....justificati....glorificandi.' St Augustine follows a similar line of thought in *De praedestinatione sanctorum* 8, n⁰ 16 (PL 44, 972) and 17, n⁰ 34 (985-986): 'Intelligamus ergo vocationem qua fiunt electi; non qui eliguntur quia crediderunt, sed qui eliguntur ut credant....quos enim praedestinavit, ipsos et vocavit....' St Augustine and William base their argument ultimately on St Paul Rom 9, 28-31 and II Thes 3, 3: 'Non enim omnium est fides.'

[27]Ep frat, 308A-310A and 303-304. See the critical edition by A. Wilmart 'La préface de la lettre aux frères du M. D.' *Revue bénédictine* 36 (1924) 238-239.

[28]See Déchanet, *Le miroir de la foi*, Introduction, p. 11-17.

[29]Er Guil, 333B: 'Venit enim nuper ad nos frater quidam fugiens de saeculo, et Deum quaerens; inter libros quos habebat unum deferens hominis illius cuius titulus erat, Summa philosophiae'; and PL 182, 531CD; see *Le miroir* p. 16.

[30]See Aubert, *Le problème de l'acte de foi*, 657-659. The author comments that the psychology of faith as a personal experience is developed more fully by St Augustine and also by the Victorines of the twelfth century than by the later scholastics. This psychological approach returns with the sixteenth century and it is still more prominent now as a result of the advance in studies on psychology. See p. 658: 'moins encore qu'au XVIᵉ siècle, on ne s'estime satisfait aujourd'hui avec des analyses de définitions; on désire voir décrire le déroulement de l'acte de foi à ses différentes étapes, caractériser les dispositions psychologiques qui l'accompagnent, déterminer le plus concrétement possible l'influence de chacun de ses éléments et la manière exacte dont ils interviennent.'

[31]Spec fid, 86-87; 375AB.

[32]Ibid., p. 88; 375B.

[33]Ibid.

[34]Ibid.:   'Opera etiam fidei inveniens in proposito et
professione, usque ad martyrii et mortis necessitatem si forte in-
grueret.'

[35]Simultaneously with the certain assent of the mind
there is to be found an element in the mind which opposes this
assent. Ibid., p. 88; 375C: 'Cogitans deinde mentis suae statum,
qualis sit, cum de fide cogitate, invenit certum quidem in ea
liberi arbitrii assensum in fide; aliquid tamen in cogitatione
contra assensum.'

[36]See *supra,* p. 00.

[37]Spec fid, 92; 376B: 'cum in fide etiam certa, sicut
certa esse potest fides, quamdiu fides est, non possit esse cognitio certa,' and p. 90; 376A: 'cum tamen ratiocinationi auctoritatem, et fidem interim scientiae jubetur anteponere, tanquam
certitudini opinionem, et sapientiae hujus mundi stultum Dei.'
In view of William's uncompromising opposition to Abelard on the
question of the certitude of faith, it would appear that the 'tanquam certitudini opinionem' is intended to emphasize the distinction of the certainty of faith from the certitude of knowledge,
scientia. See the explicit distinction of these two kinds of certainty in 376B (see *supra,* p. 185-186). The distinction between
faith and *scientia* is stressed also in Sacr altar, 345A: 'aliud
enim est fides, aliud scientia. Scientia ratione et intellectu
colligitur: fides vero sola auctoritate indicitur.'

[38]Spec fid, 88-90, 375CD; p. 100, 378AB; following in
378B the correction of Migne given in this critical edition of
Déchanet: 'Rationalitas....fidem saepius aggreditur: etsi non
studio contradicendo, sed natura ratiocinandi: non ut illi velit
occurrere; sed quasi illam sibi concurrere.' In this text the
opposition from reason is not motivated by a deliberate opposition
to faith but by its intrinsic need to follow its own nature. See
also the continuation: 'nam sicut solet agere in rebus humanis
humana ratio; quasi per mediam credendi necessitatem irrumpere
nititur in rerum divinorum cognitionem.'

[39]Ibid., p. 88; 375C.

[40]Ibid.

[41]Ibid.

[42]Ibid., 88-90; 375CD.

[43]Ibid., 90; 376A: 'quia non tam ratio voluntatem, quam voluntas trahere videtur rationem ad fidem.'

[44]Ibid., 88; 375C.

[45]The reference to 'rationalitas....in seipsa inquieta' (p. 100; 378A) might appear to imply that the power of reasoning is intrinsically in opposition to faith. But this refers in its context to the assault of nature without the assistance of grace. See the words immediately preceding: 'Nam saepe etiam qui in ea proficit, si non habeat adiuvantem gratiam, molestam patitur naturam.'

[46]Ibid., 84; 374C: 'Ratio videtur esse quae impugnat, et ratio quae repugnat; illa animalis et carnaliter sapiens, haec autem spiritualis, et spiritualiter diiudicans omnia; illa quasi de inexpertis haesitando, haec vero auctoritati omnia subdendo.' The hesitations of the *ratio animalis* lead to the attitude of 'foristan et forsitan' rather than 'est, est, non, non' (374B), referring to James 5, 12. See also Ibid., p. 76; 372C: 'licet repugnante ratione fidei rationi et consuetudini humanae....' The antithesis of *ratio animalis* and *ratio spiritualis* is rooted in William's spirituality of the ascent from flesh to spirit, a theme which will be found to be prominent throughout the Spec fid; see *infra*, n. 92, showing the similarity to Origen's spirituality.

[47]Ibid.

[48]Ibid.

[49]Ibid., 76; 372BC: 'Infirmi quippe ingenii, sed infirmioris fidei homines animales, non percipientes, aut vix percipientes ea quae Dei sunt, licet repugnante ratione fidei rationi et consuetudini humanae, saepe etiam nolentes, quasi infinitatem divinae potentiae metiuntur de infirmitate sensus humanae, seu fidei suae, quasi suggerente natura humana et sensu ejus, Deum nil posse vel esse, vel agere, nisi quod homo de eo videtur sibi posse intelligere.'

[50]Nat corp, 718BC: 'quia in rationalitate fundatur, quasi naturaliter semper solet esse avida rationis; quia vix ei fit credibile, quod vel congrua auctoritas, vel ipsa ratio non demonstrat aliquo modo esse rationabile.'

[51]See *supra, The relevance of this structure*....

[52]See *supra*, n. 24 ff.

[53]The polemic against Abelard may explain why the role
of reason as a disposition for the act of faith is less developed
in William's theology than in that of St Augustine. St Augustine's
'crede ut intelligas' is counterbalanced by 'intellige ut credas,'
Ep. 120, 2 (CSEL 34, 706), together with the recognition of the
need to establish first the reliability of the witness as a condition for the act of faith. See *Ep.* 147, II, 7 (CSEL 35, 281):
'Creduntur ergo illa quae absunt a sensibus nostris, si videtur
idoneum quod eis testimonium perhibetur,' and *De praedestinatione
sanctorum* 2, no 5 (PL 44, 962): 'Nullus quippe credit aliquid
nisi prius cogitaverit esse credendum.'

[54]Spec fid, 146-148; 389C.

[55]See Aubert, *Le problème de l'acte de foi*, p. 655: 'La
foi du chrétien est raisonnable, diront encore les théologiens du
XIIIe siècle, parce qu'il est raisonnable de ne pas s'en tenir aux
lumiéres de sa propre raison et d'apprendre des autres ce que nous
ne pouvons pas connaitre par nous-mêmes.' He refers here to his
article, R. Aubert,'Le caractère raisonnable de l'acte de foi
d'après les théologiens de la fin du XIIIe siècle,' *RHE* 39 (1943)
31-39.

[56]See R. Aubert, *Le problème de l'acte de foi*, p. 655-656.
The author shows that the evolution towards the more modern point
of view moved slowly even in the sixteenth century with the need
for defence against the protestants and humanists.

[57]Spec fid, p. 146-148; 389C. See also Nat corp, 718BC,
where 'authority' is placed together with reason as a means of
demonstrating the reasonableness of faith: 'vix ei fit credibile,
quod vel congrua auctoritas, vel ipsa ratio non demonstrat aliquo
modo esse rationabile.'

[58]See *infra, Credo ut experiar.*

[59]Spec fid, p. 148; 389C.

[60]Ibid., 389D: 'non ad voluntatem haesitantium, vel ad
quaestiones incredulorum, sed in adiutorium fidelium et consola-
tionem pro fide vel in fide laborantium, quae vel in illis vel per
illos fiunt, non ut credant, sed quia credunt.' In the Aenig, 401CD,
William refers to St Augustine's argument on the miracle of the con-
version of the world to Christianity, *De civitate Dei* XXII, 8, 1-
15 (CC 48, 815): 'Venit incredibilia faciens, et incredibilius ea
hominibus contradens....mirabile est hoc: sed multo mirabilius est
totum mundum rem tam incredibilem credidisse.' But this argument

in its context on the description of the growth of the Church
from its simple origins (Aenig, 401D-402A) is proposed less as a
motive of credibility than as an example of the paradox of belief
and of the pedagogy of the Incarnation leading us from the human
to the divine (401D-402B).

[61]Spec fid, p. 148; 389D.

[62]Ibid.: 'habentes amores quos nolunt vincere, et per
illos missi in errores, a quibus non inveniunt qua redire sed et
sensus in eis carnis qui etiam de spiritualibus nescit cogitare,
nisi corporaliter; multo minus de eis quae humanae dispensationis
sunt in Domino Jesu Christo scit vel potest cogitare, nisi carnaliter.'

[63]See William's psychology and spirituality of *anima,
spiritus* and the spiritual states of the *status animalis* and the
status spiritualis, Ep frat, 315C-316B.

[64]The Fathers and St Thomas regard the general disposition of the subject and in particular the influence of grace as of
great importance in determining whether or not the reasons of credibility are in fact accepted as decisive. According to J. Martin,
L'apologétique traditionnelle, vol. I and II (Paris, 1905-1906),
Lactantius alone among the ancient writers holds that arguments
can convince irrespective of the dispositions of the subject. This
is especially true of the traditional teaching on the value of miracles. See St Thomas *Contra Gent.* III, 155: 'Quia vero per malig-
nos spiritus aliqua similia fiunt his quibus fides confirmatur,....
necessarium est ut adjutorio divinae gratiae instruantur de hujusmodi spiritibus discernedis.' This of itself does not decide the
debated question as to whether St Thomas admitted at least the theoretical possibility of a purely natural knowledge of the motives
of credibility. An affirmative answer to this question is probable
in view of the text in *IIa IIae, q.* 5, *a.* 2 on the faith of demons.
For these questions see Aubert, *Le problème de l'acte de foi,* 17-
20, 68-71.

[65]Moreover the Vatican Council recognizes that not all
are led to faith by scientific external apologetic arguments; see
the discussion around Canon 3 of Chapter 3 of the *Constitutio 'Dei
Filius.'* See H. Denzinger - A. Schönmetzer, *Enchiridion symbolorum,*
32nd ed. (Freiburg im Br., 1963) nº 3033 (1812): 'Si quis dixerit
revelationem divinam, externis signis credibilem fieri non posse,
ideoque sola interna cuiusque experientia aut inspiratione privata
homines ad fidem moveri debere: an. s.' The word 'debere' was deliberately added in order to safeguard the position of those of the

faithful whose only reason for belief appeared to be their individual experience; see Mansi, *Sacrorum conciliorum collectio*, vol.
51, col. 232AB: 'Sunt enim aliqui qui experientia interna moventur ad fidem quin ipse constet de externis signis divinae revela-
tionis.'

66*IIaIIae, q. 2, a. 9, ad* 3.

67Aubert, *Le problème de l'acte de foi*, p. 703: 'Extrin-
sécisme, intrinsécisme....? Peut-être ici, comme en tant d'autres
questions, un certain exclusivisme a-t-il été néfaste; les deux
positions se sont durcies en des extrémismes outranciers, au lieu
de chercher à se concilier en mettant chaque élément de la synthèse
à la place qui lui revient.'

68Spec fid, p. 82-83; 373D.

69Ibid., 374A: 'Relicta vero in initio credendi auctoritate duce necesse est perire de via iusta ambulantes in sensu
carnis suae.' Authority is connected with the first of the three
theological stages. See Aenig, 414C: 'Primus gradus in auctoritate fundatus, fidei est, habens formam fidei, probatae auctoritatis probabilibus testimoniis fundatam': obedience to authority
is also the distinguishing mark of the 'animal state,' the first
of the three spiritual states, 'animalis,' 'rationalis,' 'spiritualis'; see Ep frat, 317BC. Note also William's emphasis on authority as the remedy for carnal temptations against faith; Spec
fid, p. 78-79; 372C, and p. 82-83; 373C, in the direct context of
the passage quoted above (p. 82-83; 373D). In general, despite
his theory of the pedagogic role of authority as a preliminary
stage, William gives great importance to the place of authority in
his theology of faith. See also Aenig, 398B, 402AB, 408A: Med,
210BCD.

70The way of authority is explicitly said to be the way
of grace: Spec fid, p. 70-71; 371BC, and 371C, where the motherhood of grace given through the acceptance of authority is compared
to motherhood on the natural plane: 'Agnosce matrem gratiam; pa-
tienter sustine; ut te nutriat in sinu auctoritatis, lacte sim-
plicis historiae.'

71Ibid., 371B: 'A carnali affectione accipe similitudinem ad Patrem Deum. Credit se homo majorum auctoritati, et
quod nullo didicit experimento, patris et matris suae filium se
indubitanter tenet,' and Ibid., p. 80; 373C: 'In eo ergo quod
nec sensu concipi, nec ulla valet ratione interim investigari,
obedientissime cedatur et credatur divinae auctoritati, sicuti est

de salvatore humanae dispensationis evangelica historia, et gesto-
rum ejus, quae eis qui tunc fuerunt, tunc facta sunt ad videndum
et ad credendum quod non videbant.'

[72]Spec fid, 82-83; 373D. The doctrine of the two kinds
of faith, that given by authority and that given by experience is
similar to the distinction made by Origen between the faith of beginners 'in the name of Jesus,' an indirect faith through what has
been heard on authority, and 'faith in Jesus' the faith of more
direct contact that develops into knowledge. See H. Crouzel,
Origène et la connaissance mystique, 444-450. See Origen, *Comment.
in Joh*. X, 28 (ed. E. Preuschen, *Origenes Werke* IV; GCS IV, 222,
1. 30; 223, 1. 5); *Fragm. in Joh*. VII (Ibid., 489, 1. 7, 14).

[73]Spec fid, *ibid*. This term as used by William often
has a mystical connotation.

[74]Spec fid, 82-83; 373D. See also p. 128-129; 384D:
'pro fide auditus fidem illuminantem,' and 383C: 'illuminante
gratia intellectum rationis, fidei assensus efficietur amoris sensus.'

[75]Ibid., p. 82-83; 374A.

[76]See *supra, Reasons for belief*.

[77]Spec fid, 78-81; 373A-373B. The double comparison
first of the law in preparation for the New Testament era of faith
and then of the era of faith as a preparation for the coming of
Christ in glory is to be found in St Bernard; SC 31, 8-9 (PL 183,
944-945). For the question as to how far St Bernard is influenced
here by Origen, see J. Daniélou, 'Saint Bernard et les Pères grecs,'
46-55, especially p. 48. Père Daniélou is of the opinion that St
Bernard depends directly on Origen for this doctrine and not simply through Greek and Latin intermediaries, even though he does not
find the same evidence of direct textual dependence as for the
theme of the *umbra fidei* in the Sermon 48, 6 and 7 and its dependence on Origen, *In Cant. Canticorum* 3 (PG 13, 153A-154A). William
of St Thierry develops this theme less directly in relation to the
future coming of Christ in glory, and more directly in relation to
the *affectus* and the illumination of grace given by the holy Spirit
in this life.

[78]Spec fid, 168-169; 394C: 'cum evacuabitur quod ex
parte est et veniet quod perfectum est (I Cor. 13, 10), cum videbitur Deus sicuti est (I. Jn. 3, 2). In hac enim vita, cognitionis
huius plenitudinem promittere, periculosa praesumptio est; et in

huiusmodi sicut circa credenda infidelitas, sic circa intelligenda temeritas cavenda est. Sed regat interim auctoritas fidem; veritas intelligentiam.'

[79]This can be compared with the question as to whether it is possible for the same thing to be both known and believed; see *IIa IIae*, *q.* 1, *a.* 5, *ad* 4, St Thomas says that the same thing cannot be both known and believed by the same man under the same aspect but that the same thing can be both known and believed by the same man under different aspects: 'Et similiter de Deo potest aliquis demonstrative scire quod sit unus, et credere quod sit trinus....sed ea ratione non potest simul idem et secundum idem esse scitum et creditum, quia scitum est visum et creditum est non visum, ut dictum est.' The same argument can explain the difficulty that underlies William's doctrine, with the difference that William is not opposing faith to knowledge but faith on authority to faith through experience and illumination. See the state described by the French mystic, Marie de l'Incarnation: 'Je n'ai pas la foi, ô mon grand Dieu, puisque vous me montrez la vérité de ce que vous êtes et de ce que vous m'êtes à découvert en une manière qui me dit tout de façon ineffable,' and the comment in P. Renaudin, *Une grande mystique française au XVIIe siècle; Marie de l'Incarnation, Ursuline de Tours et de Québec. Essai de Psychologie religieuse* (Paris, 1935) p. 83, note 1: 'Le mystique demeure sous le régne de la foi, il ne voit pas Dieu face à face comme les bienheureux ....Ce que veut dire ici Marie, c'est que sa foi ne s'appuie plus, comme la nôtre, sur la parole d'autrui, sur l'enseignement de l'Eglise, mais sur une expérience directe de la présence et de l'action de Dieu dans l'âme.'

[80]See Aenig, 399D; Med, 213D-214A; Ep frat, 313AB, 351B; Cant, 480BC, 536CD; Nat corp, 725A; Spec fid, 164-168; 393CD, 394C; Aenig, 416C and especially 397D: 'Visio namque facie ad faciem, et plena cognitio nemini hic datur, sed pro merito fidei, quo credimus hic quod non videmus, in futuro promittitur. Habemus enim interim hic promissorum bonorum lumen in fide: in qua tanquam per speculum et in aenigmate felicium rerum, et futurorum bonorum imaginem intuemur.'

[81]This ascent by faith leads ultimately to the final theological stage in the three degrees of faith when there is a state of transition from faith to vision. See Aenig, 414D: 'finiens fidem....a fide ad speciem transmittens.'

[82]Spec fid, p. 78-79; 372C-D: 'Sed sicut divinae auctoritatis fidele manicipium, primo omni studio animi subicit se disciplinae fidei eius quae discitur; deinde omni pietatis affectu

ambit ad eam quae donatur; primo ad eam quam revelat caro et sanguis; deinde ad eam quam non revelat misi Pater qui est in caelis.'

[83]Compare Spec fid, p. 78–81; 373A–373B, and p. 78,
372D; p. 102–103, 378C.

[84]Compare Spec fid, p. 80–81; 373B; p. 82, 373D and
p. 102–102; 378C.

[85]Ibid., p. 102–103; 378C. Note, however, that faith on
authority is also associated closely with the object of faith presented for belief; see Aenig, 414BC, and Exp Rm, 654C: 'simpliciter credens quod credendum indicit divina auctoritas.'

[86]Spec fid, p. 102–103; 378C. See p. 128–129; 384D,
where the *forma fidei* is further specified as 'forma quidem fidei
quae verbis et ecclesiasticae disciplinae institutis tradi potest
hominibus ab hominibus; in assensu bonae voluntatis, praesto est
omnibus hominibus,' accentuating still more the external aspect
of the 'forma fidei.'

[87]Ibid., p. 102–103; 378C: 'Ista non suscipit nisi
spiritu ferventes.'

[88]Ibid.: 'cum qui credit, intus in affectu cordis legit
qui credit.'

[89]Ibid.: 'habentes illuminatos oculos cordis.'

[90]Ibid. The ascent from faith revealed by flesh and
blood to faith revealed by the Father is an expression of the more
general movement of the spiritual ascent from the 'carnal' to the
'spiritual' man which pervades William's doctrine of faith (see v.
g., p. 190–191, p. 193). The psychological basis is given in the
Ep frat where this ascent is expanded into the trichotomy of *anima-
animus-spiritus* (PL 184, 315BC, 340BC) under the influence of Origen. In Origen's theology as in William's theology the deeper and
more spiritual penetration of faith is rooted in the ascent from
the 'carnal' to the 'spiritual' state; see, Origen, *Comm. in Mat-
thaeum* 27 (PG 13, 1633).

[91]See Sacr altar, 345A, where, in the context of the
foundation of faith on authority, he praises the simple acceptance
of faith: 'Beati pauperes spiritu....accedunt simpliciter ad fidem.' See also Exp Rm, 654C: 'simpliciter credens quod credendum indicit divina auctoritas.' In the Ep frat, 316C–317A, the
state of simplicity belongs to the 'status animalis,' when the

soul is not yet able to lead itself, but must submit to a wise man. See also here the tendency of Origen to associate simplicity with the 'animal' state; *In Lev. Hom.* III, 3 (PG 12, 426CD).

[92]This question of the ascent from simple faith to a higher spiritual insight is to be found at the basis of the theology of Origen. It is disputed whether or not Origen teaches that speculation is an essential aspect of the journey to the vision of God; see, H. Crouzel, *Origène et la connaissance mystique,* p. 531, and C. Vagaggini, *Maria nelle opere di Origene* (Orientalia Christiana Analecta 131 (Rome, 1942) 192-193.

[93]Both William and Origen show the double tendency to associate simplicity with the 'animal' state (see *supra,* note 91) and also to recognize that those of simple faith can receive special spiritual gifts; see Origen, *In Lev. Hom.* XII, 7 (PG 12, 543CD): 'sed animas mundas, virgines in simplicitate fidei quae in Christo est eligant, ipsis committant secreta mysteria, ipsis verbum Dei et arcana fidei proloquantur, ut in ipsis Christus formetur per fidem.' But the tendency to select the 'simplices' for such gifts is stronger in William's theology than in that of Origen and reflects William's opposition to Abelard. On the theme of simplicity in medieval monastic theology see J. Leclercq, 'The Monastic Tradition of Culture and Studies,' *American Benedictine Review* 11, nos 1-2 (1960) 99-131.

[94]Spec fid, p. 102-105; 378C-D. From the point of view of the experience of faith given in the faith revealed by the Father William accords a primacy to the 'simplices filii Dei' over the reflective rational understanding of the things of faith. See the somewhat pejorative description of rational argument in the text quoted above 'absque omni verborum sive cogitationum disceptantium strepitu.' This attitude is influenced by his polemic against Abelard; see the praise of simple faith in the Aenig, 408 408CD, and especially 408C where the phrase 'sine strepitu disputationum' recalls the passage quoted above from the Spec fid. See also Spec fid, p. 106-107; 379C, where those of simple faith precisely in virtue of their simplicity are shown to have an easier access to the faith revealed by the Father than those who understand their faith by reflective intelligence. 'Et licet sanctae simplicitatis compendio saepe a simplici praevenitur; et ipsi tamen a fonte gratiae qui omnibus patet, non repellitur.' But William admits that simplicity and rational understanding each have their own particular gift. See Spec fid, p. 106-107; 379C: 'Aliud enim est habere simplicem fidem, et fructus eius simpliciter in corde capere suavitatem; aliud intelligere quod creditur et paratum esse semper ad reddendam de fide rationem. Simplex fides sapit,

sed non lucet, et est a temptationibus remotior. Haec autem et si
nonnumquam cum labore sapit, lucet tamen, et est contra temptation-
es tutior.'

95See Spec fid, 379A: 'Nihil enim dijudicantes in fide,
nihil discernentes, omne rationis suae judicium Spiritu Sancto
iugiter illuminandum offerentes, et dirigentes omnem suum sensum,
in fidei assensum.' See the doctrine of St John on the teaching
by the Holy Spirit (I Jn, 2, 20): 'Sed vos unctionem habetis a
Sancto et nostis omnia,' and ibid. 27: 'Et non necesse habetis
ut aliquis doceat vos; sed unctio eius docet vos de omnibus....'

96Ibid., 378D: 'singulariter sapientes,' and 379A:
'sapit eis quod sentiunt.' Compare this experimental aspect of
the faith of the 'simplices filii Dei' with the description of
the final stage in the theological penetration of faith in the
Aenig, 414B, where *simplicitas* is associated with *experientia*:
'Tertius ipsa jam rerum experientia est in sentiendo de Domino in
bonitate, sicut sentiunt qui in simplicitate cordis quaerunt illum'
(the quotation alludes to Wisdom I, I); see ibid. (415C) describing
this last stage as 'sapore summae sapientiae.'

97Spec fid, 379A.

98See Déchanet in his valuable introduction to William's
theology of faith in *Speculum fidei, Le miroir de la foi,* p. 38.

99The movement is 'ex fide in fidem'; Spec fid, p. 128-
129; 384D: 'ex fide in fidem....pro fide auditus fidem illuminatam.' Contrast here the more advanced trinitarian experience
where 'cognitio amoris' is explicitly contrasted with 'cognitio
fide' (p. 162-163; 392D).

100This question arises from the need to explain how the
faithful believe reasonably even when they have not examined scientifically the objective, external apologetic arguments of credibility. The explanation through the experience and judgement by
connaturality is well founded in St Thomas' doctrine, whether or
not St Thomas' explanation bears directly on the point under discussion by modern theologians; see Aubert, *Le problème de l'acte
de foi,* p. 61-62. For texts form St Thomas, see, v.g., *II^a II^ae,*
q. 2, *a.* 9, *ad* 3: 'Ille qui credit habet sufficiens inductivum
ad credendum: inducitur enim auctoritate divinae doctrinae miraculis confirmatae, et *quod plus est,* interiori instinctu Dei invitantis; unde non leviter credit'; and *Quodl.* II, *q.* 4, *a.* 1,
ad 3: 'Dicendum quod interior instinctus quo Christus poterat se
manifestare sine miraculis exterioribus pertinet ad virtutem Primae

Veritatis quae interius hominem illuminat et docet.' R. Aubert
writes, pp. 723-724, on this question of a supernatural experience
in faith: 'Le désir de mettre ainsi à la base de la foi théolo-
gale une certain expérience surnaturelle a paru inquiétant à plusieurs théologiens, attentifs au danger--pas toujours imaginaire,
du reste--d'illuminisme. La thèse en question est cependant par-
faitement traditionelle....il y a, sur ce point, unanimité chez
les théologiens de la fin du XIIIe siécle,' referring here to his
previous article, R. Aubert, 'Le caractère raissonable,' RHE 39,
62-72. For an excellent theoretical explanation of this question
see Vagaggini, *Il senso teologico*, 417-424.

[101]For a discussion of this question see Aubert, 'Le
caractère,' p. 587f., 703f., 721f.

CHAPTER 6

THE ASCENT TO GOD BY FAITH[*]

I. Credo ut experiar.[1]

A.--THE PENETRATION OF THE SACRAMENTUM THROUGH FAITH.

MY PREVIOUS ARTICLE on this subject [Chapter 5] described
the transition *ex fide in fidem* from a more exterior to a more interior faith.[2] That transition is closely related to the pedagogy from the exterior to the interior *sacramentum*. The patristic
sacramentum has a wider connotation than the seven sacraments and
extends to the whole economy of salvation history whereby what is
visible and temporal manifests and evokes what is invisible and
eternal,[3] so that through this visible and temporal economy we are
initiated into the invisible and eternal life of the Trinity. William inherits this traditional doctrine[4] and shows how this sacramental 'economy' is essentially structured after the pattern of
Christ the prototype of the *sacramentum*.[5] But he shapes this traditional doctrine to his own pattern of thought. The particular
sacramenta of salvation history[6] are wholly subordinated to the
sacramental economy in its essential structure. The objective,
external, collective aspect of the sacramental economy is seen
structly in its relevance for the more subjective,[7] internal, personal penetration of that economy.

> Ipse enim ea sacrat spiritus sanctus, ut sint tantae
> rei sacramenta. Ipse ea revelando, fideli conscientiae
> commendat, in qua rem ipsam operatur occulta gratia.
> Omnibus enim interioribus nostris interior Deus, in
> exterioribus nostris, hoc est in sensibus corporis ex-
> teriora nobis credidit sacramenta, per quae interiora
> nostra ad sua introduceret interiora, per corporalium
> sacramentorum operationem paulatim suscitans in nobis
> gratiam spiritualem.[8]

William sees this essential structure of the sacramental economy as a penetration through the exterior to the interior Sacramentum in an ascent through faith to the inner life of the Holy Spirit. He distinguishes the *sacramenta* which are corporeal and visible signs from the *sacramenta* which are purely invisible.[9] The insight into the invisible *sacramenta* is given only through the Holy
Spirit who is the uncreated substantial divine will and the *sacramentum sacramentorum*.[10]
This sacramental structure is closely related to William's
theology of faith. Faith breaks through the barrier of the

external *sacramentum* and initiates us into the inner *res*.[11] Conversely, faith itself is interiorized through the pedagogy of the sacramental economy. The movement from the exterior *sacramentum* to the inner *res* is the movement from the ascent of faith to the experience of love. William explains this transition in the following sequence of thought. Through the pedagogy of the external *sacramenta*[12] the ascent of faith becomes inseparable from love. *Credere in Jesum* is impossible without the connotation of *amando in eum ire*.[13] Through the *affectus amoris* or the *sensus amoris* the transition is made from the exterior to the interior *sacramentum*.

> Primo ergo in rebus Dei absque omni retractatione vel
> hesitatione, simplicem et purum debemus fidei assensum:
> deinde ad intelligenda quae credimus cum omni observa-
> tione et obedientia mandatorum Dei credere debemus
> Spiritui Sancto totum spiritum nostrum et intellectum;
> non tam ambientis conatu rationis, quam affectu pii ac
> simplicis amoris. Sicque plus studiis humillimae pieta-
> tis, quam viribus potentis ingenii, promerebimur, ut
> incipiat se credere nobis Jesus, cum illuminante gratia
> intellectum rationis,[14] fidei assensus efficietur amor-
> is sensus; qui ad sacramentum cognoscendum internae Dei
> voluntatis, jam non habeat opus exterioribus sacramen-
> tis. Quorum tamen sacrosancta religione quamdiu hic
> vivitur, religantur exteriora nostra, et per ea inter-
> iora nostra, ne in aliena diffuant; propter quod et
> religio a religando nomen accepit.[15]

Throughout this argument the spiritual experience given in the *amoris sensus* appears not as a superstructure but as the logical development of the *sacramenta fidei*. The *amoris sensus* is simply the insight into the inner reality of the sacramentum which is communicated through the intrinsic development of the life of faith. Ultimately this experience tends, as the text shows, towards the transcendence of the exterior *sacramentum*.

The final transition from the vision *per speculum* and *in aenigmate* to the vision *facie ad faciem*,[16] from *sacramentum* to *res*, from the knowledge of Christ according to the flesh to the knowledge of Christ according to the Spirit[17] gives the ultimate consummation to the exterior-interior movement of the *sacramenta fidei*. To see God is to make that final penetration of the sacramentum to which faith is essentially directed.

The transition from the exterior to the interior *sacramentum*, from the *sacramentum* to *res*, from *fidei assensus*, to *amoris sensus* is grounded in the anthropological transition from flesh to spirit.[18] This flesh-spirit antithesis in the *Speculum fidei* is

sometimes seen in more Pauline terms as an antithesis of sin and
grace and in that context the flesh-spirit conflict is seen as a
resistance to faith in consequence of man's historical fallen condition.[19] In that situation the temptations of Satan are directed
not only against the corporeal but also against the spiritual element in man.[20]

When he develops most explicitly the economy of the *sacramenta fidei* William tends to shift the **anthropological** perspective
towards the condition of man as a corporeal[21] and mutable creature[22]
who needs the mediation of the temporal economy exemplified in
Christ the Mediator as a purification in the ascent to the eternal
and immutable *res*.[23] This corporeal mutable condition of man is
not simply the composite nature of man as spirit united with a body
but man in a particular historical situation as a consequence of
original sin. Man is dominated by this mutable corporeal state.
He therefore needs to be led pedagogically through the *sacramenta*
which touch him at this corporeal level[24] so as to raise him from
this state of 'flesh' to the state of 'spirit.'[25] The *credo ut
experiar* ascent through the *sacramenta fidei* to spiritual experience and to vision without the mediation of the speculative *ratio
fidei* is expressed anthropologically in an ascent which is predominantly an ascent from flesh to spirit, or in the terminology to
be developed finally in the *Epistola aurea*,[26] an ascent from the
'animal' to the 'spiritual' state, from *anima* to *spiritus*. The
animus, the principle of rational, discursive reflection will be
seen elsewhere to emerge as a rational speculative discipline distinct though never wholly separated from spiritual experience.[27]
But these texts reveal an aspect of William's theology from which
this development is absent. The ascent here is directly from
faith to spiritual experience and to vision rooted in an anthropological ascent from flesh to spirit.

B. *The Ascent Through Faith, Hope and Charity.*

From the metaphysical perspective the theologian should prescind from the question as to whether faith is living or dead in
order to consider the ultimate entitative structure of every act
of faith whether living or dead. But from William's perspective
it is impossible to prescind from this question. For his point of
departure is not the structure of the act of faith on the metaphysical plane but the **evolution** of the life of faith on the historical plane. From this point of departure faith is intrinsically
directed towards charity and inseparable from charity.[28]

This union of faith and charity is seen most **explicitly in**
William's theology of faith, hope and charity as an image of the
Trinity. Faith, hope, and charity are the 'machina salutis'[29]
in the pilgrimage[30] which, **initiated** in faith,[31] ends in the

vision of God.[32] At the end of this pilgrimage faith and hope
will not be annihilated but they will be transmuted into the 'res'
to which they are directed.[33] The union of the three theological
virtues is seen ultimately to converge and to fuse in charity.
Faith is given its final fulfilment in the charity which remains
and which is made perfect in the vision of God.[34] Enclosed within this sweeping movement towards the vision of God, the illustration of the Trinity through the differentiated unity in faith,
hope and charity is not static but dynamic.[35] The interpenetration of faith, hope and charity is an image of the distinction of
the persons within a unity of substance.[36] But the purpose of
William's argument is not primarily to give a metaphorical illustration of unity in distinction but to show the evolution of faith
towards union with charity so that, although the *species proprie-
tatis* of each of the virtues remains distinct, there appears to
be only the *una....facies caritatis*.

> Fides, et spes, nonnumquam, non tam caritati confor-
> mantur, quam uniuntur; adeo ut tribus ipsis in lumine
> vultus Dei proficiendo ambulantibus, licet suae uni-
> cuique maneat species proprietatis; saepe tamen in
> tribus nonnisi una sit seu appareat facies caritatis.[37]

Logically the trend of William's thought is to see faith as
an initiation into the trinitarian mystical experience. For faith
tends towards a perfect assimilation to charity and charity gives
an assimilation to the Trinity through the *cognitio amoris* in the
trinitarian mystical experience. But in the actual explanation
of this experience William concentrates on the transformation
through love into the similitude of the Trinity given through a
participation in the intratrinitarian life of the Holy Spirit.[38]
The image of the Trinity through faith, hope, and charity has
now receded into the background. There is, however, a significant
allusion to the ascent through faith, hope, and charity placed in
the immediate context of the transformation through the Holy Spirit
into the divine likeness.[39] It is difficult not to recall the
opening lines of the *Speculum fidei* and to see in them a reference
to the later analysis of the trinitarian experience. One thing
is certain: the trinitarian image of faith, hope and charity, as
described here, is not primarily a metaphysical illustration of
the Trinity but a saving image which leads efficaciously to man's
salvation through the remaking of man into the likeness of the
Trinity. Faith, hope and charity are the initiation into the life
of the Trinity.

> Inter omnia salutaria Dei Salutarium nostrorum, quae
> Deus noster, Deus salvos faciendi, homini ad salutem

suam proposuit observanda; sicut dicit Apostolus,
manent tria haec: fides, spes, caritas, maxime
observanda salvandis mortalibus. Hanc enim trinitatem constituit Trinitas Sancta in mente fideli,
ad imaginem et similitudinem suam; qua renovamur
ad imaginem eius qui nos creavit in homine nostro
interiori.[40]

C. *A Fide ad speciem.*

I. TOWARDS THE TRINITARIAN EXPERIENCE.

In a previous article,[41] I have attempted to show the relevance of the theology of William of St Thierry for those theologians who see the *instinctus interior* of the act of faith as an
intrinsic orientation of faith towards mystical experience. In
that article I described William's dynamic approach to faith
through the movement from faith as a purely external assent expressed in outward verbal formulae to faith as an interior illumination by the Holy Spirit. There can be no doubt that William
was describing a kind of knowledge which transcends abstract, conceptual, discursive reasoning and that he explained this knowledge
as an organic development in the life of faith. But it could be
questioned whether that *fides illuminata* can be called a mystical
experience in the strict sense.[42] There is, however, another and
deeper experience, described by William, which is beyond doubt
mystical in the strict sense. This experience is also an organic
development in the life of faith. But there is a difference in
the two kinds of experience. The first is faith itself experienced
at a deeper level. The second is the trinitarian experience in
the state of transition from faith to vision. This difference is
indicated in the double movement of faith *ex fide in fidem*[43] and
a fide ad speciem.[44] *Ex fide in fidem* is the movement towards an
affective 'experienced' faith communicated through the illuminating grace of the Holy Spirit. *A fide ad speciem* is the movement
into the depths of God's personal intratrinitarian life.[45] *Ex
fide in fidem* describes the action of the Holy Spirit on man's
faith. *A fide ad speciem* describes the transportation of man into
the life of the Holy Spirit within the Trinity. The first ascent
is towards God's life in us. The second ascent is towards our
life in God. It is therefore deceptive to equate these two kinds
of experience on the basis that they both initiate us into an
affective mode of knowledge which transcends *ratiocinatio* and
which is taught by the Holy Spirit.
    The *Speculum fidei* culminates in the most profound analysis
which William has given of this trinitarian experience.[46] But the
Speculum fidei is a treatise on faith. What is this relationship

of faith to the trinitarian experience? The question is important.
For the theory of the trinitarian mystical experience is William's
most original contribution to trinitarian theology and the orientation of faith towards that trinitarian experience is his most
original contribution to the patristic and monastic *credo ut experiar*. In contrast to the closely knit theory of the trinitarian
experience William's theology of the relationship of faith to that
experience is much less explicitly developed. But there is an implicit relationship of faith to the mystical experience of the
Trinity through the series of movements which deepen the life of
faith and converge towards the trinitarian mystical experience.

These movements will now be briefly recalled so as to show
how each of them is directed ultimately towards the trinitarian
experience. The image of the Trinity in faith, hope, and charity
is the saving image which remakes man into the similitude of the
Trinity and which therefore connotes the trinitarian experience
given through this similitude.[47] Moreover, through this image
faith is directed towards *una facies caritatis*.[48] But the trinitarian experience is a *cognitio amoris vel caritatis*.[49] Therefore
the movement of faith towards charity is perfected through the
trinitarian experience. In the sacramental economy faith breaks
through the exterior *sacramentum* into the interior *sacramentum*.
This interior *sacramentum* is a spiritual experience, the *amoris
sensus*, communicated through the Holy Spirit.[50] But the trinitarian experience is a *cognitio amoris* communicated to us through
the Holy Spirit.[51] Therefore the sacramental economy is perfected
through that experience.[52] The same implication is to be found in
the movement from faith as an assent to authority to the *affectus
fidei* given through the Holy Spirit[53] and in the movement from
the exterior form of faith to the *sensus amoris* given through the
Holy Spirit.[54] This experienced faith in the movement *ex fide ad
fidem* is perfected in the trinitarian experience *a fide ad speciem*
through the association of both these experiences with the Holy
Spirit and with the knowledge given through love. This implicit
relationship of faith to the mystical experience of the Trinity
can be summarized as follows. A unifying tendency emerges throughout these various themes. Faith is in movement from the external
form of faith to the inner *res* of faith.[55] This inner *res* is
charity or the spiritual experience given through charity by the
Holy Spirit. But this spiritual experience given through charity
by the Holy Spirit tends towards the trinitarian experience which
is its deepest realization. For the trinitarian experience is
pre-eminently a spiritual experience given through charity by the
Holy Spirit in which we participate in the intratrinitarian life
of the Holy Spirit as the uncreated love of the Father and of the
Son.

The *Speculum fidei* is no less a treatise on charity than a
treatise on faith. For William sees faith predominantly as an
organic development in the life of the believer and from this
perspective faith is intrinsically directed towards charity for
its perfection. But, if this is so, it is no less true to say
that the *Speculum fidei* is also a treatise on the mystical experience of the Trinity. For William sees the perfection of charity
in this life as the mystical experience of the Trinity in anticipation of the final vision. This mystical experience is therefore
not a superstructure extrinsic to the organic development of the
life of faith but the consummation and fulfilment of the life of
faith.

2. THE EXPERIENCE OF A PERSONAL COMMUNION.

The trinitarian experience is the experience of a personal
communion. For it is a participation in the intratrinitarian
life or the Holy Spirit who, according to William's theology of
the Trinity, is the mutual knowledge and love of the Father and
of the Son.[56] To know God through this *cognitio amoris* is to be
assimilated[57] to God so perfectly through the Holy Spirit that we
experience this intratrinitarian communion. This life of the
Holy Spirit into which we are drawn is described in the personalist language of love as the mutual embrace of the Father and of
the Son.

> In amplexu et osculo Patris et Filii, qui Spiritus
> Sanctus est, hominem quodammodo invenire se medium,
> et ipsa caritate Deo uniri, qua Pater et Filius u-
> unum sunt; in ipso sanctificari, qui sanctitas est
> amborum. Huius boni sensus, et suavitas experientiae,
> quanta potest esse in hac misera vita et falsa, iam
> quamvis non plena vera tamen est vita, et vere bea-
> ta.[58]

William's theology of faith is personalist, not so much in
his treatment of the act of faith in its basic structure, as in
his application of this structure to the personal conflict of
faith and doubt[59] and in his orientation of faith through charity
and through the Holy Spirit towards the experience of communion
with the persons of the Trinity.[60] Faith is the initiation into
this experience.

3. TOWARDS VISION.

Faith in movement towards the trinitarian experience is faith
in movement towards the vision of God.[61] For the trinitarian

experience in William's theology is an anticipation of the final vision. *Cognitio amoris* is explicitly contrasted with the *cognitio fidei* as the knowledge of God which belongs to eternal life is contrasted with the knowledge of God which belongs to this life.

> Cognitio autem haec Dei, alia fidei est; alia amoris
> vel charitatis. Quae fidei est, hujus vitae est;
> quae vero caritatis, vitae aeternae; vel potius si-
> cut Dominus dicit: haec vita aeterna est. Aliud
> quippe est cognoscere Deum sicut cognoscit vir ami-
> cum suum; aliud cognoscere eum sicut ipse cognoscit
> semetipsum.[62]

But the *cognitio amoris* is not to be equated with the final vision. For it is a mode of knowledge which is still *per speculum* and *in aenigmate*.[63] The difficulty is to see how William avoids a contradiction. For he says that this *cognitio amoris* is not the *cognitio fidei* because it belongs to eternal life and not to this life and yet he denies that the *cognitio amoris* is the final vision. If this knowledge is not the final vision, then surely it must be a knowledge in faith? But if it is a knowledge in faith, then surely it is a knowledge that belongs to this life? The answer to this difficulty is that William is not affirming that the same kind of knowledge under the same aspect is both the knowledge that belongs to eternal life and the knowledge that belongs to this life. He is affirming that the same kind of knowledge under a different aspect is both the knowledge that belongs to eternal life and the knowledge that belongs to this life. Therefore there is no contradiction. In so far as this knowledge has an immediacy which transcends the knowledge of faith,[64] it belongs to eternal life. But in so far as this knowledge is *per speculum* and *in aenigmate*, it is not yet the final vision.[65]

II. *Credo ut intelligam.*

William approaches the theology of faith dynamically rather than statically. He sees faith primarily not in its 'essential' structure but in its 'existential' development in the life of the believer. He is concerned less with what faith is than with what faith is for. Primarily this tension of faith is towards the *affectus fidei*, the experienced faith *ex fide in fidem*[66] and towards the *cognitio amoris*, the trinitarian eschatological experience *a fide ad speciem*.[67] But the tension is also, though secondarily, towards the metaphysical understanding of God and this tension rooted in the thrust of the mind to know God in his essence.[68] This double aspect in the dynamism of faith can be described as *credo ut experiar* which is the spiritual ascent and *credo ut*

intelligam which is the intellectual ascent.[69] The spiritual ascent is the movement towards the penetration of faith on the mystical level. The intellectual ascent is the movement towards the
penetration of faith on the metaphysical level.[70] The spiritual
ascent is the movement towards the trinitarian experience. The
intellectual ascent is the movement towards the trinitarian mystery. This thrust of the mind towards the metaphysical understanding of God's nature appears to be superimposed and only partially integrated[71] into the more basic theme: tension of faith
towards mystical experience. A plausible explanation as to how
this 'intellectual' tendency developed can be given in the light
of William's polemic against Abelard. This opposition to Abelard
is not restricted to a purely polemical refutation of his theories.
William answers Abelard through an opposite position. Shifting
his own perspective from the mystical to the metaphysical plane
he shows that *ratio fidei*[72] leads to the opposite conclusion from
the rationalistic *ratio* of Abelard. Abelard's rationalism reduces
the mystery to the limited vision of human reason. William's
ratio fidei leads to the inverse understanding that the trinitarian mystery is beyond human reason and even beyond the understanding of *ratio fidei*.[73]

This position attains its most complete development in the
central section of *Aenigma fidei*[74] which, in its original form,
may have been composed as a distinct treatise[75] under the influence
of Erigena. The central section of the *Aenigma fidei* takes its
point of departure from what we should now call the 'material'
object of faith, and moreover from the entitative formulation of
the trinitarian faith in the mystery of distinction within an absolute unity.[76] The *ratio fidei* which develops from this basis
is William's speculative trinitarian theology. Through a dialectic of the Latin and of the Greek approach to the Trinity, the
approach both from the unity of nature and from the distinction
of persons,[77] the mind of man is led pedagogically through the
signa of *ratio fidei*. These *signa* are the philosophical concepts
of number, person, relation, essence, purified and transformed
through faith.[78] Faith transcends the human connotations of these
philosophical concepts and leads the mind on from the sign to the
divine *res* which is signified.[79] *Ratio fidei* is not a restriction
of God's transcendence within the limitations of the verbal formulae of faith but a theophany of the divine nature communicating
itself to man through concepts which, despite their human limitations, point in the light of faith to the hidden divine mystery.[80]

III.   *Towards a synthesis.*

A.   THROUGH *RATIO FIDEI* TO *AMOR ILLUMINATUS*.[81]

1.   *The analogy of* sacramenta fidei *and* ratio fidei.

Credo ut experiar is the spiritual ascent to the trinitarian experience. *Credo ut intelligam* is the intellectual ascent to the trinitarian mystery. Finally there is the attempt towards a synthesis in an ascent from faith through *ratio fidei* into the trinitarian experience.[82]

The signs of *ratio fidei* pointed to the trinitarian mystery. In the light of faith they transcend their human limitations. But they are limited to talk about the mystery in contrast to the more direct and more inward contact with the divine reality which is given in *amor intellectus*. The mind of man, stimulated by *ratio fidei* on the metaphysical level, is restless until it has made the more direct penetration on the mystical level. The tension of *ratio fidei* towards *amor illuminatus* is shown in the dialectic of the *signum* in *ratio fidei*. This dialectic will now be explained.

Ratio fidei and *sacramenta fidei* have an analogous role in William's theology. William's conception of the sacramental structure is not limited to the seven sacraments but extends to the more general notion of *sacramentum*.[83] Beyond even this more general notion of *sacramentum*, which includes essentially a material sign perceptible to the senses an even wider concept pervades William's writings on faith. Through this wider concept he sees the whole divine economy as the hidden transcendent reality of the divine mystery manifested but also concealed *in speculo* and *in aenigmate*.[84] The terms *speculum, aenigma, imago, signum*[85] all connote this pattern of manifestation and concealment. The role of faith is to penetrate through the *speculum* to a deeper and more inward insight into the divine reality.

This structure appears in the analogy of *ratio fidei* and *sacramenta fidei*.[86] As the *signa* in the *sacramenta fidei* contain both the exterior, temporal, human element perceptible to the senses, and also the hidden, inward, eternal, divine element penetrated only in the inner light of faith, so the *signa* of *ratio fidei* contain the exterior human, temporal element, expressed in material words, and also the hidden inward divine, eternal *res* penetrated only in the inner light of faith. As the *signum* of the *sacramenta fidei* both reveal and conceal the *res* which is signified, so the *signum* of *ratio fidei* both reveals and conceals the *res* which is signified.[87] As faith in the *sacramenta fidei* penetrates through the sign to the *res* which is signified, so faith in *ratio fidei* penetrates through the sign to the *res* which is signified.[88]

This comparison is implicit throughout William's teaching on
sacramenta fidei and *ratio fidei* and it is explicit in a text from
the *Speculum fidei*. The text describes the tension in all talk
about God. Concepts and words are *de ipso*. They are not *ipsum*.[89]
They signify the *res* which infinitely transcends these concepts
and words.[90] The dialectic of the argument is as follows. We
can only talk about God through the use of words[91] which are signs
of God. But beyond a given point the limitation of these signs
blocks any further insight into God.[92] Therefore the limitation
of talk about God must be transcended through the more direct insight which is given from God himself through *amor illuminatus*.[93]
This dialectical movement, by which the human mind is led pedagogically through talk about God into an insight which transcends
all talk about God, is related in the following text to the pedagogic action of the temporal economy, described in the *Speculum
fidei* as a sacramental economy:

> Nam et ideo Verbum Dei in forma hominis apparuit, ut
> multifariam multisque modis olim Deus locutus patri-
> bus in prophetis, novissime diebus istis loqueretur
> nobis in Filio (Hebr. 1): hoc est efficaciter, sicut
> in ipso Verbo suo, quia quod temporaliter et corporal-
> iter in eo fiebat, quasi ad suscipiendum manibus fidei
> porrigebat; ipsum autem Verbum per quod facta sunt om-
> nia, per corporalia et temporalia purgandis promitte-
> bat; et purgatis in aeterna beatitudine plenius con-
> templandum et habendum reservabat. Ubi sicut Christus
> non secundum hominem cognoscetur; sic et hic a de-
> siderantibus, aliquatenus eum supra hominem cognoscere,
> verbis quae de eo sunt non nimis inhaereatur; sed eis
> quasi navigio a fide ad speciem transeatur.[94]

Amor illuminatus is the response to the tension of the sign
in our talk about God. To name God is to express God through human words. Only the eternal Word expresses God as he is in himself. But *amor illuminatus* gives an insight with approaches more
closely to the reality of God in himself.

> Si rei ipsius nomen requiris: 'Ego sum inquit qui
> sum.' Hoc nomen sicut ipse dicit, ei est ab initio;
> quia ad significandam rem, nullum ei aliquando Ver-
> bum proprius accessit. Non tamen sicut est exprimit,
> quia pertransit; quod autem significat est aeternum;
> nec plene illud significat nisi verbum coaeternum.
> De ipso ergo multa multis edicere fas est; ipsum au-
> tem cui praeter ipsum? Amor tamen, amor illuminatus,
> qui intus Deo loquitur, melius hoc agit.

2. *Faith as the impulse towards the transcendent* res.

Throughout this dialectic faith is the impulse towards *amor illuminatus*. But this impulse begins from a different point of departure and moves through a different sequence of development from that of the impulse of faith towards love in the spiritual ascent. This new point of departure given through the intellectual ascent is the contact of faith with the divine transcendent *res* which is attained beyond the verbal formulations.

Sed quia fides nutrit amorem quae sanat ad haec oculum mentis; quod intelligimus, sine obscuritate capiamus; quod non intelligimus, sine ambiguitate credamus; nec a verbis omnino recedamus; quamdiu nescientibus, eorum ministerio ingeritur nobis quod verbis nobis percipiendum est; et tamen sine omni verborum forma credendum est nobis.[96]

This radical contact of faith with the transcendent reality of God, who is beyond all verbal formulations, determines the entire sequence of the subsequent dialectic. First, the dialectic of the *via affirmativa, via negativa* and *via eminentiae* is conducted in the light of this initial contact through faith with the transcendent divine *res*.[97] The revelation of the trinitarian mystery of distinction within an absolute unity is given in order to purify the human intellect from sense imagery.[98] But this ascent through the purification of the mind to an intellectual, metaphysical recognition of the mystery is still restricted to the level of reasoning about God. It is an intellectual confrontation with the mystery. It is not mystical experience. Therefore the dialectic advances further. William insinuates that, if the divine mystery of faith transcends human words, images, concepts and discursive reasoning, then that mystery can only be further penetrated through the more divine mode of knowledge given in *amor illuminatus*.[99] Beyond the *amor illuminatus* the ultimate goal is the transition *a fide ad speciem* when the transcendent reality of God is seen in vision.[100] The steps in the ascent are clearly marked. Faith, *ratio fidei, amor illuminatus*, vision. The expanding dialectic develops logically and inevitably from the initial contact of faith with the divine transcendent reality.

3. Amor illuminatus *in a new perspective.*

Amor illuminatus and *affectus experientia* are now seen in the context of the quest of the mind for the understanding of God through human concepts and words.[101] Mystical insight comes as the response to the limitations of metaphysical insight.

From this new perspective William rethinks the theme of our communion with the persons of the Trinity. Towards the end of the *Speculum fidei* he moves abruptly away from the description and explanation of the trinitarian experience and begins the dialectic of the intellectual ascent.[102] In the course of this dialectic he reintroduces the theme of our communion with the persons of the Trinity. The question then is not how we experience mystically this communion with the divine persons but how we can explain intellectually the meaning of propositions about this communion with the divine persons.[103] The *affectus experientia* and *interior sensus amoris illuminati* now reappear as an aspect of the intellectual dialectic and as the response to the incapacity of the mind always to grasp the meaning of these propositions on the purely metaphysical plane of thinking and talking about God.[104] In this new context the *affectus experientia* and the *interior sensus amoris illuminati* are so closely related to the understanding of the meaning of these propositions that one may ask whether this spiritual experience and insight are a kind of knowledge which transcends those verbal propositions or whether the *interior sensus amoris illuminati* is not here simply an illumination of the meaning in these propositions. The more probable answer to this question is that in this context the *interior sensus amoris illuminati* is beyond the propositional statements about God but not apart from these propositional statements. William teaches not only in this context[105] but also elsewhere in his writings that knowing God through love differs both from knowing God through propositions and from discursive reasoning about God.[106] But the context also shows clearly that this knowledge of God through love is given here directly for the understanding of propositions about God which cannot be understood simply by reasoning about them.[107] Therefore William is moving towards the synthesis of *credo ut experiar*, the impulse towards the experimental communion with the divine persons in the connatural knowledge through love, and *credo ut intelligam*, the thrust of the mind towards the metaphysical understanding of God's nature as revealed through propositions about the divine persons of the Trinity.[108]

B. THE THREE STAGES IN THE UNDERSTANDING OF FAITH.

The three stages of *intelligentia fidei* move more directly and more explicitly towards the formulation of this synthesis.[109] The first stage in the ascent is to give the data of faith. The second stage is to think and to talk correctly about God and to defend the faith against the opponents. The third stage is the *experientia* given by the Holy Spirit in the transition *a fide ad speciem*. *Fides, ratio fidei, experientia* are three integrally related stages of the ascent in which *fides* moves towards

experientia not immediately but through the mediation of the intervening stage of *ratio fidei*.

> Primus gradus est, diligenter investigatum habere,
> quid sibi de Domino Deo suo sit credendum; secundus,
> quomodo de eo quod recte creditur, recte nihilominus
> ei cogitandum sit et loquendum; tertius ipsa jam rerum
> experientia est in sentiendo de Domino in bonitate,
> sicut sentiunt qui simplicitate cordis quaerunt illum
> ....Item primus gradus in auctoritate fundatus, fidei
> est, habens formam fidei, probatae auctoritatis proba-
> bilibus testimoniis fundatam. Secundus rationis est,
> non rationis humanae, sed ejus quae propria fidei est;
> habens et ipse formam sanorum in fide verborum divi-
> nae auctoritate per omnia concordem. Hujus est scire,
> non solum cogitare et loqui de Deo rationabiliter se-
> cundum rationem fidei; sed et quomodo fides eadem fiat
> ubi non est, nutriatur et adjuvetur ubi est, et qua-
> liter contra inimicos defendatur. Tertius jam gratiae
> illuminantis et beatificantis est, finiens fidem, seu
> potius beatificans in amorem, a fide ad speciem trans-
> mittens....110

The unified structure of these three stages might suggest
that William has indicated here a final synthesis of his doctrine
of the ascent to God through faith.111 This would be an illusion.
On closer inspection these stages are seen to give a formulation
in the direction of a synthesis but they do not give even in outline his entire doctrine. The point of departure in the three
stages unifies but also restricts William's vision with the result
that the apparent synthesis is constructed within a limited area
of his teaching on faith. The context of the central section of
the *Aenigma fidei* on the divine names112 situates the three stages
directly within the movement towards the intellectual, metaphysical penetration of faith through *ratio fidei*. An intellectual
perspective appears explicitly in the formulation of the three
stages as 'Tribus enim intelligentiae gradibus.'113 Moreover, the
actual point of departure for the ascent is the 'material object'
of faith, 'quid sibi de Domino Deo suo sit credendum,' and not the
structure of the act of faith. The immediate and the more remote
context imply that this material object of faith is restricted to
the entitative dogmatic propositions of faith and more specifically
to the dogmatic formulations of the Trinity.114 The second stage,
ratio fidei and the third stage, *experientia, amor, Spiritus* are
a further understanding of faith from this propositional basis.
William is groping towards the integration of the spiritual and
the intellectual ascent. But the *experientia* in this text, as

compared with the *experientia* of the *Speculum fidei* is seen through
the intellectual perspective of the three stages. The era of faith
and the transition from faith to vision are compared as *duae....*
cognitiones.[115] Consequently William tends to focus the attention
on those aspects of the final stage which are relevant for this
comparison, and which show how the sapiential understanding given
through the teaching of the Holy Spirit is the response on the mystical level to all that *ratio fidei* fails to achieve on the rational level. Basically, the antithesis is that of man thinking and
talking about God and God teaching man about Himself.

> Duae enim istae cognitiones tantum ab invicem sunt
> differentes, quantum differt a Deo in eo quod ipse in
> semetipso est, quidquid homo secundum hominem de Deo
> seu cogitando seu loquando sentire potest....Et tamen
> prima haec ad Deum cognitio est, rationabiliter secun-
> dum rationem fidei scire de Deo vel cogitare, vel lo-
> qui....Ipsa enim est scientia de Deo, de qua Psalmista
> dicit, quia nox eam indicat nocti (Ps. XLIV), hoc est
> homo homini caro et sanguis carni et sanguini, in-
> fidelis nonnumquam infideli, longe distans a sapientia
> illa, et verbo illo, quod dies diei, seu spiritualis
> homo spirituali homini, seu ipse per se Spiritus
> Sanctus sancti cujusque hominis spiritui non indicat
> sed eructat, hoc est, cum sensu quodam divinitatis
> et sapore summae sapientiae, occulta aliqua inspira-
> tione insinuat.[116]

C. WIDENING THE HORIZON OF WILLIAM'S INTELLECTUALISM.

Some of the themes of William's theology of faith, which are
often associated with the ascent from faith to mystical experience
without the mediation of the speculative *ratio fidei,* are in certain text impregnated with a more intellectualist tendency. This
tendency is sometimes though not always related to the speculative
ratio fidei. But it always reflects the perspective of the ascent
of the mind towards understanding and vision. This widening of
the intellectual horizon so as to 'intellectualize' those themes
which of their nature are not directly speculative, is characteristic especially of the opening pages of the *Aenigma fidei.*[117]
The hypothesis might be suggested that, under the influence of the
speculative *ratio fidei,* William rethinks and reshapes some of the
themes of the *Speculum fidei* in the light of the ascent of the
mind toward the metaphysical understanding of God's nature. Why,
for instance, does the text in the *Aenigma fidei*[118] which centers
on the *visio-similitudo* equation,[119] rooted ultimately in the Holy
Spirit as the *unitas* of the Father and the Son,[120] in comparison

with the corresponding texts in the *Speculum fidei*,121 give a relatively greater emphasis to the *visio* of the future life rather
than to the trinitarian 'experience' in this life, and to *visio*
and *cognitio* rather than *charitas* and *amor*?

But this tendency is still more evident in the new direction
given to the pedagogy of the Incarnational sacramental economy
when the purification of the soul for the experience of love becomes the purification of the mind for the trinitarian mystery.122
As a consequence of sin the mind of man, immersed in sense imagery,123 must emerge from this domination by corporeal images so as
to recognize first that the human intellect of man transcends such
images124 and a fortiori that the Trinity, which incomparably
transcends the human intellect cannot be conceived in terms of
such images.125 As, in the spiritual ascent, faith in the Incarnational economy breaks through the external sacramentum into
amoris sensus and into the inner life of the Holy Spirit the *sacramentorum sacramentum*,126 so, in the ascent of the mind, faith in
the temporal economy breaks through the barrier of time and initiates the mind into the eternal mystery of the three persons in
one God.127

> Temporalium autem rerum fides sive visibilium, sive
> invisibilium, magis credendo quam intelligendo valet;
> ubi nisi credatur quod dicitur, nulla prorsus ratione
> id persuaderi potest. Hujus ergo religionis sectan-
> dae caput est historia et prophetia temporalis dis-
> pensationis divinae providentiae, pro salute generis
> humani in aeternam vitam reformandi atque reparandi.
> Quae cum credita fuerint, mentem purgabit vitae mo-
> dus divinis praeceptis conciliatus et exemplis con-
> formatus; et idoneam faciet spiritualibus percipien-
> dis, quae nec praeterita sunt nec futura; sed eodem
> modo semper manentia et nulli mutabilitati obnoxia;
> id est unum ipsum Deum, Patrem et Filium, et Spiritum
> Sanctum.128

The entire *Aenigma fidei*, including also those passages which
are in themselves more closely connected with spiritual ascent towards mystical experience, is a response to the intellectual desire to know something about the 'essence' or 'nature' of God,129
however imperfectly and however obscurely through the enigma of
faith.

IV. Conclusion.

The ultimate unity in William's theology of faith is to be
found not in a perfectly ordered synthesis of doctrine, which he

never wholly achieves, but in a unifying approach towards the
theology of faith. He always sees faith dynamically as an ascent
to God. He concentrates predominantly not on the metaphysical
analysis of the act of faith but on the description and explanation
tion of faith in its development towards an authentically Christian life. Even the explanation of the structure of the act of
faith never prescinds from this context of the life of the Christian in movement towards God.

There are two different aspects of this ascent to God through
faith. There is the spiritual ascent, which I have called *credo
ut experiar,* and there is the intellectual ascent, which I have
called *credo ut intelligam.* The first is the spiritual movement
towards mystical union with God. The second is the intellectual
movement towards a speculative knowledge about God's nature. The
spiritual ascent leads from experience to experience, from the
experience *ex fide in fidem* to the experience *a fide ad speciem*
so as to reveal an intrinsic relationship of faith to mystical
experience. Neither the experienced faith *ex fide in fidem* nor
the more advanced trinitarian experience *a fide ad speciem* are a
superstructure extrinsic to the initial act of faith. These experiences are an organic development from that initial act of
faith. In contrast the intellectual ascent leads the mind of man
from its basic thrust towards a metaphysical knowledge about God's
nature to the initiation through faith into the mystery of the
Trinity. Through the purification of *ratio fidei* the human mind
is led into a reflective intellectual awareness of the mystery.
Finally there is the movement towards the union of the spiritual
and of the intellectual ascent in a higher synthesis. The movement towards a synthesis is grounded in the limitations intrinsic
to the intellectual drive towards speculative knowledge about God.
The limitations of *ratio fidei* are only transcended through *amor
intellectus.*

The ascent through faith leads us beyond every limited insight into the depths of the trinitarian life and ultimately into
the vision when God is no longer seen *per speculum* and *in aenigmate*
but *facie ad faciem.* The *Speculum fidei* and the *Aenigma fidei* are
titles which hint at William's most basic intuitions. Faith is
the initiation into the hidden life of God which is communicated
to us first through the mediation of external forms, visible signs,
rational concepts and discursive language. The *signa* of *sacramenta fidei* and the *signa* of *ratio fidei* are the medium through
which God leads us to himself. Faith breaks through the external
signum and penetrates to the inner *res*. William suggests here an
interesting analogy whereby *sacramenta fidei* and *ratio fidei* can
be compared through a similar sign structure. This economy of
God's disclosure through the *speculum* and the *aenigma* is continued
even in the trinitarian experience in so far as this experience is

not yet the final vision *facie ad faciem*.

This approach to faith suggests the theory, which has been expounded by recent theologians, that there is a connatural experience as the proximate disposition for every act of faith, and that this experience is the basis from which the experience of the mystics develops. William does not explicitly consider this question. But the implicit convergence of the spiritual ascent towards the trinitarian mystical experience strnegthens the argument at the conclusion of the previous article. William argues that faith is orientated first towards the experienced faith *ex fide in fidem* and ultimately towards the trinitarian experience *a fide ad speciem*. He argues further to the dynamism of faith through *ratio fidei* to *amor intellectus*. In the course of his argument he shows how the dynamism of faith penetrates the sign both of *sacramenta fidei* and of *ratio fidei* so as to give an insight into the inner *res* through a spiritual experience. Therefore the logic of William's thought moves implicitly towards the theory that, at the root of every act of faith, there is a connatural experience which is the basis from which mysticism develops. In this way the monastic theology of William of St Thierry can throw light on contemporary problems and point towards further theological development.

NOTES

*Published RTAM 33 (1966) 282-318.

[1]For this expression see Leclercq, *L'amour des lettres*, p. 202. The expression should not be interpreted as an implicit denial that faith is in itself an experience. *Experientia* here refers more specifically to the deeper and more inward experiences to which, according to William's teaching, faith is intrinsically orientated. This *experientia* is ultimately a mystical experience in the strict sense. The division of the ascent to God through faith into 'credo ut experiar' and 'credo ut intelligam' is justified for the following reasons. William's doctrine of the ascent to God through faith reveals two distinct tendencies. There is the spiritual ascent which describes a movement from faith to mystical experience and to vision so as to prescind almost totally from an intervening stage of metaphysical speculation about the nature of God. There is the intellectual ascent towards the knowledge of God's nature and which, under the formative power of faith, develops into *ratio fidei*. Finally there is the movement towards a synthesis in which faith ascends to mystical experience through the intervening stage of *ratio fidei*. The spiritual ascent, *credo ut experiar*, is the theme of the concluding section of the preceding article (Chapter 5,'William of St Thierry's Doctrine of the Ascent to God by Faith') and of the first section of this article. These sections are based on texts which are principally from the Spec fid and in which the spiritual ascent to mystical experience is predominant. William explicitly states that the *simplices filii Dei* can ascend directly to the inward communication from the Holy Spirit without intermediary rational and discursive arguments (Spec fid, p. 102-105; 378CD). This proves that his doctrine of the spiritual ascent does not in itself depend essentially on an intervening stage of the speculative *ratio fidei*. During the greater part of the Spec fid (p. 48-168; 365B-394C), William barely develops the intellectual ascent of the mind towards the speculative understanding of God's nature except on p. 134-141 (368B-388A) and then only slightly in comparison with the incomparably greater development of this theme in the Aenig. This development in the Aenig is foreshadowed more strikingly in the concluding pages of the Spec fid, p. 168-179; 394C-398A, although by comparison with the Aenig it is synthesized more closely with the spiritual ascent. The purpose of the first section of this article is to continue the description of the spiritual ascent, *credo ut experiar*, begun in the preceding article and so to give the basic orientations of this ascent which of itself does not appear in William's analysis to depend essentially on the speculative ascent of the mind.

[2]See Chapter 5, pp. 140-6.

[3]See Vagaggini, *Il senso teologico*, 36-38, 473-484.

[4]See Déchanet, *Le miroir*, p. 25-26.

[5]Spec fid, 120-121; 382D-383A): 'Quod potissimum in persona mediatoris elucet nobis; qui in seipso manens Deus aeternus, in tempore est homo factus; ut per temporalem et aeternum, a temporalibus ad aeterna transeamus. Ideo sicut dictum est corpus Domini manducamus, et sanguinem bibimus corporaliter, sed reficimur spiritualiter; corporaliter in baptismo lavamur, sed spiritualiter purificamur.' (See p. 130-131, 385A, where the term *Sacramentum* is explicitly referred to Christ: 'Deum autem factum hominem pro nobis....altum Sacramentum'). For Origen's doctrine on this question see H. U. von Balthasar, *Parole et mystère chez Origène* (Paris, 1957) p. 79-80. This theology of Christ as sacrament has been developed further in the writings of contemporary theologians. See E. H. Schillebeeckx, *Le Christ Sacrement de la recontre de Dieu*, 38-41, and K. Rahner, *The Church and the Sacraments* (London, 1963) p. 15-19.

[6]There is strong evidence for the influence of Origen on William of St Thierry; see Déchanet, *Guillaume de Saint-Thierry*, p. 116; *Exposé sur le Cantique des Cantiques* (Paris, 1962) p. 30-42. This influence will appear in the course of this article. It is therefore important also to note the difference in the approach of Origen and of William to this question of *sacramentum*. Origen approaches the question more specifically from the angle of Scriptural exegete and, despite his emphasis on the penetration of the external sign through the spiritual insight of the believer, he concentrates much more closely than William on the objective external economy as narrated in Scripture and more specifically on the particular *mysteria* as revealed through typology; see for example, the classic exposition of Origen's doctrine of *signum (Comment. in Epist. ad Rom;* PG 14, 968A-969A). The contrast can be seen clearly from Crouzel's analysis of Origen's theology of the relationship of the different phases of Scriptural revelationship in the typological perspective of umbra, imago, veritas (H. Crouzel, *Origène et la connaissance mystique*, 324-374).

[7]'Subjective' here does not mean an individualist self-realization irrespective of objective salvation history but rather the assimilation of salvation history in the life of the individual believer.

[8]Spec fid, 382BC.

[9]Ibid., 418D: 'constituens sacramenta fidei, alia ut sint sacrae rei signa corporalia et visibilia, sicut in baptismo, sicut in sacramento corporis et sanguinis Domini; alia ut sint tantum sacra recondita spirituali intellectu ipso Spiritu Sancto praeduce investiganda; de quibus dicit Apostolus: "ut notum faceret nobis sacramentum voluntatis suae" (Ephes. I).'

[10]Ibid., p. 96–97, 382A: 'Occultum enim voluntatis Dei et altissimum est, et omnium sacramentorum sacramentum; quod notum facit secundum bonum placitum suum, quibus vult, et sicut vult; quod sicut divinum est, sic modo quodam divino revelat ei qui donante ipso dignus est. Quin potius non divinum, sed Deus est, quia ipse est Spiritus Sanctus, qui substantialis Dei voluntas est.' With this reference to the Holy Spirit as 'substantialis Dei voluntas' who reveals himself gratuitously 'quibus vult' and in a transcendant revelation 'modo quidam divino' we touch on the center of William's theology which is the Holy Spirit. Ultimately the Spec fid converges on the mystical experience of the Trinity given in the Holy Spirit (p. 162–165, 393A). In this text William refers again to the gratuitous revelation of the Holy Spirit in phraseology similar to that of the text quoted above (p. 96–97, 382A): 'Aliquibus ergo revelant; scilicet quibus volunt,...quibus largiuntur Spiritum Sanctum qui communis notitia, vel communis voluntas est amborum.' In each of these texts the Holy Spirit is *voluntas* and reveals himself gratuitously. But in the later text (p. 164–165, 393A) the revelation is explicitly trinitarian: 'communis voluntas est amborum.' Through this doctrine William shows that the insight into the inward reality of the *sacramentum* is wholly dependent on the gratuitous gift of God's revelation. Our 'ascent' to God depends on God's 'descent' to us. See von Balthasar, *Parole et mystère*, p. 33–34.

[11]Spec fid, 124–125; 383D–384A: 'Hic ergo quamdiu purgamur suam sacramentis rerum reddamus reverentiam; ipsis vero rebus fidem: ut his purgati et adiuti, proficiamus ad ea quibus et res gestae servierunt, et sacramenta earum serviunt, et fides ipsa; ad aeternorum scilicet contemplationem.'

[12]Ibid., 120–121; 383A: 'Sic enim quibusdam Christianae pietatis rudimentis paulatim erudiendus erat fidei nostrae assensus.' This text follows immediately after the text on the sacramental pattern of the Eucharist and Baptism exemplified in Christ the Mediator.

13Ibid., 383A-B: 'Abusive quippe dictum de illis est, quia credebant in eum, quem non diligebant. Credere enim in eum, amando in eum ire est. Illi vero Christum eum esse credebant, sed non sicut Christum diligebant' (see *infra*, for a more complete analysis of the relationship of faith and love and for the Augustinian background to this doctrine).

14The *intellectus rationis* in this context is not an intermediate stage of speculative theology prior to the final stage of spiritual experience but an element within that spiritual experience. This intellectual element is not the 'conatus rationis' contradistinguished from the 'affectus amoris' but the 'intellectus rationis' under the dominion of illuminating grace and inseparable from the 'affectus amoris.' The penetration of the exterior Sacramentum and the insight through faith into the interior Sacramentum is a direct transition from faith to experience through the Holy Spirit without the mediation of the speculative *ratio fidei*.

15Spec fid, 383B-C. The 'Sacramentum....internae Dei voluntatis' should be read in the light of William's teaching on the Holy Spirit as 'occultum enim voluntas Dei,...et omnium sacramentorum sacramentum' (p. 96-97; 382A).

16Cant, 536D: 'Tunc sicut olim nova gratiae Sacramenta finem imposuerunt veteribus Sacramentis: res ipsa Sacramentorum omnium finem imponent omnibus omnino Sacramentis. In sacramentis quippe Novi Testamenti coepit aspirare nova gratiae dies: in illo vero omnis consumptionis fine erit meridies, ubi non erit speculum et aenigma, et ex parte, sed visio facie ad faciem....' Here William moves into the wider historical perspective which considers not only the New Testament in relation to the future life but also the Old Testament in relation to the New Testament. The approach is similar to that of St Bernard, SC 31, 8. This theme together with the frequent reference to the contrasting 'unbra'-'veritas' (Cant, 536D) shows a resemblance to the doctrine of Origen. See J. Daniélou, 'Saint Bernard et les Pères grecs,' 46-55.

17Exp Rm, 592D. The transition from *Sacramentum* to *res* is directly related to the transition from the knowledge of Christ according to the flesh to the knowledge of Christ according to the Spirit. 'Non jam in Sacramentis sed in ipsa re omnium Sacramentorum, non in mysteriis, sed in ipsa luce manifestae veritatis, quia, etsi novit Jesum secundum carnem, sed hunc jam non novit.' The transition from faith to 'affectus' initiates this transition from the knowledge of Christ according to the flesh to the knowledge of Christ according to the Spirit. See Ep frat, 336B-C:

'Post modum vero fide migrante in affectum, amplexantes in medio cordis sui dulci amoris amplexu Christum Jesum....incipiunt eum non jam secundum carnem cognoscere, quamvis eum necdum Deum plene possint cogitare.' *Sacramentum, fides,* the knowledge of Christ according to the flesh, are closely interrelated and they are respectively orientated towards *res, visio* and Christ according to the Spirit.

[18]This anthropological basis for the penetration of the sacramental economy is prominent in the writings of Origen: see *In Matth., Comment. Series,* 27; PG 13, 1633B, C, D). The divinity of Christ and the spiritual sense of Scripture is concealed to the *carnales* but revealed to the *spirituales.*

[19]See Spec fid, 60-61; 368D-369A, and 96-97; 377A-377B.

[20]Ibid., 98-99; 377D-378A.

[21]Ibid., 124; 383C: 'Nam in corpore positi corporalibus sacramentorum formis cohibendi eramus et continendi....'

[22]Ibid., 124-125; 383D: 'Aegritudo nostra, mutabilitas nostrae morta litatis est.' But even here William does not locate man's opposition to spiritual things exclusively in the corporeal sphere. Ibid., 384A, where 'superbus animus' is one of the elements of opposition.

[23]Ibid.: 'Medicina qua hinc illuc transitur, fides Mediatoris est. Fides autem maxime est rerum temporaliter pro nobis gestarum; per quam corda nostra mundantur, ut ad aeterna non credenda, sed intelligenda, idonea inveniantur. In qua, si fideliter nos agimus, et fides meretur veritatem; et mutabilitas transit ad creditae rei incommutabilem aeternitatem.' William's approach here resembles that of St Bernard. See Déchanet, 'La christologie de S. Bernard,' *Saint Bernard théologien,* p. 78-91. St Bernard teaches that Christ is the Mediator who reconciles the antithesis of flesh and spirit. See Asc III, 3 (305D).

[24]Spec fid, 124-125; 383C-D: 'Aegroti quippe sumus de corruptione naturae languentis; et sanitatem desiderare debemus. Aegritudo nostra, mutabilitas nostrae mortalitatis est; medicina qua hinc illuc transitur, fides Mediatoris est.' See also Aenig, 402B, C, D and 406A, B, where this theme is rethought in closer relationship to the ascent of the mind towards the understanding of God metaphysically. These texts from the Aenig refer in general to the Incarnational temporal economy rather than specifically to the *sacramenta.* But the theme follows closely the argument from

the Spec fid and describes still more explicitly the historical origin of this immersion in the corporeal aspect of human existence. 'Nam in quem locum quisque ceciderit, ibi debet incumbere et inniti ut resurgat. Formae carnales amore suo nos detinent, in quem per consensum peccati cecidimus, ipsis innitendum est, ut surgamus. Idcirco Filius Dei qui in forma Dei erat, exinanivit semetipsum formam servi accipiens....' (402C). See the explicit reference to original sin as the historical origin of our difficulty in conceiving either the human soul or the divine nature other than in terms of corporeal imagery (406A-B).

25The life of faith is described explicitly as the opposition of 'spirit' to 'flesh.' Spec fid, 110-111; 380C: 'Hoc est, si fidei conformantur affectiones animae, homo ille spiritu vivit, spiritu est et ambulat, et quasi totus spiritus est; si vero spirituales illae virtutes resolvuntur in affectiones carnales, totum caro fit.'

26Ep frat, 315C-316B, where the three spiritual states are formulated as *animalis, rationalis, spiritualis;* ibid., 340C and 348D-349A, where the psychological root of these states is formulated as *anima, animus, spiritus.* Déchanet has shown the influence of Origen on William's anthropology in *Exposé sur le Cantique,* 34-39.

27There is similar tension in Origen's doctrine on the question as to whether the ascent from faith to spiritual experience is to be made with or without the mediation of speculation. See Crouzel, *Origène et la connaissance mystique,* p. 531.

28Spec fid, 70-71; 371AB: 'Non credis quia non diligis, non diligis quia non credis. Neque enim alterum esse potest sine altero, quia alterum pendet ex altero.' See p. 122-123; 383AB: ' 'abusive quippe dictum de illis est, quia credebant in eum, quem non diligebant. Credere enim in eum, amando in eum ire est;' and Exp Rm, 582C. William here follows the teaching of St Augustine; see *In Johannem* 29, 6 (PL 35, 1631A): 'Quid est ergo credere in eum? Credendo amare, credendo diligere. Credendo in eum ire, et ejus membris incorporari,' or *Sermo* 144, 2 (PL 38, 388C). St Augustine distinguishes faith without hope and charity, 'Christum esse credit,' from faith with hope and charity, 'credit in Christum.' William admits the existence of dead faith. See Spec fid, p. 56-57; 367C; Aenig 440A; and Nat am, 390B. But, like St Augustine, he is little concerned with a faith which is not in union with charity.

[29]Spec fid, 48-49; 365B.

[30]Ibid.

[31]Ibid.: 'A fide enim incipit homo,' and p. 58-59; 368B. See St Augustine, *Sermo* 158, 6 (PL 38, 865A): 'incipit homo a fide.'

[32]Ibid., p. 48-51, 365C; p. 58-59, 368C, Aenig, 400A, 407BC; Cant 491C.

[33]Spec fid, p. 50-51; 365C: 'nec tamen fides et spes peribunt; sed in res suas transibunt, cum quod credebatur, videbitur; habebitur quod sperabatur.' See St Augustine, *Sermo* 158, 8 (PL 38, 866 CD: 'spes jam non erit, quando erit res' and Ibid. 9 (867B): 'visio erit, non fides....res erit non spes.'

[34]Spec fid, p. 50-51; 365C: 'Caritas vero non tantum erit, sed perfecta erit.' See St Augustine, *Sermo* 158, 9 (867B): 'Ergo charitas erit, sed perfecta erit.'

[35]The illustration of the trinitarian distinction in unity through the mutual interpenetration of faith, hope and charity (Spec fid, p. 54-57; 367C-368A) is enclosed within the wider context of faith as an ascent to God (Ibid., p. 48-61; 365B-369B).

[36]Spec fid, 48-49; 368A: 'et quantum ad virtutis substantiam quodammodo consubstantiales; licet videantur habere secundum formam differentis affectus, quasi differentias quasdam personales.' See Ibid. (p. 54-57; 367C): 'Tres autem cardinales istae virtutes ubi sunt, ad aliquam similitudinem Trintatis Dei, sic sibi invicem connexae sunt et conjunctae, ut sint singulae in omnibus, et omnes in singulis; ut quod, et quantum, et quomodo quis credit, hoc etiam et tantum, et eo modo speret et amet; sic etiam speret, quod credit et amat; sic amet, quod credit et sperat.'

[37]Ibid., 58-59; 368B.

[38]See *infra,* p. 000.

[39]Spec fid, p. 158-161; 392A-392B: 'Nec enim maior potest esse suavitas homini in hac vita, quam cum in imagine conditoris, in similitudine bonitatis ejus invenit se bene affecta conscientia. Hanc quicumque desiderat suavitatem, nequaquam onerosam habeat in exercitio fidei laboriosam necessitatem; quoniam tribulatio patientiam operatur, patientia probationem, probatio vero spem, spes autem non confudit; quia per probationem diffunditur in

corde caritas, et mox per Spiritum Sanctum ordinatur sua piae mentis suavitas.' William alludes here to St Paul, Rom. 5, 3-5.

[40]Spec fid, 48-49; 365B.

[41]Chapter 7, note 67ff.

[42]It could be questioned whether the *affectus fidei* of
fides illuminata in the experience *ex fide in fidem* were not simply a normal intensification of the experience through connaturality which many theologians discern in the initial act of faith as
such (see Aubert, *Le problème de l'acte de foi*, 721-737, and
Vagaggini, *Il senso teologico*, 417-424). But although the experience *a fide ad speciem* will be seen to be an organic development
of the life of faith, this experience will be shown to be explicitly contradistinguished from a *cognitio fidei*. It cannot be called
simply an **intensification** of the experience of faith, a new depth
in faith as such, for it is an experience which transcends *cognitio fidei*, and it is an initiation into a transcendent mode of
knowledge which is a real participation in the mutual knowledge
and love of the persons of the Trinity. Such an experience has
the marks of a strictly **mystical** experience, a transcendent divine
mode of knowledge which goes beyond the normal powers of the soul
even aided by grace. See **David** Knowles, *The English Mystical Tradition*, (London, 1961) p. 1-20.

[43]Spec Fid, 128-129; 384D: 'Ipse ex fide in fidem revelat fidelibus Dei iustitiam; cum pro gratia dat gratiam; pro fide
auditus fidem illuminatam.' The reference *ex fide in fidem* is to
Rom. 1, 17.

[44]Aenig, 414D. The terminology is not altogether constant; see Exp Rm, 557B, where *ex fide in fidem* suggests the eschatological tension of *a fide ad speciem*. Nor does the terminology *a fide ad speciem* in the text quoted above from the Aenig refer explicitly to the trinitarian experience. But William clearly
differentiates the **experience** of interiorized faith from the more
advanced experience given in a state of transition from faith to
vision and the terminology *ex fide in fidem* and *a fide ad speciem*
aptly expresses this distinction. See also the expression *a fide
ad speciem* in the **Spec fid**, p. 174-175; 396A.

[45]The texts on the *affectus fidei*, the *fides illuminata*,
in the experience *ex fide in fidem* do not describe a specifically
trinitarian experience (see previous chapter) whereas those of the
Spec fid, 162-169; 392D-394C, describe an experience which is essentially trinitarian with its whole raison d'être in the Holy

Spirit as the mutual union of the Father and of the Son. In this
trinitarian text from the Spec fid the eschatological note is much
more developed (see 164-169; 393CD, 394BC, as compared with 78-81;
373A-373B, and 128-129; 384D). The more transcendent character of
this experience is also emphasized by the development of the theology of the *similitudo*. The *similitudo*, the restoration of the perfect likeness to God, is a participation in the trinitarian *unitas*,
the Holy Spirit as the union of the Father and of the Son (164-
165, 393B). See also the description of the trinitarian experience
in the Ep frat, 349-350D.

[46]Spec fid, 162-169; 392D-394C.

[47]See supra, *a fide ad speciem*.

[48]Ibid., n. 37.

[49]Spec fid, 162-165; 392D-393B.

[50]See supra, n. 14.

[51]Spec fid, 162-165; 392D-393B.

[52]This relationship of the sacramental economy to the
trinitarian experience is indicated further through the relationship of the Incarnational economy to the trinitarian experience.
See Spec fid, 148-159; 390A-391D. Here William refers specifically
to the economy of the Incarnation rather than to the sacramental
economy. But the reference to Christ as mediator (p. 152-153;
390C) touches directly on the sacramental economy. For Christ the
mediator is the exemplar of the sacramental economy (120-121; 382D-
383A). Through Christ as mediator we are transformed into his
image (Spec fid, 152-153; 390C, referring to St Paul, II Cor 3, 18).
But this assimilation is realized through love (Spec fid, pp. 154-
159; 390C-391D) and the root of this love is the Holy Spirit, the
substantialis voluntas Patris ac Filii (pp. 158-159; 391CD) and
this participation through love in the trinitarian life of the
Holy Spirit is the trinitarian experience (pp. 158-169; 390C-394B).

[53]Chapter 5, *Credo ut experiar*.

[54]Ibid., pp. 143-4.

[55]See Ibid., pp. 140-3.

[56]Spec fid, 164-165; 393A: 'Quibus ergo revelat Pater
et Filius, hii cognoscunt, sicut Pater et Filius se cognoscunt;

quia habent in semetipsis notitiam mutuam eorum; quia habent in semetipsis unitatem amborum et voluntatem vel amorum; quod totum Spiritus Sanctus est.' William explicitly guards against the pantheist danger, (393B): 'aliter in Creatore, aliter in creatura; aliter in propria natura, aliter in gratia.'

[57]Father Giles Hibbert OP, in his article 'Created and Uncreated Charity,' *RTAM* 31 (1964) 63-84, disagrees that William's doctrine of the image is a true development of St Augustine's thought (p. 72-73). I am grateful to him for pointing to the limitations of William's theology in comparison with that of St Augustine and of St Thomas on the question of the full development of the created as distinct from the uncreated element in man's assimilation to the Trinity and in particular on the question of the created natural basis for that assimilation. But my point is that William has given a new development to St Augustine's doctrine of man as the image of the Trinity through his theology of the trinitarian mystical experience. Moreover, he has attempted an explanation of that experience. According to that explanation which is based on what we should now call 'connatural knowledge,' the trinitarian experience is communicated through our similitude to the Trinity and that similitude is rooted in the intratrinitarian life of the Holy Spirit who is the uncreated unity of the Father and of the Son. The tendency of William's thought is to see the uncreated intratrinitarian life of the Holy Spirit as the ultimate explanation of this experience. But William recognizes the created term in grace (see Spec fid, 164-165; 393B) and he also recognizes the natural inalienable structure of the created image. See the explicit reference to this in the Ep frat, 348C). Therefore William's theology of our assimilation to the Trinity is a true development of St Augustine's thought. For both St Augustine and William presuppose as a point of departure that the image is man in relationship to the Trinity. But St Augustine develops this relationship more completely through the analysis of the image in its created structure and William develops this relationship more completely through his theology of the achieved similitude in the trinitarian mystical experience.

[58]Spec fid, 168-169; 394B-394C.

[59]See Chapter 5, *The Structure of the Act of Faith.*

[60]See R. Javelet, 'Intelligence et amour chez les auteurs spirituels du XIIe siècle, in *RAM* 37 (1961) 429-450. See 431-432, where the author refers to William's conception of the trinitarian *cognitio amoris* in terms of personal communion. The personalist approach is suggested also in the *cognitio fidei*

contrasted with the *cognitio amoris*: 'aliud quippe est cognoscere
Deum sicut cognoscit vir amicum suum, aliud cognoscere eum sicut
ipse cognoscit semetipsum' (Spec fid, 162-163; 392D). William
merely alludes to the analogy of human friendship without developing the question further (Javelet, 431). This illustrates further
William's tendency to concentrate on the assimilation of man to the
uncreated life of God rather than on the created natural basis for
that assimilation. The personalist theory of faith has been more
fully developed in contemporary theology and especially in the
works of J. Mouroux who, under the influence of G. Marcel, has
attempted an explanation of faith as an encounter with the divine
persons in the light of the personalist philogophy of the realization of the human person and of the mutual encounter of human persons (see Aubert, *Le problème*, 615-622).

61The traditional teaching that faith is orientated towards vision is deeply rooted in William's doctrine. See Spec fid,
48-51; 365C; 56-59, 368AB; 58-59, 368C; 168-169, 394C; 174-175,
396A; Aenig, 397D-398B, 399BC, 399D-400A, 402B, 403C, 414D, 416C,
435B; Exp Rm, 557B, 609D, 655A, 655D-666A; Nat corp, 725AB; Ep frat,
349B-350A; Cant, 536C-537A; Med, 213D-214A, 235A. For this traditional doctrine see St Augustine, *Sermo* 158, 7-9 (PL 38, 865
D867C); St Bernard, *CSI* V, 3 (PL 182, 791); St Thomas, *De veritate*,
q. 14, a. 2, *ad* 9; II^a II^{ae}, q. 4, a. I (for this teaching of St
Thomas, see A. Stolz, *Glaubensnade und Glaubenslicht nach Thomas
v. Aquin* [Rome, 1933]). For this whole question see Aubert, *Le
problème*, 47-48, 709-710.

62Spec fid, 162-163, 392D, and 150-151; 390C, in the
context of our knowledge of Christ: 'Quem etiam aliter vident per
fidem cogitando qui digni sunt, cum soli sibi sunt; aliter cum per
efficientem gratiam ipse est in eis; et illi in ipso per affectum
devotionis.'

63In the Aenig, 399CD, William contrasts the vision *per
speciem* and *facie ad faciem* as given in the future life with that
per speculum and *in aenigmate* as given in this life. In the texts
from the Spec fid describing the trinitarian experience, William
also explicitly denies that the knowledge of God given in this
life can be equated with that given in the future life (p. 164-167;
393CD: 'quia quae de Deo hic sciuntur, vel cognoscuntur, nequaquam scire possunt vel cognosci sicut in vita illa ubi videbitur
facie ad faciem, et sicuti est.' See also pp. 168-619; 394BC.
In the similar description of the trinitarian experience in the Ep
frat, William refers again to the same principle that all knowledge given to the faithful in this life is *per speculum* and *in
aenigmate*. But here he appears almost to make an exception with

the 'nisi cum aliquando fit....' (PL 184, 349C). But this apparent exception is a vision only *in puncto* and in this transitory glimpse the soul longs for the full vision. 'Ut per hoc quod quasi in transcursu, vel in puncto permittitur videre, inardescat animus ad plenam possessionem luminis aeterni, et haereditatem plenae visionis Dei....nonnumquam quasi pertransiens gratia perstringit sensum amantis....ad punctum id ipsum ostendens ei videndum sicuti est' (349D-350A). Even if William conceives this momentary vision as beyond the *speculum* and the *aenigma* of faith, he excludes the possibility of a continuous state in this life which transcends the limitations of faith. See the text in the Aenig, (399D-400A) where he excludes from this life any vision entirely free from corporeal images 'constanter et indeclinabiliter,' and also the general teaching of William throughout his works that the knowledge of God in this life is *per speculum* and *in aenigmate* and not *facie ad faciem*. Med, 213D-214A; Cant, 480BC, 526C, 546CD; Exp Rm, 609CD: Nat corp, 725A; Ep frat, 313AB, 351B; Aenig, 397D, 406CD.

[65]Further light is thrown on this intermediary state in the text in the Aenig, 414D which describes the final stage in the three stages of the ascent through faith. In this text William is describing the ascent from faith to mystical experience through the mediation of *ratio fidei*. This text and its importance for William's theology of the ascent through faith, will be discussed later in this article. It is the most perfect expression of William's attempt towards the synthesis of *credo ut experiar* and *credo ut intelligam*. In that text William is describing *cognitio amoris* in another context and without explicit reference to the trinitarian experience. But what he says in that text is relevant to the *cognitio amoris* in the trinitarian experience. 'Tertius jam gratiae illuminantis et beatificantis est, finiens fidem seu potius beatificans in amorem, a fide ad speciem transmittens, inchoando cognitionem non eam quae fidei est, et cum fide hic incipit esse in homine fideli, sed de qua Apostolus dicit: "Nunc cognosco ex parte; tunc autem cognoscam sicut et cognitus sum" (I Cor. 13). Illa enim est, quam perfecta charitas inchoat in hac vita perficiendam in futura.' William speaks here of an intermediary stage between faith and vision, a stage which is a prefiguration of the future vision. This intermediary stage is described dynamically rather than statically. It is a movement rather than a fixed state. 'A fide ad speciem transmittens.'

[66]See *supra*, p. 168.

[67]See *supra*, pp. 168-9.

68Aenig, 397A: 'Humanae infirmitatis religiosa confessio est, de Deo hoc solum nosse, quod Deus est. Caeterum essentiam vel naturam, et secreta illa imperscrutabilis judicii ejus
decreta investigare quidem et perscrutare pium est,' and (417D):
'Homini siquidem condito ad imaginem Dei, naturalis inest appeti-
tus cognitionis Dei et propriae originis. Ex ea enim quod nullus
est animus humanus quantumvis rationis capax, quem natura ipsa
dubitare permittat, quin Deus sit; quin sit Creator omnium, et
omnium potestas et providentia penes ipsum sit; satagit etiam et
ambit semper quasi naturaliter humana et pietas et curiositas aliquatenus suspicere de eo, quid sit.' See Joannes Scotus Erigena,
De divisione naturae II, 27 (PL 122, 585B): 'Sed quemadmodum de
conditore suo hoc tantum cognoscit, quia est, non autem percipit,
quid sit.' It is probable that Erigena influenced William in the
metaphysical development of his theology from this basic drive of
the mind towards the understanding of God's nature. On this question I am indebted to Père Déchanet who, in his unpublished notes,
shows persuasively the influence of Erigena on this aspect of William's theology.

69The antithesis of *credo ut experiar* and *credo ut intelligam* is not a denial that the 'experience' given at the term of
the movement *credo ut experiar* is also an *intellectus fidei*. But
this *intellectus fidei* is not the metaphysical understanding which
is given in *ratio fidei*. The *intus.... legere* of the mystical *intellectus fidei* is associated essentially with nonintellectual
elements. See Spec fid, 102-103; 378C: 'ista fidei suum suggerit
intellectum, et plenam intellectus ethimologiam; cum qui credit,
intus in affectu cordis legit quod credit.' See also pp. 103-105;
378D-379A, where this *intellectus fidei* is given through the teaching of the Holy Spirit and through the *sensus amoris* in contrast to
the activity of discursive rational argument.

70Faith is always seen as an initiation. But in the
credo ut experiar ascent faith is the initiation into the way of
salvation and in the *credo ut intelligam* ascent faith is the initiation into an intellectual metaphysical understanding of God's
trinitarian nature. The opening passage of the Spec fid contrasts
here with the opening passage of the Aenig. Contrast for instance
Spec fid, 48-49; 365B: 'A fide enim incipit homo' in the context
of the pilgrimage to God through the saving trinitarian image,
faith, hope and charity, and Aenig, 397B-398A, where faith is the
response to the desire of the mind to know the nature of God, and
(408A-409B) where the trinitarian faith is the point of departure
for the metaphysical reflection of *ratio fidei* (409C-432C). This
'intellectualist' development which is the point of departure for
knowledge about God's nature is similar to that of Erigena,

De divisione naturae (PL 122, 516C): 'Nil enim aliud est fides, ut opinor, nisi principium quoddam, ex quo cognitio Creatoris in natura rationabili fieri incipit.'

[71]It is not denied that William's entire theology including the speculative *ratio fidei* is rooted in the patristic *sapientia*, rather than in the scholastic *scientia* and therefore that the scientific and speculative *ratio fidei* is not the *genus purum* of scientific theology. This *sapiential* approach will appear in the movement towards the synthesis of *credo ut experiar* and *credo ut intelligam*. But although *ratio fidei* is not wholly autonomous, it is not wholly integrated into William's mystical theology. This tension has its origin in the distinct point of departure in the *credo ut intelligam* movement. This new point of departure is the thrust of the mind in its desire to know, as far as possible, something about the nature of God. This thrust of the mind develops into the speculative *ratio fidei*, a penetration of faith which is distinct from that given in *credo ut experiar*. Therefore the approach towards an integration of the intellectual and the spiritual ascent can only be understood if the intellectual ascent is first explained as a distinct even though not wholly autonomous aspect of William's *sapiential* theology.

[72]This conception of *ratio fidei* differs from another kind of *ratio fidei* developed in the passages in the Spec fid, which explain the conflict of faith and doubt. See Spec fid, 76; 372BC: 'Infirmi quippe ingenii, sed infirmioris fidei, homines animales, non percipientes, aut vix percipientes, ea quae Dei sunt licet repugnante ratione fidei rationi et consuetudini humanae, saepe etiam nolentes, quasi infinitatem divinae potentiae metiuntur de infirmitate sensus humani, seu fidei suae.' In these texts from the Spec fid the concept of *ratio fidei* is seen predominantly from the angle of the conflict between the *ratio animalis*, which experiences doubts against faith, and the *ratio spiritualis*, or *ratio fidei* which demands the surrender of this *ratio animalis* to the higher criterion of divine authority given in *ratio fidei*. See also the development of the argument, on pp. 82-93; 374A-376C. The *ratio fidei* of the central section of the Aenig presupposes this basic assent of faith to authority, which was the whole question at issue in the texts from the Spec fid and discusses the problem of the metaphysical analysis of the trinitarian faith. Here the conflict is not that of doubt and faith but the conflict of the human connotations of philosophical concepts and the demands of the trinitarian faith. There is, however, a common basis at the root of these two conceptions of *ratio fidei*. In each of these conceptions autonomous reason has to surrender to the dominion of faith. Moreover, in the midst of those

texts from the Spec fid, which consider *ratio fidei* predominantly
from the angle of the 'doubt-faith' conflict, there are hints towards the development of the other conception of *ratio fidei*. See
Spec fid, 78-79; 372D, where William alludes to a *scientia:* 'primo ad scientiam quam nox nocti indicat; deinde ad verbum, quod
dies diei eructat; satagitque discere, non solum quod creditur,
sed etiam quibus contra inimicos fidei, fides ipsa muniatur.' The
conception of *ratio fidei* as a polemical defence of faith and of
a speculative penetration of the trinitarian faith appears to be
a logical development from the conception of *ratio fidei* as the
surrender of the questioning, doubting, reason to authority.

73For this question see 'The Speculative Development of
the Trinitarian Theology of William of St Thierry in the Aenigma
fidei,' [Chapter 3]. William's ascent of the mind to the trinitarian mystery closely resembles the theology of Erigena both in
the movement towards an increasingly purified understanding of
God and in its *theologia negativa*. But William differs from Erigena in his radical subordination of reason to faith in *ratio fidei*. The polemic against Abelard is discussed here in the light
of William's interpretation of Abelard's doctrine. For the question as to how far this interpretation is justified, see my introduction to Chapter 3.

74Aenig, 410C-432D.

75Although this central section is characterized by a
more directly and more exclusively scientific and speculative approach which contrasts with the other sections of the Aenig and
also with the Spec fid this metaphysical tendency is reflected
throughout the whole of the Aenig. This development is foreshadowed in the final pages of the Spec fid, pp. 168-179; 394C-398A.
But in these final pages metaphysical reflection is integrated
more closely with the movement towards mystical experience than
in the central section of the Aenig with the principle exception
of the text in the Aenig on the three stages of ascent, 414B-415D.

76Aenig, 407C-410B; 409B: 'Deum Patrem, et Deum Filium,
et Deum Spiritum Sanctum, omnes illae Scripturae clamant unum esse
Deum.'

77See *The Speculative Development....*[Chapter 3], especially II. *The Mystery of the Trinity*. See Aenig, 426C: 'Nusquam autem in hac vita divinitas melius humano intellectu comprehenditur, quam in eo quo magis incomprehensibilis esse intelligitur.' William's theology here is strongly influenced by the
Dionysian tradition: see *De divinis nominibus* VII, 3 (PG 3, 871);

St Gregory, *Moralia* V, 36 (PL 75, 716A), and Erigena, *De divisione naturae* I, 76 (PL 122, 522C) and I, 66 (510C).

[78]See *The Speculative Development....I, 2. RATIO FIDEI.* See Aenig, 417B: 'Idcirco autem dicimus, secundum rationem fidei, quia modus hic loquendi de Deo habet quaedam propria verba, rationabilia quidem, sed non intelligibilia, nisi in ratione fidei, non autem in ratione sensus humani....in rebus enim humanis humana ratio parat sibi fidem; in divinis vero praecedit fides, deinde ipsa sui generis format sibi rationem,' and 418BC, 419C.

[79]Aenig, 409CD: 'In nominibus enim divinis, seu verbis quibuslibet, quibus aliquid dicitur de Deo, non tam signa ipsa nominum vel verborum attendenda sunt, quam id quod per signa ipsa designatur,' and Ibid. (427A): 'Haec autem sic suscipienda sunt nobis, sicut ad inveniendum Deum divina quedam instrumenta per homines Dei Deo plenos a Deo nobis transmissa, sed tamen rerum notitiam, quarum signa sunt, minime impleta. Quae quandiu ad profectum cognitionis Dei nos adjuvant, quantum nos verba adjuvare possunt, veneranda et amplectenda nobis sunt; ubi vero deficiunt verba, sicut verba, cum gratia ejus qui nominatur et benedictione, pertranseunda sunt.'

[80]Ibid., 409D: 'Instabat enim tempus cribrandae Catholicae fidei, ut purgaretur; exercendae ut probaretur. Et ideo ineffabilis illa natura summi boni paulo indulgentius in verba humana passa est seipsam demittere, in adjutorium humanae ad Deum pietatis; non tamen usque ad angustias humanae rationis.' This 'descent' whereby the divine nature is expressed but not limited by human formulations leads to the 'ascent' whereby *ratio fidei* educates the mind towards the recognition of God's transcendance. Ibid., 417B: 'ad docendum loqui de Deo rationabiliter secundum rationem fidei, et praeparandos homines ad cogitandum ac sentiendum ineffabiliter de ineffabili.'

[81]The term *amor illuminatus* which appears in the relevant texts for the argument in this section of the article should be understood in the light of William's doctrine of *amor intellectus*. See Déchanet, *Exposé sur le Cantique,* pp. 17-27, and 'Amor ipse intellectus est,' 349-374. See the *cognitio amoris, supra,* p. 169, and *The Trinitarian Aspect of the Ascent,* [Chapter 2], pp. 12-62, for the explanation of the trinitarian mystical experience through this doctrine.

[82]This order is based on a logical and systematic sequence and not on a chronological sequence so as to discern the unifying structure of William's thought rather than the chronological evolu-

tion of the texts.

[83]See *supra*, I, A.

[84]See Spec fid, p. 128-129; 384D-385A: 'Forma quidem fidei quae verbis et ecclesiasticae disciplinae institutis tradi potest hominibus ab hominibus; in assensu bonae voluntatis, praesto est omnibus hominibus; cum adhuc videt in speculo, et in aenigmate, et in imagine pertransit homo; in speculo in quo a simili erudimur, et in obscuriore aenigmate in quo execemur, et in simplici et evidenti imagine in qua dulcius **afficimur**; ipsa vero pietas, ipsa veritas, non nisi a Spiritu Sancto traditur aut docetur; nec nisi digito Dei menti inscribitur.' The economy of *signum* in this wide connotation is present even in the most interior and spiritual phases of the ascent to God as in the mystical experience of the Trinity. See Spec fid, p. 166-169; 393C and 394C.

[85]*Signum* is used by William not only for the corporeal and visible *sacramenta fidei* but also for the intellectual *ratio fidei*.

[86]The comparison is only an analogy. There is no failure to recognize the uniqueness of the *sacramenta fidei* rooted in the strictly sacramental economy which is ordered directly towards sanctification through grace (Spec fid, 381D-383A). The *signa* of *ratio fidei* are not directly ordered towards sanctifying grace but towards the intellectual understanding of the divine nature. But presupposing this fundamental difference William's doctrine reveals an analogy of sign structure in *sacramenta fidei* and *ratio fidei*.

[87]The sign manifests what is signified under its aspect of union with what is signified and conceals what it signifies under its aspect of distinction from what is signified.

[88]See *supra*, p. 172.

[89]Spec fid, 170-171; 394D: 'Nimirum, Deus est, idipsum est; quod cogitare et amare, idipsum est. Ipsum dico; non de ipso. De ipso enim multi cogitant, qui non amant. Ipsum autem, nemo cogitat, et non amat.' See also Aenig, 415A.

[90]See *supra*, n. 79.

[91]Spec fid, 170-173; 395B: 'Nos vero verba iactamus; verbis involvimur; et impedimur ab eo quod nullis verbis exprimi

potest; et tamen nonnisi verbis de eo aliquid dici potest,' and
pp. 173-175, 395D.

[92]Ibid., 172-173, 395B: 'Suas enim formas verba habent
in significandis rebus in locutione; et eas imaginant in loquentis
vel audientis cogitatione. Et cum significant formas et formata;
mentem ab interioribus suis foras trahunt ad res quarum ipsa signa
sunt. Cum vero rerum spiritualium vel divinarum signa sunt; intus
quidem nos mittunt; sed intro nonnisi impediunt; et oculis mentis
caliginem obducent. Sic enim mentem admissa inficiunt imagina-
tionibus suis; ut vix sine eis cogitari possint spiritualia vel
divina, quarum nullae penitus formae vel imagines sunt.'

[93]Ibid., 172-173; 395C: 'De ipso ergo multa multis edicere fas est; ipsum autem cui praeter ipsum? Amor tamen, amor
illuminatus, qui intus Deo loquitur, melius hoc agit...,' and
p. 176-177; 396C.

[94]Ibid., 174-175; 395D-396A. This text alludes to the
sacramental economy first through the reference to purification
through what is corporeal and temporal as the way to the eternal
Word and also through the reference to the transition from the
knowledge of Christ according to the flesh to the knowledge of
Christ according to the spirit. Moreover, this purification is
placed directly in the context of the historical Incarnational
economy as can be seen from the allusion to Hebrews 1, 1-2. Therefore it is of particular interest to see how the pedagogy of the
signa in talk about God is interwoven almost imperceptibly with
the pedagogy of the Incarnational, temporal, sacramental economy.
The transition from the knowledge of Christ according to the flesh
to the knowledge of Christ according to the spirit which, elsewhere in William's writings is related to the historical sacramental economy, is seen in this text in terms of the pedagogy of
talk about God. As the pedagogy of the sacramental economy is a
transition from faith to vision, so too in this text the pedagogy
of talk about God is a transition from faith to vision. 'Verbis
quae de eo sunt non nimis inhaereatur; sed eis quasi navigio a
fide ad speciem transeatur.' The 'verba quae de eo sunt' should
be understood here in the context of the dialectic, of the *verba*
as *signa*. See Spec fid, pp. 170-173; 395BC.

[95]Ibid., 172-173; 395C.

[96]Ibid., 174-175; 395D. See also Aenig, 409BCD.

[97]Spec fid, 172-177; 395C-396C. See especially the
similarity in the expression and argument of the dialectic

through the *theologia negativa* (pp. 170-173; 395B): 'verbis involvimur; et impedimur ab eo quod nullis verbis exprimi potest et
tamen nonnisi verbis de eo aliquid dici potest' with that of the
affirmations of faith *ibid*. (p. 174-175; 395D). William's conception of the relationship of faith to the *theologia negativa* touches
the question as to whether the connatural impulse of faith giving a
'quasi mystical' contact with God in his absolute transcendance
may not be at the root of discursive theology. See L. Malevez,
'Théologie contemplative et théologie discursive.' The concluding
pages of the Spec fid (168-179; 394C-398A) are impregnated with
the Dionysian *theologia negativa* from which Père Malevez draws
much of his argument. See also the convergence of William's dialectic towards the transcendent 'one,' *ibid*. (176-179; 396C) in
which Déchanet detects a Plotinian influence ('Guillaume et Plotin').
But William's conception of this relationship of faith and the
theologia negativa cannot be shown to be rooted specifically in
the 'quasi mystical' connatural experience of faith. The texts do
not go beyond the doctrine that faith is a contact with God transcending all discourse about God. In the Aenig, 417C, William refers to *ratio fidei* as teaching through experience rather than
through polemical argument and vain disputation: 'ipsa magis experientia docens credentes, et informans per meritum et usum fidei
pervenire ad praemium contemplationis.' But this text is more
likely to refer to a contemplative experience arising out of *ratio*,
in accordance with the orientation of *ratio fidei* towards mystical
experience (see especially *ibid*. 414C-415D, together with the dialectic in the concluding pages of the Spec fid) rather than to a
connatural experience at the origin of *ratio fidei*.

98Spec fid, 176-177; 396C: 'Ideo ipse Dominus apparens
in carne hominibus, sicut de mundo abstulit vanitatem idolorum;
sic dum cogitantibus Deum proposuit in Trinitate unitatem, Trinitatem in unitate; fulgurans choruscatio divinitatis, omnem tulit
a cogitatione fidei de Deo vanitatem imaginationis.'

99Ibid., 176-177; 396BC: 'Sed et illa verba Domini, et
haec nostra illa exponentia usu vel ratione docuimus dicere os
nostrum, et cogitare cor nostrum quoties volumus; quae tamen non
aliquando intelligimus, nisi per affectus experientiam, et interiorem sensum amoris illuminati, etsi multum velimus.' The text on
faith in the trinitarian mystery (396C) follows immediately afterwards and the trinitarian text leads on immediately to the further
comment: 'Cum enim divinitatis intellectum docuit esse supra homines; suo inde modo docuit cogitare homines' (ibid.). 'Suo inde
modo' would appear to indicate not simply the contact through faith
with the mystery beyond human imagination but also the *affectus
experientia* and *interior sensus amoris illuminati* to which William

has referred in the immediate context. See 170-171; 394D, and
172-173; 395C, where *amor* and *amor illuminatus* are a direct response to the recognition of God's transcendence through *theologia
negativa.*

[100]Ibid., 174-175; 396A.

[101]See also the text in the Aenig, 433D, where, shortly
after the conclusion of the central section on the divine names
(432C), William leads from this central section on *ratio fidei* into a passage which describes the fusion of *fides, dilectio* and *intellectus* in a 'similitude of the Trinity.' 'Huic inscribitur nomen Domini novum, hoc est, innovans fideliter nominantem, cum formae fidei spiritualis Dei notitia informatur. Hoc autem fit, cum
fides incipiens operari per dilectionem, incipit etiam ipsa formari
in dilectionem, et per dilectionem in intellectum, et per intellectum in dilectionem, seu in intellectum simul et dilectionem. Difficile enim est homini sic affecto discernere quid de quo, cum jam
in corde credentis et intelligentis et amantis tria haec unum sint,
ad similitudinem quamdam summae Trinitatis.' The exterior 'ratio
fidei' is interiorized and vivified. 'Sed exteriorem nunc fidei
rationem de Trinitate, et publicam ejus formam investigare susce-
pimus, quam formatam in interiore homine nostro post modum ejus
erit vivificare....'

[102]Spec fid, 168-169; 394C.

[103]Ibid., 174-177; 396AB: 'Cum enim dicitur, quia Pater
in Filio, et Filius in Patre est, et ipsi in nobis et nos in ipsis;
si verbotenus haec intelligimus, quid nisi idolum in cordibus nostris fabricamus? Cum enim locus sit unicuique ubi est; si ex his
verbis cogitamus locum vel locale quid in Deo; longe a veritate
aberramus.'

[104]Ibid., 176-177; 396BC.

[105]Ibid., 172-173; 395C.

[106]Ibid., 154-155; 390D: 'Maior tamen et dignior sensus
ejus, et purior intellectus, amor est; si fuerit ipse purius,'
and pp. 104-105; 378D-379A, describing the faith of the *simplices*:
'docibiles Dei, et absque omni verborum sive cogitationum disceptantium strepitu a Sancto Spiritu discentes;....quia sentiunt de Domino in bonitate, et sentiunt sensu amoris, quicquid de Deo credunt;
et sapit eis quod sentiunt.' See also Med, 246C: 'Affectus enim,
quo to amando fruuntur, sensibili quidem suavitate cujusdam gaudii
spiritualis vel divini potest sentiri; sed sicut sapor cibi cujus-

libet nulli insinuare potest, nisi gustanti, sic sapor ille nec
ratione discuti, nec exponi verbis, nec sensibus potest concipi.
Divinum quiddam est, et arrha vel pignus spiritus....'

107See Med, 214BC. Here the *intelligentia desursum* which
transcends *ratio* and which is *totum divinum* is the response to the
intellect baffled by the mystery of the Trinity. In the Exp Rm,
610A, William indicates the double aspect of this higher understanding *dursum* which transcends *ratio* ('non formatur a ratione')
but which is given as the fulfilment of *ratio*: 'sed ipse sibi
conformat rationem non ut eum capiat, sed ut illuminata ab eo,
aliquando in eum consentiat.' See Med, 210D.

108But the spiritual and the intellectual ascent are not
completely integrated. In the concluding section of the Spec fid,
p. 168-179; 394C, from 'Interim enim..., -398A) William abruptly
breaks off from the theology of the experience of our communion
with the divine persons which had been closely developed throughout the preceding passages (152-168; 390C-394C). In the concluding section he concentrates not on the explanation of the actual
trinitarian experience of our communion with the divine persons
but on the meaning of propositions about the divine persons and
about our communion with the divine persons. The knowledge that
comes through love is introduced in the concluding sections not
directly as an explanation of the actual experience of our communion with the divine persons but directly as an explanation as
to how we can penetrate to the meaning of these propositions.

109Aenig, 414B-415D.

110Ibid., 414B-D), and 414C: 'Tertius perfectorum est....
primitias jam et pignus Spiritus habentes, quod sint Filii Dei,'
and 415C: 'seu ipse per se Spiritus Sanctus **sancti** cujusque hominis spiritui non indicat, sed eructat, hoc est, cum sensu quodam
divinitatis et sapore summae sapientiae, occulta aliqua inspiratione **insinuat.'** William reflects here Origen's thought and follows to some extent the actual expression and terminology of Origen. See Περὶ ἀρχῶν (PG 11, 364B-365A) with the reference to the
ascent in three stages towards an understanding of Scripture rooted in the *corpus, anima, spiritus* trichotomy, *Contra Celsum* (PG
11, 1309C) with the terminology of *fides, scientia, sapientia* in
a hierarchical gradation, and *In Num.* (PG 12, 784) where the advance in faith is described in terms of gradation and ascent,
'ascendere ad **singulos** fidei et virtutum gradus.' The relation of
faith and the temporal economy to the sense data of Revelation
suggests also a parallel between William's three stages of ascent
through faith and Erigena's three movements of the soul, *sensus,*

ratio, animus (De divisione naturae II, 23; PL 122, 572C–574B: *animus* is identified with *intellectus, ibid.* 574B). The relationship between faith and the sense data of revelation is explicitly, affirmed by William in the Spec fid, p. 134–135; 386AB, and 136–137; 386C.

111This movement towards a synthesis is foreshadowed elsewhere in William's writings where he indicates three stages of ascent; see one of the few passages in the Spec fid prior to its concluding pages (168–179; 394C–398A) where William hints at a more speculative development of *ratio fidei* (78–79; 372D–373A). In this text the interrelationship of love and understanding is described in terms similar to the Aenig, 433D. See Spec fid, 78; 372D, immediately preceding the text quoted above as compared with the text from the Aenig on the three stages (PL 180, 415BD). A further suggestion of the three stages is given shortly afterwards in Spec fid, 82–83; 374A. But the *ratio fidei* in the context of these passages (74–93; 371D–376C) is not the metaphysical speculative *ratio fidei* of the Aenig. Predominantly the faith-reason question in these pages is not that of the advance from faith to the further understanding of *ratio fidei* but that of conflict between the authority of faith and the questioning doubts and temptations of the autonomous reason. Moreover this conflict of authority and doubt is logically prior to the further advance from the pure act of faith to the understanding of *ratio fidei* (see *William of St Thierry's Doctrine of the Ascent to God by Faith,* Chapter 5, pp. 134–207. Whenever there is a reference in these texts of the Spec fid to a further *ratio fidei* as a development from the basic act of faith on authority this reference is not to a speculative *ratio fidei* but to a reflection on faith in the temporal economy (see Spec fid, pp. 80–81; 373B–373C), and this reflection centers on the spiritual ascent to the illumination of the Holy Spirit (373A–373C). A more explicit indication of the mediation of a **scientific** and speculative *ratio fidei* in the three stages of ascent is given in the Spec fid (136–139; 386D–387B read in the light of the context, 386B). The three stages of the Aenig are also foreshadowed, although in a different and unusual terminology, in the Exp Rm, 609D: 'Proponunt enim tres formas in doctrina fidei: rationalem, spiritualem, intellectualem. Rationalis est in sacramentis et moribus....spiritualis est in lectionis studio et meditationis....intellectualis est in amoris illuminati affectu ....' (and 609D–610A). See Cant, 478D–479A, where the three stages of prayer *animalis, rationalis, spiritualis* (477BC) are related to a development from faith (478D–479A) *forma fidei, ratio, spiritus.* But none of these texts shows a development of *ratio fidei* in the specifically metaphysical and speculative direction of the *ratio fidei* in the Aenig.

112Aenig, 410B-432C.

113Ibid., 414B.

114Ibid., 413D-414A: 'Credo ergo et confiteor unum in
tribus personis Deum tres personas expressas sub proprietate dis-
tinctas;' see the more remote context (409B-414B) on the problem
of the further understanding of faith on the metaphysical level of
speculative trinitarian theology. This speculative trinitarian
theology is the principle theme of the central section of the Aenig.
The introductory and more anthropological section of this work
(397C-407C) is to some extent a pedagogic preparation for our knowledge of the Trinity from the entitative aspect (403D-404A).

115Ibid., 414D-415A.

116Ibid., 415A-415C. The relationship of *ratio fidei* to
mystical experience in the three stages of ascent in the *Aenigma
fidei* should be understood against the background of the polemic
against Abelard. For Abelard's *Theologia* tended to conceive mystical experience as a prolongation of speculation; see J. Cottiaux,
'La conception de la théologie chez Abélard,' 541-542. William
shows that this experience is a mode of knowledge which comes directly from God. Therefore this experience transcends speculative
theology which is based on reasoning about God even though that
reasoning is in the light of faith.

117Aenig, 397C-407C.

118Ibid., 399A-400A.

119Ibid., 399B: 'In tantum ergo eum videbimus, in quantum similes ei erimus: et inde eum videbimus, unde similes ei
erimus, mente scilicet.'

120Ibid.: 'ubi etiam sicut in Patre et Filio, quae visio,
ipsa unitas est; sic in Deo et homine, quae visio, ipsa similitudo
futura est.'

121The text from the Aenig alludes to the knowledge
through similitude in this life (399B): 'Similitudo ista est, qua
renovatur homo de die in diem in agnitione Dei secundum imaginem
ejus qui creavit eum,' and (399D): 'non per speculum et in aenigmate, sicut hic videtur ab hominibus qui digni sunt hac visione...'
But the experimental *cognitio amoris* given already in this life as
a consequence of the life of faith, the 'nova quaedam fidei facies'
(Spec fid, p. 162-163; 392C) is much more fully developed in the

text from the Spec fid describing closely the power of love to
transform us into the divine likeness (154-162; 390D-392D). Moreover, the actual trinitarian experience in this life is described
more explicitly in pp. 166-168; 393D-394C.

[122]This is not to deny that the Incarnational economy in
the introductory section of the Aenig extends also to the more
sapiential purification of man. But, in comparison with the approach to the sacramental Incarnational economy in the Spec fid,
the Incarnational passages in the introductory section of the
Aenig are more concerned with the purification of the mind in the
ascent to God. Those texts in this section of the Aenig, which are
concerned with the moral and ascetic purification of man (Aenig,
401C-402A, 403A-C, 406D-407C), see this purification directly as
a preparation for vision (especially 403C, 406C, 407C). The *visio*
here, when seen in the context of intellectual purification (404D-
405D) is given an intellectualist connotation and appears directly
as a response to the desire of the intellect to understand God's
nature.

[123]Ibid., 402B-D, 406A: 'et quia illa corpora sunt quae
foris per sensus corporis adamavit, eorumque diuturna quadam
familiaritate implicatus est, nec secum potest introrsum tanquam
in regionem corporeae naturae ea inferre; imagines eorum secum
trahit, vix semetipsum vel naturam, ut dictum est, divinitatis,
aliud esse imaginans, quam id, sine quo eam cogitare non potest.
Haec enim est maledictio, Domine Deus, qua maledixisti terram in
opere Adam et filiorum ejus.' This conception of the immersion
of the mind of man in sense imagery as a consequence of the fall
recalls the doctrine of Erigena, *De divisione naturae* II, 12 and
IV, 2 (PL 122, 540AB and 744AB). See also the references to the
spinas ac tribulos (Aenig, 406A) paralleled in *De divisione naturae*
(744B). William's progressive purification whereby the mind is led
first to transcend the sense imagery in which it is immersed
through original sin and then to transcend its own intellectual
powers is similar to Erigena's doctrine, *De praedestinatione* IX,
1-2 (PL 122, 390B-D), especially 390B: 'Quomodo enim signa sensi-
bilia, id est corporibus adhaerentia remotam illam omni sensu cor-
poreo naturam ad liquidum significare possent, quae vix purgatis-
sima mente attingitur, omnem transcendens intellectum? Eis tamen
utitur humanae ratiocinationis post peccatum primi hominis labor-
iosa egestas, ut quodammodo credatur et innuatur copiosa conditoris sublimitas.'

[124]Aenig, 405A: 'tertium ab utroque discretum, quod
neque sit corpus, neque habeat aliquam similitudinem corporis,
sicuti est sapientia quae mente intellecta conspicitur, et in

cujus luce de his omnibus veraciter judicatur,' and 405B-D.

[125]Ibid., 405D: 'Nil certe tale invenimus in eo, quo in natura nostra nihil melius invenimus; hoc est in intellectu nostro, quo sapientiam ipsam capimus, inquantum ejus capaces sumus. Quod ergo non invenimus in meliore nostro, nequaquam admittere debemus in cogitando, id quod tam incomparabiliter melius est omni meliore nostro.' For a further investigation of this purifying intellectual ascent in the twelfth century theology see Jolivet, 'Intelligence et amour chez les auteurs spirituels du XIIe siècle,' 273-290 and 429-450.

[126]See *supra*, pp. 164-6.

[127]This approach in the Aenig is foreshadowed in a section of the Spec fid, pp. 134-140; 398A, 386B-388A, which is concerned with the temporal economy even though not directly and specifically with the sacramental economy. Here the pedagogy of faith and of the temporal economy is directed towards the understanding of the eternal attributes of God. Ibid., 138-139; 387B: 'cum bene credita temporalis dispensatio Mediatoris, per fidem, vel eam quae fidei est scientiam, erudit et enutrit ad aeterna capienda cor credentis' (note the explicit reference to the attributes of God in the context which immediately precedes: 'temporalibus Domini commendantibus, et intelligibilem facientibus omnipotentem Dei bonitatem....'). But the description of the intellectual purification through the temporal economy in these texts from the Spec fid differs considerably from that in the texts quoted above from the Aenig. Here in the Spec fid the purification is only suggested in very general terms whereas the texts from the Aenig analyze closely the gradual ascent of the intellect from its immersion in sense imagery. Moreover the purification described in the texts from the Aenig is explicitly directed towards the eternal mystery of the Trinity. Here in the Spec fid the movement of the mind is not only directed towards the eternal truths in God himself but it is also directed through the eternal truths towards an understanding of their manifestation ad extra in the temporal economy; Spec fid, pp. 138-139; 387BC; see p. 140-141; 387B-388A. In fact the argument here is not directly to lead the mind towards the metaphysical understanding of God in himself but rather to lead the mind towards the contemplation of the eternal truths as manifested through the temporal economy *ad extra*. Moreover the section of the Spec fid, 381D-374A, where William explains most explicitly the meaning of the sacramental economy, describes predominantly the spiritual rather than the intellectual ascent. See 148-155; 390A-390D, where the Incarnational economy leads not towards the metaphysical understanding of God in himself but to the

transformation through love into the divine likeness.

[128]Aenig, 403D-404A.

[129]For this reason the Aenig cannot be interpreted as a
complete synthesis of what had been only imperfectly achieved in
the Spec fid.   The Aenig is predominantly the theology of the intellectual ascent.   The Spec fid is predominantly the theology
of the spiritual ascent.   Each of these works has developed aspects
of William's doctrine which are less perfectly developed in the
other.

CHAPTER 7

THE THEOLOGY OF WILLIAM OF ST THIERRY:
A METHODOLOGICAL PROBLEM*

Introduction

THE PROBLEM OF THEOLOGICAL METHOD is the problem of the human subject. The questions to be asked about Revelation emerge from the very structure of the human subject and that structure is a highly differentiated, complex, unity. To take refuge in a mere juxtaposition of differentiated elements is to reject an understanding of the human subject as a unity, and a failure to discern the unity of the human subject leads to a failure to discern the unity in Revelation. Conversely, an understanding of the human subject as a unity which ignores the complexity of these differentiated elements leads to a premature synthesis in our understanding of Revelation.

Anima--Animus--Spiritus

I would like therefore to make a few comments on the theology of William of St Thierry in the light of this methodological problem.[1] The problem is implicit rather than explicit in William's theology. But I suggest that a reflection on these implications in his theology may help towards a more explicit recognition of the task which lies ahead of us. It is interesting for instance to see how William's theology appears to be rooted in his psychological structure of the human person: *anima--animus--spiritus*. *Anima* is the corporeal, sensitive, imaginative, aspect of human psychology. *Animus* is the intellectual, rational, volitional aspect of human psychology. *Spiritus* is the human person as open to self transcendence, the 'take over' by the Holy Spirit, the initiation into the intra-trinitarian communion in knowledge and love.[2] In the context of the spiritual life this structure becomes the 'animal' state, the 'rational' state and the 'spiritual' state. From a state of immersion in the life of the senses we emerge into a rational, moral pattern of human living. Ultimately we move beyond the human pattern of living into the divine life of the Holy Spirit.[3] Expressed in terms of the more recent philosophical and theological reflection on the 'subject,' we could say that William is interpreting the spiritual life as an ascent from 'empirical' to 'rational' and 'spiritual' consciousness. In the context of William's theology *anima* is proportioned to the data of Revelation, *animus* to the intellectual, rational, meaning of the data and *spiritus* to the mystical meaning of the data.[4]

A Conflict of Method

When this psychological and spiritual structure is transposed
in this way so as to give a methodological basis for theological
questions we are confronted with the problem of differentiation
and integration. William's theology, deeply under the influence
of his spirituality, can be called a theology of the ascent to
God. But the very structure of *anima, animus, spiritus* when transposed on to the theological level, leads to a conflict in method.
We could perhaps articulate the conflict in this way: we might
say that 'the ascent of the soul' to God is contrasted with 'the
ascent of the mind' to God. The 'ascent of the mind,' even though
conducted under a strict subordination of reason to faith in opposition to Abelard, is the search to know, as far as possible,
'what' God is. The 'ascent of the soul,' is the search not to
know what God is but to experience God. This experience is ultimately the mystical experience of the Trinity.

To qualify this distinction further we should say that the
contrast is not that of experience and knowledge as such but that
of experience and the intellectual, rational kind of knowledge in
which we are engaged when we ask the question: 'What' is God?
The mystical experience of the Trinity is associated in William's
theology with that deeper, more unitive, mystical, knowledge which
is given through our 'likeness' to the Trinity. This kind of knowledge is called *amor-intellectus*, the knowledge which comes through
love.

A Shifting Perspective

The theology of 'the ascent of the soul' is basic, original,
and primary in the works of William of St Thierry. The central
core of his theology is the ascent to the mystical experience of
the Trinity. When he comes to consider the problem of faith, that
problem is situated basically within this context. Faith is the
point of departure in the ascent to that experience: *credo ut
experiar*.[5] But towards the end of the *Speculum fidei*[6] he moves
abruptly away from the description and explanation of the trinitarian experience and begins the intellectual ascent: *credo ut intelligam*. This is the intellectual problem of thinking and talking about God in language derived from our knowledge of creatures.
In fact it is the problem of analogy. This more specific problem
is rooted in the thrust of the mind to know as far as possible
what God is. So it is not surprising that, after the *Speculum
fidei*, William opens the *Aenigma fidei* with this question.[7] His
point of departure here is the acceptance from faith *that* God is.
Consequently there is the exigence of the mind to search towards
a knowledge of *what* God is. This gives the clue to the kind of

questions that he is going to ask. But the consequences of this
point of departure do not emerge clearly until the central section[8]
of this work. Then he plunges again into the problem of analogy
but with a much closer and more technical analysis than in the
closing pages of the *Speculum fidei*. This analysis is concerned
directly with the Trinity in itself rather than with the Trinity
for us and specifically with the problem of thinking and talking
about the Trinity in terms of number, person, relation, essence.
Ultimately this analysis confronts us, at every turn in the argument, with the impenetrable mystery of the Trinity. We do not
penetrate the mystery of the Trinity but we see more precisely
why the Trinity is a mystery.[9]
      This new point of departure with its exigence for a different
kind of question reveals a conflict in method. From questions
about the search for union with God William shifts to questions
about 'what' God is. From questions about the Trinity for us he
shifts to questions about the Trinity in itself. From questions
about the mystical experience of the Trinity he shifts to questions about the mystery of the Trinity.

Towards A Synthesis

      This is a conflict in method. But it would be misleading to
think in terms of a juxtaposition. William moves towards a synthesis. The ascent of the mind begins to be integrated with the
ascent of the soul. The *animus* theology begins to be integrated
with the *anima-spiritus* theology. We do in fact find this attempt
towards a synthesis in the three theological stages in the *Aenigma
fidei: fides, ratio fidei, experientia*.[10] First, faith, then
rational reflection on the data of Revelation, and finally the experience of God communicated through the Holy Spirit. The trans-
position of this basic structure from the psychological and spiritual to the theological perspective is so logical and so convincing
that we **are** tempted to think that in these 'three stages' William
has given us an outline for a definitive synthesis. But closer
inspection reveals that this is an illusion. We could perhaps
say that William gives us here a vision of the whole. But it is
a vision of the whole from a limited horizon. That horizon is
the intellectualist horizon, the thrust of the mind to know what
God is and not the horizon of the total human person searching
for union with God. This intellectualist perspective appears in
the very formulation of the degrees of ascent: 'Tribus enim intelligentiae gradibus.'[11] Moreover the point of departure for the
ascent unifies but also **constricts** his vision. That point of departure is God in himself and not God for us, the entitative propositions of faith and not the Biblical economy. The subsequent
stages in this intellectual ascent, 'ratio fidei' and 'experientia'

are seen in the light of this point of departure. In this perspective the final stage, the 'experience' communicated by the Holy
Spirit as seen as a participation in a divine mode of understanding
and therefore as a response on the mystical level to the limitations of 'ratio fidei' on the rational level.

It is interesting to see how in the closing pages of the
Speculum fidei and throughout the greater part of the *Aenigma fidei*, the theology of the ascent of the soul is rethought and re-
shaped in the light of the 'ascent of the mind.'[12] There is a
movement towards synthesis. But the themes of the 'anima-spiritus'
theology are given a new resonance in the context of the intellectualist theology of *animus*. For instance the *amor illuminatur*,
the *affectus experientia*, reintroduced in the closing pages of the
Speculum fidei, might appear as an allusion to the mystical experience of the Trinity which William had recently been describing.
His argument goes as follows: concepts and words are signs pointing to a reality which infinitely transcends those concepts and
words.[13] The intellectual search to think and to talk about God
exacts the use of this human language and it exacts an accurate
use of this language. But beyond a certain point the limitation
of language blocks any further insight into God. For human concepts and words are only 'about' God. We cannot penetrate to God
himself without the illumination given through love.[14] We might
ask whether William is not simply saying that mystical insight
comes as a response to the limitations of metaphysical insight.
But the argument is directly concerned with understanding the
meaning of verbal propositions about God. In this context, the
illumination of love, although implying an insight into God beyond propositional knowledge, appears to be given directly for an
insight into the meaning of the actual propositions.[15] Very significantly the question of our communion with the persons of the
Trinity is reintroduced in this new context. But the question
now is not how we experience mystically this communion with the
divine persons but how we can see the intellectual meaning in propositions 'about' this communion with the divine persons.[16] William's answer is that this meaning is given through an affective
experience and through the illumination of love. This dialectic
does not end with insight into the meaning of propositions about
God. It ends with the vision of God. But the point is this:
throughout the argument the perspective is an intellectualist perspective.

In the greater part of the *Aenigma fidei* this remains the
perspective of William's theology. For instance the theme of
participation in the intra-trinitarian life through the knowledge-
likeness equation is given a more predominantly intellectual resonance. In the *Aenigma fidei* there is relatively a stronger emphasis on the 'vision' of the future life. In the *Speculum fidei*

there is relatively a stronger emphasis on the trinitarian experience in this life.[18]   The influence of this new point of departure
is felt even more deeply in the theology of the Sacramental economy.   In the *Speculum fidei* the Sacramental economy was an *anima-
spiritus* ascent, a pedagogic liberation through Christ in the
flesh to Christ in the Spirit.   The *affectus amoris*, the *sensus
amoris* penetrated through the external *sacramentum* of the 'flesh'
into the interior *sacramentum* of the 'Spirit.'[19]   In contrast the
sacramental 'economy' of the *Aenigma fidei* is predominantly an
anima-animus ascent.   Both in the *Speculum fidei* and in the *Aenigma fidei* William sees the initial human condition as a state of
immersion in the life of the senses.   But in the *Speculum fidei*
this immersion in the life of the senses is seen predominantly as
a barrier to the life of the Spirit and in the *Aenigma fidei* this
immersion is seen predominantly as a barrier to the life of the
mind.   In the new perspective the argument is this: we are so
dominated by sense images that we cannot see that the human intellect transcends those images and a fortiori that the intratrinitarian life of God himself cannot be conceived in terms of
such images.[20]   The sacramental economy which, in the *Speculum
fidei*, was a spiritual purification, in the *Aenigma fidei* is an
intellectual purification.   The purification of the soul for the
trinitarian experience becomes the purification of the mind for
the trinitarian mystery.

The Question Today

The problem is that of differentiation and integration and
this means a differentiated **integration**.   More precisely the problem is how we can move towards an integration without limiting our
horizon.   We have seen how William is confronted with this problem
as he moves towards the integration of the 'ascent of the soul'
and the 'ascent of the mind,' the ascent to the mystical experience
of the Trinity and the ascent towards the knowledge of 'what' God
is.   In so far as he attempts this integration the entire pattern
of his 'ascent of the soul' theology begins to be dominated by
the intellectualist perspective.   The old themes are given a new
resonance and their meaning begins to change.   Therefore can we
say that this is a total integration?

The problem today is more acute.   The human person is now revealed in a much greater complexity not only through scholastic
philosophy[21] but also through the more recent exploration of exis-
tentialism, personalism, phenomenology and depth psychology.   We
are beginning to see that contrasting interpretations of Revelation emerge as a result of contrasting interpretations of the human person.   The shifting perspective in the methodology of Bernard
Lonergan is an example.   His earlier theological works, together

with his reflections on theological method, have given us the kind of interpretation of Revelation which emerges from the thrust of the human mind in the pure, disinterested desire for knowledge.[22] But now he is developing a methodology based not only on man's intellectual self appropriation but also on man's existential self-appropriation.[23] The thrust of the mind is now seen as situated within the wider, historical, existential, development of the human person. This is a problem of differentiated integration not entirely unlike that which confronted William of St Thierry in the conflict of the *animus* and *anima-spiritus* theology. But the question today is complicated even further with the conflicting interpretations of the existential, historical aspect of human development. We might, for instance, refer to the contrasting the theology of Rahner and Metz where the theology of the 'transcendental' and of the 'political' kingdom develops from the 'transcendental' or the 'political' interpretation of the human person.[24] This situation makes us recognize the fact and almost the inevitability of a theological pluralism. But the human mind, of its very nature, searches for unity, integration, synthesis. This search exposes us to the question: How can we integrate our understanding of the human person,[25] and therefore integrate our understanding of Revelation without limiting the horizon of the human person and therefore without limiting the horizon in our understanding of Revelation?

NOTES

*Published in *Cistercian Studies* 6 (1971) 261-68.

[1]In my earlier articles, which are concerned with William's trinitarian doctrine, I did not give sufficient attention to the methodological conflict: *credo ut experiar: credo ut intelligam.* In the later articles, which are concerned with William's theology of faith, I have attempted to show this more complex structure of William's theology. Therefore I am hoping that further interpretation of William's doctrine will, in this respect, follow the later articles on faith rather than the earlier articles on the Trinity.

[2]Père Déchanet points to the source in Origen's trichotomy ψυχἠ-νουσ πνεῦμα (PG 11, 223B); *Guillaume de Saint-Thierry,* p. 116. I have referred to the similarities and differences in Origen's and William's trichotomy in *The Trinitarian Aspect of the Ascent of the Soul to God,* p. 23.

[3]Ep frat, 307-354, and especially 315C-316B.

[4]This relationship of a psychological, spiritual structure to a theological structure in William's writing was first discovered by Déchanet (*Guillaume de Saint-Thierry,* p. 94 footnote) and developed by Père Bouyer (*La spiritualité,* 139-154).

[5]Leclercq has used this term to describe St Bernard's approach to faith, *L'amour des lettres,* 202.

[6]Spec fid, 168-169; 394C.

[7]Aenig, 397A: 'Humanae infirmitatis religiosa confessio est, de Deo hoc solum nosse, quod Deus est. Caeterum essentiam vel naturam, et secreta illa imperscrutabilis judicii ejus decreta investigare quidem et perscrutare pium est' (see 417D). See the parallel text of Erigena (*De divisione naturae* II 27 (PL 122, 585B). It is probable that Erigena influenced William in his theology of the basic thrust of the mind to know 'what' God is. On this question I am indebted to Père Déchanet who, in his unpublished notes, has shown persuasively the influence of Erigena on this aspect of William's theology. Père Hourlier has also referred to the influence of Erigena as adapted to William's 'ascent of the soul' theology in one of his earliest works, Contempl, 365-380 (ed. *La contemplation de Dieu* [Paris, 1959] 41-43).

[8]Déchanet argues that an examination of the manuscript, Charleville 114, proves that the manuscript shows signs of having been rewritten. He suggests that the major part of this central section formed a separate treatise: 'The divine names' (PL 180, 417D-432D) (Déchanet, 'Les manuscrits de la lettre aux Frères, 259-271).

[9]Aenig, 410C-435A.

[10]Aenig, 414B-415D.

[11]Ibid., 414B.

[12]See 'William of St Thierry's doctrine of the Ascent to God by Faith,' [Chapter 5, *Towards a Synthesis*].

[13]I **referred** to William's analogous interpretation of *signum* in *Sacramenta fidei* and *ratio fidei* in Chapter 6, pp. 173-174.

[14]Spec fid, 170-183; 394D-395C.

[15]Ibid., 176-177; 396B-C.

[16]Ibid., 174-177; 396AB as contrasted with 161-168; 392C-394C.

[17]See Chapter 6, pp. 178-9.

[18]Aenig, 399A-400A as contrasted with Spec fid, 161-168; 392C-394C.

[19]See Spec fid, 120-121; 382A-384A, 385A.

[20]Aenig, 402B-D, 405D, 406A.

[21]The distinction between the question *an sit* and *quid sit*, to which William alludes at the opening of the Aenig (PL 180, 397A) is now seen to lead to a distinction in the theological method. Bernard Lonergan shows how the question *an sit* leads to the *via certitudinis* and the question *quid sit* leads to the *via intelligentiae* in *Divinarum personarum conceptionem analogicam* (Rome, 1959) 7-51, and especially pp. 8-9. This differentiation of method in itself poses a problem of integration even from within the scholastic, 'entitative' perspective.

[22]Lonergan, *De Constitutione Christi ontologica et psychologica* (Rome, 1958); *Divinarum personarum conceptionem analogicam, De Deo Trino* (Rome, 1961).

[23]This initial restriction to the scholastic perspective appears to be a deliberate program based on the principle that we cannot grasp adequately even the potentialities of the *nova* unless we have first understood the *vetera*. See Lonergan, *Insight* (London, 1957) p. 748. An opening to these new potentialities is given in his later essays in *Collection* (London, 1967), See especially 'Existenz and Aggioramento,' pp. 240-251' and 'Dimensions of Meaning,' pp. 252-267.

[24]This implies neither that Rahner's theology excludes the 'political' question nor that Metz's theology excludes the 'transcendental' question. The point is that Rahner's theology, even in the political context, develops from the transcendental interpretation of the human subject and that the theology of Metz, even in the transcendental context, develops from the political interpretation of the human subject. See P. Mann, 'The transcendental or the political kingdom,' *New Blackfriars* (December 1969-January 1970). Dom Peter Mann shows convincingly how a different type of theology emerges from a difference in the point of departure.

[25]Ricoeur points to this problem of conflicting interpretations of the human subject. The critic should see the value of each of these interpretations within the limitations of their horizon and at the same time question the 'totalitarian' claim which makes their horizon the ultimate horizon. But to question a false 'totalitarian' claim is to exclude only a premature unity and not the search for an ultimate unity. See P. Ricoeur, *Le conflit des interprétations, essais d'herméneutique* (Paris, 1969) 7-28.

II.   STUDIES IN MONASTICISM AND THEOLOGY

CHAPTER 8

MONASTIC THEOLOGY AND ST AELRED*

PATRISTIC THEOLOGY AND SCHOLASTIC THEOLOGY will be familiar
terms to most readers. But what, it may be asked, is 'monastic
theology?' Considerable attention has recently been drawn to
this subject by Père Leclercq's illuminating distinction of the
two Middle Ages.1 We are shown the existence of a mediaeval monastic theology which is basically a continuation of the patristic 'sapientia,' yet with its own special character and contribution. Like the patristic 'sapientia' it is quite distinct in
its approach from its scholastic counterpart, though both movements should be seen as complementary rather than in opposition
to each other. The question as to their place in the light of a
general theological synthesis is beyond the scope of this article.
Nor can we attempt to treat of the many varying trends within
this wide field of monastic theology. The aim is simply to give
a short introduction to certain aspects of this movement as illustrated by the Cistercians of the twelfth century, and to indicate
the place of St Aelred against that background.2
    The search among the early Cistercians for the original puri-
ty of monastic life is a familiar theme. What is less familiar
is the parallel theological movement to which it gave rise. In
response to the call of the last chapter of St Benedict's rule to
the sources of monastic spirituality in St Basil and Cassian,
these early Cistercians looked also towards the full inheritance
of the patristic wisdom which had inspired that life. This led
them to the *orientale lumen,* the light from the east, to find
their theological sources not only in St Augustine and the Latin
Fathers, but beyond St Augustine in the Greek Fathers, and especially St Gregory of Nyssa and Origen. Less predominantly Augustinian than the Cluniacs, this movement tended towards a synthesis of traditional patristic thought in the east and in the west.
Historically this is of no little importance. The Greek Fathers
were at that time viewed with suspicion by the conservative theologians, who were out to check the more dangerous speculations of
the rising scholasticism and especially those of Peter Abelard.
On this point the Cistercian theological movement is of special
interest. Its leaders in St Bernard and William of St Thierry
were foremost in the attack against Abelard and in the stand for
theological orthodoxy. In their suspicion of rash speculation
and of the perils of rationalism they were extreme traditionalists.
Yet they were among the pioneers in their return to the Greek
Fathers, and in their attempt at a wider synthesis of patristic
thought. Yet surely we need not be surprised at this apparent
paradox? In their study of the Fathers they looked not so much

for their special theories and explanations of the faith as for
the basic themes of revelation. What they found in the Fathers,
Greek and Latin, was precisely what they did not find in Abelard:
the whole body of traditional Christian wisdom and the antidote
to what they saw as a too independent use of philosophy and logic.

As such this was a continuation into the Middle Ages of the
patristic *sapientia*. But it was not simply a synthesis of the
Fathers. It was a creative synthesis, bearing the imprint of the
twelfth century Cistercian movement. It was a monastic theology
in the sense that its leading theological conceptions grew out of
the whole monastic ethos. It was a theology formed from the background of the journey of the soul to God. The special accentuation which this gave to the patristic *sapientia* was the view of
the great themes of revelation as lived and experienced within
the life of the soul in the course of this journey. In contrast
to those theologians among the black monks, such as for instance
Rupert of Deutz, whose interest centered on the mysteries of
Christianity in their objective presentation throughout the wide
sweep of the history of salvation,[3] the Cistercian movement dwelt
on the reflection of this history within the individual soul.

St Aelred of Rielvaux is true to this background. His thought
is formed by his whole experience of monastic life, by this progressive recovery of the divine likeness in man, so that he con-
forms more and more completely to his true self as God's image.
For this dogma of man as the image of God, so prominent a theme
in the Cistercian twelfth century theological movement, lies also
at the roots of the doctrine of St Aelred. What could be more
natural in a conception of theology built upon the theme of the
journey of the soul to God? But St Aelred's interest does not
lie primarily in the speculative analysis of *what* constitutes man
as God's image. Nor is he even principally concerned with the
objective development of this theme as seen in the whole course
of the history of Salvation, the creation of man as God's image,
the original paradise, the fall into the land of unlikeness, the
regio dissimilitudinis, the return of man to God through Christ
and in the Church. His main purpose is to show how this theme with
its foundation in the objective history of salvation is reflected
in the journey of the individual soul to God within the whole formation of the monastic experience. Moreover this is not merely
a dispassionate analysis such as might be written by someone who
had not made that journey. It is more a living personal testimony
of someone who is describing what he has himself known. It is
precisely this which makes St Aelred and the other Cistercian
theologians of the period so interesting.[4] No one could maintain
that they are giving a complete theological exposition of all that
the dogma of the image demands. But they are presenting *an* aspect
of this dogma and one to which until recently we have given too

little attention.

Gustate et videte....taste and see.... St Aelred tells us
that a wisdom, *sapientia*, is given by God and it can only be known
through direct contact. *Ipsa experientia doceat te*.....[5] *de ejus
dulcedine sola docet experientia*.[6] It cannot be explained, for it
is of its very nature *sui generis*. It can only be hinted at indirectly by such terms as: *gustus* and *sensus*. These terms in the
vocabulary of St Aelred can denote the highest states of the soul,
and the use of expressions normally used for sense knowledge help
to convey something of the directness, the immediacy of this mode
of knowledge. This does not mean that St Aelred is making the
gustus in itself a criterion of spiritual advancement. It can be
deceptive *experimentum fallax*[7] and the only true test of its value
is the submission of the will to God. Nor is this experience of
the soul necessarily limited to what is most easily perceptible.
The soul moves from one experience to another, including that of
aridity, in the course of the journey towards the *similitudo*, the
likeness to God.

Are we justified in describing this experience as knowledge?
Certainly it is not the kind of knowledge which one man communicates to another through the use of rational concepts common to
all men. But does this mean that it is not knowledge? To say so
would be to minimize the didactic force given to it by St Aelred.
Doceat te....*sola docet*...: it really teaches us but in a different way from conceptual, rational knowledge. It is knowledge
which comes through what St Aelred describes as *affectus*, an inclination, a sympathy, an assimilation to the thing known. 'Non
intelligis nisi condoleas....non sentis nisi congaudeas....[8] non
intelligit nisi qui amat.[9] The knowledge of divine things to
which St Aelred refers is a *sapientia* proportionate to the degree
of assimilation, of likeness to God which has been achieved within the soul, and which comes ultimately from the Holy Spirit.[10]

In itself this doctrine is no innovation. St Aelred and the
Cistercians of his period are in line with a traditional current
of thought among the Fathers, which is ultimately of platonic origin. It is a doctrine which is unquestionably recognized by St
Thomas. Among the many references to it among his works we need
only mention the famous text from the first question of the *Summa*
on the judgement *per modum inclinationis*.[11] The Cistercian contribution lies in their special emphasis on this subject which becomes one of the mainsprings of their theological method. They
see the themes of revelation as experienced within the life of
the individual soul precisely through this mode of knowledge.
This is a development of considerable importance for the history
both of dogma and of spirituality. For it portrays the dogmas of
the Church as lived within the life of the individual soul, and
conversely it describes an experience which can in the broad sense

be called mystical and yet still remains deeply rooted in dogma.
A particularly interesting example can be found in William of St
Thierry's theology of *amor intellectus* seen as a participation in
the intra-trinitarian life. Here we can see the origin of the
doctrine of the experience of the trinitarian life within the soul,
which was to be developed so strongly by the Flemish mystics of
the school of Eckhardt, Ruysbroeck and Tauler.[12]

St Aelred's analysis of this knowledge through the assimilation of the soul to God is less deeply theological than that of
William of St Thierry. It has more the character of a practical,
psychological description of the total monastic 'experience,' the
general development of the spiritual life in the return of the
soul to a perfect likeness to God. But in the course of this
description he throws light on this Cistercian approach to Scripture and the Liturgy. It is impossible to understand the writings
and commentaries of these monks on Scripture without seeing that
they did not set out to give a strictly scientific exegesis of
Scripture or even a purely objective intellectual delineation of
the Scriptural theological themes, the *thèmes Bibliques* which
many theologians are rightly trying to revive. They looked for a
'spiritual sense' which was not simply the purely intellectual
grasp of the senses of Scripture and of Typology, but a spiritual
understanding which was a *gustus*, an experimental contact with the
word of God.[13] That contact is the result of the assimilation to
God that has taken place within the soul. St Aelred is now able
through this contact to find in Scripture and in the action of the
liturgy the pattern of his own experience, and to see his own experience as an expression of Scripture and the liturgy.[14]

The motive force behind this 'monastic experience' is Charity.
Here St Aelred opens up for us a further perspective, revealing
the whole cosmic movement into which the soul is impelled. Charity
is the Sabbath, the 'rest' in which God dwells in his intratrinitarian life before the work of creation. It is also the end
into which he has willed to draw all things. All creation reflects
Charity through its order and harmony, but man enters into the Sabbath through the very life of charity.[15]

There is a special interest in St Aelred's treatment of the
relationship between Charity and human friendship.[16] St Aelred
was a humanist. It has been said of these early Cistercians that
they had given up everything except the art of writing in good
style.[17] But St Aelred more than any of the other Cistercians had
come under the impact of the classics, and especially of Cicero
and his *De amicitia*. But he was also a humanist in his close
psychological study of human affections. This human interest extends also to his approach to Scripture where the personalities
of Scripture constantly engage his attention. Like so much else
in his writings, this is something which touches closely on his

own experience. The theological reflections in the *Speculum charitatis* were suddenly interrupted by grief at the death of his friend Simon, felt to be foreshadowed in the nightmares which had recently been disturbing his sleep. He then finds a pattern for his own sorrow in the picture of Jacob weeping for his son, Joseph for his Father and David for his friend Jonathan. The *Speculum charitatis* finds its completion ultimately in another work, *De spiritali amicitia*. Despite the dangers of the *affectus* St Aelred sees friendship in its ideal form as the perfect expression of reciprocal Charity,[18] and therefore as an image, an anticipation of eternal life.[19] David and Jonathan offer the example of such a friendship. The ideal is not an easy one. But it should not be abandoned. For to live without friendship, St Aelred says, is to live as a beast and not as a man.[20] How, he asks can one prepare for eternity without the effort to form at least an image of eternity here on earth?[21] In this interplay of Charity and friendship St Aelred shows that he is pre-eminently a Christian humanist, for whom nothing is alien that is human, and who sees Charity as the beginning and as the end of all things.

NOTES

*Published in *PAX* 291 (1959) 87-92.

[1]Jean Leclercq, *L'amour des lettres*. See Leclercq's
'S. Bernard et la théologie monastique du XIIième siècle,' *S. Bernard théologien*, 7-23.

[2]This article does no more than resume some of the conclusions of recent scholars on this subject. See especially J.-M.
Déchanet, *Aux sources* and *Guillaume de Saint-Thierry*, for the
patristic background of monastic theology and particularly the
influence of the Greek Fathers. For the place of St Aelred, see
La Spiritualité, 155-94 and A. Hallier, 'L'expérience Spirituelle
selon Aelred de Rievaulx, *Collectanea OCR*, 20 (1958) 97-113.
This last article, with its admirable analysis of the place of
'experience' in St Aelred's doctrine, is an extract from a thesis
recently defended in Rome, treating fully of the theology of St
Aelred against the monastic background.

[3]See Rupert of Deutz, *De victoria verbi dei*, PL 169,
1217-1502 and *De trinitate*, PL 167, 197-200.

[4]See A. Squire, 'Aelred of Rielvaux and the Monastic
Tradition Concerning Action and Contemplation,' *Downside Review*
(1954) p. 302, 'His charm as a writer is that he makes us feel
all the time that he speaks of what he knows.'

[5]*Sermones inediti*, ed. C. H. Talbot, p. 142.

[6]Ibid., p. 146.

[7]Spec char, PL 195, 564D. ET: *The Mirror of Charity*,
to appear as CF 17.

[8]*Sermones inediti*, p. 47.

[9]Ibid., p. 51.

[10]Oner PL 195, 451C: 'Est quaedam in hac vita experientia....unctio scilicet illa spiritus quae nos docet de omnibus:
quae quasdam nobis futurae beatitudinis infundit primitias, cor
nostrum, simul illuminans et accendens, ut videat et amet, gustet
et intelligat quando ipse spiritus testimonium reddit spiritui
nostro, quoniam sumus filii Dei.' ET projected for Cistercian
Fathers Series.

[11]I, 1 art 6 ad 3.

[12]L. Reypens, 'Dieu, connaissance mystique,' III, 883-929.

[13]P. Dumontier, *S. Bernard et la Bible* (Paris, 1953).

[14]Jesu, PL 184, 856BC. ET: CF2 (1971); Inst incl, ed. Talbot, 32, p. 212; *Sermones inediti,* ;;. 104, 106, 102.

[15]Spec car, PL 195, 521A-531B. See Bouyer, *La Spiritualité,* pp. 167-9.

[16]Ibid., pp. 155-94.

[17]See E. Gilson, *The Mystical Theology of St Bernard* (London, 1940) p. 7.

[18]Spir amic, PL 195, 662C and 664, 691BCD.

[19]Ibid., 690BC.

[20]Ibid., 676C.

[21]Ibid., 690C.

CHAPTER 9

TOWARDS AN INTEGRAL THEOLOGY*

THE TRUTH OF REVELATION does not change, but the theologian
must penetrate more deeply into that one unchanging truth. To
reject **development** is to reject tradition, for tradition is essentially a basis for future development. But to reject tradition
is equally to reject development, for development is essentially
a deeper insight into the traditional inheritance of the past.
The either/or of conservative or progressive is, in theology, a
false antithesis. In this light, the theological conflict that
underlies the debates in the second Vatican Council, appears not
as a mutually exclusive opposition of the 'traditional' and 'new'
theology, but as a movement towards a higher synthesis.[1]
    The new vision of theology as a history of salvation should
not be opposed to the deductive and syllogistic theology of the
scholastics, with its emphasis on Revelation in its metaphysical
aspect. Despite the divergence as to the basis for the integration of these two conceptions of theology, theologians should work
towards a total penetration of Revelation at every level. For
Revelation as the intervention of God in history, demands an investigation of that history together with its ultimate metaphysical
foundation, and with man's personal response to that intervention.[2]

The Metaphysical Foundation

    The theologian must be a **metaphysician.** Very significantly,
Fr Lonergan's *Insight*[3] is a book about philosophy written by a
theologian. For the author has seen that a deep understanding of
the classic metaphysics of St Thomas is an essential basis for the
great speculative questions in theology. Lonergan's great achievement is to have thrown new light on the traditional speculative
problems of theology through a re-thinking of this scholastic inheritance. On this speculative level, he has given us, after the
preparatory *via certitudinis,* an *intellectus fidei,* an understanding of our faith through a reduction of multiplicity to unity, a
penetration of faith through a unified explanation of the data of
Revelation on the philosophical plane.[4]

God's Intervention in History

    But Revelation is God's intervention in history. The ques-
tion therefore is whether there can be an *intellectus fidei* of
this intervention in history, comparable to the *intellectus fidei*
on the speculative plane. Until recently theologians have tended
to restrict the investigation of the sources of Revelation to what

is called 'positive' theology, directed towards certitude as to the facts of Revelation, as contra-distinguished from *intellectus fidei*, the understanding of faith in 'speculative' theology. But Fr Vagaggini's important work *Il senso teologico della liturgia*[5] shows that there can be an *intellectus fidei* of Revelation on the historical no less than on the metaphysical level. For saving history is not a collection of atomized facts,[6] a multiplicity of events without unifying principles. The multiplicity of these events is reduced to unity through the unity of the divine plan, directed according to freely chosen laws as unifying principles of intelligibility.[7] To penetrate to these ultimate unifying principles is to penetrate to the understanding of Revelation in its historical dimension.

The Personal Response to God's Intervention

This understanding of Revelation in the historical dimension raises a further problem. The history of salvation, as revealed in the Bible and as lived in the Liturgy, is primarily collective, external, objective, and to some extent impersonal. God's intervention in history appears first of all as a sequence of external objective events about the salvation of God's People. The problem is to see how these external events of the salvation of a People are assimilated in the inward life of the individual person. How does the historical event of Revelation become *his* event? How does this external history become *his* personal history? The recent interest in monastic medieval theology touches closely on this problem. The medieval monastic theologians, and especially the Cistercians, St Bernard, William of St Thierry and St Aelred, approached the history of salvation under the aspect of the ascent of the soul to God.[8] This 'interiorization' appears above all in their theology of man as the image of God. The dominant theme here is not the metaphysics of the image, nor the external, objective history of mankind as the image of God, but the history of the individual soul as reflecting the collective history of mankind, first in the creation of man in God's image, then in the loss of that image through the fall, and finally in the restoration of that image through the Redemption. This doctrine of the image is also their basis for their theology of Christian experience. William of St Thierry develops a whole theology of mystical experience through this conception of the return of man to the likeness of God. We know God in proportion to our likeness to God. Likeness is a participation in unity. To become like God is to participate in the life of the Holy Spirit as the mutual union of the Father and the Son.[9] The perfect likeness of man to God with its correlative mystical experience, is therefore rooted ultimately in the life of the Persons of the Trinity. Faith is an

initiation into this experience: *credo ut experiar.*10   The life
of faith is a progressive assimilation of the external content of
Revelation through an inward experience, first through an 'experienced' faith, and ultimately through the experience of the trinitarian life as an anticipation of the final vision.

This doctrine shows us how the Christian Revelation is not
completely understood until it is seen as lived in the individual
soul in its ascent to God. Here is the special relevance of the
medieval monastic theology for our contemporary theology. For
the monastic theology is more than a question of purely historical
research. It can shape our theological development.11   We must
work towards a theology of Christian experience, which is not simply an analysis of psychological states of the spiritual life,
but an explanation as to how this Christian experience is rooted
in the dogmas of the Christian Revelation. The *credo ut experiar*
of St Bernard and William of St Thierry, touches here on the important question as to an intrinsic relationship of faith to mystical experience. Is mystical experience the ultimate development of the experience through connaturality discerned by so many
theologians in the initial act of faith?12

The theology of the Fathers and the monastic theologians was
not simply about the Christian experience. It was orientated of
its very nature **towards** that experience itself. *Credo ut experiar*
did not only mean: Believe in order to talk about the Christian
experience. It meant: Believe in order to experience. Our
scholastic conception of theology as *scientia,* as distinct from
the *sapientia* of the Fathers and monastic theologians, must of
its very nature as scientific knowledge be restricted to talking
about the Christian experience. But the theologian as a person
should transcend these limits of scientific knowledge, and direct
his life to the 'kneeling theology.'13

This assimilation of the external objective content of Revelation into the inward life and experience of the individual human person, confronts us again with the need of contemporary theology to express that content through the **categories** of existential-
ist14 and personalist philosophy, and through depth psychology.15
Here Revelation is assimilated by the individual person, not directly through a theology of the spiritual life, as with the Fathers
and monastic theologians, but through a **pre-theological reflection,**
philosophically or psychologically, on the meaning of human existence. This pre-theological reflection is not primarily and directly a metaphysical analysis of 'what is,' but an existentialist
analysis of 'what is happening.'16   It is not an understanding of
being in its ultimate metaphysical causes, but an understanding of
the concrete situations of human existence. It differs in this
way from the classic philosophy, and it is therefore directed towards a different aspect of Revelation. Whereas the classic

philosophy helps towards an understanding of the ultimate foundation of Revelation in its metaphysical causes, the new philosophy and psychology helps towards an understanding of the impact of Revelation on man in his existential situation. But the task of the theologian here is not easy. First, the truth of the new philosophy and psychology has to be sifted from its error, and its philosophical insights have to be integrated into the classic philosophy. There must be a synthesis and not eclecticism. Then, in the light of this new philosophical and psychological understanding, there must be an attempt towards a further explanation of Revelation. The work of the theologian is to complete the investigations already made in this direction. The philosophy of Heidegger, which explains man, not through his static metaphysical nature, but through his historical orientation towards his future destiny may throw light on the Christian Revelation of man as orientated towards his future destiny in Christ.[17] Marcel's philosophy of intersubjective personal relations, expressed in the categories of 'fidelity' and 'presence,' may give a deeper understanding of the Christian life of charity as a communion of persons.[18] Jung's doctrine of the integration of the psyche may explain more completely the Christian doctrine of the salvation and integration of man as a whole, in solidarity with the human race and with the whole cosmos.

Conclusion

This new perspective will respond to the need of contemporary man to see the Christian message, not as extraneous to him, but as a fulfilment of his inward aspirations. The revelation of the Trinity must be seen, not only as the revelation of God, but also as the revelation of man who finds the meaning of his existence in a communion of persons, which is ultimately a communion with the Persons of the Trinity. The Incarnation must be seen, not only as the revelation of God, but as the revelation of man, for man finds his true meaning in Christ the Mediator, God and Man, through whom he enters into this communion of persons. The Church must be seen, not only as an organization with an authority which imposes its decisions on man from above, but as the sphere of man's inmost life, the new man in Christ, the *Ecclesia Trinitatis,* where man lives his authentic existence of a communion of persons in the life of the Holy Spirit through Christ to the Father.

NOTES

*Published in *PAX: A Benedictine Review* 309 (1964) 63-68.

[1]See Dom Christopher Butler's observations on the theological undercurrent of the Council in *Downside Review* (April, 1963) 165-167.

[2]The reason why this last aspect is treated at greater length in this article is not because it is intrinsically more important. It is because it is better to concentrate in a short article on one particular approach to this very wide problem, and also because this aspect is especially relevant for the contemporary outlook and likely to engage increasingly the attention of theologians.

[3]B. Lonergan, *Insight, A Study of Human Understanding* (London, New York, 1957).

[4]B. Lonergan, *Divinarum Personarum; De Deo Trino* and *De Constitutione Christi*.

[5]C. Vagaggini, *Il senso teologico*.

[6]See also Karl Rahner, *Theological Investigations* I, trans. Cornelius Ernst (London, 1961) 14-15.

[7]Vagaggini, *Theological Dimensions*, 102-233.

[8]See Leclercq, *L'amour des lettres*, p. 208.

[9]See **especially** William of St Thierry, Spec Fid, 162-164; 393A-393C.

[10]See Leclercq, *L'amour* 202. The author observes that St Bernard's penetration of faith is more in the direction of *credo ut experiar* than of *credo ut intelligam*. Despite a more developed intellectualistic trend, William of St Thierry saw faith as orientated essentially towards mystical experience.

[11]See Rahner's remarks on the study of theologians of the past in view of the development of the theology of the future. *Theological Investigations* I, 9-10.

[12]See Aubert, *Le Problème de l'acte de foi*, 58-62, 587-600, 723. Also Trethowan, *Certainty*, 113-129.

[13]See the references to this expression in J. Leclercq, *Theology and Prayer; Father Cyril Gaul Memorial Lecture Delivered at St Meinrad Seminary, 23rd September, 1962*, 7, 18.

[14]See Rahner, *Theological Investigations* I. Introd. by Cornelius Ernst, pp. ix–xvii; and L. Malavez, *The Christian Message and Myth* (London, 1958).

[15]See V. White, *God and the Unconscious* (London, 1952); *Soul and Psyche* (London, 1960).

[16]See E. Hill 'Aristotle and Jung,' *Clergy Review* (December, 1963) 778–783.

[17]See Rahner, *Theological Investigations* I, Introd. p. x, referring to R. C. Kwant: 'De Historie en het Absolute,' *Tijdscript voor Philosophie* 17 (1955) 257.

[18]See Mouroux's theology of faith as influenced by the personalist philosophy of Marcel; R. Aubert, *Le Problème*, 615–616.

CHAPTER 10

TOWARDS A THEOLOGY OF CONNATURAL KNOWLEDGE*

The basis in Revelation

THE DEVELOPMENT of historical consciousness has had a decisive influence on theology. We are told that Revelation is not primarily information about God but a saving 'happening.'[1] God is giving himself to us through the development of history and history is given its definitive meaning in the central Christ Event. Therefore the dogmatic theologian cannot restrict himself to the speculative and apologetic aspects of Revelation. He must move towards an understanding of Salvation history. This was an important step forward. But I think that we must reflect more closely on what is meant by history and in particular what is meant by Revelation as Salvation history. That is a vast problem.[2] But I should like at least to touch on one aspect of that problem. The question is whether we do not tend to think of Revelation as something given purely objectively in external, collective, historical events irrespective of the conscious response to God's action in the individual believer. Revelation should not be falsely 'objectified as an event' out there and assimilated as if by an afterthought in the individual believer. To 'objectify' in this way would be a failure to recognize that Revelation is God's self-disclosure to *us* and God cannot be disclosed to us unless we recognize that disclosure through our conscious response. Therefore this conscious response enters intrinsically and essentially into Revelation.[3] To deny this would be the opposite error to that of Bultmann who excludes the miraculous supernatural intervention of God in the external, material events of history. The logic of Bultmann's position is to conceive Revelation solely as the existential response of the believer and to sever that response from a miraculous supernatural intervention of God directing external events even if not from all objective action of God in history.[4] To avoid these opposing errors we have to deny that Revelation is either a purely external objectified history or a purely individual, existential event and we have to affirm that Revelation is an external objective intervention of God in history which can only be interpreted by us through the individual, existential, event of the act of faith.[5] Revelation is the meaning of history recognized through the faith of the believer. Many theologians argue persuasively that this act of faith is grounded in a judgement of connaturality.[6] Through this connatural judgement we recognize that God is disclosing himself personally to us through the 'sign' given in the external, material events of history.[7] Some theologians carry this argument further and suggest that the various

gradations of spiritual and mystical experience may be a development from this radical experience given to us in the act of faith.[8]
The theologian, who attempts to understand this historical dimension in Revelation, should not only record the events. He should search for an intelligible pattern in the events.[9] But the point I want to make here is that our understanding of Revelation is still incomplete if it is limited to the external, objective, collective aspect of Salvation history. We should reflect on our inward, subjective, personal experience in God's self-disclosure to us through that history in an attempt towards an intelligible explanation of that experience. This demands an understanding not only of the experience in the initial connatural knowledge given in the act of faith itself but also an understanding of the experience in the deeper manifestations of connatural knowledge which emerge in the course of the spiritual and mystical life.

This viewpoint enables us to overcome the dichotomy not only between dogmatic theology and ascetical or mystical theology but also between all theology and mystical experience. For it shows as that the dimension of spiritual experience is not a purely individualistic point of contact between God and the soul which takes place somewhere on the fringe of God's Revelation to mankind.[10] That experience is rooted intrinsically and essentially in Revelation through the judgement by connaturality in the initial act of faith.

The Relevance of St Aelred

The Monastic Experience

The twelfth century monastic theologians have said something important about this question. The Cistercian School as represented by St Bernard, William of St Thierry and St Aelred is particularly relevant. For these theologians were concerned predominantly not with the history of Salvation in its purely objective, external, collective aspect but with the assimilation of that history through the connatural experience of the individual believer.[11] Moreover, this was a personal assimilation in the experience of the theologian himself. It was not simply an analytical reflection on the meaning of this experience according to the testimony of others. These theologians did not only know about connatural knowledge. They knew connaturally. Their reflections about this kind of knowledge was grounded in their own personal experience.[12]
How did this experience arise? An answer to this question can only be given through an understanding of connatural knowledge[13] both in a pre-theological and in a theological context. Prior to an explicit reflection on this question we are aware of the connatural as distinct from the purely rational pattern of

knowledge not only on the theological but also on the pre-theological level. Many of our judgements about aesthetic and moral questions and also many of our judgements about people are of this kind. We call them 'instinctive' or 'intuitive' to distinguish them from judgments given through a more analytical and more explicitly rational process of thought. Does this mean that we have to take refuge in some mysterious intuition entirely outside the normal process of human knowledge as given in experience, insight and judgement? I would suggest that connatural knowledge is structured according to this process of experience, insight and judgement. But in contrast to the purely rational pattern of knowledge, the experience, insight and judgement in connatural knowledge is grounded in a natural affinity of knower and known through sympathy or love.[14] In this specific sense we can say that connatural knowledge is rooted in the 'likeness' of knower and known. Knowledge always implies an intentional identity of knower and known.[15] But this intentional identity is given in two different ways. The 'intentional' identity in purely rational knowledge is given through a purely intellectual and rational pattern of insight and correct reasoning irrespective of a natural affinity of knower and known through sympathy of love. The intentional identity of knower and known in connatural knowledge is not given through a purely intellectual and rational pattern but demands also a natural affinity of knower and known through sympathy or love.

In the theological context this kind of knowledge is grounded in an affinity or likeness to God in the believer, whereby his 'nature' is made like to God through grace. To know God connaturally means to know God through becoming like him. Therefore the experience of knowing God connaturally developed in these monastic theologians through the renewal of the divine likeness. This experience was the basis for a theological reflection on the meaning of that experience. Historically this theological reflection has its origins in patristic doctrine[16] and in platonic philosophy.[17] But previous to the twelfth century it would be difficult to point to a theological understanding of this kind of knowledge equal in depth to that given by these monastic theologians and in particular by William of St Thierry.[18] I do not imply that these monks in contrast to their predecessors were more experienced in this knowledge. But I doubt whether previously theologians had given so coherent a theological explanation of this knowledge in terms of the knowledge-likeness equation which is the key to the whole question. I would suggest that this explanation was conditioned by the particular theological perspective of these monastic theologians. This perspective can be explained as follows.

St Aelred's monastic theology cannot be adequately explained if it is simply equated with the patristic sapiential tradition without any further qualification. Both the Fathers and the twelfth century Cistercian writers followed the sapiential rather than the strictly scientific approach to theology. But these monastic theologians did not simply repeat the teaching of the Fathers. They rethought that teaching and they moved towards a new creative synthesis. This was to some extent a new synthesis of particular doctrines of the Fathers. But basically it was a tendency to concentrate more exclusively on a particular kind of question. The kind of questions which engaged their attention most deeply were those which concerned the movement of the soul towards union with God.[19] These questions converged on the doctrine that man is in the image and likeness of God.[20] But merely to state that this doctrine is central to St Aelred's theology would be to miss the point. What is specific to their theology is the approach to this doctrine from a particular perspective. For St Aelred the primary question is not what essentially constitutes man in the image and likeness of God[21] but what is happening to that image and likeness in the various phases of man's historical existence. Moreover he is not concerned with what is happening to the image and likeness to God in the universal history of mankind without reference to what is happening to the image and likeness within the individual Christian in his ascent to union with God. He shows that each individual Christian experiences the effects of the creation of man in the image and likeness of God, the loss of the divine likeness through the fall into the *regio dissimilitudinis* and the renewal of that likeness through Christ.

The question of connatural knowledge is seen directly within this theological perspective. The experience of connatural knowledge is now interpreted theologically through the categories of image-resemblance. But for the monastic theologians this interpretation is never purely intellectual and rational. St Aelred's interpretation given through a reflexive understanding was the articulation of a personal experience and it was intended to initiate his readers into a similar experience.[22]

NON INTELLIGIT NISI QUI AMAT

To know God connaturally is to know God through becoming like him. This likeness is a personal affinity which is given through love. That is the reason why the monastic theologians say that to know God connaturally is a *cognitio amoris*.[23] Following St Gregory the Great they even say that *amor* is *intellectus*.[24] This should be interpreted as an interpenetration and not as a formal identification of the faculties of love and intellect.[25] To understand love connaturally means that we have to experience love. St Aelred is explicit on this point. Fear, he tells us, has its language which is understood only by him who fears. Grief has its language which is understood only by him who grieves and love has its language

which is understood only by him who loves.[26] God, who is love,
can be known in this way only through loving him. 'Lingua amoris
est; non intelligit nisi qui amat.'[27] Love, he says, is the capacity for God, 'est hic locus capax tui.'[28] We can possess God only
through loving him[29] and this loving possession of God is a personal experience which cannot be communicated directly to anyone who
has not had that experience.[30] But it can be evoked through the
language used to describe sense experience. St Aelred describes
it as a kind of spiritual 'sense.'[31] The intellectual note is
sounded less strongly than in the explanation given by William of
St Thierry.[32] But St Aelred indicates clearly that this experience transcends that of the physical senses[33] and that it is in
the intellective soul.[34]

The reflection on the experience of love is perhaps St Aelred's
greatest contribution towards the theology of connatural knowledge.
His theoretical explanation of this kind of knowledge is not equal
in theological depth to that given by William of St Thierry. But
he has thrown a further light on the question through his insight
into friendship. Knowledge through connaturality in personal re-
lationships is not based simply on a particular affinity of nature
but on an intersubjective communion of persons.[35] St Aelred in
contrast to William of St Thierry develops more closely the intersubjective communion in human friendship. William of St Thierry
explains connatural knowledge towards the end of the *Speculum fidei*
as a participation in the intersubjective communion of the persons
of the Trinity.[36] He compares this *cognitio amoris* with the knowledge given through human friendship. But the comparison is that
of contrast. Knowledge of a friend is given through an image of
that person retained in the memory.[37] Our knowledge of the persons
of the Trinity is a knowledge through love grounded in a connatural
likeness to the divine persons, through grace.[38] St Aelred's approach to the question is very different. He does not contrast
human friendship and friendship with God in terms of two different
kinds of knowledge. He experiences human friendship as an initiation into friendship with God. If we read the relevant passages in
De spirituali amicitia[39] it is difficult to avoid the conclusion
that the friendship of two human persons in union with Christ leads
directly into the spiritual experience of *amor intellectus*. Here
St Aelred is talking about human friendship within a Christian context. He does not say that a human friendship can of itself lead
into divine love. He says that a human friendship in Christ *is*
divine love. 'Quae omnia a Christo inchoantur, per Christum pro-
moventur, in Christo perficiuntur.'[40] Christ is present immanently
in the friendship. St Aelred calls this communion the *osculum
spirituale*.[41] But ultimately this friendship moves into a union
with Christ which is beyond the *osculum spirituale*. St Aelred
calls this communion the *osculum intellectuale*.[42] This is not the

presence of Christ immanently within the human friendship.[43] It
is the transcendent presence of Christ which is beyond the human
friendship.[44] But the point of St Aelred's argument is that the
immanent presence is an initiation into the transcendent presence.
The transcendent presence of Christ beyond the love for a human
person is experienced *through* the immanent presence of Christ in
the love for a human person.[45] Through loving a human person with
the love of Christ we come ultimately to love Christ in himself.
This union with Christ in himself, the *osculum intellectuale*,
is described by St Aelred in terms which suggest a deep spiritual
experience.[46]

St Aelred's reflections on love are not purely theoretical.
They are reflections on his own personal experience. There can
be little doubt that he experienced the knowledge which is given
through an affinity with God through love.[47] He experienced also
the spiritual friendship between two human persons as an initiation into this affinity with God through love. *De spirituali amicitia* has been described as 'le journal de son coeur,' the expression of his own experience of love rather than thoughts about love
conceived in isolation from others.[48] The truth of this judgement
will be evident to anyone who has read the deeply moving words
which describe St Aelred's emotions after the death of his friend
Simon.[49] He knew its dangers.[50] He knew that it was not always
a prelude to the divine 'similitudo.' It could lead downwards into the 'regio dissimilitudinis.'[51] He thought that in his youth
love had made him a pagan.[52] But he discovered that a spiritual
friendship was an initiation into friendship with God. When Yves,
his disciple, in the *De spirituali amicitia* interprets St John's
'God is charity' to mean 'God is friendship,'[53] St Aelred concludes:
'He who abides in friendship abides in God and God in him.'[54] For
St Aelred the problematical question is not whether we can come to
God through human friendship but whether we can come to God without
human friendship. To live without friendship, he says, is to live
as a beast and not as a man.[55] How, he asks, can we prepare for
eternity without attempting to form at least an image of eternity
here on earth?[56]

We might be inclined to think of *amor intellectus*, the knowledge of God through connaturality, as a kind of rarefied spiritual
insight unrelated either to our human experience or to the structure of the world around us. St Aelred shows us that this is not
so. He tells us that this spiritual experience can be attained
through a human friendship which is lived in its ultimate depth in
Christ.[57] He throws a further light on this spiritual experience
through his interpretation of the cosmos in terms of the impulse
of love. All creatures, St Aelred says, tend towards an end which
responds to the impulse of their natures.[58] This movement is a reflection of God's love in so far as it manifests that love through

the order and harmony in the cosmos.[59] St Aelred traces this impulse in ascending gradations from inanimate creatures to living
creatures and to the brute animals. This connatural impulse in
non-rational creatures tends towards an end within creation.[60]
But the connatural impulse in man tends towards an end beyond creation.[61] For man is in the image of God which means that he is
'capax Dei.' He realizes himself as image of God only through
entering into friendship and communion with God in the depths of
his personal life. To know God connaturally through friendship
with him is therefore the ultimate realization of the charity
which is reflected throughout the entire cosmos.[62]

Conclusion

The tendency of theologians today is to say that Revelation
is primarily the event of God's self-disclosure to us and only de-
rivatively propositions about that event. That event unfolds within the historical dimension. But God's gift of himself to us is
not given in purely external, objectified, historical events. It
is given in our penetration into the meaning of those events. To
say that Revelation is history is ultimately to say that it is the
meaning of history. That meaning is disclosed to us through the
instinctus fidei. There are strong arguments for the theory that
the act of faith is grounded in an instinctive judgement through
connaturality and also for the theory that mystical experience is
a development from this initial *instinctus fidei*. Mystical experience would therefore be a deeper penetration into the meaning of
the central Revelation Event whereby we discern God's self-disclosure to us through the connatural instinct of faith.

The twelfth century monastic theologians have something to
tell us through their personal experience of connatural knowledge
and through their theological reflection on the meaning of that
experience. In this experience these theologians did not only
know about God. They knew God. They knew God through becoming
like him. This is what is meant by knowing God connaturally.
Theologically they reflected on this experience and expressed that
reflection in the categories of image-resemblance. This theological insight explains the experience in terms of Salvation history
understood under the aspect of the renewal of the divine likeness
in man. From the point of view of cognitional analysis the role
of love is central to the understanding of knowledge of God through
likeness to him. Through love we become like to God. What is called a connatural knowledge of God is to be equated with the *amor
intellectus* of the monastic theologians.

The importance of St Aelred for this whole question is principally in his experience of love and in his reflection on the experience of love. The divine impulse of love, which impels man

towards friendship with God, is reflected in the connatural impulse of every creature towards its end. *Amor intellectus* is the experience which emerges through this friendship with God and it is communicated through a communion of persons. The friendship of human persons in Christ is an initiation into personal communion with Christ himself and therefore into the *amor intellectus* which is given through this communion. This aspect of St Aelred's teaching is particularly relevant for contemporary thought. God's self-disclosure to man is meaningless for our contemporaries unless that disclosure is given to them through their human experience. This is not only a conviction of men today. It is also a conviction which is theologically true. *Gratia praesupponit naturam*. Even the most transcendent disclosure of God must be received according to the capacity of the human person. The difficulty which many people find in responding to God's Revelation is that Revelation appears as extraneous to their human experience. St Aelred meets this difficulty. He tells us how a transcendent union with God is discovered through exploring a human relationship in its ultimate depth in Christ.

NOTES

*Published in *Cîteaux*, 18 (1967) 275-290.

[1]See Karl Rahner, *Theological Investigations*, Vol. I, 'The Development of Dogma,' p. 48: 'Revelation is a saving Happening, and only then and in relation to this a communication of "truths".'

[2]A very stimulating study of this question has been made in Alan Richardson's *History Sacred and Profane* (London, 1964).

[3]See G. Moran, 'What is Revelation,' *Theological Studies*, 25 (1964) p. 217-231   See p. 225: 'our irrepressible tendency to objectify makes us think and speak of God "up there," man "down here" and revelation "out there." But there is no revelation "out there;" there is God revealing, man believing, and there is no revelation unless it is received' and p. 227: 'where then does revelation come to its full fruition, where does it exist in fulness? The answer would seem to be: in the human consciousness of Christ.' See also G. Moran, *Theology of Revelation* (London, 1967).

[4]See L. Malevez, *The Christian Message and Myth* (London, 1958). Père Malevez argues for an objective element in Bultmann's conception of the Christian kerygma as against the purely subjective interpretation of his thought, p. 71-110. See also P. Benoit, *Exégèse et théologie*, Vol. I (Paris, 1961), 'La pensée de R. Bultmann,' pp. 62-90, and 'La pensée de R. Bultmann critiquée par le P. Malevez,' pp. 91-93. The question of Bultmann's attitude to history is discussed further by Alan Richardson and by Jean Mouroux who interpret his thought essentially as a disengagement from history, see J. Mouroux. *The Mystery of Time* ([translation of *Le mystère du temps*, 1962], New York 1964), and A. Richardson, *History Sacred and Profane*, 125-153, 'Disengagement from history.' See especially p. 153, where the author explains the meaning of this 'disengagement': 'The keryma of the whole Bible is a proclamation that God is a God who intervenes in history and is Lord of history. The biblical language about God's mighty acts in history certainly need interpreting; but it does not need demythologizing, because it is not a myth. It does not speak in mythological terms of an existential meaning disclosed in a certain historical situation, but of how God intervened in the stream of events and altered the course of history.'

[5]Richardson argues persuasively for the role of interpretation in all historical research (*History Sacred and Profane*, 190-194, 293-294). Seen in this light the interpretation given by faith

does not appear as extraneous to the historical facts but simply as a unique example of the role of interpretation which is present even in the simple affirmation of the facts (206-212). The failure to recognize the need for the interpretative role of faith is a serious limitation in Pannenberg's conception of Revelation. Note the criticism of Pannenberg's uninhibited perception of the 'revealing events' in C. G. O'Collins 'Revelation as History,' *The Heythrop Journal,* (Oct. 1966) pp. 394-406.

[6]See Aubert, *Le problème,* 61-62, 723-724, and Vagaggini, *Il senso teologico,* 417-424. The argument is grounded in the teaching of St Thomas, II. II. *q.* 2. *art.* 9 *ad* 3. See P. Duroux, *La psychologie de la foi chez S. Thomas d'Aquin,* (Tournai, 1963) 100-108.

[7]Theologians are increasingly aware of the importance of the sign structure in our understanding of God's revelation to us. See K. Rahner, *Schriften* Band IV (Einsiedeln, 1961) 275-355: 'Zur Theologie des Symbols' and E. H. Schillebeeckx, *Le Christ Sacrement de la rencontre de Dieu.* G. Moran, *Theology of Revelation,* p. 225, J. Bourke, 'The historical Jesus and the kerygmatic Christ,' *Concilium* Vol. I (2), pp. 16-25: see p. 24: 'We must regard the event of Jesus, from his incarnation to his resurrection, not merely as a gesture but as a *sacramental* gesture....It is this specifically Catholic principle of sacramentality which makes the historical Jesus in his concrete factuality one and continuous with the *kerygmatic Christ* in his eternal saving meaningfulness.' Fr Bourke rightly sees that this sacramental understanding of Revelation is the key to the problem posed by Bultmann as to how we can synthesize the 'external' and the 'inner' event in Revelation.

[8]See Aubert, *Le problème,* 58-62, 587-600, 723, and Trethowan, *Certainty,* 113-29.

[9]See Rahner, *Theological investigations,* I, p. 15. Fr Rahner, arguing for a theology of both essence and existence, shows that we should not only give an accurate reporting of the events as facts but that we should also attempt an understanding of the nature and structure of the events. 'There are structures which persist even in the most surprising novel event. Otherwise it would be meaningless to speak of a single saving history taking its course according to a comprehensive and eternally abiding divine plan....'

[10]See von Balthasar, *Word and Redemption* (New York, 1965) pp. 49-86, 'Theology and Sanctity.'

[11]See J. Leclercq, *L'amour*, p. 208. The contrasting tendency of the black monks is illustrated in the works of Rupert of Deutz, *De victoria* (PL 169, 1217-1502) with his emphasis on the divine economy in its objective historical aspect. But this contrast is mainly a question of emphasis and the generalization should not be pressed too closely.

[12]To speak of the relevance of this monastic theology does not prejudge the question as to whether theology should be 'sapiential' or 'scientific.' The Fathers and the monastic writers of the Middle Ages conceived theology to be directed 'ex fine operis' not only towards intelligible explanations and rational conclusions but ultimately towards the perfection of the entire human person in his quest for union with God. A 'reasoning' theology was intrinsically orientated towards a 'praying' theology. This is the 'sapiential' method, see Vagaggini, *Il senso teologico*, pp. 493-495; M. R. Gagnebet, 'La nature de la théologie spéculative,' *Revue Thomiste* 44 (1938) 1-39 and 213-255; Perino, *La dottrina trinitaria di Sant' Anselmo*, 37-40; and J. Maritain, *Le degrés du savoir* (Paris 1932) 577-613. This method is engaged of its very nature in a response to Revelation not only through the purely intellectual and rational pattern of knowledge but also through the connatural pattern of knowledge. Apart from its basis in the radical connatural knowledge given in the act of faith, the scientific method is not directed of its very nature towards knowing connaturally. But it is directed towards knowing **scientifically** about connatural knowledge not only in the radical act of faith but also in its deeper manifestations in a strictly contemplative knowledge. The scientific method is therefore committed *ex fine operis* to an intelligible explanation of connatural knowledge. Moreover, *ex fine operantis* the scientific theologian as a person, who desires union with God, should transcend the purely scientific pattern of knowledge and should engage himself in the connatural pattern of knowledge.

[13]St Thomas distinguishes connatural from scientific knowledge, see especially I. *q.* I. *art.* 6 *ad* 3 and II. II. *q.* 45 *art.* 2. An extensive list of the relevant texts of St Thomas are given by Marin-Sola in *L'évolution homogène du dogme catholique*, Vol. I (Fribourg, 1924) 358-362. The author discusses the question in relation to the evolution of dogma, pp. 353-392. See also P. Rousselot, *The intellectualism of St Thomas* (London, 1935) 78-80, and J. Dedek, 'Quasi experimentalis cognitio (see p. 13), A historical approach to the meaning of St Thomas,' *Theological Studies* 21 (1961) 357-390.

[14]An object or a person can be judged connaturally to be antipathetic. But this judgement presupposes a particular affinity as its basis. For example, a person may be judged connaturally to be lacking in some particular virtue by another person who has an affinity with that particular virtue.

[15]This 'intentional' identity of knower and known is compatible with a 'natural' distinction of knower and known.

[16]The classic formula is that given by St Gregory the Great, *Homiliarum in Evangelia* 27 (PL 76, 1207A): 'amor ipse notitia est.' Further references to this doctrine among the Fathers can be found in J.-M. Déchanet, *Méditations et prières,* 49-50. Note especially the comment by R. Roques, *L'univers dionysien,* 125: 'Une telle connaissance n'est pas séparable de l'amour et c'est en effet l'amour de Dieu qui l'accomplit.'

[17]See J.-M. Déchanet, 'Guillaume et Plotin,' 241-260.

[18]In the theological explanation of connatural knowledge given by William of St Thierry, knowledge and likeness act in reciprocal causality. 'Quem in tantum videbit, sive cognoscet, qui cognoscet vel videbit, in quantum similis ei erit; in tantum erit ei similis, in quantum eum cognoscet vel videbit.' (Spec fid, 164-165; 393C). The likeness, the *similitudo,* is a created participation in the uncreated *unitas,* the Holy Spirit, who is the mutual union of the Father and the Son. Therefore, in accordance with the principle that knowledge and likeness are proportioned to each other, this 'likeness' or connaturalization with the intratrinitarian life implies that we participate in an intratrinitarian mode of knowledge; see pp. 164-165, 393A: 'Quibus ergo revelat Pater et Filius, hii cognoscunt, sicut Pater et Filius se cognoscunt; quia habent in semetipsis notitiam mutuam eorum; quia habent in semetipsis unitatem eorum et coluntatem vel amorem; quod totum Spiritus Sanctus est.' William describes this *cognitio amoris* as an organic development from the living faith which is inseparable from love. See my 'Faith and Mystical Experience in William of St Thierry,' [Chapter 4].

[19]See P. Bodard, 'La Bible expression d'une expérience religieuse chez St Bernard,' *S. Bernard Théologien,* 23-46; see p. 25: 'il est clair que l'attention de l'écrivain est retenue avant tout par les choses de l'âme. On s'explique dès lors pourquoi cette théologie monastique--et celle de S. Bernard plus encore que celle de ses prédécesseurs--est fortement teintée d'intériorisme et toute orientée vers l'expérience religieuse.'

[20]Père Hallier places this doctrine at the very center of the teaching of St Aelred, see A. Hallier, *Un educateur*, 29-30. See also Déchanet, *OEuvres choisies*, p. 253, who writes of the image-resemblance theme 'une des clefs--sinon la clef--de sa spiritualité.' See also M. Standaert, 'La doctrine de l'image chez Saint Bernard,' *ETL* 23 (1947) p. 102.

[21]St Aelred recognizes the ontological basis in man as the image of God and this 'natural' image cannot be destroyed. *Sermones inediti*, ed. Talbot, p. 108: 'Sic animam rationalem secundum naturam sui essentiam ad Dei imaginem factam diximus....' (*sui*, as Hallier comments, p. 32, is an error. The text should read *seu*). But St Aelred, following the patristic tradition, considers the nature of man in the historical perspective as orientated towards a participation in God's life through grace. See Hallier, p. 31. The context of the passage quoted from the Sermon, *in die pentecostem*, reveals this historical perspective, the gift through grace of the divine likeness, the *similitudo*, the loss of the *similitudo* and the renewal of the *similitudo* through Christ. *Sermones inediti*, pp. 108-109. The terminology *imago similitudo* is not perfectly consistent in St Aelred's writings. But the terminology *similitudo*, when it is specifically related to the terminology *imago*, denotes a further perfection given to the soul by grace. Hallier, p. 34.

[22]See Hallier, 133-134. 'La doctrine d'Aelred a un caractere concret très marqué, en ce sens qu'elle est moins préoccupée de spéculation objective et impersonnelle que d'un *témoignage*, écho d'une expérience. La réalité spirituelle y est décrite telle qu'elle a été vécue par une âme qui l'a éprouvée, sentie, goûtée, non certes d'une manière sensible mais par toute son activité spirituelle qui en a été "affectée"....Invitation à l'expérience, une telle doctrine sollicite un engagement....' See p. 129.

[23]See William of St Thierry, Spec fid, p. 162-163; 392D: 'Cognitio haec Dei alia fidei est, alia amoris vel charitatis.'

[24]St Gregory, *Homiliarum in Evangelia* 27 (PL 76, 1207A). 'amor ipse notitia est.' See William's 'amor quippe Dei intellectus est,' Adv Abl, 252C, Cant, 491D, 499C.

[25]See Déchanet, *Méditations et prières*, pp. 50, 62 ff; and R. Javelet, 'Intelligence et amour,' 273-290.

[26]St Aelred, *Sermones inediti*, p. 47: 'Nam sicut michi videtur, habet timor linguam suam, quam non intelligit nisi qui

timet, habet linguam suam et dolor, quam non intelligit qui dolet. Habet ergo et linguam suam amor, quam non intelligit nisi qui amat.'

[27]Ibid., p. 51. St Aelred describes here the deification of man in the union of the created and the uncreated spirit through love: 'quando in osculo spirituali sibi obviant sibique miscentur spiritus creatus et increatus, ut sint duo in uno, immo dico unum, sicut justificans et justificatus, et santificatus sicut sanctificans, sicut deificans et deificatus? Dicam itaque, quod ipsi melius et expressius experimini. Lingua amoris est; non intelligit nisi qui amat.'

[28]See St Aelred, Spec car (PL 195, 505C).

[29]Ibid., 'Qui enim amat te, capit te; et tantum capit, quantum amat, quia ipse amor est, quia charitas es.'

[30]*Sermones inediti*, p. 142: 'Sunt et alia quaedam spiritualia experimenta que sentire quidem possunt et explicari minime,' and p. 106. See St Gregory the Great, *Moralia*, XXIV, 6, 12 (PL 76, 293A): 'quam tamen praesentiam et sentire possit et explere non possit.'

[31]See such expressions as 'dulce et sapidum usque ad palatum cordis' (*Sermones inediti*, p. 47), 'sapiat interiori palato meo,' 'et est palatum cordis cui sapis, quia dulcis es'; (Spec car, PL 195, 505B), 'gustet quam dulcis est' (*Sermones inediti*, p. 47). See St Bernard's letter to St Aelred, *Epistola Bernardi ad Aelredum* (PL 195, 501-502): 'sub umbris arborum senseris quale nunquam didicisces in scholis.' For a further analysis of the twelfth century monastic theology, see J. Walsh, 'Guillaume de Saint-Thierry et les sens spirituels,' *RAM* 137 (1959) 27-42. The doctrine can be traced to Origen. See K. Rahner, 'Les débuts d'une doctrine des cinq sens spirituels,' *RAM* 13 (1932) p. 263ff.

[32]See Spec fid, 162-165; 392D-393B and Aenig 399B.

[33]*Sermonis inediti*, p. 106: 'Non enim oculis cernitur aut tangitur manibus aut hauritur auditu, cum sapor sit spiritualis, non nisi gustu ipsa hac experientia discernendus.'

[34]Ibid., p. 137: 'Pars inferior sensus, pars superior intellectus....sicut igitur a parte superiori, id est sensu judicamus inter corporalia, ita de spiritualibus intellectu discernimus....Ita in summitate anime virginalis, scilicet, in mente vel intellectu imago dei similitudo que relucet....' St Aelred is also explicit that this spiritual experience implies an understanding

of God.   See *Sermones de oneribus* (PL 195, 451C):   'Est autem in
hac vita experientia....unctio scilicet spiritus quae nos docet
de omnibus; quae quasdam nobis futurae beatitudinis infundit primitias, cor nostrum, simul illuminans et accendens, ut videat et
amet, gustet, et intelligat quando ipse spiritus testimonium reddit spiritui nostro, quoniam sumus filii Dei.'   See also Oner,
484D, *Sermonis inediti*, p. 47.   In the terminology of the twelfth
century theologians *intellectus* is distinguished from *ratio*.
Intellectus in contrast to *ratio* is interpreted as a deeper and
more immediate and more experimental kind of knowledge.   From
this point of view St Aelred's description of spiritual experience
as a kind of spiritual 'sense' is not incompatible with his description of it as an intellectual experience, see Javelet, 'Intelligence et amour,' 273-290.

   35See Javelet, 'Intelligence et amour,' 429-450.   See
especially p. 430:   'De même, je ne connais un ami, peut-être à
travers son style de vie, son tempérament et ses actes, que grâce
à une sympathie profonde qui atteint sa liberté, sa personnalité.
On n'ignore pas ce que Scheler a écrit à ce sujet.   Harmonisation
de nature sans doute, mais communion de sujets.'

   36Spec fid, 162-165; 392D-393C.

   37Ibid., pp. 162-163; 392D.

   38Ibid., pp. 162-165; 393A-393C.   Javelet suggests that
William of St Thierry's theory of the *cognitio* through the intersubjective communion with the persons of the Trinity can be extended to the intersubjective communion of one human person with
another.   See 'Intelligence et amour,' p. 431.

   39Spir amic, PL 195, 661A-702B, especially 672B-673D
and 701A-702B.

   40Ibid., 672C, see 661A: 'Ecce ego et tu et spero quod
inter nos Christus sit.'

   41Ibid., 673AB.

   42Ibid., 673A.   St Aelred distinguishes the *osculum corporale*, the *osculum spiritale* and the *osculum intellectuale*:
'osculum corporale impressione fit labiorum; osculum spiritale
conjunctione animorum; osculum intellectuale per Dei Spiritum, in-
fusione gratiarum.'

[43]Ibid., 673C: 'Hoc osculum dixerim Christi, quod ipse tamen porrigit non ore proprio sed alieno; illum sacratissimum amantibus inspirans affectum, ut illis videatur quasi unam animam in diversis esse corporibus.'

[44]The presence of Christ in the *osculum intellectuale* is the presence of Christ in himself. See Ibid., 673: 'O si ipsemet accessisset; ad illud intellectuale suspirat, et cum maximo desiderio clamans: osculetur me, dicit, osculo oris sui' (Cant. I). The 'ipsemet' and 'oris sui' is contrasted with the 'non ore proprio sed alieno' of the 'osculum spiritale.' The transcendent presence of Christ beyond all that is created is suggested in the words which follow, Ibid., 373D: 'ut jam terrenis affectibus mitigatis, et omnibus, quae de mundo sunt, cogitationibus desideriis que sopitis, in solius Christi delectetur osculo....'

[45]Ibid., 672C: 'Non igitur videtur nimium gravis vel innaturalis ascensus, de Christo amorem inspirante, quo amicum diligimus, ad Christum, semetipsum amicum nobis praebentem, quem diligamus,' and Ibid., 701B-702A: 'Ita pro amico orans Christum, et pro amico volens exaudiri a Christo, ipsum diligenter et desideranter intendit: cum subito et insensibiliter aliquando affectus transiens in affectum et quasi a vicino ipsius Christi tangens dulcedinem, incipit gustare quam dulcis est, et sentire quam suavis est. Ita a sancto illo amore, quo amplecitur amicum, ad illum conscendens, quo amplectitur Christum....'

[46]The metaphorical expression *osculum intellectuale* appears almost literally to suggest *amor intellectus*. A literal interpretation should not be pressed too closely in the metaphor itself. But there is no doubt that the *osculum intellectuale* is an expression used to describe an intimate spiritual union with Christ. See Ibid., 672D: 'unus cum eo Spiritus efficitur in osculo uno.' There is no doubt also that this union is accompanied by a spiritual experience. Ibid., 672CD. The transition from the *osculum spiritale* to the *osculum intellectuale* is described as follows: 'ut suavitas suavitati, dulcedo dulcedini, affectus succedat affectu' see also Ibid., 702A. An affective experience is present already in the *osculum spiritale*. Ibid., 673C: 'ex sui participatione coelestem immittente saporem.' The *affectus* is in the *mens*, Ibid., 673B: 'Non enim fit oris attactu, sed mentis affectu.'

[47]See pp. 234-5.

[48]A. Hoste, 'Le Speculum Spiritalis Amicitiae,' *Studia Monastica* 3 (1961) 292, 294.

49Spec Car, PL 195, 539C-546C.

50Ibid., 600D-602A, 528B-532D.

51Ibid., 508A-509A, 512B-513B.

52Ibid., 531B-532D.

53Spir amic, 669A-670A: 'Dicamne de amicitia quod ami-
cus Jesu Joannes de charitate commemorat Deus amicitia est?'

54Ibid., 670A: 'Inusitatum quidem hoc, nec ex Scripturis habet auctoritatem: quod tamen sequitur de charitate amicitiae profecto dare non dubito, quoniam: "Qui manet in amicitia
in Deo manet et Deus in eo" (I Joan. IV).'

55Ibid., 676C: 'Ego eos non tam homines, quam bestias
dixerim, qui sic dicunt esse vivendum..., amare nullum, amari a
nullo curantes.'

56Ibid., 690C: 'Haec est vera et aeterna amicitia, quae
hic inchoatur, ibi perficitur; quae hic paucorum est, ubi pauci
boni; ibi omnium, ubi omnes boni. Hic necessario probatio, ubi
est sapientium et stultorum permissio; ibi probatione non egent,
quos beatificat angelica illa et quodammodo divina perfectio. Ad
hanc proinde similitudinem comparemus amicos, quos non secus ac
nos ipsos diligamus.'

57See G. Raciti, 'L'apport originel d'Aelred de Rievaulx
à la réflexion occidentale sur l'amitié,' *Collectanea* 29 (1967)
77-99.

58Spec car, 524C: 'Singula quaeque ad suum ordinem ten-
dunt, sua loca petunt, extra ordinem suum inquieta sunt, ordinata
quiescunt.'

59Ibid., 524A: 'Porro si omnem creaturam a prima usque
ad novissimam, a summa usque ad unam, a summo angelo usque ad minimum vermiculum subtilius contempleris, cernes profecto divinam
bonitatem, quam non aliud dicimus quam ejus charitatem.'

60Ibid., 524C-525A: 'Nam si lapidem libres in aera,
nonne mox quasi vim passus proprio pondere se deponit ad solida
....Quid olera, quid arbusta? Nonne quo feracius uberiusque
fructificent, haec solidiarem, haec molliorem, haec pinguiorem,
haec argillosam, haec arenosam quasi appetunt terram?....Porro
animantibus irrationalibus quid labor est tueri salutem, vitare

perniciem, carnalium appetituum quaerere satietatem. Qua adepta, cum nihil habeant ultra quod appetant, conquiescant?'

[61]Ibid., 525A: 'Tibi enim, o anima rationalis, prae caeteris animantibus haec praerogativa servatur; quo te sensibus carnis emergens, ad altiora contendas:....restat ad quod anheles, restat postremo ipsa beatitudo, ad quam appetendam animam rationalem vis quaedam naturalis impellit.' This beatitude is beyond all that is created. (526B-527B and 521B).

[62]Ibid., 505B, C.

CHAPTER 11

THE MONK AND THE WORLD*

The Question

A NEW SENSE of the Church in the world has led many people
to question the *fuga saeculi* as a criterion for the authentic monk.
To question is not necessarily to reject this criterion. But we
should ask how a flight 'from' the world can be reconciled with
our human situation 'in' the world. There is the obvious fact
that we are all of us 'in' the world. There is also the increasing
awareness that the development of the human person is radically conditioned through his historical context. There is the growing consensus of philosophical opinion that our personal experience is not
an isolated phenomenon. Our experience is 'our world' and our
world is *the* world as shaped through our individual, personal development.[1] But is it possible to be radically involved in the
world and at the same time to flee from the world? How do we
avoid a contradiction?

I would like to pose the problem in different terms. I would
prefer to ask the question: 'Where is your center? Is your center
in the world or is your center beyond the world?' This approach
opens up the possibility of rejecting an 'either/or' dilemma without taking refuge in a *via media*.[2] Our involvement in the world
is not partial but total. But we are involved in the world from
a new center which not partially but totally transcends the world.
We are therefore engaged totally *in* the world from a center totally
beyond the world.

The purpose of this article is to attempt an explanation of
this paradox. But I would like to say now that this total involvement does not necessarily imply what is called 'activism.' I hope
that this explanation will gradually emerge in the following pages.
We shall then see that even the most strictly contemplative community should, in this sense, be totally committed to the world,
and that even the most 'active' community should find its center
'beyond' this world. The point which I am attempting to make is
this: There is a basic relationship of the monk to the world,
which is presupposed to the question of the more 'contemplative'
or the more 'active' interpretation of the monastic life. Therefore, although my argument does not in itself solve that debate,
I am hoping that, however indirectly, it may contribute something
towards it.[3]

The New Center[4]

SPIRIT IN THE WORLD

From a purely philosophical point of view we might argue as
follows: In reaction against the Platonist and Cartesian concept
of man, and following the lead of Aristotle and St Thomas, we have
rejected a spirit-body dualism. But this rejection of a spirit-
body dualism has not always been accompanied by a rejection of a
person-world dualism. We find ourselves affirming simultaneously
that man is spirit-body,[5] *and* that man is an isolated, independent
person, detached from his social, historical and cosmic context.
Both kinds of dualism are to be rejected.[6] The human person is
spirit-body and he is spirit-in-the-world.[7] He fulfils himself as
spirit in and through the world. As 'spirit' the human person
transcends the world. As 'spirit-in-the-world' he is conditioned
by the world. His development can be frustrated in two directions.
He can attempt to retreat into a purely spiritual existence. This
is the error of angelism. Alternatively, he can 'lose' himself in
the world. This is a capitulation to what is less than human and
leads to the disintegration of the human person. Nor can this
dilemma be solved through an eclectic oscillation between the phenomenal world and the transcendent, spiritual dimension. The infinite
being whom we call God is the origin and end of our personal life.
As 'spirit' the human person has the capacity for union with that
infinite being through knowledge and love. This union is the ultimate center of our human life and therefore we must be involved
in the world *from* that spiritual center.[8]

THE FUTURE OF THE WORLD[9]

The Christian Revelation gives a new meaning to this human
situation. From this further perspective we find ourselves committed to a radical transformation of the world. The center of
human life is now revealed not purely as the timeless ground of
man's being but as the Father transforming the world through Christ
in the Holy Spirit. In the philosophical perspective the crucial
question is: Do we live the spirit-world relationship from the
spiritual center or do we reject the primacy of the spiritual in
a surrender to the purely phenomenal world? In the theological
perspective the crucial question is: Do we go forward towards the
transformation of the world through the risen Christ or do we re-
sist this transformation? The choice is not whether to be involved
in the world or to flee from the world. This would be a false dilemma. The question is whether to accept or to reject the transformation of the world through Christ.
The following objection could be made to this argument. The

Christian tradition has continually pointed to the need to reject
the world. In reply to this difficulty I would say that this 'no'
to the world in the sense of rejection is a 'no' to the world considered under the aspect of sin. Here there must be an uncompromising dualism. But this rejection of the world as sinful is not
in contradiction to my argument. Sin is privation. Through sin
the world is deprived of its true meaning. Therefore a 'no' to sin
is a 'yes' to the world. The rejection of sin is the liberation
of the world from the evil forces which hold it captive and which
prevent it from going forward to its fulfilment.

A further objection might be made: Transformation leads ultimately to the new world on the other side of **death**. But we cannot move forward into that world without the experience of death,
and death demands a total break with the world on this side of
death. I would reply that the ultimate break with the world on
this side of death is not a rejection of this world but a rejection of the limitations of this world. This final eschatological
transformation is a revolution which radically changes the structures of the world. But this radical change is a liberation from
the restrictions of our present human condition. Therefore that
change is not a denial but an affirmation of the world in its latent potentialities.[10]

In the Christian context a denial of the world can only mean
a denial of privation and of limitation. This denial of privation
and of limitation is not a rejection but an affirmation of the
world. In Pauline terms this could be called the transformation
of the human condition from 'flesh' to 'spirit,' the transformation from the condition of 'privation' and of 'limitation' into
the integrated and unrestricted life of the risen body.[11]

The Monastic Perspective

ESCHATOLOGICAL SIGN

We should not misunderstand the distinction between an 'eschatological' and an 'incarnational' way of life. There is a
sense in which we must say that the way of life for all Christians
is eschatological and that the way of life for all Christians is
also incarnational. All Christians should be moving towards the
new world in the future and all Christians should be involved in
the transformation of *this* world.[12] This point becomes clear as
soon as we understand that the new world of the future *is* this
world transformed.

A distinction between two ways of life cannot be founded on
the basis of a **false** dualism between this world and the new world.
But the distinction could be accepted in this restricted sense:
we can take part in this one indivisible process in two different

ways. We can take part in this process through a way of life
which visibly signifies the transformation of the world from beyond the human condition. That is the 'eschatological' way. Alternatively we can take part in this process through a way of life
which visibly signifies the transformation of the world from 'within' the human condition. That is the 'incarnational' way.[13]

This contrast could be exemplified in the life of the monk
and the life of the married man. Both the monk and the married
man are involved in the transformation of *this* world through the
risen Christ into the *new* world of the future. But the life of
the monk visibly signifies the transformation of this world from
'beyond' the human condition and the life of the married visibly
signifies the transformation of this world from 'within' the human condition. The monk is committed to the world no less than
the married man. But he is committed to the world in another way.
Both the married man and the monk live from the one center, common
to all Christians, which is the risen Christ. But the married man
is involved in the world from that one center in the incarnational
perspective and the monk is involved in the world from that one
center in the eschatological perspective.[14]

What is this eschatological perspective in the life of a monk?
What is this monastic sign which visibly points to the transformation of the world from beyond our present human condition? An answer might be given in this direction: We know that the new world
in the future will be a communion of persons in a new kind of existence. They will be united in a new kind of way because they will
be living together in the immediate presence of the Mystery of God.
The monastic community anticipates this communion of persons united
in a new kind of way through living together in the presence of the
mystery of God. In contrast for instance to the community created
in marriage the basic reason for the existence of the monastic community is to create a community through the presence of the divine
mystery given in a life of prayer.[15] But unlike the future eschatological community the presence of the divine mystery is given
not immediately but through the mediation of the sign. Therefore
the monastic community is a provisional anticipation of that future
community, a sign pointing to the new world.

THE MONK IN THE CONTEMPORARY WORLD

The monastic community, seen as a provisional anticipation of
the future eschatological community, should appear not as a mere
legacy from the past, but as a pointer towards the future. This
does not mean that monasteries are in some mysterious way 'events'
of the future thrown as isolated 'signs' into our contemporary
world. The Christian community of the future emerges from within
the historical situation here and now. Within the *fieri* of the

historical process we should discern a tension towards this future
fulfilment.[16] This latent tension can come to the surface in some
phenomenon at a particular moment in history. I think that we are
now witnessing that kind of phenomenon. We could not identify
this movement with contemporary civilization as such. For this
movement emerges as a protest against the contemporary civilization.
We might say that it is a trend 'in' the contemporary world rather
than a trend 'of' the contemporary world. Questioned as to its nature, we might describe it as a protest against 'one-dimensional
man.' This protest could become the point of intersection between
the contemporary world and monastic communities.

The protest is against both the dangers and the limitations
of a materialistic, positivist, extraverted, technological civilization. In opposition to the obvious dangers of this technological world with its power to manipulate, to control, to dominate,
to enslave and to destroy human beings, there is the counteraction
towards non-violence, receptivity, openness, empathy in our rela-
tionships with other people. In opposition to the intrinsic limitations of the technological world there is the search for a more
complete human existence. We are becoming aware that some of our
more vital human faculties have been atrophied in the development
of a one-sided civilization. In the process of the great achievement of our western civilization, a highly developed rational consciousness, men have lost the 'sense of the whole.' We have lost
touch with the more intuitive, symbolic, contemplative consciousness, and we have isolated ourselves from the communion with the
whole cosmos given in that kind of consciousness.[17] The technological civilization has led to an increasing domination over the
material cosmos. But domination is not to be identified with communion.

The development of the human person from childhood and the
development of the human race from its primitive origins appears
to follow this kind of pattern. A more symbolic consciousness
gives way to a more rational consciousness. The sense of being
part of a whole gives way to a more acute awareness of personal
identity, to more clearly differentiated processes of thought, and
to more sharply distinguished intellectual disciplines.[18] This
process is a stage in human development. Integration is given in
a forward and not in a backward movement. We should not attempt
to regress to the original primitive childhood state. The human
person should not desire to return to the undifferentiated fusion
with his environment which he experienced in his state of childhood. The human race should not desire to regress to a primitive
state prior to a more rational scientific and technological civi-
lation. We should move on towards a more total experience. The
human person should recapture the sense of the whole without los-
ing his sense of identity. The human race should recapture the

more symbolic, intuitive, consciousness without surrendering its
rational, scientific, technological, achievement. An **authentic**
monasticism would point towards this integration.

Further Reflections

I hope that this basic monk-world relationship may be accept-
able to all monks irrespective of the debate between the more 'active' and the more 'contemplative' interpretation of monastic life.
A wide pluralism could be reconciled with an **agreement** on this
question of principle. Whether we choose the more active or the
more contemplative form of monasticism, we should think of the monastic community in terms of this kind of relationship to the world.
The contemplative would argue that this relationship is given most
effectively in a withdrawal from the 'activist' involvement, and
that he is involved in a transformation of the world at a deeper
level.[19] The 'activist' would argue that this transformation
should be given a more visible and tangible manifestation through
a more direct contact with the problems of people outside the
monastery. This pluralism should be accepted. But we are always
exposed to this dilemma: Either our life is dissipated in an extraverted activism which is insufficiently 'informed' by an interi-
or life of prayer; or the life of interior prayer fails to achieve
a visible witness to our environment.[20] Therefore I think that
many people are asking whether a monasticism centered in a deep
experience of prayer is necessarily incompatible with a greater
openness and freedom in our institutional structure and in our
contacts with the surrounding world. It is rash to predict the
future. But, if we were to hazard a guess, we might foresee a
tendency towards that kind of development.[21] This, I think, would
offer a monasticism which appears both as authentic and as relevant.
The young **people** are searching for the experience of God. They are
more sceptical about attempts to 'institutionalize' that experience.[22]
These are merely a few tentative reflections. My argument on
the question of principle does not lead necessarily to any one conclusion on this more debatable problem. But a pluralistic solution
to these more specific questions should not obscure the search for
a **meaning** to our relationship to the world which could be shared
by all monks. For the monastic problem today demands more than a
contemporary *aggiornamento* and more than a renewal through a return
to its origins. We need an interpretation of the role of monasticism within the **total** historical context and in particular within
the contemporary world. *Aggiornamento* and renewal would then appear in a new light. We could then begin to answer the crucial
question: 'What are we here for? What are we really doing?'
We should then see ourselves not as disconnected 'entities,'

playing an anachronistic role, but as relating to the world, and
to the entire movement of history towards the new Creation.[23]

NOTES

*Published in *The Downside Review* 88 (1970) 150-159.

[1]See Charles Wincklemans de Cléty, *The World of Persons* (London, 1967); Bernard Lonergan, 'Existenz and Aggiornamento' from *Collection* (London, 1967) 240-251 (esp. 243-246), and Adrian Cunningham, *Adam* (London, 1968) especially pp. 69-70: 'Man does not merely exist *in* time, he is a being who is himself temporal. Similarly, the world is not merely the place in which man has existence, but is constitutive of his existence. No separation is possible. Man always presents himself to us as being-in-the-world' (p. 69). See also William C. Shepherd, *Man's Condition. God and the World Process* (New York, 1969).

[2]The temptation is to retreat into a 'both/and' position based merely on the desire to avoid extremes. The argument is: Basically we withdraw from the world. However this does not prevent us, discreetly and with moderation, from a measure of involvement in the world. But an eclectic solution never satisfies.

[3]See C. Peifer, and R. Roloff, 'Purity of heart and the modern monk,' V, *American Benedictine Review* (June, 1963) 263-291, and more recently H. van Zeller, 'The Benedictine Choice,' Ibid. (March, 1968) 64-68, and 'Renewal or Accomodation?' Ibid. (September, 1968) 317-322.

[4]This first part of the article discusses the question of the life of the monk more generically from a basis common to all Christians. The second part of the article, *The Monastic Perspective*, suggests a more specifically monastic orientation.

[5]Spirit-body, not spirit *and* body, i.e. not a dualism of two separate entities.

[6]It could be argued, from the basis of the philosophy of Aristotle and St Thomas, that the denial of spirit-body dualism does not imply a denial of person-world dualism. The spirit-body union is a substantial union. The person-world union is not a substantial union. I would of course agree. But the answer posed in these terms is the answer to the entitative question: 'What *is* the human person?' and therefore the wrong kind of answer to the other question: 'What is happening to the human person?' In answer to this last question both kinds of dualism should be rejected. The human person cannot *develop* apart from his social and historical context in the world (see the penetrating analysis of the question by Cunningham in *Adam*, pp. 69-102). The subject of this

article is about a way of living and therefore is primarily a question about 'What is happening to us?'

[7]See K. Rahner, *Spirit in the World* (London, 1968) introduction, p. liii: 'By "spirit" I mean a power which reaches out beyond the world and knows the metaphysical. "World" is the name of the reality which is accessible to the immediate experience of man.'

[8]This point is made very clearly by Wincklemans de Cléty in *The World of Persons*, pp. 100, 199-200, 214-15, 369-438.

[9]From now onwards I am using the term 'world' to mean the entire concrete, historical human situation presupposed to the new creation in Christ. See the preamble to the Constitution of the Second Vatican Council on the Church in the World Today. 'The world the Council has in mind then is the world of men, the entire human family, its whole environment; the world which is the theatre of human history, marked with man's industry, his triumphs and disasters. It is the world which the faithful believe to be made and sustained by the Creator's love. It was enslaved to sin but Christ crucified and risen from the dead has freed it so that according to God's design it may be transformed and achieve its fulfilment.' The meaning of the term 'world' has now shifted from the philosophical perspective of Karl Rahner's *Spirit in the World*, the 'phenomenal world' as contrasted with the spirit of man, to the entire historical condition of man as contrasted with the new creation of man in Christ. But both in the philosophical and in the theological use of the term, the human person neither rejects the world now immerses himself in the world. He lives in the world from a transcendent center.

[10]See Fr McCabe's interpretation of eschatology in terms of revolution and continuity, a continuity seen only from the 'other' side of the revolution (H. McCabe, *Law, Love and Language* [London, 1968] 126-73).

[11]This 'flesh'--'spirit' antithesis in the Pauline terminology should not be confused with a 'body'--'spirit' dualism.
In the final transformation into the new world we shall of course be subject to the ontological limitations of man as a finite creature. But we shall be liberated from the limitations of our present human condition.

[12]To say that this principle applies to all Christians is to say that it applies to all monks. Even the most strictly 'contemplative' community should, in this sense, be involved *in*

this world and even the most 'active' community should find its center *beyond* this world.

[13]See K. Rahner, 'Theology of the Spiritual Life' *Theological Reflections*, Vol. III (London, 1967) pp. 47-57, 'Reflections on the Theology of Renunciation: 'one might also express wnat is meant here more briefly by saying that the *res* of perfection is always and everywhere and only the love of God and of one's neighbor in God. The quasi-sacramental sign (*quasi-sacramentum*) of this *res*, taken as something transcendingly eschatological in the Church, is renunciation (as a permanent form of life). The sign of the same *res* taken as something cosmic is the love-informed worldly life of Christians in the Church (ibid., p. 56).

[14]In this way we can affirm both the **continuity** of the monastic life with the life of all Christians and the point of differentiation.

[15]The life of prayer should be understood not primarily as outward liturgical 'observance' but rather as a deep, interior, personal experience. This experience, the 'reality' of prayer, the *res*, should find its perfect, sacramental articulation in the liturgical sign the *sacramentum* which evokes and expresses that experience.

[16]This is not to equate a human historical development as such with the creation of eschatological Christian community. The point is that there is no such thing as a *purely* human historical development. *De facto* all history is in the context of the Christian Revelation. Therefore the eschatological Christian community, although transcending history, comes into **existence** through this human historical development. To deny this would be to conceive the Christian Revelation as a disembodied platonic entity which is not really incarnated in human history. This would be a failure to grasp the implications of the Incarnation. The risen Christ is present *within* history.

[17]See the valuable articles by Fr Fergus Kerr, 'Ataraxy and Utopia,' *New Blackfriars* (March, 1969) 304-13; 'Liberation and Contemplativity,' Ibid., (April, 1969) 356-66; 'Resolution and Community,' Ibid. (June, 1969) 471-82. Fr Fergus Kerr points to the importance of Marcuse, *Eros and Civilization* (London, 1955) and makes an interesting comparison between **Marcuse** and the later Heidegger. He refers also to the affinity between the later Heidegger and the German mystics, in particular to Eckhart, and alludes to *Der Staz von Grund* where in 'the last set of lectures Heidegger gave before retiring, and in many ways the finest statement of his

position, he replaced Leibniz by Angelus Silesius, just as he had
previously substituted Eckhart for Kant ('Liberation and Contemplativity,' p. 365).

[18]See J. Coventry, 'The Problem of God Today,' *Clergy
Review* (July, 1968) 500-513, esp. p. 502.

[19]See J. Leclercq, 'Present Day Problems in Monasticism,'
Downside Review (April, 1969) 135-54; 'Does the fact of existing
for others (*Da sein für andere*) necessarily imply being with (*sein
mit*)? There is place for a consented withdrawal which is a way of
"being-present-to" and of "living-for"' (p. 151).

[20]The comments of Fr Schillebeeckx on the Christian
apostolate are also relevant to this more specifically monastic
problem. E. H. Schillebeeckx, *Le Christ Sacrement de la Rencontre
de Dieu* (Paris, 1960) p. 249.

[21]See Leclercq, 'Present Day Problems in Monasticism,'
p. 152: 'If we are attentive to the movement of the forward-
going Church, one has the feeling, the presentiment, that contem-
platives will have to have more and more contacts with the world,
have more and more immediate radiation in the world, without being
less centered on prayer.'

[22]See Rosemary Haughton's valuable distinction between
formation and *transformation* and her discussion of the Benedictine
rule in the light of this distinction (*The Transformation of Man*
[London, 1967] pp. 211-41, 'The Formation Community'). Mrs. Haughton shows clearly that the purpose of the external 'formation'
structure is to evoke and express the inner 'transformation' event.
The danger is that the 'formation' structure, designed as a 'means'
can become an 'end.' 'It was not an end in the sense that people
thought that this life was all that mattered, but that a life lived
according to the secular structures arranged by the Rule, with careful attention to the specifically religious duties, was *itself* the
necessary qualification for eternal life after death. So the observance of the Rule was no longer felt as the framework within
which the encounter with God, the Salvation-occurrence, could take
place but as itself the only kind of occurrence that had any necessary connection with Salvation' (Ibid., p. 235). Whether or not
one agrees with this criticism of the historical evolution of Benedictine communities, it cannot be denied that this danger is always
present in any system of 'observance.'
See also Louis Merton, 'Final Integration: Towards a
"Monastic Therapy",' *Monastic Studies* 6 (1968) 87-99, esp. p. 89:
'For instance it is not enough to keep the monks strictly enclosed

and remote from all external activity. This does not by itself constitute a sign of the eschatological kingdom. On the contrary very often this limitation constitutes a serious impoverishment of the personalities of the monks and at the same time serves to prevent that impoverishment from becoming public!' Fr Louis Merton qualifies this statement with his recognition that 'silence' and 'solitude' are essential to the monastic way of life and that 'discipline' contributes to the end for which monastic communities exist. But he rightly says that the aim of monastic life is transformation and rebirth to 'a new and more complete identity' and that 'when rigidity and limitation become ends in themselves they no longer favor growth, they stifle it.' This points again to the basic question of the relationship of 'transformation' and 'formation.'

23This article was written before I had read R. Pannikar, 'The Problem of Monastic Aggiornamento,' *Monastic Studies* (Michaelmas, 1969) 103-112. I cannot do justice here to this important article. But I hope that my argument can be reconciled with the author's claim that monasticism is 'a dimension in all human existence': the eschatological dimension. But we seem to differ in our concept of eschatology (this may be, to some extent, a difference in perspective). Dr Pannikar would say that eschatology is a dimension 'beyond' this world. I would agree. But I would also say that, in the *historical* perspective, the 'beyond' is the 'future' of the world. Consequently I would give a somewhat different interpretation to the meaning of 'monasticism as a dimension in all human existence.'

ABBREVIATIONS

I. Works by William of St Thierry

Adv Abl	*Disputatio adversus Petrum Abaelardum*
Aenig	*Aenigma fidei*
Brev com	*Brevis commentatio in cantica canticorum*
Cant	*Expositio super Cantica canticorum*
Cant Amb	*Super cantica canticorum ex operibus sancti Ambrosii*
Cant Grg	*Super cantica canticorum ex operibus sancti Gregorii*
Contemp	*De contemplando deo*
Ep frat	*Epistola ad fratres de Monte Dei (Epistola aurea)*
Ep(p)	*Epistola(e)*
Ep Rup	*Epistola ad Rupertum*
Er Guil	*De erroribus Guillelmi de Conchis*
Exp Rm	*Expositio in epistolam Pauli ad Romanos*
In lacu	*Soliloquium 'In lacu miseriae'*
Med	*Meditativae orationis*
Nat am	*De natura et dignitate amoris*
Nat corp	*De natura corporis et animae*
Orat	*Oratio domni Willelmi*
Resp Matt	*Responsio ad cardinalem Matthaeum*
Sacr altar	*De sacramento altaris*
Spec fid	*Speculum fidei*

Vita Bern   *Sancti Bernardi vita prima*

II. Works of Bernard of Clairvaux

Asc   *Sermo in ascensione Domini*

Csi   *De consideratione*

Gra   *De gratia et libero arbitrio*

SC   *Sermones super Cantica canticorum*

III. Works of Aelred of Rievaulx

Oner   *Sermones de oneribus*

Spec car   *Speculum caritatis*

Spir amic   *De spiritali amicitia*

IV. Periodicals and Serials

ASOC   *Analecta sacri ordinis cisterciensis*

CC   *Corpus Christianorum. Series Latina.*

COCR   *Collectanea Ordinis Cisterciensium Reformatorum.*

DThC   *Dictionnaire de théologie catholique.*

ETL   *Ephemerides theologicae Lovaniensis*

RAM   *Revue d'Ascetique et de mystique*

RHE   *Revue d'histoire ecclésiastique*

Rech.SR   *Recherches de science religieuse*

RTAM   *Recherche de Théologie ancienne et médiévale*

BIBLIOGRAPHY

I. The Works of William of St Thierry.

Dom Odo Brooke cited the works of William of St Thierry in the
PL edition, with the exception of the *Speculum fidei*, for which he
preferred Déchanet's edition (noted below). Other editions of William's works known to him, and cited by him, are noted after the
PL reference. Works appear in what Dom Odo considered 'the most
probably chronological order.'

De contemplando deo. PL 184, 365-380.
     Ed. J. Hourlier, *La contemplation de Dieu. L'oraison de Dom
     Guillaume.* Sources chrétiennes, 61. Paris, 1959.

De natura et dignitate amoris. PL 184, 379-408.
     Ed. J.-M. Déchanet, *OEuvres choises de Guillaume de Saint-
     Thierry.* Paris, 1943. Latin text with French translation
     and notes.

De sacramento altaris. PL 180, 341-366.

Meditativae orationes. PL 180, 205-248.
     E. J.-M. Déchanet, *Méditations et prières de Guillaume de
     Saint-Thierry.* Brussels, 1945. Latin text with French trans-
     lation and notes.

De natura corporis et animae. PL 180, 695-726.
     Ed. Déchanet, *OEuvres choises.*

Expositio in Epistolam ad Romanos. PL 180, 647-694.

Super Cantica Canticorum ex operibus S. Ambrosii. PL 15, 1945-
2060.

Super Cantica, ex operibus S. Gregorii. PL 180, 441-474.

Expositio (altera) super Cantica Canticorum. PL 180, 473-546.
     Ed. Déchanet, *OEuvres choisies.*
     Ed. Déchanet, *Guillaume de Saint-Thierry: Exposé sur le
     Cantique des cantiques.* Paris, 1962.

Disputatio adversus Petrum Abaelardum. PL 180, 249-282.

De erroribus Guillelmi de Conchis. PL 180, 333-340.

Speculum fidei. PL 180, 365-398.
   Ed. Déchanet, *Le miroir de la foi*. Bruges, 1946.
   Critical edition with Latin text and French translation.

Aenigma fidei. PL 180, 397-440.

Epistola (aurea) ad fratres de Monte-Dei. PL 184, 307-354.
   Ed. Déchanet, *La lettre d'or aux Frères du Mont-Dieu*.
   Paris, 1956. French translation with introduction and notes.
   N. B. Book III (cols. 353-364) is of doubtful authenticity and
   has not been used in these studies. See *OEuvres choisies*, 45-
   46.

II. Works and **Articles** on William of St Thierry.

Bouyer, Louis. *La Spiritualité de Cîteaux*. Paris, 1954. ET: *The
   Cistercian Heritage*. London: Mowbray, 1958.

Davy, M.-M. 'La connaissance de Dieu d'après Guillaume de Saint-
   Thierry,' *Rech. SR* 28 (1938) 440-56.

----------. *Théologie et mystique de Guillaume de Saint-Thierry*,
   I: La connaissance de Dieu. Paris, 1954.

Déchanet, J.-M. '*Amor ipse intellectus est*. La doctrine de
   l'amour intellection chez Guillaume de Saint-Thierry,' *Revue
   du moyen âge latin* 1 (1945) 349-74.

--------------. *Aux sources de la spiritualité de Guillaume de
   Saint-Thierry*. Bruges, 1940.

--------------. 'La connaissance de soi d'aprés Guillaume de
   Saint-Thierry,' *Vie spirituelle* 56 (1938) Supplément, pp. 102-
   122.

--------------. *Guillaume de Saint-Thierry, l'homme et son oeuvre*.
   Paris, 1942. ET: *William of St Thierry: The Man and His Work*.
   Spencer, Mass.: Cistercian Publications, 1972.

--------------. 'Guillaume de Saint-Thierry et Plotin,' *Revue du
   moyen âge latin* 2 (1946) 241-260.

--------------. 'Les manuscrits de la lettre aux frères du Mont-
   Dieu de Guillaume de Saint-Thierry et le problème de la Préface dans Charleville, 114,' *Scriptorium* 8 (1954) 236-271.

Hourlier, J. 'S. Bernard et Guillaume de Saint-Thierry dans le
    Liber de amore,' Saint Bernard théologien. Analecta SOC 9
    (1953) fasc. 3-4, pp. 223-233.

-----------. 'Guillaume de Saint-Thierry et le *Brevis Commentatio
    in Cantica,' Analecta SOC* 12 (1956) 105-14.

Malevez, L. 'La doctrine de l'image et de la connaissance mystique
    chez Guillaume de Saint-Thierry,' *Rech.* SR 22 (1932) 178-
    205; 257-79.

Walsh, James. 'Guillaume de Saint-Thierry et les sens spirituels,'
    RAM 137 (1959).

III.   Secondary Works: Medieval and Modern Theology.

*S. Bernardo, Pubblicazione commemorativa nel VIII centenario della
    sua morte.* Milan, 1954.

S. Bernard théologien. Analecta SOC 9 (1953) fasc. 3-4.

Aubert, D. 'Le caractère raisonnable de l'acte de foir d'après
    les théologiens de la fin du XIIIe siècle,' RHE 39 (1943) 31-39.

---------. *Le problème de l'acte de foi.* Louvain, 1958.

Balthasar, Hans Urs von. *Parole et mystère chez Origène.* Paris,
    1957.

---------. *Word and Redemption.* New York, 1965.

Benoit, P. *Exégèse et théologie,* I. Paris, 1961.

Bliemetzrieder, F. *Anselms von Laon systematische Sentenzen,* Teil
    I. *Beiträge zur Geschichte der Philosophie des Mittelalters*
    18, 2-3. Münster, 1919.

Bodard, P. 'La Bible expression d'une expérience religieuse chez
    St Bernard,' *Saint Bernard théologien,* 23-45.

Bourke, J. 'The historical Jesus and the kerygmatic Christ,'
    Concilium I (2), 16-25.

Bréhier, E. *La philosophie de Plotin.* Paris, 1928.

Butler, Cuthbert. *Western Mysticism.* London, 1922.

Cappuyns, M. *Jean Scot Erigène, sa vie, son oeuvre, sa pensée.* Louvain, 1933.

Châtillon, J. 'Influence de saint Bernard sur la scholastique,' *Saint Bernard théologien,* 268-88.

Chenu, M.-D. 'La psychologie de la foi dans la théologie du XIIIe siècle,' *Etudes d'histoire littéraire et doctrinale du XIIIe siècle,* 2 (1932) 163-87.

----------. *La théologie au XIIe siècle.* Paris, 1957. Partial ET: *Nature, Man and Society in the Twelfth Century,* tr. Jerome Taylor. Chicago and London: University of Chicago Press, 1968.

Chevalier, I. *S. Augustin et la pensée grecque. Les relations trinitaires.* Fribourg, 1940.

Copleston, Frederick. *A History of Philosophy,* I. London, 1946; II. London, 1950.

Cottiaux, J. 'La conception de la théologie chez Abélard,' RHE 28 (1932) 247-95; 533-51; 787-828.

Crouzel, H. 'L'anthropologie d'Origène dans la perspective du combat spirituel,' RAM 31 (1955) 364-85.

----------. *La théologie mystique d'Origène.* Toulouse, 1960.

----------. *Théologie de l'image de Dieu chez Origène.* Toulouse, 1955.

Daniélou, J. 'Saint Bernard et les Pères grecs,' *Saint Bernard théologien,* 46-55.

----------. *Platonisme et théologie mystique.* Paris, 1954.

Déchanet, J.-M. 'La Christologie de S. Bernard,' *Saint Bernard théologien,* 78-91.

Dedek, J. '*Quasi experimentalis cognitio:* A Historical Approach to the Meaning of St Thomas,' *Theological Studies* 21 (1961) 357-90.

Dumontier, P. *S. Bernard et la Bible.* Bruges-Paris, 1953.

Ethier, A.-M. *Le De Trinitate de Richard de Saint-Victor,* Paris-Ottawa, 1951.

Fliche A. and V. Martin. *Histoire l'Eglise*, XIII. Paris, 1951.

Frickel, M. *Deus totus ubique simul.* Freiburg im Br., 1956.

Gagnebet, M-R. 'La nature de la théologie spéculative,' *Revue Thomiste* 44 (1938) 1-39; 213-55.

Ghellinck, Joseph de. 'L'histoire de *persona,*' *Revue néoscholasti-que de philosophie* 36 (1934).

----------. *Le mouvement théologique du XIIe siècle.* 2nd edition. Paris, 1948.

Gilson, Etienne. *Introduction à l'étude de saint Augustin.* Paris, 1923.

------. *Le théologie mystique de saint Bernard.* Paris, 1934. ET: *The Mystical Theology of St Bernard,* tr. A. H. C. Downes. London-New York: Sheed and Ward, 1940. 1955.

Hallier, A. *Un éducateur monastique.* Paris, 1959. ET: *The Monastic Theology of Aelred of Rievaulx,* tr. Columban Heaney. CS 2. Spencer, Mass.-Shannon, Ireland, 1969.

Häring, N. M. 'The Case of Gilbert de la Porrée, Bishop of Poitiers,' *Mediaeval Studies* 13 (1951) 1-40.

Hausherr, I. 'Ignorance infinie,' *Orientalia Christiana periodica* 2 (1936) 351-62.

Henry, P. *Etudes plotiniennes. Les états du texte.* Louvain, 1938.

--------. *Plotin et l'Occident.* Louvain, 1934.

Hibbert, Giles. 'Created and Uncreated Charity,' RTAM 31 (1964) 63-84.

Hill, E. 'Aristotle and Jung,' *Clergy Review* (Dec. 1963) 778-83.

Hoste, Anselme. '*Le* speculum spiritalis amicitiae,' *Studia Monastica* 3 (1961).

Javelet, Robert. 'Intelligence et amour chez les auteurs spirituels du XIIe siècle,' RAM 37 (1961) 429-50.

Knowles, David. *The English Mystical Tradition.* London, 1961.

Landgraf, A. M. *Dogmengeschichte der Frühscholastik.* 8 vols. Regensburg, 1952-55.

--------. 'Probleme um den hl. Bernhard von Clairvaux,' *Cistercienser Chronik* (May 1954).

Leclercq, Jean. *L'amour des lettres et le desir de Dieu.* Paris, 1957. ET: *The Love of Learning and the Desire for God,* tr. Catherine Misrahi. New York: Fordham University Press, 1961.

--------. 'The Monastic Tradition of Culture and Studies,' *American Benedictine Review* 11 (1960) 99-111.

--------. 'Present Day Problems in Monasticism,' *Downside Review* (April 1969) 135-54.

--------. 'S. Bernard et la théologie monastique du XIIe siècle,' *Saint Bernard théologien,* 7-23.

--------. *Theology and Prayer: Father Cyril Gaul Memorial Lecture Delivered at St Meinrad Seminary, 23rd September 1962.* n.p., n.d.

Lonergan, Bernard. *Collection.* London, 1967.

--------. *De Constitutione Christi ontologica et psychologica.* Rome, 1958.

--------. *De Deo Trino.* Rome, 1961.

--------. *Divinarum personarum conceptionum analogicam.* Rome, 1959.

--------. *Insight: A Study of Human Understanding.* London-New York, 1957.

Lubac, Henri de. *Histoire et esprit, l'intelligence de l'Ecriture d'après Origène.* Paris, 1950. ET: *History and Spirit,* tr. Richard Strachan, to appear in Cistercian Studies Series.

Mahé, J. 'La sanctification d'après saint Cyrille d'Alexandrie,' RHE 10 (1909) 469-92.

Malet, A. *Personne et amour dans la théologie trinitaire de saint Thomas d'Aquin.* Paris, 1956.

Malevez, L. 'La doctrine de l'image et de la connaissance mystique,' *Rech. SR* 22 (1932) 178-205; 257-79.

Malevez, L. 'Théologie contemplative et théologie discursive,' *Nouvelle Revue théologique* 86 (1964) 225-49.

--------. The Christian Message and Myth: The Theology of Rudolph Bultman. tr. Olive Wyon. London: SCM Press, 1958.

Mann, P. 'The Transcendental or the Political Kingdom,' *New Blackfriars* (Dec. 1969-Jan. 1970).

Mansi, J. D. *Sacrorum conciliorum nova et amplissima collectio,* 31 vols. Florence-Venice, 1759-98; rpt. Graz: Akademische Druck- u. Verlagsanstalt, 1960.

Maritain, Jacques. *Les degrés du savoir.* Paris, 1932.

Martin, J. *L'apologétique traditionnelle* I, II. Paris, 1905-1906.

Mayer, A. *Das Bild Gottes im Menschen nach Clemens von Alexandrien.* Rome, 1942.

Merton, Louis (Thomas). 'Final Integration' Towards A 'Monastic Therapy,' *Monastic Studies* 6 (1968) 87-99.

Michel, A. 'Relations divines,' DThC, XIII, 2 cols. 2135-2156. Paris, 1937.

Moran, G. *Theology of Revelation.* London, 1967.

--------. 'What is Revelation?' *Theological Studies* 25 (1964) 217-31.

Mouroux, J. *Le mystère du temps.* Paris, 1962. ET: *The Mystery of Time.* New York, 1964.

O'Collins, C. G. 'Revelation as History,' *The Heythrop Journal* (October 1966) 394-406.

Ostlender, H. 'Die *Theologia scholarium* des Peter Abaelards,' *Aus der Geisteswelt des Mittelalters* I (1935) 263-81.

Penido, M.T.L. *Le role de l'analogie en théologie dogmatique.* Paris, 1931.

Perino, R. *La dottrina trinitaria di Sant'Anselmo.* Rome, 1952.

Rahner, Karl. *The Church and the Sacraments.* London, 1963.

Rahner, Karl. 'Les débuts d'une doctrine des cinq sens spirituels,' RAM 13 (1932) 263ff.

------------. *Schriften,* IV. Einsiedeln, 1961.

------------. *Spirit in the World.* London, 1968.

------------. *Theological Investigations,* I. Tr. Cornelius Ernst. London, 1961.

------------. *Theological Reflections,* III. London, 1967.

Regnon, Th. de. *Etudes de théologie positive sur la Sainte Trinité.* 4 vols. Paris, 1892.

Reypens, L. 'Dieu (connaissance mystique),' DSp, III, cols. 883-929. Paris, 1957.

Richardson, Alan. *History Sacred and Profane.* London, 1964.

Raciti, G. 'L'apport originel d'Aelred de Rievaulx à la réflexion occidentale sur l'amitié,' *Coll.* 29 (1967) 77-99.

Ricoeur, P. *Le conflit des interpretations: essais d'hermeneutique.* Paris, 1969.

Rocques, R. *L'univers dionysien.* Lille, 1954.

Rousselot, P. *The Intellectualism of St Thomas.* London, 1935.

Schillebeeckx, E. H. *Le Christ, sacrement de la rencontre de Dieu.* Paris, 1960. ET: *Christ the Sacrament of the Encounter with God.* New York: Sheed and Ward, 1963.

Schmaus, M. *Die psychologishce Trinitätslehre des heiligen Augustinus.* Münster, 1927.

Schmidt, M. A. *Gottheit und Trinität nach dem Kommentar des Gilbert Porreta zu Boethius* De Trinitate. Basel, 1956.

Sherwood, P. *The Earlier Ambigua of St Maximus the Confessor.* Rome, 1955.

Sikes, J. G. *Peter Abaelard.* Cambridge, 1932.

Spicq, C. *Esquisse d'une histoire de l'exégèse latine au moyen âge.* Paris, 1944.

Squire, Aelred. 'Aelred of Rievaulx and the Monastic Tradition
    Concerning Action and Contemplation,' *Downside Review* (1954).

Standaert, M. 'La doctrine de l'image chez saint Bernard,'
    Ephemerides theologicae Lovanienses 23 (1947) 70-129.

----------. 'La spiritualité de saint Bernard,' *S. Bernardo, Pub-*
    blicazione commemorativa, 42-65.

Talbot, C. H., ed. *Sermones inediti b. Aelredi Abbatis Rievallen-*
    sis. Rome, 1952.

Trethowan, I. *Certainty.* London, 1948.

Vagaggini, C. *Il senso teologico della liturgia.* Rome, 1957.
    Partial ET: *The Theological Dimensions of the Liturgy.* College-
    ville, Minn., 1959.

------------. *Maria nelle opere di Origene.* Orientalia Christiana
    Analecta 131. Rome, 1942.

Vonier, A. *A Key to the Doctrine of the Holy Eucharist,* 2nd ed.
    London, 1931.

Wellens, E. 'Saint Bernard mystique,' *S. Bernardo, Pubblicazione*
    commemorativa, 66-91.

White, V. *God and the Unconscious.* London, 1952.

--------. *Soul and Psyche.* London, 1960.

Williams, M. E. *The Teaching of Gilbert Porreta on the Trinity as*
    Found in His Commentaries on Boethius. Rome, 1951.

CISTERCIAN FATHERS SERIES

Under the direction of the same Board of Editors as the CISTERCIAN
STUDIES SERIES, the CISTERCIAN FATHERS SERIES seeks to make available the works of the Cistercian Fathers in Good English translation based on the recently established critical editions.   The
texts are accompanied by introductions, notes and indices prepared
by qualified scholars.

Bernard of Clairvaux

CF 1   *Treatises* I *(Apology to Abbot William, On Precept and
            Dispensation)*

CF 4   **Sermons on the Song of Songs* I

CF 7   **Sermons on the Song of Songs* II

CF 13   **Treatises* II *(On the Steps of Humility, On Loving God)*

CF 19   **Treatises* III *(In Praise of the New Knighthood, On Grace
            and Free Will)*

Aelred of Rievaulx

CF 2   *Treatises* I *(Jesus at Twelve Years Old, Rule for Recluses,
            Pastoral Prayer)*

CF 5   **Spiritual Friendship*

William of Saint Thierry

CF 3   **On Contemplating God, Prayer, Meditations*

CF 6   *On the Song of Songs*

CF 9   *The Aenigma of Faith*

CF 12   **The Golden Epistle*

Guerric of Igny

CF 8   *Liturgical Sermons*

*Available in paper as well as hard cover

THE WORKS OF WILLIAM OF ST THIERRY IN ENGLISH TRANSLATION

The *Cistercian Fathers Series* will include translations of all the
works of this great monastic writer.

CF 3   *On Contemplating God. Prayer, Meditations.*
        Introductions by Jacques Hourlier and J.-M. Déchanet
        1971   vi - 202 pp.   ISBN 0-87907-703-4
        Paper $4.00

CF 6   *Exposition on the Song of Songs*
        Introduction by J.-M. Déchanet
        1970   xlvii - 172 pp.   ISBN 0-87907-306-3
        Clothbound $7.95

CF 12   *The Golden Epistle (A Letter to the Brethren of Mont-Dieu)*
        Introduction by J.-M. Déchanet
        1971   xxxvi - 118 pp.   ISBN 0-87907-712-3
        Paper $4.00

CF 9   *The Enigma of Faith*
        Introduction by John Anderson
        1974   ISBN 0-87907-309-8
        Clothbound $7.95

CF 15   *The Mirror of Faith*
        Introduction by E. Rozanne Elder
        1979   104 pp.   ISBN 0-87907-315-2
        $12.95

CF 27   *Commentary on the Letter to the Romans*
        Introduction by John D. Anderson
        1980   298 pp.   ISBN 0-87907-327-6
        $17.95

        On the Nature and Dignity of Love

        Letters, Life of William by a Contemporary (Title provisional)

CS 10   J.-M. Déchanet, *William of St Thierry. The Man
        and His Work* (1972)
        x - 173 pp.   ISBN 0-87907-810-3 $10.95

        David N. Bell, *The Image and Likeness: A Study of the Mystical
        Theology of William of St Thierry and Its Relation to That of
        St Augustine*